The
Tudor Play
of Mind

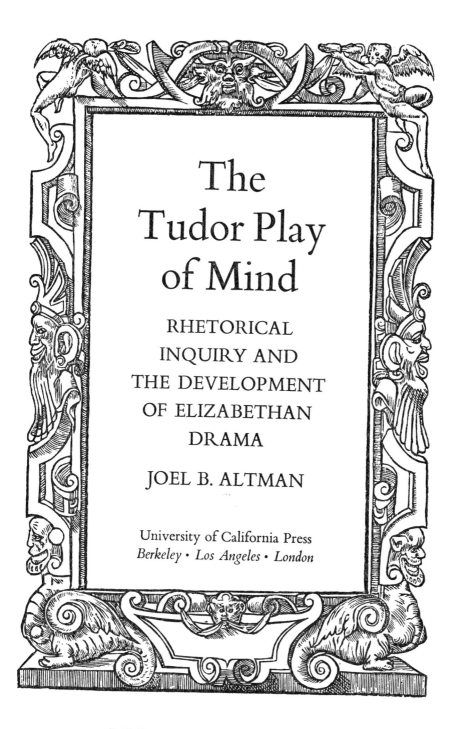

The Tudor Play of Mind

RHETORICAL INQUIRY AND THE DEVELOPMENT OF ELIZABETHAN DRAMA

JOEL B. ALTMAN

University of California Press
Berkeley • Los Angeles • London

University of California Press
Berkeley and Los Angeles, California

University of California Press, Ltd.
London, England

Copyright © 1978 by
The Regents of the University of California

ISBN 0–520–03427–9
Library of Congress Catalog Card Number: 76–52022
Printed in the United States of America

1 2 3 4 5 6 7 8 9

For Virginia

Contents

Contents

Acknowledgments

A STUDY SUCH AS THIS NATURALLY BUILDS UPON THE INSIGHTS AND GOOD
will of others. I have attempted to indicate my awareness of this depen-
dency in the notes to my text. Certain obligations, however, are felt as
primary, and these must be acknowledged separately. In writing this
book, I have had the good fortune to be associated with scholars who are
consistently generous with their ideas, their time, and their personal concern. My appreciation must first be expressed to Professor Wesley Trimpi
of Stanford University, whose graduate seminars in literary theory originally stimulated me to think about the relationship between drama and
rhetorical inquiry, and who has continued to be an inspiring teacher and
an unsparing critic. My indebtedness to his unique work in the history of
literary theory is apparent throughout this book. To my colleagues in
the English Department at Berkeley, I wish to express deep gratitude
for the intellectual and moral support that they provided during the long
period of planning, writing, and revision. My special thanks go to Pro-
fessors Janet Adelman, Paul Alpers, Jonas Barish, Stephen Greenblatt,
and Norman Rabkin, who took the trouble to read and even re-read the
manuscript at its various stages, and made me question my assumptions
and clarify and refine my argument. The faults of the book I own as
mine, but it is much better for their generous engagement with my problem. Thanks are due also to the University of California for the Humani-
ties Research Fellowship in 1972–1973 and the Regents Faculty Fellowship in 1975 which allowed me the leisure to pursue research and writing
relieved of teaching duties. Inevitably, one's greatest debts lie closest to
home; I owe more than I can say to my parents, whose encouragement
was always felt, and to my wife, a tactful editor and Patience on a monu-
ment.

Introduction

Iᴛ ɪꜱ ᴏᴡɪɴɢ ᴛᴏ ᴛʜᴇɪʀ ᴡᴏɴᴅᴇʀ," ᴀʀɪꜱᴛᴏᴛʟᴇ ᴡʀᴏᴛᴇ ɪɴ ʜɪꜱ *Metaphysics*, "that men both now begin and at first began to philosophize; they wondered originally at the obvious difficulties, then advanced little by little and stated difficulties about the greater matters . . . about the phenomena of the moon and those of the sun and of the stars, and about the genesis of the universe." In wonder is the source of learning, and through learning man is brought into his natural condition of wisdom.[1]

This book is about the exercise of wonder—not through the rigorous discipline of philosophy, but rather through the more playful medium of drama. The relationship of wonder and drama is as august as that of wonder and philosophy. Aristotle considered wonder an essential component of tragic pleasure:

> Incidents arousing pity and fear . . . have the very greatest effect on the mind when they occur unexpectedly and at the same time in consequence of one another; there is more of the marvelous in them than if they happened of themselves or by mere chance. Even matters of chance seem most marvelous if there is an appearance of design as it were in them . . . for incidents like that we think to be not without meaning.[2]

Here, the marvelous—that which arouses wonder—is found in a group of incidents that stimulate the mind to new surmise. We are not simply surprised by the unexpected; we are stirred by the dramatist's artful disposition of events to infer a larger rational pattern lying behind them. In doing so, we move toward knowledge, which resides in the discovery of first principles.[3]

---

1. *Meta.* 982b12–18; *Rhet.* 1371a31–35. The translation is by W. D. Ross, *The Basic Works of Aristotle*, ed. Richard McKeon (New York, 1941).

2. *Poet.* 1452a1–11, trans. Ingram Bywater, *ibid.*

3. *Meta.* 982a1–982b10. In a more general sense, all artistic imitation stimulates inferences of this kind: "The reason of the delight in seeing the picture is that

This relationship between wonder, learning, and drama remained an important factor in the critical tradition. It is expressed in late classical criticism by the Terentian commentators Donatus and Evanthius, who observe that in comedy the playwright withholds certain facts in order to maintain the curiosity of the audience, and in the catastrophe unfolds the mystery so that the dramatic conflict may be resolved in full understanding.[4] In the scholastic tradition, Albertus Magnus remarks that "wonder is the movement of the man who does not know on his way to finding out, to get at the bottom of that at which he wonders and to determine its cause. . . . Thus Aristotle shows in that branch of logic which is called poetic that the poet fashions his story for the purpose of exciting wonder, and that the further effect of wonder is to excite inquiry."[5] The concept also suffused Renaissance poetic theory. Although the term *wonder* was also used in its narrower sense to designate a response to the "shocking," the "nonverisimilar," its more philosophical meaning was never lost, and may be seen in the language, structure, and plots of many of the plays we prize most highly today.[6]

Wonder, then, is our theme. We shall be less immediately concerned with the Aristotelian theory of wonder, however, than with the Ciceronian and sophistic rhetoric that was the instrument of arousing and expressing it. The period of our study is the sixteenth century, give or take a few years, and the setting is England. Essentially, my aim is to show how the philosophical *quaestio* mentioned by Aristotle in the first passage quoted above—and its cognate forms of rhetorical inquiry—inspired and gave shape to a large body of Elizabethan drama. This means that I shall be asking the reader to consider a great many Renaissance plays to be questions: questions about love, justice, sovereignty, nature, imagination —even questions that question whether such questions can be answered. Whimsical though this may seem, the term is not offered facetiously. For I shall propose that these plays did not merely raise questions, in the gen-

one is at the same time learning—gathering the meaning of things, e.g., that the man there is so-and-so" (*Poet.* 1448b15–18).

4. See Ch. V, p. 133.

5. *Commentary on the Metaphysics of Aristotle*, quoted by J. V. Cunningham, *Tradition and Poetic Structure* (Denver, 1960), p. 206.

6. Cunningham's important essay documents this tradition in detail. See pp. 188–231.

eral sense, but literally were questions—or rather fictional realizations of questions—and part of my argument will be to show how such realization comes about.

The origins of such a drama are to be found in the study of formal rhetoric, which in the sixteenth century was considered to be not only an art of persuasion, but also an art of inquiry, in which the methods of logic were employed with greater amplitude than that permitted the dialectician.[7] Dramatists of the period were trained in the discipline from their early grammar school days and, as recent scholarship has shown, the evidence of this education can be found throughout their work. It is manifested in the use of specific rhetorical forms learned in school, in a predilection for debate, in frequently disconcerting shifts of viewpoint, and in an explicit preoccupation with the subject matter of rhetoric.[8] To prove the importance of this influence, therefore, will not be my concern, but rather to consider its deeper resonances in the minds which were fashioned by it, and to come to some better understanding of what this meant for the dramatic literature such minds produced.

Several important questions arise when we consider the impact of a rhetorical education like the one enjoyed by the young grammarians of Tudor secondary schools and those who pursued more advanced studies at the universities. First, what happens to a mind conditioned to argue *in utramque partem*—on both sides of the question—as Renaissance students were trained to do? Surely one result must be a great complexity of vision, capable of making every man not only a devil's advocate but also a kind of microcosmic deity—as John Heywood playfully suggests—

7. The overlapping concerns of rhetoric and logic can be seen in most contemporary handbooks, and represent one facet of the ancient war between rhetoric and philosophy so eloquently described by Cicero in *De oratore*. Their frequent redundancy, in fact, stimulated the Ramist reform later in the century. On this matter, see Wilbur S. Howell, *Logic and Rhetoric in England 1500–1700* (Princeton, 1956) and Walter J. Ong, S.J., *Ramus, Method, and the Decay of Dialogue* (Cambridge, Mass., 1958).

8. The most exhaustive treatment is T. W. Baldwin, *William Shakspere's Small Latine and Lesse Greeke*, 2 vols. (Urbana, Ill., 1944); but see also Milton B. Kennedy, *The Oration in Shakespeare* (Chapel Hill, 1942); Madeleine Doran, *Endeavours of Art* (Madison, 1954); Wolfgang Clemen, *English Tragedy Before Shakespeare* (London, 1961); and especially Charles O. McDonald, *The Rhetoric of Tragedy* (Amherst, 1966).

who can see all sides of an issue.[9] Then, what kind of drama is this mind likely to create? Is its probable ambivalence and multiplicity of view to be regarded as an artistic virtue or shortcoming?[10] Still more problematic, when a writer trained in sophistic rhetoric has assimilated the various elements of composition taught in the discipline—speeches of praise and blame, arguments in defense of a proposition, *sententiae* confirming an argument, mimeses of persons in highly emotional states—and has learned to seek out and enjoy these passages in the literature he reads, what will be the nature of the aesthetic experience he provides in the play he composes *of* them? A rhetorical element designed to arouse passion may be placed beside one designed to investigate truth, which will perhaps be juxtaposed to another commanding assent. How will these parts relate to one another, and how will their collocation affect the auditor's response? Here, we confront not simply the matter of intellectual consistency but also of formal unity and the continuity of imaginative participation on the part of the auditor. How are we to assess the frequent discontinuities in Elizabethan drama? Finally, what happens when academic exercises become public entertainments, as in the case of the dramatized debates that constitute a large part of early English secular drama? Do they retain the ethical neutrality which they enjoyed in the schools—the ancient home of liberated *otium*—or must they become responsible to the *doxa* of the audiences they have come out to entertain? Does the audience join the world of the play, or must the world of the play reflect that of the audience?

With this last question, we have arrived at the larger interest of this study: the relationship of dramatic art to the concerns of everyday life in the period. The problem of didacticism is one that incessantly haunts our enjoyment and understanding of Elizabethan drama, and has probably inspired more critical crossfire in our time than any other scholarly

9. See the discussion of *The Play of the Weather,* Ch. IV.

10. *Vide* Doran: "The habit of mind fostered by the debate leads, I believe, to greater structural defects than mere runaway speeches. . . . It may be responsible for the unresolved oppositions in *The Merchant of Venice, Richard II,* and *Julius Caesar*; in *The Revenger's Tragedy,* in *The White Devil,* and in the Bussy and Byron plays. All these plays are characterized by a puzzling failure of direction because two or more ethical or political points of view are unreconciled" (p. 318).

issue. Contemporary records tell us with remarkable uniformity that comedy is "a figure of the rewards and punishments of virtues and vices" (Gascoigne), and that "material instruction, elegant and sententious excitation to virtue, and deflection from her contrary, [are] the soul, limbs, and limits of an autentical tragedy" (Chapman).[11] How seriously, and in what sense, ought we to take such assertions? In the twentieth century, many historical critics have taken them quite seriously, and have argued that Elizabethan drama must be viewed as essentially didactic. Although in recent years no one has asserted, with the conviction of Lily B. Campbell, that in order to understand Shakespearean tragedy we must "look to such *explanations* as were given by writers of tragedy and by philosophers in Shakespeare's time" (emphasis mine), still it is a widely held assumption that by and large Elizabethan drama lies in a homiletic tradition.[12] Yet when we look at the plays themselves, not obscure anomalies but important works like *The Spanish Tragedy*, *Tamburlaine*, and *Hamlet* —or in comedy, *Endimion* and *Every Man in his Humour*—the didactic approach seems thin indeed, and few serious critics today would argue that they "explain" anything. On the other hand, no theory of Elizabethan drama has arisen to account for the existence of such plays or for a tradition to which they belong, even though there have been searching and sensitive studies of individual plays and authors.[13] It is ironic that

11. David Klein, *The Elizabethan Dramatists as Critics* (New York, 1968), pp. 93, 96.

12. "The presentation of the evil that befalls man is but one of the concerns of tragedy; the other and the more important is the *explanation* of the why of the evil so presented" (*Shakespeare's Tragic Heroes: Slaves of Passion* [Cambridge, 1930], p. 3, again my emphasis). While other writers have been less doctrinaire, this is also the underlying assumption of such important works as Willard Farnham, *The Medieval Heritage of Elizabethan Tragedy* (Berkeley, 1936); E. M. W. Tillyard, *Shakespeare's History Plays* (London, 1944); Alfred Harbage, *As They Liked It* (New York, 1947); Bernard Spivack, *Shakespeare and the Allegory of Evil* (New York, 1958); David Bevington, *From Mankind to Marlowe* (Cambridge, Mass., 1962); and Virgil K. Whitaker, *The Mirror Up to Nature: The Technique of Shakespeare's Tragedies* (San Marino, 1965).

13. I have in mind such works as A. P. Rossiter's *Angel With Horns* (New York, 1961); Eugene M. Waith, *The Herculean Hero in Marlowe, Shakespeare, Chapman, and Dryden* (New York, 1962); Ernest Schanzer, *The Problem Plays of Shakespeare* (London, 1963); Norman Rabkin, *Shakespeare and the Common Understanding* (New

while we can account to our satisfaction for a whole string of moralities like *Impatient Poverty* and *Enough is as Good as a Feast*, we cannot find a place in the moral life of the period for the plays we really cherish. We can only—if implicitly—regard them as inspired aberrations.

To account satisfactorily for plays of this order as a *corpus of drama* is therefore a matter of high priority. This is what has been attempted in this study, through a close examination of dramatic structure and its origins in rhetorical theory. The conclusion drawn—that the plays are essentially questions and not statements at all—suggests a much wider moral function for them than has commonly been supposed. For if my argument is sound, the plays functioned as media of intellectual and emotional exploration for minds that were accustomed to examine the many sides of a given theme, to entertain opposing ideals, and by so exercising the understanding, to move toward some fuller apprehension of truth that could be discerned only through the total action of the drama. Thus the *experience* of the play was the thing. The corollary of this hypothesis is that such an experience was, in some measure, set apart from that of ordinary life, so as to provide a leisured *otium* wherein the auditor was freed to discover or to recall—and then to contemplate—ideas and feelings not always accessible or expressible in the life of a hierarchical Christian society. Hence the title of this book. But true to the highest humanist ideal, the fruits of this play of mind were intended to be realized in action, through the intellectual and spiritual enrichment of the citizens of the polity. This was the impulse behind the original cultivation of rhetoric, and such, I would suggest, was the aim of the drama it engendered.

Such a theory legitimizes and makes available to us a much greater range of response than we have been accustomed to feel is appropriate, and allows us to be true to our sense, as careful, affectionate readers and viewers, of what these plays do to us. We can accept without strings, for example, Hieronimo as a tragic hero, despite his rejection of "Vindicta mihi, saith the Lord," for that represents only one possible response to his predicament, and one which most of us feel would be intolerable; we can afford to ponder rather than ignore, as most critics do, the strongly

York, 1967); Wilbur Sanders, *The Dramatist and the Received Idea* (London, 1968); and Stephen Booth, "On the Value of Hamlet," *Reinterpretations of Elizabethan Drama*, ed. Norman Rabkin (New York, 1969).

worded condemnation of primogeniture in *Gorboduc*, a play that otherwise seems to stress the necessity of primogeniture; we can question both the sincerity and wisdom of Luciana's exhortation to Adriana in *The Comedy of Errors* that she submit herself to her husband's will—for we shall have weighed her pious rehearsal of the Elizabethan hierarchies against Antipholus's surly and callous nature, perhaps noting her own sexual anxiety in the process; and we can respond in just as many ways to Tamburlaine as Marlowe urges us to in the course of two plays, leaving us ultimately to decide the meaning of his fate for ourselves. Our options in cases like these are not wide open; we have not slipped into critical anarchy. On the contrary, we have been put on our mettle. We are free to respond to the shifting pressures of the playwright's rhetoric without restraint, allowing him to guide our feelings and thoughts toward the fullest apprehension of the experience he is offering us, and then we must make of it something meaningful in our lives. In doing so, we shall participate in the productive *otium* our predecessors enjoyed four hundred years ago, and in a large measure re-live their experience of the drama.

The major task of this book will be to persuade the reader of the likely truth of this hypothesis, and to illustrate it by showing what the plays do in fact achieve. To accomplish this, I have marshalled both historical evidence of a nondidactic critical tradition and also detailed rhetorical analyses of the works under consideration. My story begins in the witty ambiance of the Thomas More circle, where alongside an existing homiletic drama a new kind, which I shall call explorative, may be seen to emerge. In form and function it is different from its homiletic counterpart, and we shall devote some time to examining these differences. Though in the course of dramatic development the two kinds become less clearly distinguished, there remain throughout the period certain salient characteristics that mark the demonstrative and explorative modes, and the first chapter will determine what these are.[14]

Having analyzed their distinctive features, we shall then go behind

14. The term "explorative" has historical justification. Ben Jonson, adapting a phrase from Seneca, considered himself an *explorator*—one who acted as a forward scout among other men's ideas in order to discover what useful things might be learned from them, *non tamquam transfuga, sed tamquam explorator* (*Ep. Mor.* 2.5). His motto—*Tamquam explorator*—retains the strong moral basis of this concept.

the scene, as it were, and attempt to discover what there was in the background of the explorative play that caused it to function so differently from its homiletic sister. Here we shall have to consider other kinds of writing as well—recreative, political, religious—in which the same exploratory tendency is manifest, and survey briefly the literary training that fostered it. In this section, there has been no attempt to expound fully what others have already discussed in great detail; my concern has been rather to select materials that best suggest the psychological and intellectual impact of such training and its potential influence upon original literary production. The reader is then invited to join me in a close rhetorical examination of several nondramatic works of the period. My aim will be to establish a paradigm of the way in which one form of rhetorical inquiry—the abstract *quaestio* or *thesis*[15]—can be developed into a psychologically complex and richly detailed fiction. I have deliberately chosen three important and rather puzzling works for this purpose—Castiglione's *Book of the Courtier*, More's *Utopia*, and Sidney's *Arcadia*—hoping to show how an approach via the tradition of rhetorical inquiry can enhance our understanding of such fictions and enable us to see in their ethical ambiguities, intellectual ironies, and affective disjunctions a larger moral design. But equally important will be our appreciation of the fact that they are realizations, through the medium of concrete, particular fictional devices, of the explorative spirit of the original bare *quaestio*.

Having established the paradigm, we shall then leave the precincts of drama and enter once again upon the scene. The first group of plays to be considered are five interludes by John Heywood and John Rastell. These plays vary in their degree of mimetic intention, but all of them seem consciously devised to make the transition from debate platform to stage. They represent the first phase in the dramatization of a question. Their language frequently echoes the genre of forensic oratory, and in structure and characterization they reflect the influence of the *progymnasmata*, those fiction handbooks of the early sixteenth century. More importantly, their resolutions suggest a turn toward comic form, making them more than simply staged disputations. They provide an early clue to the relationship of debate and comic structure.

15. The terms will be explicated fully in Ch. III, but briefly they signify theoretical inquiry into any matter concerning knowledge or action.

Examination of Tudor comic pedagogy comes next. Here we shall concentrate on the study of Terence as it was conducted in the grammar schools, where our playwrights received their first formal knowledge of the nature of a comedy. What emerges from this study is a view of comedy as "an image of human reasoning and its outcome," and of comic scenes as mimetic debates, wily proofs, schemes, and suasions—all suggesting that within the bustle of a comic action lay specific problems to be examined and resolved by the human wit. The representation of this activity is the business of comedy, and sixteenth-century criticism reveals a keen interest in the exhibition of wit and its ability to solve its problems. Alongside this view, and often strangely unconnected to it, is an ethical one, which attempts to root the events of the play in universal moral precepts. Thus there is a tendency implicit in the criticism to bifurcate the comedy into *moralitas* and *ingenium*, which is reflected in the imitations that follow. One strain, developing into a Christian Terence, tends to become homiletic; another, concentrating upon the line of wit, runs the danger of sophistic barrenness. The latter kind, which is of greater historical importance, is the one we shall study—in academic imitations and translations and in the early work of Shakespeare, Chapman, and Jonson, who reveal in interesting ways the different forms explorative comedy could assume.

An interlude follows in which we shall enter the charmed circle of John Lyly, whose Court plays bear such a strong family resemblance to the early humanist debates, yet are transmuted into something rich and strange. Until recently, these plays had been considered simply decorative occasional pieces designed to flatter the Queen, and most discussions of them centered on the sources of Lyly's Euphuism and the "real" identities of his allegorical figures. Lyly's critical fortunes have improved, however, and now both his style and his drama are recognized as more seriously analytical. Yet they are extremely puzzling analyses, ambiguous in the unfolding and often hopelessly unresolved. This suggests that argument *in utramque partem* may underlie the intention and structure of his drama, and so we shall examine two plays in detail, paying special attention to the educative function of Lyly's allegory, which exercises in often exquisite ways the imagination of his courtly audience.

In Chapter VIII, we shall turn our attention to tragedy, beginning with a careful examination of the declamatory structure of Seneca's drama and its intellectual and affective implications. My justification for doing this is that while Seneca is by no means the only source of Elizabethan tragedy, the English plays that concern us in this study do not reflect the homiletic emphasis of the morality or *de casibus* tragedy, and therefore might very well reveal unexpected affinities to Senecan drama, of far more significance than sententious tags and alleged bloodthirstiness. The results of this closer look, I believe, confirm the hypothesis. Seneca's psychological discontinuities, his indefatigable use of sophistic set pieces, the abrupt shifts he brings about in affective allegiance, his adramatic concentration on debate for the purpose of airing an issue (and his dim view of its efficacy)—above all, his manner of circumambulating a theme so that the fullest awareness of its significance is obtained—produce deep reverberations in the Inns of Court tragedies and the more mature plays that follow. The so-called "Senecanism" of these plays is merely a token of much greater influence, which is reflected in their complex and fascinating variations upon Seneca's dramaturgy and (as one might expect) upon one another. This will be seen in our examination of such matters as framing devices, the sophistic use of imagery to evoke desired responses, choral function, and, of course, tragic concept—as we study a variety of English tragedies produced in the second half of the century. In each case, we shall focus upon how the dramatist works to shape our understanding.

The final chapter will deal with Marlowe, whose rhapsodic music and audacious rant make him the most troublesome of Elizabethan dramatists. My aim here is twofold: first, simply, to see how he fits into the picture—for even his most homiletic play seems so unhomiletic in effect as to be nearly a travesty of morality form. More specifically, though, I want to examine further the implications of the tragic view of wit that is evident in the work of other playwrights. Marlowe, it seems to me, probes this matter more deeply than his predecessors, and certainly views it more bleakly than any dramatist in the sixteenth century. Explorative comedy had assured us that some vision of truth, beyond our usual field of perception, might well be available to us through the exercise of wit; such was the promise, after all, of rhetorical argumentation. In the latter half of the century, however, one tragedy after another casts doubt upon this possibility of transcendence. Hamlet, the courtier, soldier, and scholar, standing on the edge of Elizabethan humanism, gives eloquent testimony to the failure of deep-searching wit to extricate itself from the limitations of its own condition. Marlowe makes the journey in less than seven years. Beginning with a resounding optimism regarding the ability of man literally to invent his own reality, *hunc dies videt fugiens iacentem*—by his last play he has apparently lost all such confidence, creating a nightmare world in which imagination and objective reality frightfully coincide. The climate was changing. Montaigne was retreating into fideism and minute self-examination, convinced that he could perceive no larger truth, and in England Greville elegized man's bleared instruments of knowing. The stage was set for a tragedy of invention. Marlowe created it, and Shakespeare followed. The dead end of the *quaestio* was in sight.

Which brings us to one final matter. Although the material discussed in this book has obvious relevance to the study of Shakespeare, I have made no attempt to include a discussion of his plays here, except for an analysis of *The Comedy of Errors* that seemed appropriate within the context of my developing argument. To have attempted to deal adequately with more of his work would have been an impossible task. Until such a time as this is feasible, I can only hope that the reader will be stimulated by the text to make his own connections, and that he will find such applications useful.

But now, let us dispense with further preliminaries, and enter into the Tudor play of mind.

Demonstrative and Explorative: Two Paradigms

TOWARD THE CLOSE OF THE FIFTEENTH CENTURY, HENRY MEDWALL, CHAP-
lain to Thomas More's benefactor Cardinal Morton, "compiled" two
plays that have been preserved to us. Both are written in two parts, apparently meant to be performed in the course of some festivity, and
are directed to the same kind of audience. Yet they are distinctly different
in conception and function. *Nature* is a humanist morality play. Its hero,
Man, is ushered onto the stage of life by Dame Nature, who opens the
action by describing her various works, referring the audience for further
details to Aristotle, "my phylosopher electe" (1.58).[1] She goes on to
extol human perfection according to "Ovyde in hys boke cleped the
transformacyon" (1.78). Then, turning to the hero, she tells him why
she has brought him here tonight. He is ordained to be a passenger on a
long voyage through the world, guided chiefly by Reason but also by
Sensuality, and nursed by Innocence. In reply, Man humbly addresses
himself to God, and in a rather moving speech acknowledges his relationship "wyth sensuall bestys," but remarks especially his unique gift of
understanding,

> whereby I may avew
> And well dyscerne what ys to be done
> yet for all that have I fre eleccyon

1. Part and line numbers refer to Alois Brandl, *Quellen des weltlichen Dramas in
England vor Shakespeare* (Strasbourg, 1898).

> Do what I wyll be yt evyll or well
> And am put in the hande of myne own counsell.
>
> (1.136–140)

And he prays for grace. Dame Nature, about to depart, offers him a final warning:

> Thou hast now lybertye and nedest no maynmyssyon
> And yf thou abond the to passyons sensuall
> Farewele thy lybertye thou shal wax thrall.
>
> (1.166–168)

To this, Sensuality objects strenuously. "I am the chyef perfeccyon of his nature," he declares; without sensuality, man would be "a lorde made of clowtes." Nature willingly concedes his point, but insists that only Reason can lead Man in the way of virtue and grace. Whereupon she exits, leaving the hero in the tuition of his rational guide, from whom he falls away soon after entering the world, succumbing rapidly to the blandishments of Worldly Affection and his coterie of sins.

Although this sketch suggests only the beginning and downward movement of the action, it will serve to justify some general observations. First, all the action in the play proceeds from an assertion about the nature of man. Nature expounds and Man rehearses his privileges, obligations, and the dangers to be incurred should he fail to fulfill his prescribed role. Each of the events that follow, therefore, has a specific moral content, and the plot measures the hero's deviation from the norm postulated at the beginning. Second, the plot provides not only a pattern of deviation but also an *anatomy* of how Man is led to abandon his nature by sleight and persuasion. When he enters the world, Mundus convinces him that he must behave as a traveler who conforms to the local customs, advising him to clothe himself ("Ye must consyder thys ys not paradyse") and to select counselors who know the lay of the land. This advice seems harmless enough, but as Man covers his nakedness he undergoes a psychological change made explicit in dialogue. Acting in accordance with the worldly logic that no man likes to be called an innocent, he banishes Nurse Innocence, and through similar distortions of reasoning—signaling his defection from Reason—he hires as his servants the seven deadly sins, all masquerading under innocuous pseudonyms: Gluttony is "Good Fellowship," Wrath is "Manhood," Lechery is "Bodily Lust."[2] Although Man takes these Vices at their word and is misled into following evil counsel, the audience is always alerted to their true identity so that it may observe their techniques of deception in operation. The action, therefore, not only traces the progress of Man's depravity, but also maps out for subsequent travelers the specific epistemological and psychological detours along the road to salvation that lead one inadvertently to hell.

The third characteristic to be noted is that the didactic and the histrionic are one in this play. No one in Medwall's audience could ever again mistake as "Worship" the man of sumptuous array who crisps his long golden hair like Chaucer's Absolon, employs a young page to carry his sword, and fusses ceaselessly about Man's new garments. Everything that Pride does manifests the disadvantages attached to his nature. He not only persuades Man to "trust all to his own brayne" (for "brayne," read "will")—and thereby to dispense with Reason—but gets into trouble himself because of his self-love. A battle with Reason is toward. Pride turns up late—not out of cowardice, but simply because he has taken too long getting dressed. Envy, seizing the advantage, tells him that Man, angered by his failure to show up for the fight, has dismissed him from office. Poor Pride is abashed:

> I am unhappy I se yt well
> For thexpense of myne apparell
> towardys this vyage
> what in horses and other aray
> Hath compelled me for to lay
> all my land to morgage
> and now whan I have all do
> To lesse myne offyce and fees also
> For my true intent
> I may say that all my cost
> And all my tyme ys evyll lost
> In servyce that I have spent.
> (2.875–886)

2. For the tradition behind this form of dissimulation, see Spivack, *Shakespeare and the Allegory of Evil* (New York, 1958).

Such is the wages of pride. But a second lesson is in store. Pride has, in fact, been the victim of a cruel hoax. Envy confides to Sensuality that he made the whole thing up, just because Pride looked so intolerably fine in his gay gear: "yt ys my guyse," he shrugs complacently. In a similar demonstration of propriety, Lechery, alias "Bodily Lust," runs from the battle because

> I will not com where strokys be.
> . . . .
> Of lust and pleasure ys all my mynde
> It longeth to me of property and kinde.
>   (2.672, 677–678)

Characters are essences in *Nature*. The vices, darting about like so many busybodies each hatching schemes to divert Man to his own sphere of sinful specialization, reveal everything one should know about sin. In a complementary movement, the final pageant of the Seven Cardinal Virtues, played before an aging Man, presents in emblematic fashion a detailed exposition of the process of repentance.

How might one describe the peculiar pleasures of such a play? It is a highly literate work, expressing many interests of the humanist circle for whom it was composed, and therefore cannot be passed off as a popular simplification. On the contrary, it is well reasoned and intellectually stimulating. Witty throughout, it describes in some vivid detail the created universe over which Dame Nature presides, satirizes such favorite humanist targets as corrupt lawyers, nuns, priests, and parasitic aristocrats, and maintains a relationship of raffish badinage with the audience.[3] But beyond its genial admixture of doctrine and solace, one is struck chiefly by the fact that it is a profoundly reassuring play. This is so not simply because of its comic ending—indeed, desertion by the sins of his youth makes Man's final atonement an ironic inevitability—but rather because of its view of the world and its method of exposition.

Although we usually take the premises of the morality play for granted, it will be useful to consider for a moment its character as an imaginative construction. Essentially it presents as a model of reality a clearly marked-

3. These topics are discussed in detail by Pearl Hogrefe, *The Sir Thomas More Circle* (Urbana, Ill., 1959).

off universe in which man may exist safely by acknowledging a defined role and remaining within its bounds. This definition has been distilled from the confused blending of desire and truth that prevails in the actual world, and set forth in the form of a dramatic exemplum which clarifies, by imaging the hero's adventures, the nature of our own moral experience. Its comic form suggests that our life, too, can have a happy ending if we are careful and, like the hero of the play, finally make the correct choice. For while Pride may disguise himself as "Worship," and Wrath as "Manhood," this only warns us that vigilance is necessary; it does not suggest that the choice itself is ultimately problematic.[4] Such a model, which expounds the moral operation of the universe and reveals how man may live successfully within it, is an instrument of affirmation, which expresses the author's sense of order and finds assent in our own gratified response.

It is not simply to a reassuring imaginative projection, however, that we are responding. An important component of our enjoyment is the intellectual satisfaction we experience upon finding an assertion proved logically. For within the dramatic action of *Nature* lies an extended categorical syllogism or sorites. The play opens by postulating a general premise which it then proceeds to prove deductively and, therefore, with increasing particularity, as the plot unfolds. The submerged syllogism may be said to go something like this:

> When man abandons reason, he loses his freedom.
> To follow sensuality is to abandon reason.
> When Man follows sensuality, he loses his freedom.

We can supply a number of intermediate terms which will account for the hero's various adventures along the way:

> Worldly affection is a form of sensuality.
> When man heeds worldly affection, he loses his freedom.

---

4. The locus classicus of this optimistic position is Richard Hooker's assertion: "There is not that good which concerneth us, but it hath evidence enough for itself if Reason were diligent to search it out" (*Of the Laws of Ecclesiastical Polity*, 1.7.7 [London, 1907]).

17

Pride is a form of worldly affection.
When man follows pride, etc.

Genus logically preceding species, the plot of the play virtually "acts out" the process of deductive reasoning—elucidating the decline and fall of Man from the generic assertion of Nature at the beginning to the specific moment of his conversion as an old reprobate facing perdition. Thus the author of *Nature* not only articulates our desire for a rational universe in which salvation is accessible to every reasonable man, but, treating that desire as *truth*, he employs the venerable method of syllogistic demonstration to confirm our mutual wish. We are certain to end where we began.

Medwall's second play, *Fulgens and Lucres*, reveals a rather different procedure. It opens not upon a theoretical proposition, but upon an anecdote. Two low characters, A and B, emerge from the audience to discuss a play that is to be presented shortly. B tells A the plot: Lucres, a beautiful, well-educated Roman lady, is wooed by two suitors. Publius Cornelius Scipio is a wealthy nobleman of distinguished ancestry who enjoys great public esteem. His rival Gaius Flamineus is a commoner of modest means who has earned high repute for his public service. Lucres replies to their suit by informing them that she will choose the nobler man, and after much partisan discussion among the citizens of Rome, the two men present their cases to the Senate for adjudication. The Senate declares Gaius the nobler in view of his virtuous life. A, who has heard this summary in silence, is shocked:

> And shall this be the process of the play?
> . . . .
> By my faith, but if it be even as ye say,
> I will advise them to change that conclusion.
> What, will they affirm that a churl's son
> Should be more noble than a gentleman born?
> Nay, beware! for men will have thereof great scorn,
> It may not be spoken in no manner of case.
> (1.126, 128–133)[5]

5. Part and line numbers refer to F. S. Boas, ed., *Five Pre-Shakespearean Comedies* (Oxford, 1934).

B assures him that such "considerations" will be presented during the play, that every reasonable man will be satisfied with the judgment. And the play proper commences, A and B stepping into the roles of servants to the rival suitors.

With the plot revealed beforehand, it is apparent that the central interest for the audience will be the *manner* in which the conclusion is reached; that is, the reasons behind Lucres's choice. And sure enough, although a comic subplot intervenes, featuring the wooing of Lucres's maid Joan by A and B, the central episode of the play is a "royal disputation" between Gaius and Cornelius in which each tries to prove that he is the nobler man.[6]

Cornelius bases his claim on descent, and accordingly his speech recounts the deeds of the Cornelii. He proudly cites their feats as recorded

6. In our delight at discovering a pre-Shakespearean subplot, we tend to forget that the disputation was at least as important to Medwall's audience as the horseplay. But Servant A reminds us of this fact at the beginning of Part 2:

> Lucres will come hither again,
> And her said lovers both twain
> To define this question;
> Whether of them is the more noble man;
> For thereon all this matter began,
> It is the chief foundation
> Of all this process both all and some.
>
> (2.54–60)

The term "foundation" has a technical significance here beyond its obvious one. It is the common English translation of *firmamentum*, which Cicero, the author of the *Ad Herennium*, and Quintilian designate the chief argument of the defense in the judicial case, but which is often described simply as the main point for adjudication (*De inv.* 1.19, *Ad Her.* 1.26, *Inst. or.* 3.11.1, 9, 12ff.). Thomas Wilson calls the foundation "the principall point in every debated matter, called of the Rhetoricians the state, or constitution of the cause" (*The Art of Rhetorique*, ed. G. H. Mair [Oxford, 1909], p. 86). According to rhetorical tradition, the "state" or *status* is concerned with one of three questions: *An sit*? *Quid sit*? *Qualis sit*? The "process" of *Fulgens and Lucres*, conducted through the metaphor of a judicial inquiry, appears to be primarily concerned with the third question: "What kind of men are Cornelius and Gaius?" In attempting to answer it, however, Medwall must also pose the second: "What is true nobility?" The matter of *status* will be discussed in more detail in Ch. III.

by chronicles, the deeds of manhood and policy which earned them reputations as saviors of the city. He compares their gests to those of Alexander (and Arthur!), dwelling especially upon the achievements of his great-grandfather Scipio Africanus, the honors accorded his family, the reverence still paid their images. In a neat bit of sophistry he argues that if honor is due their dead images, how much more is due their living image—himself! He then switches topics from inherited honor to inherited wealth, and vaunts his palaces, towers, and treasures. He even allows himself the luxury of a little *ad hominem* sniping at Flamineus who "now of late Among noble gentlemen playest checkmate!" Lucres scolds him for the lapse, and Flamineus eagerly steps in to reply, but Cornelius insists he be allowed his peroration, in which he promises Lucres a life of "ease and pleasant idleness."

When Gaius speaks in rebuttal, he directly attacks Cornelius's major premise that nobility is acquired through ancestry and wealth. First he questions whether all Cornelius's ancestors did in fact accomplish great deeds; this in doubt, Cornelius must show what he himself has achieved. But Cornelius has refused to do this, he maintains, because of the ignoble facts of his life. Thereupon he cites Cornelius's voluptuous and vicious dealings—"thefts and murders," "riotous disports," a "mind disposed to all uncleanness"—and asks whether this constitutes nobility. In effect, he is moving toward a new definition of nobility, which he describes as "long continued virtue," rather than nobility of descent, a gift of nature for which a man is no more responsible than if he were born lame or blind. He proceeds to show how his own life has fulfilled this definition, and concludes by promising Lucres moderate riches and a man suited to her condition.

After the debaters have left the stage, Lucres announces that while she honors Cornelius for his blood, Gaius is the nobler man and will be her husband. Now that he is "inside" the play, it is servant B's turn to be shocked:

> Yes, by my troth, I shall witness bear,
> Wheresoever I become another day,
> How such a gentlewoman did openly say
> That by a churl's son she would set more
> Than she would by a gentleman bore.

Lucres denies that this is the meaning of her decision:

> Fore God, sir, the substance of my words was this—
> . . . .
> That for virtue excellent I will honour a man
> Rather than for his blood, if it so fall
> That gentle conditions agree not withal.

Clown B then hypothesizes:

> Then I put case that a gentleman bore
> Have godly manners to his birth according.

Suppose you found a gentleman, he speculates, as virtuous as his ancestors. Lucres replies:

> I say of him is to be set great store:
> Such *one* is worthy more laud and praising
> Than *many* of them that hath their beginning
> Of low kindred, or else God forbid!
> I will not affirm the contrary for my head,
> For in that case there may be no comparison.
>   (2.768–787, emphases mine)

And the play ends with A's suggestion to the nobles of the audience that perhaps one of them might become the ideal Lucres describes.

How may we characterize *Fulgens and Lucres*? It, too, is an educative play: the author hopes to move his noble audience to virtue. But in this play the center of interest has shifted from demonstration to inquiry. The action develops not from an abstract assertion, but from a specific question: who is the nobler man, Cornelius or Gaius? An admittedly bare action it is, necessitating the creation of a second action—the wooing of Joan—to sustain it for 2300 lines. But this second action, parodying the first, is also in the way of inquiry, concerning not moral qualities but physical ones. Declares Joan:

> he that can do most mastery,
> Be it in cookery or in pastry,

21

In feats of war or deeds of chivalry,
With him will I go.

(1.1095–1098)

And the activity that follows is concerned with discovering who possesses such mastery. Along the way further variations crop up. At the end of Part 1, A asks:

Let me see now, what is your opinion
Whether of them is most noble of condition?

B replies:

That can I tell hardily:
He that hath most nobles in store.

(1.1374–1377)

The delight in questioning (and in finding answers both serious and outrageous) is most obvious in the orations, which are expounded with loving attention to fine points.[7] After the speakers have concluded, Lucres even asks if there are further proofs or witnesses, and when both men agree to stand on "the common voice of the country," she promises to investigate this evidence. Near the very end of the play, when A asks what the outcome of the debate has been and B tells him that Lucres has accepted Gaius for his virtue, A exclaims:

Virtue, what the devil is that?
An I can tell, I shrew my cat.

(2.842–843)

Thus, one question leads to another, and it is this sort of probing, serious and comic, that continually flavors the play. Debate sets the tone: who is more noble, who is better in singing, wrestling, or jousting at "fart prick in cule"? Indeed, when in the subplot Joan finally reveals that she

7. Notice that Gaius attacks Cornelius's claim to nobility on two counts. First, he denies that all Cornelius's forbears acted heroically. Then, dropping this argument, he proceeds to the broader objection that a man's nobility is not derived from his kin, whom he now grants to be "noble without fail" (2.649). The two arguments are clearly inconsistent, but sophistic disputation demands neither continuity nor consistency—simply answers that are possible. This point will be amplified in Ch. II.

is already betrothed, and rejects both A and B, one suddenly realizes that these "investigations" have been conducted rather for their expository value than for any answers that might have been conclusively demonstrated.

Significantly, this emphasis is reflected in the main plot as well. For Lucres makes it abundantly clear that her decision is not absolute; it is something of a compromise. Given a corrupt nobleman and a virtuous commoner, she chooses the commoner. But Gaius is not Lucres's ideal, which is "a gentleman bore" with "godly manners to his birth according." In effect, the play does two separate and not entirely congruent things: intellectually, it summons up the vision of an ideal; physically, it embraces the actual that most closely resembles the ideal. The good frog never turns into Prince Charming.

The fact that the plot arrives at one solution and the heroine points to another suggests that the function of the play has not been to demonstrate anything but rather to lead the audience to envision, and ultimately to achieve, the ideal solution itself.[8] Medwall seeks to accomplish this goal in a curious fashion. He presents an exemplum that is not likely to be ingratiating to the audience, but offers it in such a way that it will be both tolerated and contemplated seriously. He does this by placing the exemplum in a special relationship to the world of the audience. In the case of *Nature*, the exemplum is a psychological extension of the outside world. It clarifies the moral universe in which the audience lives and

8. This is precisely what the epilogue says is its purpose:

> All the substance of this play
> Was done specially therefore,
> Not only to make folk mirth and game,
> But that such as be gentlemen of name
> May be somewhat moved
> By this example for to eschew
> The way of vice and favour virtue,
> For sin is to be reproved
> More in them, for their degree,
> Than in other persons such as be
> Of poor kin and birth.

(2.888–898)

The noble auditor is asked to entertain the possibility of achieving the ideal synthesis of blood and virtue that is described, but not realized, in the play.

which it tacitly accepts, by reproducing a symbolic image of that world. The exemplum of *Fulgens and Lucres* performs a different function because it exists in a different relationship to the outside world. This play very consciously marks off for itself a territory in which to operate that is set apart from the world of habitual expectations. Just before the disputation takes place, Lucres agrees to serve as judge only upon the following condition:

> Lo, this wise I mean and thus I do intend,
> That whatsoever sentence I give betwixt you two
> After mine own fantasy, it shall not extend
> To any other person, I will that it be so,
> For why no man else hath therein ado:
> It may not be noted for a general precedent,
> Albeit that for your parts ye do thereto assent.
>
> (2.427–433)

She is demanding, in effect, total liberty of action, thereby establishing an ethically neutral environment in which she may impartially examine opposing ideas and select that which seems best, *immune from the pressures of the actual world.* In doing so, she is also making it possible for the audience to suspend its ordinary judgments and to entertain for a while the alternative possibilities the action will present. This is why she insists that the decision finally offered will have meaning only within the context of the play and "may not be noted for a general precedent." If a churl is not to be preferred to a gentleman born, but only *this* churl and *this* nobleman, *within the special circumstances of the play*, then the audience is free to think otherwise than it usually does in the world of serious consequences.[9]

Fulgens and Lucres differs from *Nature*, then, in several important respects. It is conceived in the interrogative and not the declarative mood; therefore its intellectual energies are devoted to discovery, not explanation, and its structure tends to be fragmented into *quaestiunculae* budding

9. Additional clues that Medwall was anxious to sharply distinguish the play world from that of the audience are found at 1.177–180, 220–222. The importance to the Renaissance polity of a "sphere of good faith where one can debate without fear of intimidation or constraint" is discussed by Nancy S. Struever, *The Language of History in the Renaissance* (Princeton, 1970), esp. pp. 116–121.

off the main question, not episodes proving an assertion. The play is able to expound fully both sides of the question because it functions within an ethically neutral environment, not one that seeks to represent, in however attractive a fashion, the prevailing realities of the outside world. Finally, as comic artifact, it locates its resolution not in a correct choice but in the image of an ideal synthesis of two imperfect alternatives. It is a comedy of inclusiveness, not conversion.

What impulse lies behind such an imaginative construction? The author is the same man who composed *Nature*, but is here exercising a different intellectual muscle. He now seems determined to question accepted habits of thought rather than to endorse them. In this respect, *Fulgens and Lucres* is a radical document, even though its question is one previously rehearsed by Boethius, Dante, Chaucer, and others. For Medwall, like his predecessors, is breaking out of a perspective and a vocabulary that has hardened in the process of time, and which under the pressures of daily political existence tends to regard nobility in its social aspect alone. He is acknowledging a moral signification that enlarges the term. The imaginative movement is outward, toward a comprehensive multiplicity, rather than inward, as in *Nature*, toward what is ultimately a rigid philosophical dualism.

As we might expect, this movement, too, assumes its characteristically logical form, one that is epistemologically prior to that in *Nature*. For *Fulgens* begins in observable data, not in generalization. We know the final situation: Lucres has chosen Gaius as the nobler of the two suitors. What we want to find out is why. We discover this by examining the premises underlying the conclusion, thus working back toward some statable general proposition. Our first observations are of the differences in manner between the two men; then we compare their habits and pastimes, their civic accomplishments and moral sensibilities. We are led, as we begin to consider more substantive characteristics, to form increasingly generic judgments concerning the worthiness of each man. Through this process of analysis we gradually come to understand why Lucres chose as she did, arriving ourselves at the general truth that a virtuous churl is preferable to a vicious gentleman. In effect, we have participated with Medwall in a search for the pattern of causality lying behind the bare series of events about which we were informed at the outset. In so doing, we have progressed from ignorance and uncertainty about a fact to a reasoned understanding of it, and have formulated a tentative and delimited premise based upon our investigation. *Fulgens and Lucres*, therefore, has more than the flavor of inquiry; it functions as inquiry. At the end of the play, we are not where we were.[10]

II

The contrast that we see in Medwall's plays is evident in the whole body of drama that has come down to us from the first third of the sixteenth century. These plays inevitably fall into two major groups:[11]

Medwall, *Nature* (1495)

Anonymous, *Everyman* (1495)

———, *The World and the Child* (1508)

———, *Hicke Scorner* (1513)

Skelton, *Magnyfycence* (1515)

Rastell, *The Four Elements* (1517)

Anonymous, *Youth* (1520)

———, *Johan the Evangelist* (1520)

———, *Godly Queen Hester* (1527)

———, *Calisto and Melibea* (1527)

Redford, *Wit and Science* (1539)

Medwall, *Fulgens and Lucres* (1497)

Heywood, *The Pardoner and the Friar* (1519)

———, *The Four PP* (1520)

———, *Johan Johan* (1520)

Rastell, *Gentleness and Nobility* (1527)

Heywood, *The Play of the Weather* (1528)

———, *Witty and Witless* (1533)

———, *The Play of Love* (1533)

10. The movements in *Fulgens and Lucres* and *Nature* correspond to the two major procedures of traditional Aristotelian logic—invention, or the discovery of arguments to support a proposition (here, the "fact" of Lucres's choice)—and judgment, or the orderly framing of syllogistic proofs to verify deductively the results of invention (see Walter J. Ong, S.J., *Ramus, Method, and the Decay of Dialogue* [Cambridge, Mass., 1958], pp. 182–184, 240–245). The function of these modes of reasoning in dramatic structures is discussed by Wesley Trimpi in ways I have found particularly illuminating for understanding Medwall's plays (see "The Ancient Hypothesis of Fiction," *Traditio* [1971], esp. 41–55, and "The Quality of Fiction," *Traditio* [1974]: 51–61).

11. The dates cited throughout the text are those supplied in Alfred Harbage,

Those on the left, for all their differences in subject matter, literary accomplishment, length, and implied audience, are plays that primarily show. Those on the right are plays that primarily ask. Furthermore, only a thin line seems to have divided the play from other forms of literary discourse. On the title page of *Everyman*, for example, we read, "Here begynnyth the treatyse how ye hye Fader of Heven sendeth Deth to somon every Creature to come and give account of theyr lyves in this Worlde, and is *in maner of a Morall play*." The romance *Calisto and Melibea* is described as a "comedy in English *in manner of an interlude*," while the debate play *Gentleness and Nobility* is subtitled "A Dyalogue between the Marchaunt, the Knyght, and the Plowman . . . compiled *in maner of an interlude* with divers toys and gests added thereto to make mery pastime and disport."[12] These rubrics suggest that those who wrote or published the plays thought of them as forms of discourse continuous with nondramatic forms, in one case a repentance treatise, in another a medieval narrative comedy, in the last a disputation—now "acted out."

Such evidence invites us to consider these plays in relation to the aims and methods they share with their nondramatic analogues. *Nature*, its companion moralities, and the plays concerning biblical heroes, saints, and virtuous lay figures are historically associated with sermon exempla, *lectiones*, and cautionary tales—all demonstrative forms of discourse aimed at explicating the meaning of received texts and reinforcing the moral exigencies acknowledged by the community. They represent and "prove," deductively and analogically, the conclusions to questions answered long ago.[13] The plays of inquiry, on the other hand, are dramatic

---

Annals of English Drama 975–1700, rev. by S. Schoenbaum (London, 1964). I have included *Wit and Science* because its *terminus a quo* is 1531.

12. See, respectively, *Chief Pre-Shakespearean Dramas*, ed. J. Q. Adams (Cambridge, Mass., 1924); *A Select Collection of Old English Plays*, ed. W. C. Hazlitt, 4th ed., Vol. 1 (London, 1874); Kenneth W. Cameron, *Authorship and Source of "Gentleness and Nobility"* (Raleigh, N.C., 1941). Emphases are mine.

13. G. R. Owst has shown in great detail the similarities in themes and devices between this type of drama and the materials of late medieval preaching, in *Literature and Pulpit in Medieval England* (Cambridge, 1933), esp. pp. 142–209, 471–547, and Spivack has alerted us to the homiletic function of morality rhetoric (*Shakespeare and the Allegory of Evil*). Further discussion of demonstrative drama and its nondramatic analogues is found in L. B. Campbell, *Shakespeare's Tragic Heroes* (Cambridge, 1930); Willard Farnham, *The Medieval Heritage of Elizabethan*

versions of the questions themselves—heirs to literary forms which set word against word, and were developed to give voice to the expanding imagination.

The source of Medwall's play, for example, is a *controversia*, written originally in Ciceronian Latin by the Italian jurist Buonaccorso da Montemagno and printed by Caxton in an English translation by John Tiptoft in 1481.[14] This literary kind evolved from the philosophical questions and deliberative and forensic debates practiced originally by Greek rhetoricians and later by their Roman heirs, including such notable authorities as Cicero and Quintilian. Beginning as an academic exercise designed to prepare the orator to argue a case at law, the *controversia* became a social entertainment under the early Roman Empire, when teachers of rhetoric and professional orators propounded their cases before audiences in private schools and public halls of declamation.[15] The declaimers were given the facts they were to work with—in the form of brief fictitious narratives leading to a legal issue—and the law governing the dispute.[16] Their task was to argue the case in behalf of either litigant, drawing the particulars of the action into broader considerations of law and equity. In effect, they supplied definition and intention to the law, character and motivation to the litigants, and thus built up a substantial argument for one side or the other. This was achieved principally by means of three devices, according to the Elder Seneca: *sententiae*, or sharp, witty "opinions" delivered upon the case; the *divisio*, or exposition of the chief lines

Tragedy (Berkeley, 1936); Hardin Craig, *English Religious Drama* (Oxford, 1955); V. A. Kolve, *The Play Called Corpus Christi* (Stanford, 1967).

14. The text is reprinted in R. J. Mitchell, *John Tiptoft* (London, 1938).

15. The decline of the serious legal exercise into a public pastime has been generally ascribed to the restricted opportunities for pleading significant issues in the courts during the principate. For an analysis of the issues, and a detailed account of the development of the *controversia*, see S. F. Bonner, *Roman Declamation in the Late Republic and Early Empire* (Liverpool, 1949), pp. 1–50. For the texts, see *The Elder Seneca: Declamations*, trans. M. Winterbottom, 2 vols. L.C.L. (London, 1974). Characteristics of the declaimers and their work are described by Henri Bornecque, *Les Déclamations et les Déclamateurs d'après Sénèque le Père* (Lille, 1902); E. M. Waith suggests the relationship of the declamatory tradition to *Fulgens and Lucres*, though not in the terms considered here, in "'Controversia' in the English Drama," *PMLA* 68 (1953): 286–303.

16. The subject matter—tales of kidnap, rape, piracy, wicked stepmothers, disinherited sons—was notorious. See *Inst. or.* 2.10.3–5.

of argument; and *colores*, highly refined interpretations of motive and cause. The product of the competition—as is so often the case in law-courts today—was the very same "story" told from different points of view, each speaker applauded or criticized in proportion to the persuasive new lights he shed on the case. Such performances were attended by the educated and politically powerful, men of literary sophistication who found the declamations a means of sharpening their wits, increasing their legal knowledge, and refining their literary style.[17]

Buonaccorso's *controversia* is simpler and certainly more tame than those in the Senecan collection, but it clearly belongs to the same genre. His declamation consists of a narration of the facts leading up to the Senate hearing, plus the orations of the two suitors. No decision is given. Caxton's epilogue makes clear its function as a medium of inquiry:

> As touchyng the sentence dyffynytyf gyven by the Senate aftir thise two noble knyghtes had purposed and shewed theyr Oracions I fynde none as yet pronounced ne gyven of whiche myn auctour maketh ony mencion of in his book. Thenne I wolde demaunde of theym that shal rede or here this book. whiche of thies tweyne that is to saye Cornelius Scipio and Gauys Flammyneus was moost noble And in whiche of theym bothe. aftir the contente of theyr oracions that noblesse resteth And to hym Juge ye this noble and vertuous lady Lucresse to be maryed.[18]

Medwall's dramatic version takes the process a step further. It reveals how one may proceed, through the arguments of a *controversia*, toward the discovery of some governing principle. For B's summary of the plot to A, outlining the facts of the case, tells us very little. It simply constitutes the given of the situation, and resembles those brief summaries that precede the arguments recorded by Seneca. It is in the "considerations" which B then promises A that the substance lies. These "considerations" are of two kinds. One kind concerns what we might call the "law" governing this *controversia*: that the truly noble man should win the hero-

17. "Orators like Pollio and Cassius Severus, scholars like Messala, social figures like Ovid, men of affairs like Gallio and Fabius Maximus, historians like Livy and Bruttedius Niger, were present at these declamations, some of them were attended by Maecenas and Agrippa, and by Augustus himself" (Bonner, p. 40).

18. William Caxton, *The Prologues and Epilogues*, ed. W. J. B. Crotch (London, 1928), p. 46.

ine. It is to determine the meaning of this "law" that Cornelius and Gaius debate the nature of true nobility. The second kind of "consideration," involving equity, concerns the characters of the two men in light of the definitions. Details of character—the *colores* of this declamation—emerge in the action, dialogue, and disputation. They are Cornelius's extravagance in dress, about which the clowns gossip; his conventional courtly wooing, represented in the mumming offered for Lucres's entertainment; the "riotous disport and play" described by Gaius; and, on the other side, Gaius's own qualities of study, modesty, and active virtue, which are revealed in his speech. These interpretive elements, which bring out the hidden qualities of the two suitors,[19] must have been followed with keen interest by the spectators at Medwall's play—a group of lawyers, political and ecclesiastical officials, and men of letters, whose tastes were probably not very different in kind from those of the more judicious auditors who had enjoyed the original declamations. Knowing Lucres's decision, they would want to know why she chose as she did, and doubtless they took pleasure in examining all the verbal and dramatic evidence that Medwall could muster to show how such a judgment might be reached.

Their interest in a play like this raises an important question: what assumption about drama—or, for that matter, about literature in general—did they bring with them to Cardinal Morton's house on that evening? Comparison of *Nature* and *Fulgens and Lucres* suggests that it was something more complex than what we usually think is implied in the familiar formula "profit and delight." Literature not only offered them edifying precepts vividly set forth, but also induced a play of mind that overran the boundaries traditionally set by the orthodoxy of the outside world and allowed them to enjoy what might best be described as an experience of aesthetic skepticism—an interlude of extended quest, free from the constraints of politic choice, that enriched their vision of reality and returned them to the actual with a deeper sense of its complexity. It is this experience that we must now examine more closely.

19. Notice that they are unknowns at the outset, unlike the characters of *Nature*. We learn what their appearances represent only in the course of the inquiry.

The Moral Cultivation
of Ambivalence

THE ENCOUNTER WE HAVE JUST SEEN BETWEEN A MORALLY EARNEST TUDOR chaplain and a model of postclassical witplay is no isolated incident. One of the more fascinating aspects of sixteenth-century intellectual life is the marriage effected between moral reformation and sophistic argumentation. Certainly, ever since Plato insisted that rhetoric bears the same relationship to knowledge as *haute cuisine* to medicine, the rhetorical art has been suspect. Yet Aristotle had argued that "we must be able to employ persuasion [rhetoric] just as strict reasoning [dialectic] can be employed, on opposite sides of the question, not in order that we may in practice employ it both ways (for we must not make people believe what is wrong), but in order that we may see clearly what the facts are, and that, if another man argues unfairly, we on our part may be able to confute him."[1] Seeing clearly what the facts are means in effect seeing what the facts may be, since Aristotle assumes that persuasion is not employed in cases where truth is demonstrable, but only where a likely probability may be arrived at; indeed, he distinguishes the logical syllogism from the rhetorical enthymeme on that basis. Rhetoric becomes, then, "the faculty of observing in any given case the available means of persuasion" —an art aimed at both finding arguments that can lead to the discovery of truth, and securing conviction through the deployment of such arguments. Its end is moral, though its means are morally neutral. This liberal

1. *Rhet.* 1355a, trans. W. Rhys Roberts, *The Basic Works of Aristotle*, ed. Richard McKeon (New York, 1941).

concept—which allows the rhetorician a privileged position due to his presumed ethical rectitude, and thus a larger measure of freedom than the uninitiated layman—was reinforced in the rhetorical treatises of Cicero and Quintilian. It also informed the attitudes of the humanists in England and Northern Europe as they cultivated the arts of persuasion at the beginning of the century. Not unexpectedly, their pursuit of the discipline under the strongest of moral imperatives produced in them an eristic turn of mind that permanently affected the way they conducted themselves, the way they read, and the way they wrote.[2]

This habit was expressed in many forms. Arguing both sides of the question was frequently employed as a method of political inquiry and (not infrequently) of political hedging; it appears as a mode of theological speculation and even of scientific investigation. But it is also turned to use simply as a creative pastime, in which one need not proceed beyond disputation to secure conviction; here, its value lay rather in exercising the inventive faculty to produce effective proofs.

We know, for example, that even as mature men, Erasmus and Sir Thomas More practiced just such declamations as the one on which Medwall's play was based. Among their translations of Lucian is a *controversia* called *Tyrannicida*, which they not only rendered into Latin but also took upon themselves to answer. It offers us an amusing glimpse of the extraordinary dexterity with which the trained rhetorician was able to simultaneously entertain two opposing points of view. In Lucian's

2. The moral exhortation to master rhetoric is sounded early in the Latin tradition by the young Cicero: "Men ought none the less devote themselves to the study of eloquence, although some misuse it both in private and public affairs. And they should study it the more earnestly in order that evil men may not obtain greater power to the detriment of good citizens and the common disaster of the community" (*De inv.* 1.5, trans. H. M. Hubbell, L.C.L. [London, 1949]). In later works he consistently develops the idea that the great orator is a man of philosophical outlook (e.g., *De or.* 1.35, 3.71; *Or.* 11–16), and he explicitly relates the practice of arguing both sides of the question to the philosophical method of the Middle Academy (see Ch. III, n. 12). His influence is clearly seen in Quintilian's insistence that *bene dicere non possit nisi bonus* (*Inst. or.* 2.15.34). Vives echoes this assumption in his commendation of rhetoric, at the same time revealing his concern that "both of these arts [rhetoric and dialectic] breed very much malice, and for this reason it is not fitting that a malicious mind, and one with any tendency toward acting deceitfully should be instructed in them" (*De tradendis disciplinis*, trans. Foster Watson as *Vives: On Education* [Cambridge, 1913], p. 177).

declamation, a man comes to court claiming the reward due tyrannicides. He argues that he has caused the death of the tyrant by entering his citadel, routing the guards, and then killing the tyrant's son in battle, cleverly leaving his sword in the youth's body so that when the tyrant discovered the corpse he snatched up the sword in grief and dispatched himself. Thus he has removed not only the tyrant but his heir as well. In his response, Erasmus counters with an entirely new interpretation of the facts:

> What really happened was this: By good luck, you penetrated the citadel and chanced upon the son, who was alone and unguarded and in a drunken slumber. Him you killed. Fearing discovery, you fled, not even pausing long enough to pull out your sword from his body. You hid in your house, trembling in terror until, hearing that the tyrant was dead, you suddenly stepped forward with your impossible fiction of being the author of his death and demanded the reward decreed for tyrannicides. You did not kill the tyrant because you were afraid to do so.[3]

He further argues that the man's intention (desire for reward), his means (murder), and the results of his misadventure (success brought about by the benevolence of the gods and not the pleader's forethought) disqualify him for the reward. Indeed, he should be punished as a criminal. Erasmus has demolished the original argument by disparaging the claimant's motive, showing its incompatibility with the intent of the law, and supplying the new *colores* of chance, drunkenness, and fear. Familiarity with this kind of exercise was widespread. More's daughter Margaret worked on declamations then ascribed to Quintilian, and Erasmus recommended them as important exercises for young scholars.[4] In addition to "Quinti-

3. Craig Thompson, *The Translations of Lucian by Erasmus and St. Thomas More* (Ithaca, 1940), p. 33.
4. *Ibid.*, pp. 40–41. In a letter to Richard Whitford dated 1 May 1506, Erasmus remarks:

> I have done this [translation] all the more willingly because I very much wish this sort of exercise to be introduced into our schools, where it would be of the greatest utility. For in the want of this practice I find the reason why at this time, while there are many eloquent writers, there are so few scholars, who do not appear almost mute, whenever an orator is required, whereas if, in pursuance both of the authority of Cicero and Fabius and of the examples

lian's" declamations, the whole body of *controversiae* and *suasoriae* (fictitious speeches of advice) recorded by the elder Seneca were available in widely read editions of the epistles and essays of the younger Seneca, with which they were frequently printed.[5]

The habit of arguing *in utramque partem* permeated virtually all areas of intellectual life. Erasmus even extended it to Scriptural interpretation. Under the leadership of John Colet, Scriptural exegesis was becoming a philological and literary discipline, and therefore a subject suitable for argument according to textual and historical probability. In a letter written in October 1499, Erasmus disputes with Colet the meaning of Christ's prayer in Gethsemane. Colet had argued that when Christ prayed that the cup be taken from him he wished to prevent the historical burden of guilt for his death from falling upon the Jews, while Erasmus upheld the traditional interpretation that Christ, in his human capacity, was expressing personal fear. Colet urged him to think the matter over. And so Erasmus returned home, reflected, then took up his pen and with considerable erudition and eloquence set down at great length what he thought might be said on both sides of the question. After doing so, although the force of Colet's argument became clearer to him, he was still convinced he was right.[6]

---

of the ancients, we were diligently practiced from boyhood in such exercises, there would not, surely, be such poverty of speech, such pitiable hesitation, such shameful stammering, as we witness even in those who publicly profess the art of oratory. (*The Epistles of Erasmus*, trans. Francis Morgan Nichols [London, 1901], 1: 407).

It is obviously quickness of wit that Erasmus is after. Stapleton comments that More composed declamations "pro ingenio exercitio" (Thompson, p. 38).

5. Vives especially commends these to young scholars, "for in them very many arguments are keenly and shrewdly invented and gracefully and charmingly expressed" (*Vives: On Education*, p. 186). Erasmus recommends them in *De ratione studii*, Bacon refers to them in *The Advancement of Learning* (see n. 21), and John Brinsley's *Ludus literarius* indicates that they were still being practiced in the seventeenth century. For their influence on the plot and style of Jacobean drama, see Eugene M. Waith, *The Pattern of Tragicomedy in Beaumont and Fletcher* (New Haven, 1952).

6. Frederic Seebohm, *The Oxford Reformers* (London, 1911), pp. 116–121. Rhetorical methods of inquiry also influenced humanist historiography. Valla framed his attack on the Donation of Constantine as a declamation, thereby invoking the

His habit of mind was not the least of Erasmus's differences with Luther. The *Table Talk* recalls Erasmus's meeting with the Elector Frederick III, who asked his secretary Spalatin what sort of man he had just encountered. "Plague take him!" Spalatin replied. "One knows not what he is driving at. I prefer the Wittenbergers; they say yes or no."[7] Of Erasmus's *Novum Testamentum*, Luther complained: "With Erasmus it is translation and nothing else. He is never in earnest; he is ambiguous and a caviller . . . he brings in all the Fathers: 'Thus says Ambrosius'; 'Thus says Augustine.' Why? That he may disturb the reader and make him think that the doctrine is very uncertain."[8] Erasmus, on his part, expressed the view of many of the humanists in his address to Luther on free will: "So great is my dislike of assertions that I prefer the views of the sceptics wherever the inviolable authority of Scripture and the decision of the Church permit. . . . Therefore I merely want to analyze and not to judge, to inquire and not to dogmatize. I am ready to learn from anyone who advances something more accurate or reliable, though," he adds slyly, "I would rather persuade mediocre minds not to argue too stubbornly on such matters."[9] Luther's reply offers a revealing insight into the conflict inherent in the two modes of imaginative orientation. From his point of view, accepting as he does the doctrine of literal inspiration, Erasmus's willingness to rest in uncertainty on so vital an issue as free will is virtually to deny the transcendence of God's word, and reduce theology to philosophical speculation. "Let Skeptics and Academics keep well away from us Christians," he writes. "Nothing is better known or more common among Christians than assertion. Take away assertions and you take away Christianity. . . . The Holy Spirit is no Skeptic, and it is not doubts or mere opinions that he has written on our hearts, but assertions more sure and certain than life itself and all experience."[10] Be-

freedom to question the received doctrine through probable argument. See Hanna H. Gray, "Renaissance Humanism: The Pursuit of Eloquence," *JHI* 24 (1963): 511–512.

7. *Conversations with Luther*, trans. and ed. Preserved Smith and Herbert Percival Gallinger (New York, 1915), p. 106.

8. *Ibid.*, p. 111.

9. *Erasmus-Luther: Discourse on Free Will*, trans. and ed. Ernst F. Winter (New York, 1961), pp. 7–8.

10. *Luther's Works*, general eds. Jaroslav Pelikan and Helmut T. Lehmann, 56 vols. (St. Louis and Philadelphia, 1955–), 33. 20, 21, 24.

neath their doctrinal differences was a conflict of imaginative impulse: both were pious men, both skeptical of the capacity of human reason to ascertain truth. Yet Erasmus was capable of living a moral Christian life in accordance with probability, while Luther was uncomfortable out of the shadow of dogma. Together, they adumbrate that division of soul to which the Renaissance gave such striking expression.[11]

If one face of this disputatious spirit was humble (or proud, depending upon your point of view), another was politic—as evidenced by Thomas Starkey's remarkable *Dialogue Between Pole and Lupset*, presented to Henry VIII, probably early in 1536.[12] Starkey was a humanist educated in Latin, Greek, and philosophy at Oxford, who later obtained a degree of civil law in Padua, and then presented himself to Cromwell for service. He was appointed Henry's chaplain, and during his tenure produced several political documents. The *Dialogue* is in the tradition of the memorandum of advice, artfully wrought as the conversation of two famous humanists. The two interlocutors discuss the pattern of the ideal state, contemporary defects of the English polity, and remedies for the restoration of the commonwealth. On some matters Pole, who is the leading figure in the dialogue, pursues his argument with Socratic doggedness, and persuades his friend to abandon his point of view. But on several important issues, Starkey is obviously using the open-ended form as a means of setting before Henry's consideration rather controversial issues that cannot gain easy acquiescence, and so they remain simply in the air, to stimulate the monarch's thought. For example, in discussing the constitutional faults of England, Pole argues:

> that cuntry can not be long well governyd nor maynteynyd with gud pollycy where al ys rulyd by the wyl of one, not chosen by electyon, but commyth to hyt by natural successyon; for sylden seen hyt

11. Significantly, much of what the Catholic humanists objected to in Luther was precisely what they disliked in the Schoolmen. Colet, in a moment of pique, had exclaimed to a youthful Erasmus, "What! Do you extol to me such a man as Aquinas? If he had not been very arrogant indeed, he would not surely so rashly and proudly have taken upon himself to define all things" (Seebohm, p. 107).

12. For the immediate background of this document, see Kathleen M. Burton, ed., *A Dialogue Between Reginald Pole and Thomas Lupset* (London, 1948), pp. 193–196.

is that they wych by successyon comme to kyngdomys and reamys are worthye of such hye authoryte.[13]

Starkey is actually proposing to Henry VIII that elective kingship and not hereditary monarchy is best for the state. Lupset, who plays the conservative, anticipates Henry's likely response by declaring this treasonable talk, but Pole insists that just as a moral and prudent monarch (such as Henry) may be most beneficial for the commonwealth, an evil, foolish king will spell catastrophe. In the ideal state, one must not rely upon chance but institute a method of selecting the man best qualified to rule. Lupset then further objects that such an election will create dangerous faction among the peers. To this Pole must accede, concluding that at this particular time a limited successive monarchy may be preferable, although elective kingship is the ideal toward which the wise statesman should work. Starkey's method is idealistic, yet practical. As a humanist employed in public business he felt sincerely bound to give the king the benefit of his deepest reflections; at the same time he was sufficiently aware of the contemporary state of affairs not to press for their immediate application. Although his later misjudgment of Pole shows him to be a somewhat naive statesman, it is he who actually puts into practice what the humanists envisioned as their goal, by applying his learning and rhetorical skills for the good of the state.

Hereditary monarchy is not the only established institution that Starkey questions. The law of primogeniture, unnatural and unreasonable because it "semeth to mynysch the natural love betwix the father and the chyld, and to incresse envy and hate betwix them whych nature hath so bounden togydder,"[14] also comes under fire. A compromise is proposed only after Lupset argues its necessity for the maintenance of degree and order. The practice remains no less unjust. On the crucial matter of nonresistance, Pole's position runs directly counter to evolving Tudor doctrine:

Hyt is not man that can make a wise prynce of hym that lakketh wyt by nature, nor make hym just that ys a tyranne for plesure. But thys

13. *England in the Reign of Henry VIII*, ed. Sidney J. Herrtage and J. M. Cowper, E.E.T.S. Ser. 2: 12, 32 (London, 1878), p. 101.

14. *Ibid.*, p. 109.

ys in mannys powar, to electe and chose hym that ys both wyse and just, and make hym a prynce, and hym that ys a tyranne so to depose.[15]

He will not accept the argument that tyrants are sent by God to chastise the people's sin, for it contradicts both reason and the teaching of Christ. And this leads him to propose that after the present king's death, parliament assembled must choose a man apt for kingship, to rule subject to law. Even here, however, he acknowledges that this ideal may never be accepted. And so he suggests as an alternative a successive monarchy bound by a much stricter conciliar system than was then in force.

Starkey offers an illuminating view of the humanist in politics. His method of counsel—through a form that allows him to propose radical measures, then to modify them and supply more practical alternatives—suggests how constructively the spirit of debate, exercising its ethical neutrality, may be applied to public business. For the radical idea, once stated, is not lost; it hovers in the consciousness, awaiting its time.[16]

Sometimes, of course, the method is not so constructive. Later in the century we find William Cecil offering advice to Elizabeth in a similar fashion. In a state paper entitled *An Order how to proceed to the Discussion of the Questions moved concerning the Quene's Mariadge with Monsieur d'Anjow*, dated 2 October 1579, Lord Burghley sets forth the following outline:

1. To consider what Dangers are to be probably dowted that may follow to hir Majesty's Person, to hir Government, and to the State of the Realme in generall, if she shall not marry.

2. To consider how these Dangers may be removed or withstode, though hir Majesty do not marry, and to consider how every Danger may have his proper Remedy.

3. To consider what Dangers may follow probably to her Majesty's Person, to her Government, and to the State of the Realm, if she shall marry.

15. *Ibid.*, p. 167. For a useful survey of how contrary this was, see Franklin Le Van Baumer, *The Early Tudor Theory of Kingship* (New Haven, 1940), pp. 85–119.

16. In 1540, the Statute of Wills permitted the eldest son to be entirely cut off from inheritance.

4. To consider what Proffitts or Benefitts may follow, to hir Majesty and to the Realm by this hir Mariadg.

5. To compare together all the Dangers, as well those that may follow by hir not mariadg, and for lack of Provision or sufficient Remedyes, as also those that shall follow probably by the Mariadg, and to see by Probabilities what are the grettar, that they may be most shuned, and the lesser admitted.

Finally, If it shall appeare that the Mariadge shall seme to be accompannyed with the smaller Perrills, than to consider in what Order, and with what Cautions and Provisions, the same is to be pursued.[17]

A few days later, Lord Burghley evidently diagrammed the contents of the order for quick perusal. In a memorandum dated 6 October, he set down two columns, headed "Perils" and "Remedies." He first examines the situation should the Queen remain unmarried:

PERILS	REMEDIES
Comfort of Titlers and Favorers of the Quene of Scots.	Laws to be more sharp against Favourers of Titles.
Comfort of Obstinate Papists.	Penalties increased upon Recusants.
Comfort to the Pope to follow.	To keep Papists under.
Revenge by Spayne and France.	To norrish their Troubles.
King of Scots his Marriage.	To retayne him in Friendship by Ayde and to compass his Marriage. . . .

The tally should the Queen decide to marry includes these items:

DANGERS BY THE MARRIAGE	REMEDIES
Doubtfullness of Issue. / Danger in Childbearing.	In God's Hands.
Contrariety of Religion.	To be by Articles help'd.
His Youth unequal to the Queen.	The Quene's good Constitution of body that may outlive hym.

17. *A Collection of State Papers Relating to Affairs in the Reign of Queen Elizabeth from the Year 1571 to 1596. . . .* (London, 1759), pp. 322–323.

The great misliking of Strangers.	So did they mislyke the King of Spayne.
His Nearness to the Crown of France.	That is in God's Hand.
The Inconvenience of joining the two Crowns.	That cannot be removed, but in Edward IIId's Days was born withall. . . .[18]

These deliberations ended with the acknowledgment that in exercising such circumspection the Council had reached its human limitations, "and therefore in such difficult Matters, Intercession is to be made to God, Director of Prince's Harts, to direct hir to that, which shall be most for hir Honor, hir Comfort, and the Weale of hir Subjects."[19] On October 7 Burghley recorded the Queen's reaction:

This Messadg was reported to hir Majesty in the Fornoone, and she allowed very well of the dutyfull Offer of ther Servicies—Nevertheless, she uttered many Specheis, and that not without sheddyng of many Tears, that she shold fynd in hir Counsellors, by ther long Disputations, any Disposition to mak it doutfull, whyther ther cold be any more Suerty for hir and hir Realme than to have hir marry, and have a Child of hir own Body to inherit, and so to continynew the Lyne of King Henry the VIIIth; and she sayd she condemned hirself of Symplycity in committyng this Matter to be argued by them, for that she ought to have rather had an universall Request made to hir to procede in this Mariadge, than to have made dout of it; and being much trobled herwith she requested us to forebeare hir untill the Afternoon.[20]

The Queen wanted an answer, but all she got was a disputation.

If the method inhibited action, it certainly did increase awareness. Its educative potentiality is most clearly seen in Bacon's *Essays*. In the sixth book of *The Advancement of Learning*, after defending the study of rhetoric as a necessary adjunct to his scientific program, Bacon makes the following recommendation:

18. *Ibid.*, p. 331.
19. *Ibid.*
20. *Ibid.*, p. 336.

I would have . . . all topics which there is frequent occasion to handle (whether they relate to proofs and refutations, or to persuasions and dissuasions, or to praise and blame) studied and prepared beforehand; and not only so, but the case exaggerated both ways with the utmost force of wit, and urged unfairly, as it were, and quite beyond the truth. And the best way of making such a collection, with a view to use as well as brevity, would be to contract those commonplaces into certain acute and concise sentences; to be as skeins or bottoms of thread which may be unwinded at large when they are wanted. Some such piece of diligence I find in Seneca, but in hypotheses or cases.[21]

He then supplies, under the rubric "The Antitheses of Things [Matter]," forty-seven subject topics with arguments on both sides of the question phrased as brief *sententiae.* Many of these appear in identical form in the *Essays,* which indicates that they were meant not simply as "store" for rhetorical display but as instruments for the wider examination of any subject under consideration. These "counsels morall and civill" are thus frequently consultations in the larger sense—active, ongoing ponderings, rather than digested presentations. An interesting example is the essay "Of Marriage and Single Life," which opens as follows:

He that hath wife and children hath given hostages to fortune; for they are impediments to great enterprises, either of virtue or mischief. Certainly the best works, and of greatest merit for the public, have proceeded from the unmarried or childless men; which both in affection and means have married and endowed the public. Yet it were great reason that those that have children should have greatest care of future times; unto which they know they must transmit their dearest pledge. Some there are, who though they lead a single life, yet their thoughts do end with themselves, and account future times impertinences.[22]

21. *The Works of Francis Bacon*, ed. James Spedding, Robert L. Ellis, and Douglas Heath (London, 1878), 4. 472. These commonplaces are to be distinguished from the traditional topics of logic which he discusses earlier; they are rhetorical *loci communes*, which he calls "promptuary topics" (for a fuller description, see p. 47). The "hypotheses or cases" he refers to are the Elder Seneca's *controversiae.*
22. Spedding, 6. 391.

The opening statement is a *sententia* from the "against" column of the topic "Wife and Children"; hence the essay begins with a negative view of marriage. The second half of the period also argues this point of view, but via another independent sentence which does not function as an explanation of the first, as the conjunction "for" implies. The logical construction would be: A wife and children are impediments to great enterprises, either of virtue or mischief; for he that hath them hath given hostages to fortune. Bacon's reversal of this order reveals that he is more interested in accumulating reasons than in smoothly persuading. He then amplifies the second statement with the assertion that the greatest public service has been performed by single men, who have wedded the commonwealth. At this point, however, the argument turns in the opposite direction. "Yet" it would also seem that men who have children would be most likely to have an eye to the future. He supports this proposition with the observation that those who are single think only in terms of their own lives and do not worry about posterity. Which brings us back to the initial statement seen in a new light: those who leave hostages to fortune (married men) might make the better statesmen.

What Bacon is doing is looking at marriage and the single life not simply from opposite sides of the question but also in different contexts. From the point of view of the individual it holds dangers—it drives him deeper into Fortune's debt; from that of the commonwealth this makes him a more reliable leader. Yet he has also considered the self-evident truth that unwedded men can devote all their energies to public service. And that's true, too. The effect is that of a circumnavigation of the topic, which ends not offering a "stand" on marriage at all, but simply exploring its significance in the wide universe in which it exists. This accounts for its disjunctive quality: many eyes are seeing and reporting.

Recently, Stanley Fish has argued that the *Essays* in their revised form embody Bacon's recommendations for a scientific discourse that would combat the mind's predisposition to settle for partial truths in its desire for certainty and order.[23] Bacon, he reminds us, distinguished between two forms of communication—the "Magistral," which aims at securing belief and is proper for conveying the settled truths of dogma, and the way of "Probation," which conveys empirical knowledge in the same

23. *Self-Consuming Artifacts* (Berkeley, 1972), pp. 78–155.

tentative manner in which the knowledge itself has been gathered.[24] Bacon recommends for this kind of communication a fragmented, aphoristic style, for "Aphorisms, representing a knowledge broken, do invite men to inquire farther; whereas Methods [the "Magistral" style of the rounded period], carrying the shew of a total, do secure men, as if they were at furthest."[25] It would seem, then, that Bacon's injunction to gather and memorize pithy *sententiae* was intended not simply to enhance the ability to persuade, but rather to compel independent inquiry through the use of sonorous cliches "urged unfairly, as it were, and quite beyond the truth," and disposed in such a way that they might qualify one another. Through such an arrangement the reader is forced continuously to rethink the assumptions encouraged by the text. If Fish's hypothesis is correct, Bacon's stylistic program is the natural culmination of that method of examining a question *in utramque partem* which we have been observing, for it seeks through the medium of the grammatical period itself to secure the suspension of belief necessary to arrive at a clearer view of the truth.

II

This method of inquiry was not simply "in the air." It had been deliberately cultivated by the humanists in the Tudor grammar school, an institution developed to produce men of firm moral conviction whose rhetorical skills would equip them for responsible public life.[26] Here young boys were confirmed in Christian ethics and at the same time taught to look for at least two sides in every question—an ideological conflation that left its peculiar mark on much of the literature of the period. Indoctrination began with the student's earliest themes, on subjects drawn from history, mythology, and proverb lore. The pedagogical function

24. These correspond to the two methods informing the structures of our dramatic paradigms.

25. Spedding, 3. 405; cited by Fish, p. 87.

26. For detailed treatments of the grammar school curriculum, see T. W. Baldwin, *William Shakspere's Small Latine and Lesse Greeke* (Urbana, Ill., 1944); Donald L. Clark, *John Milton at St. Paul's School* (New York, 1948); and Virgil K. Whitaker, *Shakespeare's Use of Learning* (San Marino, 1953). Charles O. McDonald examines the relationship of Tudor rhetorical training to the sophistic tradition of *dissoi logoi* in *The Rhetoric of Tragedy* (Amherst, 1966), pp. 75-92. The following discussion draws in part upon these studies.

of these themes was to teach the beginning writer where to find matter and how to compose it. In his sketch of the curriculum for St. Paul's, Erasmus writes:

> care must be taken to propound themes not only worthy in subject, but suitable, as being within the range of the boy's interests. For in this way he may acquire not only training in style, but also a certain store of facts and ideas for future use. For example, such a subject as the following would prove attractive: "The rash self-confidence of Marcellus imperilled the fortunes of Rome; they were retrieved by the caution of Fabius." Here we see the underlying sentiment, that reckless counsels hasten toward disaster. Here is another: "Which of the two shows less wisdom, Crates who cast his gold into the sea, or Midas who cherished it as his supreme good?"[27]

Erasmus's instructions reveal two major concerns of Tudor pedagogy that will be reflected in the literature produced by those trained in the system: the student is to see in historical or fictional events the "underlying sentiments" or universal principles that inform them, and he is encouraged to regard these as controversial issues—rashness versus caution, profligacy versus cupidity. These emphases lay the foundation for a mimetic fiction of explorative character, one that teaches and delights by examining through exempla which engage the emotions the diverse existential claims that govern human life. The concern to link the universal principle with the particular example—which lies at the heart of Renaissance poetic theory—and the interest in developing the ability to see both sides of the question remain constants throughout the program.

From his early themes, the student proceeded to the epistle, which was subdivided according to the three types of classical oration—the judicial, deliberative, and demonstrative. In his *De conscribendis epistolis*, Erasmus recommends letters which, like Ovid's *Heroides*, are imitations of what specific persons might say in particular circumstances. Materials are to be drawn from history, Scripture, and literature. A condemned Horatius begging the aid of his father, Penelope exhorting Ulysses to return home,

27. William Harrison Woodward, *Desiderius Erasmus Concerning the Aim and Method of Education*, Classics in Education No. 19 (1904; rpt. New York, 1964), pp. 169–170.

Jonathan consoling David as he hides from the wrath of Saul—these are among the subjects proposed as suitable. In writing such letters, the student was taught to imagine himself in circumstances utterly unlike his own and to see with eyes other than his own; in formal terms this meant composing according to the decorum of person, audience, and matter, but psychologically it involved a systematic expansion of the imagination beyond its usual subjective limitations, and fostered an awareness of other human realities.

Following his work on the epistle, the student was introduced to the fourteen minor forms of composition. The standard authority for these exercises in the sixteenth century was the Latinized *Progymnasmata* of Aphthonius, a fourth-century grammarian who described and illustrated the several kinds of writing that would ultimately be employed in the full-scale declamation and oration.[28] Here we find a wide variety of literary forms, both universal and particular, introduced in the light of their suasive function. The *fabula*, for example (of which the most familiar to us are those ascribed to Aesop), "drew its origin from the poets, and is also commonly used by public speakers because it is suitable for gentle remonstrance and appropriate for teaching the unlearned." It is effective because it is vivid and specific, "inducing belief by placing the facts, as it were, before the eyes."[29] By way of contrast, the *sententia*—defined as "a speech setting forth something which pertains to exhortation or dissuasion, gathered together in a few words"—offers the prac-

28. The most popular version was one translated by Rudolph Agricola and Johan Cataneus, with scholia by Richard Lorich. For the influence of the *Progymnasmata* on Shakespeare and Milton, see Baldwin and Clark; for its widespread popularity, see Clark's "The Rise and Fall of Progymnasmata in Sixteenth and Seventeenth Century Grammar Schools," *Speech Monographs* 19 (1952): 259–263; and F. R. Johnson's introduction to Richard Rainolde, *A Book Called the Foundacion of Rhetorike* (New York, 1945). An English translation of the Greek original is Raymond E. Nadeau's "The Progymnasmata of Aphthonius in Translation," *Speech Monographs* 19 (1952): 264–285.

29. Fabula traxit a Poetiis originem, qua Rhetores etiam communiter utantur, quod admonitionibus sit idonea, & erudiendis imperitioribus apta. . . . Fidem faciunt, quia verum veluti ponunt ante oculos. *Aphthonii Progymnasmata, a Rodolpho Agricola partim, partim a Johanne Maria Cataneo, Latinitate donata. Cum scholiis R. Lorichii.* . . . (Wesel, 1670), pp. 7, 9.

titioner a universal truth to which he may refer his particular argument, and thereby increase its credibility.[30] In a third form, the *chreia*, the student unites the universal with the particular, by attaching the *sententia* to a definite person. In doing so he creates a little fictional vignette.[31]

In the more advanced of the exercises, the student was required to analyze the deeper implications of his subject and often approached it from different points of view. The *destructio* or *subversio*, for example, taught him to overthrow any argument based on probability with one of his own, based on a counter-probability. Aphthonius provides an outline, recommending that the student state his opponent's assertion first, then amplify it and argue from the following topics: the obscurity of the claim, its lack of credibility, its impossibility, its inconsistency, impropriety, and inexpediency. The common procedure is to prove the point according to one topic, then graciously concede it and go on to the next, as if there were an unending supply of successful arguments.[32] The examples given reflect the pervasive literary flavor of Tudor pedagogy: "The things the poets tell us about Daphne are not probable"; "What Herodotus wrote in Book I about Arion playing the lute is false"; "It is without foundation that Elpenor was turned into a swine." A specimen argument from the last theme, drawn from the topic *incredible*, reads: "Who is there who will have suffered so cruel a deficiency that it may seem to him true that a man can be changed into a swine? And *that* by a woman, who, as she is weaker than a man, and less able, so is she less suited to seizing upon and claiming for herself arts of divine power."[33]

30. Sententia, est oratio, brevi complexa aliquid quod ad hortandum dehortandumve pertinet, explicans. . . . Sententia sine persona effertur (*ibid.*, pp. 84–85).

31. The examples in Aphthonius include Plato observing that the fruits of virtue are produced by labor and sweat, Pythagoras demonstrating by a brief disappearance the duration of man's life, Diogenes striking and rebuking the tutor of an ill-bred boy. The general principle is thus figured forth through the speech or action of an individual. The *chreia* reappears as the figure *expolitio*, a fictitious dialogue used to enliven an argument, in the pseudo-Ciceronian *Rhetorica ad Herennium*, 4.55.

32. The method is beautifully demonstrated in Erasmus's *Praise of Folly*, and discussed in his tenth chapter on dilating matter in *De duplici copia verborum ac rerum*. See pp. 56–57 and n. 50.

33. Quis tanto crudelitatis vitio laboraverit, cui verum esse videatur, hominem in porcum transformari potuisse? idque per feminam, quae ut viris infirmior est,

It is incredible because improbable, and what is probable is what is familiar in human experience. Such juxtaposition of exotic myth and literalminded criticism inevitably draws a smile to our lips, but it is a forceful reminder that these figures from the classical past were real presences in the Renaissance. Examples from history and fiction were mingled freely by Cicero and Quintilian, and all were subject to scrutiny by the familiar store of commonplaces that were universal currency.

The other side of these questions is represented by the form called the *confirmatio*, whose topics are the reverse of the *destructio*, and whose aim is to prove that all the stories *are* probable. In these paired exercises, we can see in rudimentary form the methods of building a case used in forensic oratory and—at the same time—a procedure for examining the issues that arise in a narrative fiction or drama, as in the *controversia* just discussed.

In the form called *locus communis*, the student learned to argue against a person by enlarging upon the evil he represents. The commonplace is common because it focuses upon a general philosophic issue that may be drawn upon in treating a particular case. A speech against a traitor, for example, can include a little oration on the nature of treason, and Aphthonius recommends that the student include even the imagined conversation of the despot convincing himself to break the law—an exercise in which we can see the germ of Brutus's tortured soliloquy in his garden on the eve of Caesar's assassination.[34]

In the *laus*, the student learned to praise a subject for its specific virtues. The subject may be a person, a moral quality, a season of the year, a place, a dumb animal, even a plant. Again, there is a strict order of topics: an exordium; the subject's genus (race, country, ancestors, parents); his education (inclination to study, talent, precepts learned); and his achievements (of mind, body, and fortune). The reverse of this ex-

---

ac ineptior, ita minus idonea ad capessendas atque sibi vendicandas divinae virtutis artes (*Progymnasmata*, p. 118).

34. See Baldwin, 2. 238. The *locus communis* was frequently used in emotional appeals at the end of the oration (*De inv.* 1.106–109). Vives, anticipating Bacon, recommends collecting these, "which in and for themselves have nothing to do with a controversy [a particular case], but which easily lend themselves to application and transference to definite circumstances. Thus, e.g., expressions concerning the chances of fortune, cruelty, and maxims on the passage of time" (p. 184).

ercise is the *vituperatio*, a speech that denounces someone or something, but not through a shared characteristic, as in the commonplace. This is a denunciation *ad hominem*, which utilizes the topics of the *laus* in their negative aspect. Thus the student was trained to approach character not only in general but also in specific terms, and learned how the same person may be described from opposing points of view. "Though he may be painted one way like a Gorgon, The other way's a Mars," Cleopatra tells Charmian. Essentially this is the vision behind all these exercises, suggesting a sophistic relativism against which Tudor apologists continually had to defend themselves.

Of special importance in the development of future playwrights was the *ethopoeia* or mimetic speech. There were three subdivisions of this exercise. In the *ethopoeia* proper the student wrote the words that a well-known person might say in a specific situation. Although the person is known, the student fabricates his *character* through speech; that is, he reveals what kind of person Hecuba is through the words she utters upon seeing Troy destroyed. A second category is the *eidolopoeia*, in which the person of a dead man, unable to speak, is evoked. In the *prosopopoeia* or personification, both the person and his nature are created from an abstraction.[35] Character is defined in two aspects, and this makes for two kinds of speech, or one combining both aspects. The first is passion, and a passive *ethopoeia* is a speech that shows the person's feelings about his situation. The second aspect is moral or generic, and an ethical *ethopoeia* reveals the type of person he is, according to the accepted principles of decorum—rustic, old man, youth, matron, and so on. In both cases, however, the emphasis is not simply upon emotional or ethical expression, but upon a human response to a specific event or problem.[36] The exercise was originally devised to train the fledgling orator to put himself in his client's place, and thus more effectively move the court in his behalf. In the fuller rhetorical treatises of Cicero and Quintilian, examples of *etho-*

35. *Prosopopoeia* is also treated as a figure of thought by Quintilian, *Inst. or.* 9.2.29, and by Erasmus in *De copia*, where it is recommended to call forth a person who is not present. Its use in *The Praise of Folly* may be seen on p. 59.

36. In his fifth chapter on dilating matter, Erasmus particularly warns of the importance of individuating persons even of the same type, and points to the contrasting servants, youths, and old men in Terence and Plautus (*Opera omnia* [Leiden, 1703; rpt. Hildesheim, 1961], I. 80).

poeia are often drawn from the tragic or comic actor, and the orator is urged to imitate the stage performer. The technique comes full circle when reduced to those exercises that train future playwrights in the fundamentals of dramatic characterization.[37]

The final Aphthonian form commonly learned was the *thesis*. This exercise—composed without reference to person or circumstance—is defined as a "mature deliberation, contemplation, or inquiry into anything that may be investigated through speech."[38] It is divided into two kinds, the practical and the speculative. Examples of practical questions are: Should one take a wife? Go on a journey? Build walls? Examples of speculative questions are: Are the heavens spherical? Are there many worlds? One of the most seminal of Aphthonius's examples is the practical *thesis*, *An ducenda uxor* (should a man take a wife?). In Lorich's edition of the *Progymnasmata*, we find one *thesis* supporting the proposition and a counter-*thesis* opposing it. The first begins by building up the dignity of marriage, attributing to it the birth of the gods, the preservation of earthly species, and the cultivation of courageous, righteous, and temperate men. A *contradictio* is then put forward: "But marriage is the cause of misfortune." The speaker, in the *solutio*, then explains that Fortune is to blame for misfortune, not marriage, and asks if farmers should stop farming because of hailstorms or mariners stay at home because of buffeting

37. The cross-fertilization between drama and oratory is everywhere apparent. Aphthonius remarks that the *eidolopoeia* was found in the old comedy of Eupolis, while *prosopopoeia* was used by Menander (p. 281). He refers the student to Quintilian who provides an example of *ethopoeia* from Terence's *Eunuch*, where a character onstage mimics another (*Inst. or.* 9.11.58). Quintilian devotes much space to impersonation, urging the orator to include in his argument fictitious speeches of his client: "And as their plea would awaken yet greater pity if they urged it with their own lips, so it is rendered to some extent all the more effective when it is, as it were, put into their mouths by their advocate: we may draw a parallel from the stage, where the actor's voice and delivery produce greater emotional effect when he is speaking in an assumed role than when he speaks in his own character" (6.1.26, trans H. E. Butler [London, 1920]). In the *Ad Herennium*, the figures *notatio* and *sermocinatio* are recommended for use in recreating a scene in which the accused and his victims are feigned to respond in their own voices to the situation hypothesized by the orator. In the examples given, the former is virtually Terentian dialogue, the latter a typical episode from a tragedy (4.63–65).

38. Thesis, id est, consultatio est rei alicuius investigandae per orationem consideratio vel disquisitio (*Progymnasmata*, p. 328).

winds. A second rebuttal blames marriage for widows and orphans. The speaker then places the responsibility on Nature, and goes on to show that marriage in fact can repair Nature's depredations by supplying new fathers and husbands. A third rebuttal brings up the drudgery of marriage, and is countered with praise of wedding songs, the pleasures of the marriage bed, and the joys of raising a family. The counter-*thesis* proceeds along opposite lines, adducing the effeminacy and injustice marriage breeds, the difficulty of child rearing, and the disappointments of parenthood. Together, the two speeches constitute a reasonable examination of marriage and family life, simplified but not bowdlerized, requiring not only a selection of major arguments but the wit to reply to and profit from rebuttal. Theoretically at least, he who has argued both sides must now regard marriage with some circumspection.

The faculty chiefly employed in constructing these themes was, of course, invention, which in the Ciceronian tradition was considered the most important of the five skills of the orator, since it supplied matter for discourse.[39] Cultivating the student's ability to invent had far-reaching effects upon his work and mind. At the most fundamental level it enabled him to find many things to say about a given subject, and may be credited for the extraordinary copiousness of much sixteenth-century writing; more importantly, it provided him with an instrument for analyzing words, ideas, and events, thereby enlarging his understanding as well as his verbal inventory.

The method followed was to consult the logical commonplaces as set forth in such popular textbooks as Cicero's *Topica* and Agricola's *De inventione dialectica*. Here one found a grid of conceptual "viewpoints," as it were, each offering a different perspective upon the matter at hand. Cicero's list of seventeen commonplaces includes such concepts as genus, species, parts, cause, and effect; Agricola's is somewhat longer. The student might run through all the topics, or only a few, to gain new ways of thinking or writing about his subject. For example, "Vertue," explains Thomas Wilson, author of the first English logic, "referred to the minde, whiche conteineth it, is a worde adjoined [viewing virtue as an

39. In *De inventione*, it is designated "the most important of all the divisions" (1.9), and in the *Ad Herennium*, "the most important and most difficult of the five tasks of the speaker" (2.1, trans. Harry Caplan [London, 1954]). The other faculties are arrangement, elocution, memory, and delivery.

'adjunct,' one sees it as a quality determining human behavior]: compared with vice, it is a contrarie [here one understands it in relation to its moral opposite]: referred to justice it is a generall woorde [a 'genus' comprising the species 'justice,' 'temperance,' 'fortitude,' etc.]." In a memorable *tour de force*, he takes the term "magistrate" through virtually all the places—defining it, giving its genus, dividing it into kinds, describing the qualities of a ruler, his necessary actions, efficient and final causes, effect, etc.—until one has contemplated "magistrate" in a wide variety of contexts.[40]

The places of invention were useful not only in broadening a student's understanding of a single term, but also in helping him discover the rationale behind a complete statement. Cicero had described invention as "the power which investigates hidden secrets";[41] as amplified by Wilson it becomes the indispensable tool for unearthing explanations that would otherwise lie silent and unseen in the world *logos*.[42] When one has a proposition whose truth must be tested, the first thing to do is examine the relationship between subject and predicate:

> Aske the cause of our selfe, why and wherefore that thing, which is spoken of the former parte in any sentence, shoulde be so applied to thesame [sic]. And to make the matier more plain I will make this question. *Est ne avarus pauper?* Is a covetous manne poore, or not? I maie thus reason with my selfe, why should a covetous manne be

40. *The Rule of Reason*, ed., Richard S. Sprague (Northridge, Ca., 1972), pp. 101, 135–138. Based upon Agricola's *De inventione dialectica*, this discursive document provides an illuminating glimpse of a sixteenth-century Englishman's view of logic. Subsequent page references will appear in the text.

41. Cicero, *Tusc. disp.* 1.25.61.

42. Writes Wilson: "The Huntesman in huntyng the foxe, wil soon espie when he seeth a hole, whether it be a foxe borough, or not. So he that will take profeicte in this parte of Logique, must bee like a hunter, and learne by labour to know the boroughes. For these places bee nothing elles, but covertes or boroughes, wherin if any one searche diligently, he maie find game at pleasure" (p. 90). Earlier, he compares invention to digging for veins of gold in the earth. Both the mining and hunting metaphors imply that reasons, like precious ore and wild game, are provided by nature, to furnish man's mind as physical creation ministers to his body—if only he will seek them out. This view is even more fully developed in the logic of Ramus and his followers, where the natural world is described as virtually a fabric of arguments to be unravelled. See Perry Miller, *The New England Mind: The Seventeenth Century* (New York, 1939), pp. 146–153.

called poore? What affinitie is betwixt theim twoo? Marie in this poincte thei bothe agree that like as the poore man, ever lacketh and desireth to have so the covetous manne ever lacketh, wanting the use of that which he hath, and desireth still to have, being never content though God geve enough. Then seyng it is even so, that bothe dooe lack, and bothe doe desire to have, thissame [sic] reason is the onely cause, whereby mine argument is made perfeict. (pp. 56–57)

Considering the possible relationship between the miser and the pauper, the student comes upon (*invenit*) the topic "words adjoined" (*adiacentia*). These are

those accidents whereby the singular worde, or proper name, hath another name, then of the very substaunce, as unto Cato (which of his substaunce is a man) wisedome doth happen, whereby he is called wise. Unto Cicero also (which by his substaunce is a man) there happeneth eloquence, whereby he is called eloquent. (pp. 100–101)

He then sees that the quality shared by both the pauper and the miser is want. Having discovered the affinity, the student frames his argument:

> Whosoever lacketh, and desireth evermore to have,
>   that same man is poore.
> A covetous man lacketh, and desireth evermore to
>   have.
> Therefore a covetous manne is poore.   (p. 57)

By searching the places, one can literally dis-cover hidden reasons lying behind a given proposition, and thus bring to light previously unseen connections that make discrete perceptions rationally comprehensible.[43]

Another important function of invention was to help one understand events that might otherwise remain obscure. To achieve this, the category of topics called *applicita* was especially useful. *Applicita* are "things outwardly applied to a matier, whiche are not the cause of thesame [sic] matier, and yet geve a certain denominacion to it" (p. 115). By the phrase "a certain denominacion," Wilson means that *applicita* provide a specific coloring (the Senecan *color*) and character to an act. The topics

43. This is the procedure informing the structure of *Fulgens and Lucres*. One moves backward from the proposition "Gaius is nobler than Publius Cornelius" via such topics as adjuncts, definition, contraries, and comparison, to arrive at the general premise "A virtuous churl is nobler than a vicious gentleman."

in this category are "time," "place," and "things annexed," such as companions, garments, visible emotions. These topics, he points out, are employed by orators in proving the guilt or innocence of a suspect:

> for when a man is taken of suspeccion, we go aboute to prove him faultie by diverse conjectures. As if he were aboute thesame [sic] place, at the self same time, when a man was slain, and also had his sworde about him: we conjecture that he might have killed him. Again, if we perceive one to be a riotous felowe, redie to fight with every bodie, accompaniyng with naughtie packes, and evermore, at one ende of all fraies, waxyng pale when he is apprehended, shakyng for feare, or runnyng awaie, when he should be taken: we suspect soche a one, that he is not altogether clere. (p. 116)

By examining with reference to such topics an act whose result alone is actually known, one can infer its internal structure and thereby transform a bare event into a morally significant pattern. This practice of conjecture had great influence upon the creation of mimetic fiction in the sixteenth century, as we shall see in more detail in the following chapter.

Each of the academic procedures outlined above—the training in universal and particular argument, the practice of examining both sides of a question, the exercises in sympathetic imitation, and the use of logical commonplaces to acquire virtually an Argus-eyed view of any subject of discourse—had a profound effect upon the developing young writer. Such an education made him aware that human experience was susceptible of a wide range of interpretations and excited in him a desire to use his wit to penetrate the givens of his environment. Equally significant, it taught him to seek the "underlying sentiment" in the particular while recognizing that it is through the particular that we are most moved. How these insights might coalesce in the creation of an ambivalent yet deeply moral poetic fiction is demonstrated by the master himself in *The Praise of Folly*.

III

Ostensibly, Erasmus's *Praise of Folly* is a *laus*—more specifically, a paradoxical encomium. But if we examine the piece closely, we will discover that Erasmus draws in fact upon a number of rhetorical forms in order to explore his subject with unusual subtlety and power. In "praising" folly, he is actually posing the speculative *thesis* "What is folly?"—though he does not choose to pursue this question in abstract terms. Instead, he examines it mimetically, concretely, in the way of fiction. To do so, he fuses two Aphthonian forms—the *prosopopoeia* and the *laus*—to create a unique speech of self-praise through which he may search out the meaning of folly not in the dialectical manner of the logicians, but discursively, by juxtaposing a variety of viewpoints within the single discontinuous mind of his speaker, a lady who is consistent only in her determination to demonstrate the extent of her influence among men. Thus in one stroke Erasmus establishes as his instrument of inquiry the ideally pluralistic consciousness, through which he can range, in moods of satire, admiration, uncertainty, and exhortation, over the entire spectrum of human insipience.[44]

He achieves this by paying close attention to the rules of decorum. In creating his *prosopopoeia*, he informs us in the introduction, he strictly observed decorum of person[45]—and when Folly herself appears, she defends her forthcoming speech of self-praise on the same principle:

> Nor do I have any use for those wiseacres who preach that it is most foolish and insolent for a person to praise himself. Yet let it be as foolish as they would have it, if only they will grant that it is proper [*modo decorum esse fateantur*]; and what is more suitable than that Folly herself should be the trumpeter of her own praises?[46]

Then, keeping in character, she promises to speak "whatever pops into my head" (p. 9).

But she does more. For within the initial conceit of casting Folly as speaker, Erasmus has placed a second conceit. Upon concluding her *exordium*, Folly announces that she is going "to play the rhetorician before you" (*apud vos Sophistam agere*)—not that current brand of schoolmaster

---

44. Walter Kaiser notes that there is no precedent for such a speaker in encomiastic literature. *Praisers of Folly* (Cambridge, Mass., 1963), p. 36.

45. In recognition of the mimetic aspect of the work, the editor of the Leiden *Opera* notes: "Decorum, quod Graeci πρέπον vocant situm est in dignate rerum et sermonarum cuius praecipua ratio habetur in tragoediis, comoediis, & dialogis" (4. 403).

46. Desiderius Erasmus, *The Praise of Folly*, trans. Hoyt H. Hudson (Princeton, 1941), p. 8. All subsequent citations in the text will refer to this edition.

who stuffs the ears of little boys with nonsense, but the kind who former-ly eulogized the great. Thus she herself assumes a role, and imitates, for *its* advantages, the habits of another known type. This makes the decla-mation yet more complex and amusing, since Erasmus has superimposed upon Folly's native vagaries the *techné* of the sophist, which, though there be method in it, also possesses its own brand of madness.[47]

In the character of sophist, Folly is appropriately scornful of the dry, dialectical procedures of philosophy. As she enters upon her *partitio*, she announces that she will not unfold herself by definition and division into parts, for "what end would be served in setting forth, by definition, a sketch and, as it were, a shadow of me, when you, present here, with your own eyes perceive me in your presence?" (p. 10). Her position, pun-ridden though it is, may be viewed as an implicit declaration of poetic intent. For she is continually alive to the power of the image. At the very outset, observing the smiles in her audience, she remarks, "Thus what great orators elsewhere can hardly bring about in a long, carefully planned speech, I have done in a moment, with nothing but my looks" (p. 7).[48] Again, when discoursing upon the folly of friendship, she says, "I shall not demonstrate it by ambiguous syllogisms, sorites, horned dilemmas, or any other sophistical subtleties . . . but by crude common sense, as the the phrase is, I shall point it out with my finger" (p. 26). Whereupon she immediately sketches in a few instances of amicable inanity. Her mimetic bent is most apparent, however, in the midsection of the speech, where, having disdained the definition and division of conventional logic, she makes her own distinctive use of genus and species by describ-ing the various *appearances* of folly which constitute her catalogue of fools. She begins by distinguishing between harmful folly and her own brand, "an amiable dotage of mind" that "frees the spirit from carking cares" (p. 52), and then presents examples. Here we meet "the fellows who renounce everything else in favor of hunting wild game, and pro-test they feel an ineffable pleasure in their souls whenever they hear the

47. In *De copia rerum*, Erasmus recommends that in representing a sophist, the speaker should show him "loquacior quam sapientior" (*Opera omnia*, 1. 80).

48. Her words suggest that same preference for mimetic over "philosophic" exposition that Sidney was to express in his famous passage about the elephant and rhinoceros some seventy years later. See "Apology for Poetry," *Elizabethan Critical Essays*, ed. G. Gregory Smith (Oxford, 1904), 1. 164–165.

raucous blast of the horns and the yelping of hounds" . . . "men who suffer from an incurable itch to be abuilding" . . . "those who keep on trying, by new and secret skills, to transmute the forms of things, and who ransack the earth and sea for a certain fifth essence," as well as gamblers, story tellers, indulgence seekers, ancestor worshippers, and others, all lovingly and compendiously drawn. Further on are those *formae Stultitiae* (note again the emphasis on "appearances," "shapes"[49]) which are treated more bitingly—the professions and the clergy—their looks, habits, values, manners of speech, and minor peccadilloes set forth for instant recognition. These are all sophistic *notationes*, those figures of thought that consist of little character sketches and are recommended by Cicero, the author of the *Ad Herennium*, and by Erasmus himself for achieving vividness of expression. They are basic equipment in the rhetorician's bag of tricks.

Folly's imitation of the sophist, however, is not confined to the use of his fictional devices. She *conducts her arguments* like a sophist. Notice the way she treats her impudent claim that even prudence is beholden to folly. She begins by arguing that prudence depends upon experience, and

> to whom does the honor of this attribute belong? To the wise man, who, by reason partly of modesty and partly of faint-heartedness, will attempt no action? Or to the fool, who is not deterred from any enterprise by modesty, of which he is innocent, or by peril, which he never pauses to weigh? (pp. 35–36)

The wise man, she suggests, will run to some ancient tome for information, while the fool will plunge *in medias res* and arrive at true prudence. She uses a *chreia* enlisting no less an authority than Homer to prove it.

But then she shifts her ground. Perhaps prudence is not simply experiential, but comes from the faculty of judgment as well. If this is so, how reliable is judgment? Adducing the Sileni of Alcibiades in evidence, she shows how deceptive are the appearances of things, and thus how imprudent the "prudence" of those who base their decisions upon external judgments. Via this reasoning, the cautious wise man, too, falls within Folly's purview. Not satisfied with this proof, however, she moves on to the next possibility: that deceptive appearances may indeed be detected. What then? She begins her argument by picturing the intrusion of a

49. Folly is universal, she says, especially that of the baser sort, *tot enim undique Stultitiae formis abundat* (*Opera omnia*, 4. 455).

spectator into a play: if he were to strip the masks off the actors and expose the reality beneath, would he not outrage the audience, deprived of its pleasurable illusion? "Now what else," she continues, "is the whole life of mortals but a sort of comedy, in which the various actors, disguised by various costumes and masks, walk on and play each one his part, until the manager waves them off the stage?" (p. 37). Suppose some sage were able to perceive the ugly passions within the man taken for a god, or suggested that one in mourning should laugh upon the death of his beloved (who had only now begun to live), or declared another man, glorying in his ancestry, base because he lacked virtue—would he not be thought mad?

> As nothing is more foolish than wisdom out of place, so nothing is more imprudent than unseasonable prudence. And he is unseasonable who does not accommodate himself to things as they are. . . . The part of a truly prudent man, on the contrary, is (since we are mortal) not to aspire to wisdom beyond his station, and either, along with the rest of the crowd, pretend not to notice anything, or affably and companionably be deceived. But that, they tell us, is folly. Indeed, I shall not deny it; only let them, on their side, allow that it is also to play out the comedy of life. (p. 38)

This passage reveals quite a bit about Folly the sophist. She is the most slippery of debaters. To prove the paradox that prudence, too, is under her aegis, she covers all the possibilities. If, as some say, prudence is to be found in experience, then the impetuous fool is prudent; if in rational judgment, then the so-called wise man, bound to the information of his senses, is destined to adjudicate foolishly; if in shrewd iconoclasm, then the disrupter will be thought to demonstrate the height of folly and the uncritical game player true prudence. But, as the moralists point out, that is the worst sort of folly. Very well. As sophist, Folly has no point of view on what constitutes prudence. She has simply offered (as Aphthonius prescribes) a series of alternative propositions that demonstrate her pervasive influence. As a result, she has presented four different faces of folly (brashness, naïveté, idealism, cynicism), and has compelled the reader to acknowledge the existence of all of them.[50]

50. In the tenth chapter of *De copia rerum*, Erasmus discusses the technique of varying an idea through rhetorical propositions, and provides a series of argu-

An important feature of sophistic argumentation may be discerned in this example: the inequality of levels of argument. Some are jokes (the prudent man is the experienced fool); some cogent paradoxes (the "wise" man is often fooled by appearances); some rueful observations (the idealist is a fool in the eyes of the world); some merely cynicisms (the truly prudent man follows the market); and some moral judgments (the man who follows the market is a fool). This interlayering of arguments reflecting varying levels of realism recurs continually,[51] even in highly serious passages, such as the emotionally charged analysis of Christianity as a kind of folly. Here, Folly's tone has modulated. She has already satirized mercilessly the ecclesiastical establishment—those "bad" fools whose follies lie in their gross misunderstanding of the responsibilities that their titles impose upon them. Now she turns to the religion itself, and one knows that it is "good" folly, moral folly, that she is describing. And yet, in support of her contention that Christianity is akin to folly, she offers three distinctly different kinds of argument: first, it is a species of folly because "children, old people, women, and fools find pleasure beyond other folk in holy and religious things and, to that end, are ever nearest the altars" (folly as dotage); second, because "the original founders of religion, admirably laying hold of pure simplicity, were the bit-

---

ments for dissuading the Pope from attacking the Venetians that follows precisely the pattern set by Folly: temporal rule is inconsistent with the office of the Pontiff, the tranquility of the Church, and Christian piety; but even if it *is* consistent with those things, it is inappropriate for the deputy of Christ, who had enjoined mercy, to seek domination through bloodshed; yet even if *that* is right, such a step is dangerous because of the uncertainties of warfare. Similarly, to dissuade a person from studying Greek literature, one will first argue that Greek letters have nothing of benefit for Christian happiness and may even thwart it; second, that though it may be worthwhile to study literature, Greek is so hard that one will waste a lifetime without learning it, and even if he succeeds in learning it, it contains insufficient wisdom to compensate for such a loss of time; finally, Greece having been overthrown and oppressed, a similar fate awaits those who study its literature (*Opera omnia*, 1. 86, 87, and *passim*).

51. One thinks of Folly's pastoral defense of nature against art, with which it is easy to sympathize until she supports it with the analogy that the happiest animals are the most "natural"—bees, flies, and birds, for example, as compared with "rationalized" horses (p. 46). Or her earnest defense of flattery as undeservedly maligned, which ends with this proof: "What is more gracious than the way two mules scratch each other?" (p. 62).

terest foes of literary learning" (folly as ignorance); finally, because "no fools seem to act more foolishly than do people for whom zeal for Christian piety has got possession of" (p. 118), for they are endlessly absorbed either in doing good works or in mortifying the flesh (folly as selflessness).

Now these are puzzlingly inconsistent proofs. The first is clearly delivered tongue in cheek, since women, children, and the aged have already been described in less than flattering terms; the second is ambiguous at the very least, given Erasmus's own dedication to letters; the third *is* commensurate with the general argument, since it, too, is evidence of moral folly. The point is that Folly, playing the sophist, draws proofs *undecumque*, provided that they support her argument. The effect is amusing and unsettling, for it is not at all certain whether the speaker is looking with kindness upon Christian folly which should, we expect, be treated with reverence. One begins to appreciate in this passage how Erasmus himself must have affected some of his less waggish contemporaries.[52]

As sophist, then, Folly pursues a decorum that is consistently inconsistent, and this makes it impossible for the reader, too, to respond consistently, since one never knows whether at any given moment she is to be taken seriously. To complicate matters, part of her sophistic strategy is to indulge in other mimeses which add new voices to her own range of unstable opinions. Some of these are brought in simply for the purpose of supplying *contradictiones* to Folly's exposition: "And now I seem to hear the philosophers disagreeing with me . . ." (p. 43) "But here those stoic frogs begin to croak at me again" (p. 51). These are relatively simple instances of *prosopopoeiae* inserted with *prosopopoeiae*, and they serve the rhetorical function of bringing the adversary, as it were, before the audience, so that the tenuousness of his position may be exposed—a task, incidentally, which Folly usually accomplishes with more celerity than credibility.[53] Interpretation begins to grow more problematic, how-

52. Another apparent indecorum occurs when Folly argues that fools are pleasing to God for the same reason that Caesar hated Brutus, Nero Seneca, and Dionysius Plato: "so Christ detests and condemns those wise men who rely on their own prudence" (p. 115). The implicit parallel between Christ, Caesar, Nero, and Dionysius on the one side, and Brutus, Seneca, and Plato on the other, would be discomfiting, to say the least.

53. When the "Stoics" object to her blazoning the happiness of naturals—

ever, when Folly the sophist decides to play the Scotist, and Folly the sophist playing the Scotist in turn imitates a Graecula—a humanist scholar—objecting to a bit of scholastic exegesis.

This complex moment occurs at the end of the catalogue of fools, when Folly attempts to find Scriptural commendation of herself:

> Then, since we undertake a difficult task, and probably it would be unfair to call upon the muses again for such a long journey from Helicon to here—especially since the business is out of their line—I think it more suitable while I play the divine [*dum Theologum ago*] and tread among thorns, to beg that the soul of Scotus, itself more prickly than a porcupine or hedgehog, shall come from his beloved Sorbonne and dwell in my breast for a season. . . . (p. 106)

Although she wishes she could actually take on the appearance of a Scotist, she contents herself by adopting his manner. This manner is all the more ironic since she has just finished demolishing as an example of high folly the scholastic exegesis of a monk who had divided the name of Jesus into two equal parts so that the letter *s* remained in the middle, and had then observed that this letter was called *shin* or *sin* in Hebrew, which proved without a doubt that Jesus took away the sins of the world. Now, in the role of Scotist seeking Scriptural sanction for folly, she quotes Ecclesiastes: "I gave my heart to know wisdom, and to know madness and folly." Then she goes on to argue:

> In this passage it is to be noted that the advantage rests with folly [above wisdom], since he put it in the last place. Ecclesiastes wrote that, and you know the ecclesiastical order is for him that is first in dignity to get the last place. . . . (p. 107)

Having ridiculed as egregious folly such scholastic quibbling in the satire on monks and priests, in the role of Scotist advocate Folly is quite happy to use the venerable method herself. What has happened is that Erasmus has simply moved Folly into another plane of argument by employing

---

"Nothing, they say, is sadder than madness" (p. 51)—she responds with some twisted lines from Cicero and Horace on the pleasures of delusion, but never really faces the question of what it means to be demented. It is an issue of which the reader would perhaps be unconscious, except for the fact that Folly herself has raised it. The net effect is to make one uncomfortably aware that he has acquiesced in Folly's superficial reasoning.

the ethopoetic device. Folly has not changed her opinion of scholastic method; she has literally changed her mind.

It is upon this plane that the strange encounter mentioned earlier takes place. Folly the Scotist cites St. Paul to the Corinthians in commendation of folly:

> "I speak as a fool," he said, "I am more." This is as if it were a disgraceful thing to be outdone in folly. But now some Greeklings, grackle-like, will break in upon me with their clamor . . . "O foolish citation," these Greeklings will say, "one worthy of Folly herself! The sense of the apostle is far different from what you dream it to be. For he did not intend by these words to have them believe him a greater fool than the rest. . . . " (pp. 108–109)

And she quotes an Erasmian interpretation of the passage—a dramatic, contextual reading in which Paul excuses himself for his arrogance in having spoken the truth by pleading folly. In effect, he does not extol folly at all, but rather takes refuge in it. Folly rehearses this interpretation with some impatience:

> But whatever Paul thought when he wrote these words, I leave them to dispute about. I follow the great, fat, dull, and generally approved theologians, with whom the large majority of learned men choose to err, by Jove, rather than to understand these trilinguists. (p. 109)

What is one to make of this oddly involuted passage? One accepts Folly's first scholastic argument as something of a companionable joke, for, after all, she has deliberately adopted the manner of the Scotist to show us how, from yet another point of view, folly may be commended. But then she is unable to resist mocking the *persona* she has assumed in her own cause, and brings in the Erasmian voice against herself. Confronted with his thoughtful refutation, Folly the Scotist advocate backs away in confusion. It would seem that here the genuine personality of Dame Folly gleams through her sophistic role. She does make some foolish tactical decisions. We have encountered them a few times along the way: when she celebrates human existence as a comedy that the prudent man must play, and introduces a moral voice that makes us uneasy about her blithe endorsement of the unexamined life; in her facile *solutio* of "Stoic" objections to her sponsorship of idiocy; and now, in her playing the fool before the humanist higher criticism. In other places, too, we catch a glimpse of her: in her confused apology for quoting Scripture inexactly (p. 114), and in her peroration—or lack of it, because she just cannot remember what she has said (p. 125). At these moments we can discern the original She upon whom Erasmus has placed his delicate overlapping of other minds, other manners.

Ultimately we must ask what function is served by this extremely complex rhetoric. Is it simply a *tour de force* or is its method, as well as its content, telling us something? In this connection, it may be helpful to recall Folly's comment on the fellow traveler in the play who, as we have seen, commits "immoral" folly from one point of view: "Only let them, on their side, allow that it is also to play out the comedy of life" (*vitae fabulam agere*). Despite the moral *frisson*, there seems to be real value placed in this playing that allows men to be other than what they are. From a strictly Platonic viewpoint, it is hypocrisy; to a more tolerant and dynamic humanism, it is a potentially fruitful flirtation with possibility. In this respect, it is not really different from the highly moral folly described at the end of the speech. There, Folly recounts in inspiring, even rapturous terms, the experience of the religious, who does not play out the comedy of life at all, but rather turns his back on it. Yet his folly, too, consists in a kind of playing. He undertakes a tentative journey of the soul from the mundane concerns of the body into the realm of the spirit, where he enjoys a foretaste of the destiny that may be his. For the duration of his ecstasy, he, too, is not what he is, and like the players in the human comedy, or Horace's delusionary, he is anguished when he "comes to himself" amid present reality. Yet by stepping out of himself, so to speak, he has found a better self. Something like this experience, multiplied many times, is what the structure of *The Praise of Folly* permits its author and its audience. An Erasmus feigning Folly who feigns a sophist feigning a Scotist who feigns a Graecula feigning St. Paul not only gives shape and voice to the vast jumble of undiscriminated moral notions circulating in the human mind, but also makes us respond emotionally to them, test the validity and provenance of our responses as the viewpoints grind with murderous innocency one against another, and finally compels us to weigh the value and the limitations of each. "Fingite!" Erasmus urges in the Latin text: "Pretend!" "Make a fiction that. . . ."

This is not to suggest that there is no hierarchy of good implicit in *The*

Praise of Folly. The shape of the monologue attests otherwise. Having discovered to us folly as ignorance, conviviality, avarice, pregnancy, ambition, lust, self-love, wealth, pedantry, warfare, plagiarism, gambling, statesmanship, interior decorating, sermonizing, boasting, physic, litigation, oratory, courtiership, kingship, prelacy, popery—Erasmus finally reveals the higher folly of Christian contemplation. This, too, is a possibility open to man. And it is the best possibility. But it is not the only one, nor, one feels, the only good one. For if we have learned anything, it is that Folly herself is like the Sileni of Alcibiades. There is that folly which seems madness from the world's point of view, and that which appears so from the perspective of the spirit—and each has its claims on us. What Erasmus has achieved by means of his highly involuted mimeses is to set it out vividly before us—the worldly folly that fosters such ordinary affairs of life as procreation, friendship, government, and the spiritual folly that begets saintliness—and to make us feel the difficulty that must inevitably result when the mind responds to that full vision. In doing so, he has realized the deeper philosophical function of the original, bare question.

Propaedeutic for Drama:
Questions as Fiction

Erasmus's ethopoetic exercise draws upon certain rhetorical principles and procedures that were well known in the Renaissance, and helped to produce an imaginative literature with a decidedly controversial cast. Sometimes only one side of an issue is pursued, as in Shakespeare's first seventeen sonnets, which argue by varying propositions the Aphthonian thesis "Shall a man marry?" Milton's *L'Allegro* and *Il Penseroso*, on the other hand, are complexly developed counter-*theses* closely related to the topic of his first prolusion, "Whether day or night is the more excellent."[1] Often, as in *The Praise of Folly*, a single work will argue two or more sides of the question at once, thus becoming an instrument of continuous inquiry. The creation of such fictional questions seems to have been the common result of training minds to think about ideas, events, and persons *in utramque partem*, and teaching that it is through particulars that one can most sensitively judge the issue at hand.

Cicero, Quintilian, and Aphthonius give explicit directions for making the transition between the general and the particular:

Questions are either *definite* or *indefinite*. *Indefinite* questions are those which may be maintained or impugned without reference to persons, time or place and the like. The Greeks call them *theses*, Cicero *propositions*. . . . *Definite* questions involve facts, persons, time and the like.

1. Donald L. Clark, *John Milton at St. Paul's School* (New York, 1948), pp. 247–248.

64

The Greeks call them *hypotheses*, while we call them *causes*. In these the whole question turns on persons and facts. An *indefinite* question is always the more comprehensive, since it is from the *indefinite* that the *definite* is derived. I will illustrate what I mean by an example. The question "Should a man marry?" is *indefinite*; the question "Should Cato marry?" is *definite*, and consequently may be regarded as subject for a deliberative theme.[2]

These questions were also called general and special, the particular instance considered a *species* of the *genus* represented in the indefinite question. In composing such an exercise, the writer does not simply debate whether a second party ought to do something. Aphthonius suggests that actual mimesis takes place:

> A *thesis* differs from a *hypothesis* in that the *hypothesis* deals with a particular circumstance but the *thesis* is without complicating circumstances. The particular circumstances are persons, act, cause and so on; for instance, "whether one should fortify," as an examination not having a definite person, is a *thesis*, but it is a *hypothesis* when Lacedaemonians are planning to fortify Sparta as the Persians are advancing, for there is a person in the Lacedaemonians consulting together, an act in Sparta being fortified, and a cause in the approaching Persians.[3]

Here one creates a mimetic fiction—changing *thesis* to *hypothesis*—by supposing certain persons, in a certain place, at a certain time, under certain circumstances, to be confronting a general question *in their own terms*. One example is Folly addressing a lecture hall audience on the nature of folly—a speculative *thesis* turned *hypothesis*. A practical *thesis*, when conceived as *hypothesis*, becomes a *suasoria*. Instead of asking "Should a successful world conqueror risk unknown dangers?"—or even whether a particular conqueror should do so—the *suasoria* presents Alexander's counselors advising him whether to cross the ocean. Or, instead of arguing whether one should obey filial or patriotic obligations, Agamemnon himself debates whether he should sacrifice Iphigenia to free his be-

2. Quintilian, *Inst. or.* 3.5.5–8, trans. H. E. Butler, L.C.L. (London, 1963). Cf. Cicero, *Part. Or.* 61ff.; *Top.* 79–82.
3. Raymond E. Nadeau, "The Progymnasmata of Aphthonius in Translation," *Speech Monographs* 19 (1952): 281.

calmed army.[4] Essentially, the *hypothesis* returns the question that has been abstracted from the particulars of experience to its natural setting, so that the issue can be examined with greater attention to its specific ethical and emotional content, and therefore adjudicated with greater subtlety. In the transition, intellectual inquiry assumes the form of affective imitation.

The principle involved here is one deeply rooted in the rhetorical tradition: the more circumstances revealed in a given case, the further "qualified" the issue becomes, and the greater the opportunity for an equitable judgment based upon the widest possible construction of the question. In the classical rhetorical treatises that formed the basis of Renaissance literary education this principle was discussed in all considerations of the *status* or "stand" the orator might take in arguing his case. There were three major kinds of *status*: one could argue whether or not an act took place (*an sit?*); how it should be defined (*quid sit?*); or what its nature was (*qualis sit?*).[5] It was this last area of inquiry, involving fundamental questions of justice and injustice and not merely issues of fact or legal definition, that Cicero and Quintilian believed to be the greatest challenge to the orator, for it required him to examine the act in its fullest circumstantiality and draw it toward an appropriate judgment—one that might well exceed what the law would have allowed had it been argued as bare fact. For there are "certain matters," writes Cicero, "that must be considered with reference to time and intention and not merely by their absolute qualities. In all these matters, one must think what the occasion demands and what is worthy of the persons concerned, and one must con-

4. See *The Elder Seneca: Declamations*, trans. M. Winterbottom, L. C. L. (London, 1974) 2. 485-507, 535-545.

5. See *Inst. or.* 3.6; *De or.* 2.104-113; *De inv.* 1.10-19; *Top.* 82-86. Although the three "points at issue" are usually associated with forensic oratory, they are intrinsic, as Cicero remarks, to deliberative and epideictic as well:

> For of all the issues disputed among men, whether the matter is criminal, as a charge of outrage, or a civil proceeding as one related to an inheritance, or a discussion of policy, as one touching a war, or of a personal kind, as a panegyric, or a philosophical debate, as on the way to live, there is not one of which the point is not either what has been done, or what is being done, or going to be done [fact], or as to the nature [quality] or description [definition] of something (*De or.* 2.104, trans. E. W. Sutton and H. Rackham, L. C. L. [London, 1942]).

sider not what is being done but with what spirit anything is done, with what associates, at what time, and how long it has been going on." Such inquiry resulted in judgment according to principles of equity.[6] Paradoxically, the more one became involved in considerations of quality the more opportunity one had to argue abstract issues—such as the nature of passion, necessity, motherhood, patriotism—for discrete actions could be shown to possess generically defensible characteristics. Thus rhetorical argument was a continuous negotiation between *theses*, or abstract questions, and *hypotheses*, or examinations of the particulars in a given problem.[7]

The declension of a question into an explorative fiction may be seen in three major works of our period which we normally associate with quite separate categories of discourse—Castiglione's *Book of the Courtier*, Thomas More's *Utopia*, and Sir Philip Sidney's *Arcadia*. I propose that we examine them as a kind of preliminary exercise to our study of drama, for they reveal in perhaps the clearest fashion the successive stages in the hypothesization of a *thesis* and the educative function such fictive questions serve.[8]

6. *De inv.* 2.176, trans. H. M. Hubbell (London, 1949). Cf. Aristotle: "Equity bids us be merciful to the weakness of human nature; to think less about the laws than about the man who framed them; and less about what he said than what he meant; not to consider the actions of the accused so much as his intention; nor this or that detail so much as the whole story; to ask not what a man is now but what he has always or usually been" (*Rhet.* 1374b10-15, *The Basic Works of Aristotle*, ed. Richard McKeon [New York, 1941]).

7. This matter is discussed in great detail by Wesley Trimpi, "The Quality of Fiction," *Traditio* (1974): 6–40, to which the reader is referred for extensive background material that cannot be included here. Much of the present chapter is indebted to his painstaking analysis of the historical interrelationship of literary and legal traditions.

8. That such a declension has ample precedent in literary tradition has been demonstrated by Trimpi, *ibid.*, 81–97. Here he traces the relationship between the *iudicia amoris* of Andreas Capellanus, the *questioni d'amore* in Book 4 of Boccaccio's *Il Filocolo*, and the *novelle* of the *Decameron*, indicating how the structure of scholastic debate is subsumed in narrative. Especially germane to the present discussion is the function of the novella in amplifying the question so that all aspects of the problem may be seen in detail (92). My argument necessarily differs from his, in that I am concerned to show the persistence of the interrogative form, which is not his concern.

Castiglione's *Courtier* is in the grand tradition of the serious literary dialogue that deals with political, ethical, and religious issues.[9] The dialogue represents what we might call the primary stage in the hypothesization of a question. Its antithetical positions are represented by specific persons, located in a distinct setting, whose function it is to put forth varying opinions in an attempt to gain a better understanding of the matter at hand. Thus, in Plato's *Symposium*, friends gather at Agathon's house, following his victory in the dramatic competition, to talk about love—and, ethopoetically, Socrates *will* be late, Aristophanes is bound to present his comical history of spheroid lovers, and Alcibiades shames both himself and his idol by drunkenly recounting certain of their intimate, if disappointing, moments together. The conversation, which begins ostensibly in praise of love, is in fact an exposition of different concepts of love, culminating in Socrates' account of Diotima's teaching.

The Platonic dialogue, however, for all its avowed skepticism, is not in the fullest sense an open-ended form. It is most often a medium of Plato's dialectic, a refining process in which grosser concepts are rigorously examined and purged, by means of *elenchus* or cross-examination. The method reflects the transcendentalism of Platonic philosophy, which urges the necessity of removing the mind from the world of opinion to the realm of pure ideas, and the dialogue gathers opinions only to discard them as steps passed over on the climb toward an absolute.[10]

9. A modern editor of Cicero has summarized the development of the form as follows:

> The dialogue as a literary form was primarily a vehicle of inquiry, reflecting debate and conversation upon some problem of common interest to the speakers. In its early form it attempted to produce the actual steps of such inquiry in the questions and answers of the interlocutors. The procedure, even at the hands of Plato, seems often slow, and may become tedious and artificial. In the course of time its inconvenience was felt, with the result that Aristotle and his school modified the Socratic form by assigning to a leading speaker a larger and more continuous role, lightened by interludes, interruptions, and transitions, shared in by other speakers. Through this device, the dialogue was made serviceable, not only for dialectical inquiry, but also for continuous presentation of almost any subject matter (G. L. Hendrickson, "Introduction," *Brutus*, L.C.L. [London, 1939], p. 9).

10. F. M. Cornford shows that the procedure utilizes "an inadequate tentative

The Ciceronian dialogue, on the other hand, seeks truth within the realm of opinion or probability, and utilizes the technique of arguing *in utramque partem* to achieve its end. This is because it derives its epistemology from the Later Academy, whose stand Cicero describes in *De natura deorum*:

> Our position is not that we hold that nothing is true, but that we assert that all true sensations are associated with false ones so closely resembling them that they contain no infallible mark to guide our judgment and assent. From this followed the corollary that many sensations are *probable*, that is, though not amounting to a full perception they are yet possessed of a certain distinctness and clearness, and so can serve to direct the conduct of the wise man.[11]

In practical terms, this means that opinion derived from experience is a generally reliable guide, provided that it is weighed against alternate views, so as to arrive at some probable truth. "The sole object of our discussion," he explains elsewhere, "is by arguing on both sides to draw out and give shape to some result that may be either true or the nearest possible approximation to the truth."[12] This procedure is reflected in the fullest of Cicero's rhetorical treatises, *De oratore*, a lengthy fiction written ostensibly in response to his brother's request for his view on the art of oratory:

---

definition [of the subject under consideration], suggested by the respondent, submitted to criticism by the questioner in the *elenchus* and either amended or abandoned altogether. It is transformed and destroyed by criticism, and never restored or confirmed by subsequent deduction. Such suggestions are mere stepping-stones which are kicked away in the ascent to the correct definition" ("Mathematics and Dialectic in *The Republic VI–VII*," *Mind* 41 [1932]: 182).

11. *De nat. deor.* 1.12, trans. H. Rackham, L.C.L. (London, 1933).

12. *Acad.* 2.7, trans. H. Rackham, L.C.L. (London, 1933); cf. *De of.* 2.8., trans. Walter Miller, L.C.L. (London, 1913): "And as to the fact that our school argues against everything, that is only because we could not get a clear view of what is 'probable,' unless a comparative estimate were made of all the arguments on both sides." For further citations, see Trimpi, "The Quality of Fiction," 44. His pp. 43–51 are especially illuminating for the relationship of rhetoric to the philosophical method of the Middle Academy. The continuing importance of the Academic position in the development of Renaissance rhetoric is discussed by Jerrold E. Seigel, *Rhetoric and Philosophy in Renaissance Humanism* (Princeton, 1968).

Nor shall I recall, from the cradle of our boyish learning of days gone by, a long string of precepts, but I shall repeat the things I heard of as once handled in a discussion between men who were the most eloquent of our nation, and of the highest rank in distinction of every kind.[13]

Here Cicero suggests the constrictiveness of bare rules, preferring instead to convey the richness of his thoughts on rhetoric by imitating the conversation of experienced men. Having suggested the method, he sketches in the scene and the *personae*, and the discussion gets under way in a setting reminiscent of the grove in Plato's *Phaedrus*. Here Scaevola, Sulpitius, Cotta, Antonius, and Crassus gather to share their views on oratory. The major speakers are Antonius and Crassus, who frequently offer opposing views on the education and offices of the orator; Antonius argues, for example, the need for general culture, while Crassus requires a specific knowledge of civil law. On the second day of the colloquy Catalus, a new arrival, remarks how the two men seem to complement each other (2.26). This theme is developed later by Crassus, who describes the various perfections that exist in art, as in nature. All oratory, he says, "is occupied with the same supply of ideas and expressions, and yet it comprises extreme dissimilarities—not in the sense that some speakers deserve praise and others blame, but that the ones admittedly deserving of praise nevertheless achieve it in a variety of styles" (3.26). The perfections of oratory being the proposed subject, Crassus delivers in the final book a swelling defense of the orator as a philosopher combining verbal skill with the dialectical abilities and moral aims of Aristotle and Carneades (3.71). Yet even after this inspiring vision has been promulgated, and Cotta has been won over to the Academy, the talented Sulpitius remarks bathetically, "for my part our ordinary acquaintance with legal and public affairs is extensive enough for the eloquence that I have in view" (3.147). Obviously the ideal orator is being molded (the plastic term is used on two occasions[14]) by a variety of hands. All reasonable views are held in equilibrium so that, as Cicero tells his brother, the reader may indeed learn "what men renowned above all others for eloquence have thought about the whole subject of oratory" (1.4).

The Ciceronian dialogue is imitated many times in the succeeding cen-

13. *De or.* 1.23.
14. *Ibid.*, 2.123, 3.200.

turies, and we find in Castiglione's book a similar gathering, where friends have retired from the busyness of life to discuss together topics of mutual interest. Translator Thomas Hoby's dedicatory epistle shows that he was much aware of the tradition in which his author was writing:

> Cicero, an excellent Oratour, in three bookes of an Oratour unto his brother, fashioneth such a one as never was, nor yet is like to be; Castilio an excellent courtier, in three bookes of a Courtier unto his dear friend, fashioneth such a one as is hard to find, and perhaps unpossible. Cicero bringeth into dispute of an Oratour, Crassus, Scevola, Antonius, Cotta, Sulpitius, Catallus, and Caesar his brother, the noblest and chiefest Oratours in those daies. Castilio, to reason of a Courtier, the Lord Octavian Fregoso, Sir Frideric his brother, the Lord Julian de Medicis, the Lord Cezar Gonzaga, the L. Frances comaria Della Rovere, Count Lewis of Canossa, the Lord Gaspar Pallavisin, Bembo, Bibiena, and other most excellent Courtiers, and of the noblest families in those daies in Italie. . . .[15]

Hoby suggests here both the aim and method of the Ciceronian dialogue: to "found a commonwealth in the realm of discourse," as in Plato—but through an open-ended, ethopoetic conversation conducted *in utramque partem quaestionis*.[16]

The perfect Courtier is, in a very real sense, the book itself, for it is a hopeless enchiridion if one wishes to follow it literally. It is constructed of a series of antitheses, both sides of which are often equally valid, many of which are left unresolved, with others resolved only in the most tentative and hopeful manner. God never constructed so deeply fragmented an individual as this Courtier. Which, of course, is just the point, for the charming company in Castiglione's dialogue set about the task not of

---

15. *The Book of the Courtier*, trans. Sir Thomas Hoby, Everyman ed. (London, 1928), p. 3.

16. *Rep.* 592b. Castiglione himself seems to disavow the Platonic epistemology while acknowledging his formal relationship to the Platonic dialogue: "Others say that since it is so difficult, and well-nigh impossible, to find a man as perfect as I wish the Courtier to be, it was wasted effort to write of him, because it is useless to teach what cannot be learned. To such as these I answer (without wishing to get into any dispute about the Intelligible World or the Ideas), that I am content to have erred with Plato, Xenophon, and Marcus Tullius" (*The Book of the Courtier*, trans. Charles S. Singleton [Garden City, N.Y., 1959], pp. 5–6). All further references, unless otherwise noted, are to this edition.

fashioning a creature of flesh and blood, but of "forming in words," as messer Federico suggests, an ideal of human personality—and that is quite another matter.

Of special interest is the ontological progression of the inquiry. Book 1 is concerned with the basic characteristics of the ideal man. Is he to be of noble birth? What is to be his profession? How is he to comport himself? What pastimes is he to cultivate? What will be his style of speaking and writing? Through such questions as these, the mental and physical qualities of the Courtier are set forth, although rarely in didactic fashion. On the matter of inherited nobility, for example, good reasonings are offered on both sides, but the question is never resolved in any absolute sense. It is finally conceded that a man of noble birth will more readily gain his Prince's ear; thus inherited nobility offers a practical advantage. The debate on the ancients and the moderns in literary style, too, moves toward a position of accommodation, ultimately embracing an inclusive Ciceronian ideal. The expository tendency in Book 1 is most frequently in the direction of the abstract. When a certain quality or accomplishment is suggested for the Courtier, the debate turns to the nature of the quality or accomplishment *per se*. Thus, when musicianship is proposed by Count Ludovico, and is opposed as effeminate by signor Gasparo, the Count replies with what is virtually an encomium of music. When the subject of painting comes up, the discussion develops into an argument on the relative merits of painting and sculpture. We find here the same inductive movement noticed earlier in *Fulgens and Lucres*. In debating the qualities of the perfect Courtier, the arguments of the interlocutors recede from actuality toward general questions (from "Ought our Courtier be a painter?" to "Is painting good?"), thereby allowing the company to examine the broader philosophical concerns that must lie behind any decision to endow him with a specific character. One is reminded here of Cicero's insistence that every specific case must ultimately be argued in generic terms, for it is in genus that one may most clearly discern the basic issue.[17]

In Book 2, however, we find a progression from the generic to the specific. Signora Emilia sets the direction by ordering Federico Fregoso to declare "in what way, manner, and time, the Courtier is to put into

17. *De or.* 2.133–141.

effect his good qualities and practice those things which the Count said befitted him" (p. 88). Messer Federico begins by providing an outline:

> In all that he does or says, I would have our Courtier follow certain general rules which, in my opinion, briefly comprise all I have to say. And the first and most important of these is that he should avoid affectation above all else, as the Count rightly advised last evening. Next, let him consider well *what* he says or does, the *place where* he does it, *in whose presence*, its *timeliness*, the *reason* for doing it, his own *age*, his *profession*, the *end* at which he aims, and the *means* by which he can reach it; thus, keeping these points in mind, let him act accordingly in whatever he may choose to do or say. (p. 98, emphases mine)

Although signor Morello remarks that these topics resemble the *circonstanzie* of auricular confession, messer Federico's outline resembles nothing so much as Cicero's heuristic scheme for developing a proposition concerning the defendant's guilt in a legal trial. In *De inventione*, he writes that all arguments in which one seeks to establish moral or legal culpability are drawn from attributes of the person or his actions. Those of the person are name, nature, manner of life, fortune, disposition, passions, interests, purposes, achievements, accidents, and past remarks. Attributes of actions include place, time, opportunity, manner, and the facility with which the act may be done (1.34–43). One develops one's contention about the guilt of the accused by examining the facts of the case in the light of these topics, drawing the appropriate implications. A man may be murdered, for example, with a butcher knife, at night, on a lonely road, when everyone is in town at a festival. Means, time, place, disposition, passion, and opportunity conspire to make probable the guilt of the irascible meat-cutter who was wont to solitude, had absented himself from the festival, and whose favorite implement is now missing. By searching the topics, one uses such circumstantial evidence to reconstruct and bring into view a character and an action which, if not demonstrably true, is as close to the truth as human reasoning can reach. In establishing this view, one is creating a fiction upon which to base a judgment.[18]

18. Cf. Thomas Wilson's enumeration of similar *topoi*, quoted in Ch. II, pp. 52–53. Although these topics are most frequently discussed in connection with

This is precisely what messer Federico would have the Courtier do. While, in general, he must behave decorously and without affectation, specifically, he must continually re-create himself by fashioning a scenario in which he may be judged in the best possible light. Several of these scenarios are provided by the speakers in Book 2. Immediately following his outline, messer Federico suggests that implied in the general rule[19] is this specific situation: when in a skirmish at arms (*what*), in the field (*place where*), the Courtier should withdraw from the vulgar and perform before the eyes of the nobility, especially before the king (*in whose presence*)—"for it is well indeed to make all one can of things well done" (p. 99). It is wasted motion to act bravely without the proper audience, since the motive of skill in arms is honor (*cause*). In a tourney (*what*) he will be mindful of the *place* and *company*, gaily caparison his horse and dress elegantly himself (*means*), never be last to appear (*time*). If he must wrestle with peasants (*what*), he should do so merely as a courteous amateur (*profession*). In making music (*what*), he will await a leisurely moment (*time*), and have regard for his years (*age*)—"if old men wish to sing to the viola, let them do so in secret" (p. 106). To be judged worthy of his Prince's respect, then, the Courtier must engage in a highly complicated *ethopoeia*.

Of even more interest, from our point of view, is the method of exposition Castiglione himself is now employing. While in Book 1 the discussants were usually content with examining qualities in the abstract, and we as readers enjoyed their arguments *pro et contra*, now they insist upon placing the Courtier in specific situations, where, we discover, these qualities begin to take on the complex shades of real human characteristics. It is one thing to say a man must act in a becoming fashion; it is another to see the many faces of decorum which emerge in quite different situations that are, in effect, fictional "scenes." It is toward the enjoyment of such fictions that the hypothetical circumstances proposed by the Duchess's guests now draw us.

Within this more particularized discourse, the explorative mood still prevails. There is disagreement over the Courtier's behavior with his

the conjectural status (*an sit?*), they are also to be used in the qualitative issue (*De inv.* 2.74).

19. sotto la nostra regula (*Il Cortegiano*, ed. Silvano del Missier, Il Club del Libro [Novaro, 1968], p. 172).

Prince—should he be retiring or bold, need he obey evil commands, how can he tell the good from the evil? Signor Gasparo asks whether the Courtier ought to deliberately disobey a command if he believes that to do so will benefit his lord. Castiglione's source here is the *Noctes Atticae* of Aulus Gellius, in which a rhetorical *quaestio* or *thesis* is presented on the subject, "What would be more proper on receipt of an order—to do scrupulously what was commanded, or sometimes even to disobey, in the hope that it would be more advantageous to the giver of the order."[20] If we compare the two versions we can readily see how Castiglione has attempted to "naturalize," and therefore to render as mimetic fiction, a more abstract form of intellectual inquiry—and also understand why the episode, as we read it, is so peculiar.

Gellius opens his chapter by remarking that this question is a doubtful one which has been weighed on both sides by wise men (*anceps quaestio et in utramque partem a prudentibus viris arbitrata est*). He then presents the judgment on one side of the question, that once a decision has been reached it must be followed, else an unfortunate outcome will be blamed on the offender, success attributed only to the gods, and a precedent set for future disobedience. Yet *others*, he continues, have argued that the benefits that may be derived from a successful countermand ought to be weighed against the disadvantages to be borne if disaster ensues, and the potentially more advantageous course pursued—always bearing in mind, however, the nature of the commander. Then Gellius adds, "I believe that this little theorem [abstract proposition] concerning obedience to commands of this kind will be more fully furnished forth and clearer if I also present the example of Publius Crassus Mucianus, a distinguished and illustrious man."[21] And he thereupon recounts the tale of an engineer who had substituted his own better judgment for that of the consul Crassus and was beaten with rods for his pains.

Castiglione renders the whole piece "fictional" by representing both sides of the question in the continuous naturalistic discourse of messer Federico, who answers signor Gasparo's inquiry almost verbatim from

---

20. *The Attic Nights of Aulus Gellius*, trans. John C. Rolfe, L.C.L. (London, 1927), 1.13.

21. Instructius deliberatiusque fore arbitramur theorematium hoc de mandatiis huius modi obsequendis, si exemplum quoque P. Crassi Muciani, clari atque incluti viri, apposuerimus (1.13.9).

Gellius, leaving out, however, such tell-tale locutions of the *quaestio* as "some say" and "others say." The result is strange. Without the verbal clues that suggest a response *in utramque partem* is taking place, we naturally expect some definite answer to emerge from Federico's free-flowing speech. Yet this is what we find:

> I would give the rule in this [question of "beneficent" disobedience] by citing the example of Manlius Torquatus [who executed his own son for disobedience, also cited by Gellius], if I thought him worthy of much praise, which truly I do not; and yet I dare not venture to condemn him either and oppose the judgment of so many centuries. For, no doubt, it is a quite dangerous thing to depart from our superiors' commands. . . . [Here he cites from Gellius the reasons, on the first side of the question, for strict obedience, ending with the warning about setting a precedent.] But in such a case I think that the man involved must consider carefully. . . . [Here he cites the "advantage-balancing" argument on the other side of the question, recommending that one follow the practice of merchants who risk little to gain much.] I deem it well above all that he reckon with the character of the Prince he serves . . . lest there happen to him what is recorded to have happened to a master engineer of the Athenians . . . . [Here he recounts the tale of Publius Crassus.] (pp. 118-119)

Notice that after the initial wavering about the rectitude of Manlius Torquatus, the rhetoric implies a climactic progression toward the enunciation of a definite doctrine. Yet after the first argument, against countermanding an order, has been set out, the phrase "But in such a case," which implies that a preferable mode of action is now to be suggested, is in fact a specious transition, for it simply introduces an alternative point of view. Similarly, the "above all" in the last section suggests the clinching argument—but all it does is add yet another complication to the question, which is, "Whatever you do, you had best weigh how your commander is likely to react." In sum, messer Federico has not resolved signor Gasparo's doubt at all, but has merely rehearsed, in language more personal, and in a syntax that appears single-purposed, the *anceps quaestio* itself.[22] It is a particularly revealing instance of the expository method employed so frequently in *The Courtier*.

22. The resemblance to the technique of Bacon's aphoristic *Essays*, which are

In Book 3, the exemplary manner of argument suggested by Gellius in the last part of the *quaestio* is developed more fully. This section, largely occupied with the *querelle de femmes*, is filled with tales illustrating the bravery, faithfulness, and chastity of women. In the hands of Castiglione, these moral anecdotes, which are drawn from such collections as the *Facta dictaque* of Valerius Maximus and Plutarch's *Mulierum virtutes*, are presented with a new twist. The Magnifico, as *defensor feminae*, is the chief story teller, but his antagonists will not accept his exempla as proofs for the virtues he expounds. When he exhorts them to remember that the wife and daughter of Mithridates exhibited less fear than Mithridates himself, that the same was true of Hasdrubel's wife, and that Harmonia, daughter of the tyrant of Syracuse, refused to leave her native city even when it was burning, signor Frisio retorts, "When it is a matter of obstinacy, it is certain that some women are occasionally found who would never abandon their purpose" (p. 224). It was not bravery, but stubbornness, that motivated these actions. Then the Magnifico tells the tale of a certain messer Tommaso, a courageous gentleman who is captured and enslaved by Moors en route to Sicily. Some fellow prisoners escape and inform his wife and family of his fate, and after many years, one of Tommaso's brothers secretly secures his freedom and smuggles him to Leghorn, whence he writes to his wife. The good woman, Argentina, learning that her longed-for spouse is so near, raises her eyes to heaven, calls out her husband's name, and dies in a fit of joy. Frisio, unimpressed, asks, "How do you know she did not die of grief on hearing that her husband was coming home?" The Magnifico refutes this possibility by declaring that it was simply not in character, whereupon signor Gasparo remarks drily, "It may be that this woman was too much in love, for women always go to extremes in everything, which is bad" (p. 230). Castiglione is obviously applying the technique of the *controversia* to these moral exempla, which are presented without question in the sources; here, the facts of the case remain constant, but their significance changes according to one's interpretation. It is further evidence that fictions may be debatable questions "more fully furnished forth" to render the issues more readily apprehensible.

derived from antithetical commonplaces, is striking. See the passage quoted in Ch. II, p. 41.

It would be misleading to suggest that there is a systematic progression of fictional realization throughout *The Courtier*, for alongside circumstantial accounts one always finds more abstract debates. But repeatedly, general opinions are criticized for their degree of simplification, and a more particularized account demanded. This reflects an awareness on the part of both the author and his *personae* that problems will be more deeply felt and dealt with in greater subtlety when they are examined in a familiar human environment.[23]

The explorative function of this antithetical fiction is disclosed most vividly in Book 4, following discussion of the Courtier's end, that of guiding his Prince. The Magnifico suddenly remarks that if the Courtier knows so much he must be greater than his Prince, and if he is as wise as signor Ottaviano and others would have him, he must be too old to exhibit the physical prowess and courtly graces that would attract the Prince to him in the first place. To these reasonable objections signor Ottaviano makes no convincing reply; after some hedging he concludes that if the young courtier is insufficiently wise, then "he is not the Courtier we presuppose" (p. 330). The ending verb is crucial. "Suppositio" is the Latin equivalent of the Greek "hypothesis," and Ottaviano's use of the term acknowledges both the Courtier's ontological status and his problematic nature.[24] As a model figured forth by "supposing" the perfections of the

23. In addition to the demands at the end of Book 1 and the beginning of Book 2 mentioned earlier, see, for example, Francesco della Rovere's request for specific instances of wit (pp. 140–141), signor Gasparo's complaint that the Magnifico has contented himself with generalities concerning the Court Lady (p. 209), and Emilia's response to their "scholastical" quibbling (p. 218).

24. non e quel cortegiano che noi presuponemo (*Il Cortegiano*, p. 536). Trimpi notes that

the word "thesis" means a "stand" or "position" and is translated *positio*; "hypothesis," whose Latin form is *suppositio* (*sub* + *ponere*) means a "placing under," and, by extension, "what one has placed under," or a "subtending." In the rhetorical usage, where hypothesis is considered a species of the genus thesis and refers to questions about action and events, the "sub" carries the meaning of being placed under a more inclusive heading and of sharing characteristics, indicated by that heading, with other species ("The Ancient Hypothesis of Fiction," *Traditio* [1971]: 27 n. 29).

He observes that Sidney uses precisely the same verb in the *Apology* when describing the poet's creation of character (*Elizabethan Critical Essays*, ed., G. Gregory Smith [Oxford, 1904], 1. 164).

human personality, he has attained a large measure of particularity; having been educed from the varying thought of the Duchess's company, however, he can never be put together as a formal man, but must remain floating free, unassembled, in the halls of Urbino. In essence, the perfect Courtier is the image of a state of mind. That mind has been temporarily freed from the either-or exigencies of the quotidian world, and by arguing both sides of the question has been able to envision a fuller reality.

Castiglione's book suggests there are several ways to envision such a reality through fiction. One is simply to create characters who discuss it theoretically. At a second stage it is examined in somewhat more concrete circumstances—the hypothetical situations remaining, however, typical, without truly individuating features. A third stage, indicated by the exemplary ancedotes, involves hypothesizing particular persons, bearing distinct names and characteristics, who are engaged in problematic activities. As we enter upon this stage of hypothesization we approach Sir Thomas More's *Utopia*.

II

If *The Courtier* is a complex literary dialogue, what can we call this peculiar work? It is not simply a dialogue, and not quite an integrated narrative, either. In Antwerp, More encounters Raphael Hythlodaeus, fresh from his Utopian experience, who debates with him the duties and probable results of public service, describes in monologue the ideal state he has visited, and then takes off for parts unknown, leaving More (and the reader) to ponder the implications of what has been discussed. The work represents a conscious attempt to create a narrative fiction out of a series of questions that have their own independent existence, and because its seams now lie open to us, it is particularly useful in examining a more advanced stage in the declension of question into fiction.[25]

25. See J. H. Hexter, *More's Utopia: The Biography of an Idea* (Princeton, 1952). Hexter argues that the narrative introduction in Book 1 and the discourse on Utopia in Book 2 were composed in the Netherlands between May and October 1515, as Erasmus implies in a letter to Ulrich Hutton. The dialogue of counsel, followed by a transitional introduction to Book 2, the peroration, and the conclusion of Book 2, were composed some time after More's return to England in the autumn of 1515, and before September 1516.

The discourse proper, we know, was originally a deeply felt yet whimsical essay in social idealism, written during More's stay in Belgium in 1515. Its aim—to fashion a state that would breed good and happy men —was serious enough, although, for reasons we shall discuss in a moment, the state was furnished with such fanciful institutions as premarital body inspections and golden chamber pots. The character of the work changed when More in the fall of 1515 was called to the King's service. Suddenly offered the possibility of working for social reform at the source of power, he was faced with the choice of remaining the visionary or entering upon the practical business of statemanship. What ought he to do? Evidently one of the things he did do, while thinking it over, was to examine the problem *in utramque partem* through a fiction.[26] Between his brief narrative introducing Raphael Hythlodaeus and the sketch of Utopia, he created the dialogue of counsel, which asks the question, "Shall a humanist enter the royal service?" This addition changed the shape of the work drastically. For in converting his own problematic situation into a practical *hypothesis* he also transformed Hythlodaeus from a picturesque foreigner with a tall tale into a man representing one side of the question, and then created another character, a stolid *persona* More, to represent the second. Moreover, this change turned the original essay on Utopia (the discourse proper) into an *argument* suggesting the kinds of fundamental reform the humanist might insist upon if he does enter public service. The completed piece now became an ambivalent anecdote comprising an introductory narration, an ethopoetic dialogue (furnished with conventional garden setting), an extended argument via exemplum, and a

26. In a period of political crisis, Cicero wrote to Atticus that he argued general questions to retain his equanimity:

> I have taken for myself certain theses, so to speak, which deal with *la haute politique*, and are applicable to the present crisis, so that I may keep myself from querelous thoughts and may practice the subject. Here are some: Whether one should remain in one's country, even under a tyranny. Whether any means are lawful to abolish a tyranny, even if they endanger the existence of the State. Whether one ought to take care that one who tries to abolish it may not rise too high himself. Whether one ought to assist one's country, when under a tyranny, by seizing opportunities and by argument rather than by war . . . (*Letters to Atticus*, 9.4, trans. E. O. Winstedt, L.C.L. [London, 1913]).

Their resemblance to More's questions suggests the longevity of such therapy.

qualifying palinode. It was a form through which More was confronting the challenge of his own vision.

This is what accounts for the elusive nature of the work, so realistic in the first book, so facetious, yet also obviously earnest in the second. Its elusiveness should not divert us from its basic seriousness, however, nor from its urgent spirit of inquiry. It begins with the overwhelming question currently haunting More, but quickly splits into *quaestiunculae* on specific social problems. For the question is not only whether the unattached humanist shall commit himself to politics, but also what his goals ought to be if he does become so engaged. To examine these, More creates additional dialogues within the main dialogue, as Erasmus had superimposed other *prosopopoeiae* upon that of Folly. The first is Hythlodaeus's account of a dinner party at Cardinal Morton's, which becomes the occasion for a serious debate on enclosures, unemployment, and the penal code. Similarly, the two hypothetical encounters in the royal councils of the French and the unnamed king allow More, through Hythlodaeus, to state his feelings about foreign policy, colonization, and fiscal management. By the time the first book is drawing to a close, More's alter ego has offered commonsense approaches to a number of contemporary issues that will demand the writer's attention if he joins the King's service, and has also envisioned the negative response he is likely to elicit if he urges dramatic reform.

It is interesting to notice here how More deliberately exploits in his exposition the advantages offered by fictional devices. More than half a dozen marginal glosses, probably provided by Erasmus, call the reader's attention to the choicer specimens. A satirical exchange between two of the guests at Morton's table, for example, is glossed "A Merry Dialogue between a Friar and a Hanger-On" (*Festivus dialogus fratris & morionis*), and the decorum observed therein is described some lines later as "A Masterful Adaptation of Speech to Character in the Tale!" (*Ut servat decorum in narratione*). The anecdote about the Achorians, which Hythlodaeus proposes to relate to the French king, is singled out as "A Noteworthy Example" (*Exemplum annotandum*).[27] Similarly remarked are an

27. *The Yale Edition of The Complete Works*, Edward Surtz, S. J. and J. H. Hexter, eds. (New Haven, 1965) 4.81, 83, 88. All subsequent citations, unless otherwise indicated, are to this edition. On the authorship of the glosses, see 22.21n, p. 280.

ethopoeia (p. 70), two similes (pp. 46, 98), an apothegm (p. 50), a proverb (p. 82), and, in the discourse proper, a *fabula* (p. 152) and a *fictio* (p. 168). The glosses pointedly remind the reader that what he sees before him is hypothetical—in both the poetic and ontological sense—and thus provide a psychological safety zone in which both author and reader may give Raphael's radical proposals a fair hearing. Even the diction of the text is thoroughly imbued with the hypothetical. Upon introducing his second colloquy, Raphael says, "Age finge me apud regem esse Gallorum atque in eius consilio considere" ("Come now, suppose [literally, *create a fiction that*] I were at the court of the French king and sitting in his privy council"), and then he proceeds to fill in specific details of a council meeting at which international strategy is being planned (86.22). Throughout this section there are a number of contrary-to-fact *si* clauses which, translated as "suppose" or "picture," invite *persona* More and the reader to put themselves into the scene temporarily and, as it were, try out Raphael's courtiership. The reader thus enjoys both the emotional and intellectual attractions of fictional specificity and also the security that comes with knowing that it is only a vicarious experience.[28]

As might be expected, the dialogue of counsel settles nothing. It only renders more vivid both the practical difficulties confronting the social reformer and the spiritual conflict that exists between the meliorist who adapts himself to the play at hand (as the historical More initially did) and the idealist who refuses to play at all (as the historical More eventually did). This exposition of personality is an important aspect of More's *hypothesis*, for it enables us to see the human motivations behind the political positions. Rooted though he may be in the prejudices of his society, *persona* More is sensitive to injustice and dedicated to human welfare. Is it not better, he asks, if one cannot put things right, to make them as little wrong as possible?[29] Hythlodaeus, for all his avowed humanitari-

28. One is reminded of Erasmus's own fictional equivocation. In the dedication of *The Praise of Folly* (trans. Hoyt H. Hudson [Princeton, 1941]), he remarks to More that if anyone is offended by the work it is, after all, Folly who is speaking, and "he should at least remember that it is a fine thing to be slandered by Folly" (p. 4).

29. Surtz points out that his meliorist position, far from representing a facile stand-patism, reflects the carefully reasoned view of Aristotle and Aquinas, the one upholding a hierarchical society guided by just laws based upon the variegated

anism, tends to remove himself from the habitations of human beings, and would allow evils to persist rather than stain himself through compromise. These considerations qualify for the reader—as they probably did for the candid More—the simple opposition between "courtier" and "philosopher" suggested by their political stands, and render judgment in the matter a good bit more problematic.[30]

The most elaborate "figuring forth" in the book, of course, is the description of Utopia itself. Since it is largely undramatic, its poetically "hypothetical" nature may easily be overlooked, but the surrounding text makes clear its status as fictive (particular) realization. The charming tetrastich at the beginning of the book provides the first clue:

> *Utupos me dux ex non insula fecit insulam.*
> *Una ego terrarum omnium absque philosophia.*
> *Civitatem philosophiam expressi mortalibus.*
> *Libenter impartio mea, non gravatim accipio meliora.*
>
> (p. 18)

The middle two lines are the ones that concern us, and are rendered most vividly in Robinson's translation:

> I one of all other [lands] without philosophie
> Have shaped for man a philosophicall citie.[31]

In general, the meaning is that without the difficult askesis of Platonic dialectic, Utopia has become the philosophical commonwealth Plato had envisioned. More precisely, the lines describe the literary work itself,

---

nature of man, the other a hierarchical society based upon the fallen nature of man. It was a position shared by most humanists, whose criticism of contemporary European conditions was tempered by their recognition of the imperfect state of Christianity (*The Praise of Pleasure* [Cambridge, Mass., 1965], pp. 161, 163, 182–183).

30. This point is well developed by Richard Sylvester: "We may also wonder whether the price which Hythlodaeus asks us to pay is too high—not so much the cost involved in losing all that has been bequeathed to us, but rather the loss in terms of human personality itself. Given Hythlodaeus's isolation from the rest of humanity, can we really trust him to lead us into the promised land?" ("*Si Hythlodaeo credimus*: Vision and Revision in Thomas More's *Utopia*," *Soundings* 51 [1968]: 284).

31. *The Utopia of Sir Thomas More*, ed. J. H. Lupton (Oxford, 1895), p. xciv.

focusing upon the discourse: it is not a work of abstract philosophical reasoning but a work of fiction, wherein an ideal is *shaped*.[32] That this ideal will assume concrete form is further suggested by Hythlodaeus when *persona* More questions the feasibility of a communist state where, he believes, there will be neither an incentive to work nor respect for authority:

Non miror inquit, sic videri tibi, quippe cui imago rei, aut nulla succurrit, aut falsa. [I do not wonder, he rejoined, that it looks this way to you, being a person who has no picture at all, or else a false one, of the situation I mean.]   (pp. 106–107)

And he gladly offers to set forth this *imago*, which he says he still keeps before his eyes. But, *res ocium poscit*: the free exploration of this ideal requires leisurely removal from the pressing affairs of life.

Such leisure is provided after lunch when More, having left orders not to be disturbed, returns to the garden to hear Hythlodaeus's account of Utopia. In the continuing debate, this description functions as a rhetorical *exemplum*—a vivid fabrication of "proofs" in support of the Utopian way of life. Viewed in this light, the strange discourse suddenly makes

32. Once again we encounter the plastic metaphor employed by Cicero and Hoby. The contrast between the dialectical method of Plato and the descriptive method of More is even more strongly pointed out in the lines by Anemolius, the Utopian poet laureate. He compares Utopia to the Republic:

> *nam quod illa literis*
> *Deliniavit, hoc ego una praestiti,*
> *Viris & opibus, optimisque legibus.*

Again, Robinson seems to convey the significance best:

> For what Platoes penne hath platted briefely
> In naked wordes, as in a glasse,
> The same have I perfourmed fully,
> With lawes, with men, and treasure fyttely.
> (p. xciii)

Robinson's diction not only suggests the contrast between the brevity and bareness of "philosophical" discourse and the fullness and liveliness of the rhetorical manner (Zeno's closed and open fist), but also the "forming" power of poetry. Of course, he does not do justice to Plato's own fiction-making.

complete sense. Rhetorical proofs, as we have discovered, support in a variety of ways the position being defended. The disputant simply examines the question before him and invents useful arguments. These may be quite inconsistent with one another, as was evident in Erasmus's claim that religion is folly because old women hover about the altars and *also* because pious men give away the shirts off their backs. Some propositions may be entirely serious, capable of sustaining prolonged scrutiny, while others may be merely expedient and vanish beneath a piercing glance. What is characteristic of rhetorical *proofs* in a verbal argument is also characteristic of the *institutions* in the fiction of Utopia. The problem set is to show how an orderly, just, and prosperous society can operate. It can do so, Hythlodaeus argues, by forbidding possession of private property, democratically electing local representatives, rotating urban and agricultural tasks, sharing the commodities of life without payment of money, and by pursuing the greatest pleasure, which is the principle that underlies all the institutions of Utopia. But included among these sensible customs are the somewhat unsettling nude examinations of brides by prospective husbands (and vice versa) and those unforgettable gold chamber pots—features of Utopian life which carry the rationalism that we have come to associate with Utopian institutions beyond normal expectations. Though supremely reasonable in themselves, they offend a deeply ingrained sense of decorum, and are therefore seen as comic. The subtle shift in emotional response that we feel upon reading about them is an experience frequently encountered in sophistic disputation, and we meet it often in Utopia.

To prevent habituation to bloodshed and cruelty, for example, citizens are permitted neither to hunt nor butcher animals, while to demean the value set on jewels—and at the same time keep them handy for future emergencies—gems are given to children as playthings. In the light of the most elementary theories of conditioning the first measure is reasonable enough, but the second smacks of ingenuity. An analogous contrast is seen in their military practices. To prevent cowardice in warfare, whole families are sent to the front to fight side by side; yet an important Utopian tactic is to exploit the cupidity of the enemy by offering a reward for the betrayal of opposition leaders. Once again two kinds of rationalism are juxtaposed. To harness natural piety for the benefit of the commonwealth seems sensible and humane, for it brings out what is most noble in the human character; the exploitation of human weakness, however—even that of an enemy—is a tactic more befitting the Europeans Hythlodaeus criticizes than an ideal race.[33] In sum, there is much that is specious in this exemplum, and More knew it. This is because the discourse is not a practical blueprint for an ideal polity at all, but an imaginative construction designed to apply therapeutic pressure on the unsightly bulges that deform human nature—pride, greed, cruelty, fear—shaping a citizen through institutions that do not permit him to cultivate his propensities for pain. Another name for such a construction is a rhetorical argument, and this one was fashioned by a mind, trained in the art of witty disputation, that found itself suddenly at leisure in the summer of 1515, and later ascribed its protean product to the otium of Raphael Hythlodaeus.[34]

By the end of the discourse, Hythlodaeus has revealed that the Utopian way works. Thus the argument has swung in the direction of radical reform. It is this at which the humanist must aim upon entering the government. Then come the strangely anticlimactic words of More:

When Raphael had finished his story, many things came to my mind which seemed very absurdly established in the customs and laws of the people described—not only in their method of waging war, their ceremonies and religion, as well as their other institutions, but most of all in that feature which is the principal foundation of their whole structure. I mean their common life and subsistence—without any exchange of money. This latter alone utterly overthrows all the nobility, magnificence, splendor, and majesty which are, in the estimation of the common people, the true glories and ornaments of the commonwealth. (p. 245)

33. The editors of the Yale edition point out that these are, in fact, Machiavellian tactics—precisely those against which Hythlodaeus has been inveighing (see 202.29n, p. 502).

34. Since the discourse was conceived independently of its larger context, its multiple levels of argument probably functioned originally as More's own private way of debating with himself the validity of the Utopian ideal—the slyly facetious qualifying and putting the earnest in its place. Sylvester ("*Si Hythlodaeo credimus*") ascribes its inconsistency of vision to Hythlodaeus's obsession with institutions and consequent moral blindness. If, in fact, this was More's intention, it is further evidence of his care to "figure forth" in imitation his earlier internal debate.

We are struck first by the fact that this is a counter-argument and that *persona* More has not been won over to Raphael's point of view. Understandably, he thinks many of Utopia's customs absurd. But more than this, he has really missed the whole point of author More's serio-comic exemplum. He still clings to the traditional definitions of nobility, magnificence, splendor, and majesty that Hythlodaeus has just overturned— which implies that these terms, like folly, have two meanings. For obtuse as he is, *persona* More is a force to be reckoned with—a fictional caricature of author More's own uncertainty. At bottom More remains the visionary explorer pitted against the practical statesman. The fiction *Utopia* does not resolve the conflict in him, nor, if we consider the events of the years that followed, did life itself. *Utopia*, in fact, allowed him that suspension of commitment which life does not usually afford, but is one of the things that fiction is for. This pseudo-narrative ends, then—having weighed the problem of public service, proposals for domestic and foreign policy, methods of influencing decision makers, and a radical response to injustice—just as it began: with a question.

Thus far in our declension, we have examined two complex fictions that proceed from *theses*. In *The Courtier*, the question is placed in a particular setting, where specific persons discourse upon it at their leisure. In *Utopia*, More attempts to return the question to its original context by supposing an encounter between two men to whom it is of immediate personal concern. Hythlodaeus, returning from his voyages with new political knowledge, is urged by *persona* More, himself on a government mission, to apply this knowledge for the public good, and this prompts the argument, discourse, and response. But while More succeeds in creating the illusion of a temporal narrative, there is in *Utopia* little of the action we usually associate with narrative fiction. It is still essentially speech vivified, for the piece is a hybrid, lying somewhere between literary dialogue and narrative tale. In Sidney's *Arcadia*, the fusion of question and narrative is completed. Questions are realized in and through action.

III

In the *Arcadia* we find a dialogue turned narrative. More specifically, a dialogue turned pastoral romance turned epic, as it makes the transition from the Old *Arcadia* to the 1590 *Arcadia*. Sidney appears to have made the change not only because of formal considerations, but also because the dialogue is not yet fully realized on both sides of the question in the older version. Essentially his narrative fiction is a medium of realization for the abstract debate on the active versus the contemplative life; both the romantic plot and the political plot insist on this.[35] But the latter side of the question is far more fully realized in the Old *Arcadia*, where the heroic exploits of the cousins are largely confined to brief sketches in the Eclogues. In the 1590 version, Sidney begins to redress the balance by presenting in detail the adventures of the Princes before their advent in Arcadia and the new feats to which their love of the Princesses inspire them during the captivity episode.[36]

The extent to which the formal dialogue was present in Sidney's mind when he began the *Arcadia* we cannot know.[37] Nor is it really important.

35. The keynotes are sounded by the suasive letter of Philanax to Basilius (1.24–26) and Musidorus's debate with Pyrochles (1.54–59). References are to volumes and pages of *The Complete Works of Sir Philip Sidney*, ed. Albert Feuillerat (Cambridge, 1912–1926), and will hereafter appear in the text.

36. This has created certain problems in defining the genre of the work. R. W. Zandvoort, *Sidney's Arcadia: A Comparison Between the Two Versions* (Amsterdam, 1929), calls it "at once a romance and a treatise" (p. 120). C. S. Lewis, *English Literature in the Sixteenth Century* (Oxford, 1954), insists that it is "not Arcadian idyll, not even Arcadian romance, but Arcadian epic" (p. 335). Walter Davis, *A Map of Arcadia: Sidney's Romance in its Tradition* (New Haven, 1965), comments, "Never before had the pastoral romance sustained such a weight of tournaments and battle; and of course it had never contained even a hint of the vast political intrigues we find in Arcadia" (p. 54). This is not to deny Sidney's consciousness of genre nor his adherence to the doctrine of imitation. His interest in the Italian epic controversy has been documented by Kenneth Myrick, *Sir Philip Sidney as Literary Craftsman* (Cambridge, Mass., 1935); his debt to pastoral romance, by Davis, and to Greek romance, by Samuel Lee Wolff, *The Greek Romance in Elizabethan Prose Fiction* (New York, 1912). But it does imply that ultimately the *Arcadia* must be considered as a form designed to contain the subjects Sidney wanted to treat, and these fall into both the "active" and "contemplative" categories, thus spilling over traditional genre lines, suggesting instead a fundamental debate structure.

37. Though Neil Rudenstine suggests that the debate on the active and contemplative lives reflects issues discussed in the correspondence between Sidney and Hubert Languet during the time the Old *Arcadia* was being composed (*Sidney's Poetic Development* [Cambridge, Mass., 1967], pp. 16–22).

What is important is that the ancient tradition of arguing *in utramque partem* clearly informs both the structure and the spirit of the work. In the dialogue, as we have seen, it is customary for the interlocutors to withdraw to a garden setting, far from the business of forum or court, to discuss general questions which often proliferate into *quaestiunculae*. Theirs is, in fact, a pastoral retirement, during which the problems life offers can be aired and clarified in a leisurely way. In the dialogue this retirement is arbitrary: a group of men meet and decide to talk. If we were to translate this into a thoroughly mimetic narrative fiction, we would have to motivate the retirement and transform the conversation, with its varying arguments, into a tale with varying episodes—"pregnant Images of life," as Greville would have it.[38] Sidney seems to have accomplished this first goal brilliantly by supplying motivation—the threatening oracle—and setting—the Arcadian woods—thereby providing an appropriate environment for asking the questions that follow.

In the romance epic, these questions take the form of adventures. Instead of simply debating the merits of the active and contemplative lives—and exploring their qualities in the realm of discourse—the characters in Arcadia live them. In fact they live them and re-live them, for the epic convention demands ongoing adventures in the Arcadian *now* as well as recounted adventures in the non-Arcadian *then*. Both, however, bud off the main stem of Basilius's self-imposed exile, which provides the occasion not only for current actions but also for the recollection of actions completed.[39] It does more. Basilius's retirement not only energizes the various adventures—in which we may see the fully developed *hypotheses* of the literary dialogue—but it also achieves, through the plot, the larger purpose of the more abstract form. Initially, Basilius's retreat seems imprudent and immoral: he seeks otium for all the wrong reasons. Yet, transmuted by the action of the romance, it becomes the instrument through which the aim of the true philosophic otium is attained, for the real nature of Basilius's apparently peaceable kingdom (both political and private) is discovered. He and those whom he has attracted by his retirement come to know themselves as never before. Ironically—but not

38. *Life of Sir Philip Sidney* (Oxford, 1905), p. 15.

39. This is easily overlooked in the epic structure of the 1590 *Arcadia*, but is readily apparent in the Old *Arcadia*, which begins *ab ovo* with the oracle, followed by the retreat, and the appearance of the Princes.

really unexpectedly—both sides of the question have had to be given due regard: by losing his way, the King has found himself and his kingdom.[40]

A further similarity to the literary dialogue may be seen: the conflict between the active and contemplative lives turns out to be specious. In the romance epic it is under the aspect of a life devoted to love that the contemplative is opposed to the heroic, since this is the experience undergone by the Princes and Basilius as they retreat from the world of political action. It soon becomes clear, however, that the antithesis of the two modes of existence is more apparent than real, for it is in the pursuit of love that Pyrochles and Musidorus vanquish the bear and lion, rout the Arcadian rebels, break the strength of Cecropia's revolution by defeating Amphialus, defend the ladies in court, and ultimately return to their kingdoms to assume the dual roles of prince and husband. As is so frequently the case in its more abstract forbears, this debate is really a means of conducting an inquiry into the larger implications of subjects supposed, for reasons of convenience, to be opposites.

In its general outline, then, the *Arcadia* suggests the structure and ends of the literary dialogue. But if we look more closely we will find that Sidney also uses internal devices analogous to those employed in the dialogue for the purpose of posing questions and entertaining possibilities without cloture. These are characteristically "fictional"—mimetic, that is, and therefore affective. The most obvious are the narrated adventures themselves. They are essentially heuristic exempla, through which we are invited to experience what love and heroism can mean. Their function is most explicitly revealed in the "wooing fiction" Musi-

40. Here, genre lines comfortably cross one another and reveal their common concerns. Davis has characterized the "plot" of pastoral romance as the disintegration, education, and reintegration of the hero, as he enters the pastoral landscape from the quotidian world, comes to understand his own nature through personal encounters there, and returns to the outside world a more stable self (*A Map of Arcadia*, pp. 38–39). This is, of course, precisely the function of the philosophic otium, where the forum represents the active, epic environment, and the academy the place for seeking the truth on which to act. The contrast is alluded to in one of the heated debates between the Princes, when Pyrochles impatiently tells Musidorus, "But these Disputations are fitter for quiet schooles, then my troubled braines, which are bent rather in deeds to performe, then in words to defende the noble desire which possesseth me" (1.81).

dorus devises to speed his courtship with Pamela. Since he is unable to approach her directly, he feigns love for Mopsa, who has been assigned to guard her. Then, pretending that the lodgekeeper's daughter has scorned his shepherd's weeds, he appeals to Pamela for intercession:

> But yet . . . most honoured Lady, if my miserable speeches have not already cloied you, & that the verie presence of such a wretch become not hateful in your eyes; let me reply thus much further against my mortall sentence [Mopsa's supposed rejection], by telling you a storie, which happened in this country long since . . . *whereby you shall see that my estate is not so contemptible,* but that a Prince hath been content to take the like upon him, and by that only hath aspired to enjoy a mightie Princesse. (1.159, emphasis mine)

And he recounts, in the guise of another man's adventure, the story of his own education, travels, love-sickness, transformation into a shepherd, and courtship of the King's elder daughter. It is not only a witty way to identify himself, but also demonstrates in small Sidney's fictional method, for Pamela has been offered a clarifying lens through which she may learn how a noble prince, educated in a great court, might happen to fall in love and be forced to assume an unworthy appearance before his lady. Armed with such knowledge she will now be better able to act judiciously should she ever find herself in such a situation. She gets the point, and in the remainder of Book 2 is concerned with precisely that question of judgment.[41]

When Dorus takes up his tale of Musidorus and Pyrochles again, the episodes he recounts function in much the same way as do the partially hypothesized scenarios and exemplary anecdotes we have seen in *The Courtier.* There (as in *Utopia*) the speakers frequently postulate hypothetical situations and ask how one might respond to them. In the *Ar-*

---

41. Sidney's interest in the presentation of heuristic exempla as actualizations of concept may be seen even in his catch-phrases. In describing King Euarchus, Dorus remarks, "I might as easily sette down the whole Arte of government, as to lay before your eyes the picture of his proceedings" (1. 187); that is, Euarchus is an exemplum of good government. Dametas, robbed of his expectation of riches, is a "Right Patern of a Wretch dejected" (4.248); Pyrochles as an Amazon presents a "paterne, whether nature simply, or nature helped by cunning, be more excellent" (1.75). Notice that the last "paterne" is in fact the exemplum of a disputation. Such references are scattered throughout the work.

cadia we find related adventures clustered together as if in response to
the question, "What does a Prince do in *this* situation? *this* one? *this*
one?" At the beginning of Dorus's history, for example, the Princes encounter one after another different types of rulers with whom men in
their line of work may expect to deal—the melancholic tyrant of Phryg-
ia, the inconstant King of Pontus, the unnatural King of Paphlagonia—
each time managing to rescue themselves and with varying degrees of
success to restore justice in the respective kingdoms. "Historically," these
encounters have constituted the Princes' education; but the schematic
way in which they are expounded suggests not a temporal development
so much as a pattern of exhibition: "These are the various difficulties and
these the kinds of human personality," Sidney implies, "that one will
encounter in the active life." Dorus's comment on the events in Paphlagonia is especially revealing. This adventure, he says, "though not so
notable for any great effect they [the Princes] perfourmed, [is] yet worthy
to be remembered for the un-used examples therein, as well of true
natural goodnes, as of wretched ungratefulnesse" (1.206). The encyclo-
pedic motive, with its inherent qualification of the active life, could not
be more strongly suggested.[42]

Later we are offered, through a framed group of tales, a variety of
perspectives on love. Philoclea begins with the story of Erona, a princess
who scorned Cupid and suffered the god's revenge by falling in love
with the lowly minded Antiphilus. But her account is interrupted by
Miso who, with the bravura of the Wife of Bath ("As long as I have the
government, I will first have my tale"), delivers a vituperation of Cupid,
denying his godhead and insisting that he is simply a trap for those not
wise enough to take their pleasures without involvement (1.237–242).
Finally Pamela begins the love story of Plangus, "if that may be called

42. Cf. his description of the Princes' shipwreck en route to Euarchus: "There
was to be seene the diverse manner of minds in distresse: some sate upon the toppe
of the poupe weeping and wailing, till the sea swallowed them; some one more
able to abide death, then feare of death, cut his owne throate to prevent drowning;
some prayed, and there wanted not of them which curses, as if the heavens could
not be more angrie then they were" (1.193). Or the appearances of Pyrochles,
Musidorus, and Gynecia at the trial—they proudly erect in splendid array, she
dejected in russet: then "did these unfortunate Princes suffer themselves to be
ledd, shewing a right by the Comparyson of them and *Gynecia* how to dyvers
persons, compassion ys dyversly to be ministred" (4.350).

love which he rather did take into himselfe willingly, then by which he was taken forcibly"—suggesting Plangus's moral responsibility for the adultery that costs him his patrimony and nearly his life (1.242-251). Is love divine compulsion, simple sexual gratification, or a moral relationship? This is the question exemplified by the tales, and Sidney does not answer it. His speakers, like those in the *Symposium*, suggest that it is perhaps exactly what one makes it.

One device, then, that Sidney employs in the *Arcadia* to investigate the nature of the two modes of life is the narrative exemplum. Another is the set disputation.[43] When Musidorus finds the lovestricken Pyrochles in solitary lethargy at Kalander's house, he chides him for abandoning the political studies requisite to the active life. "The workings of the minde," Pyrochles replies loftily, "I finde much more infinite, then can be led unto by the eye, or imagined by any, that distract their thoughts without themselves," and he goes on to praise the contemplative mode. But this argument soon dissatisfies him, and he calls Musidorus's attention instead to the beauties of the surrounding landscape, claiming these as sufficient reasons for lingering. Musidorus, who has prepared a complete rebuttal to Pyrochles' defense of solitude (the topics of which Sidney supplies), then does a strange thing. He is so moved by his friend's impassioned eloquence that he wryly yields the argument: "And even so do I give you leave (sweet Pyrochles) ever to defend solitariness; so long, as to defend it, you ever keep company" (1.56, 58). The issue is not resolved; rather the intellectual debate melts into feeling, which obviates logic and temporarily reconciles the two friends. The conflict is merely postponed until several scenes later when to his horror Musidorus finds Pyrochles, now disguised as Zelmane, actually effeminized by love. Thor-

43. The major debates in the *Arcadia* are those between Pyrochles and Musidorus on the active and contemplative lives and on the nature of love (1.54-58, 77-83); the verse dialogue between Basilius and Plangus on Providence (1.227-231); the shepherds' song debate on love and marriage (1.137-140, 340-344); the disputation between Cecropia and Pamela on chastity and the deliberative orations of Kalander and Philanax (1.405-410, 466-469); the debate between Philoclea and Pyrochles on suicide (4.273-278); and the discussion of memory between Pyrochles and Musidorus (4.344-347). Of these, only the debate on chastity can be said to be resolved, and this is because it moves out of the range of ordinary human judgments and invades the precincts of divine relevation—an area expressly forbidden to rhetoric.

oughly disgusted, he delivers a lengthy vituperation of love, to which Pyrochles replies with an encomium of women (including a praise of motherhood), and when this has worn thin, with the Neoplatonic defense that he is just beginning with women and hopes for better things. Musidorus denounces his sophistry, but once again the debate breaks down as it becomes clear that reasoning cannot heal Pyrochles, and Musidorus, in his compassion for his friend's misery, agrees to help him win his lady (1.77–84).

This irresolute resolution occurs time and again in the *Arcadia*. When Kalander and Philanax offer contrary advice to Basilius on raising the siege of Cecropia's castle, the winning argument is neither the plea to the father to save his daughter nor that to the king to persevere. Instead it is an argument unknown to them—Basilius's passion for Zelmane, who is immured in the castle—that silently persuades him to retire (1.468). And when Pyrochles argues stoically for suicide in an effort to save Philoclea from disgrace, it is not Philoclea's Christian viewpoint that induces him to acquiesce, but the charm of her earnest oratory: "Pyrochles was not so much perswaded as delighted by her well conceyved and sweetely pronounced speeches" (4.278).[44] After a number of such episodes, one begins to wonder what Sidney's point is in including these arguments if they settle nothing.

His interest in debate, it would seem, stems directly from his conception of poetry. In these *suasoriae*, the characters attempt to move behind the particulars of their experience and discover the general principles that must inform their actions. In doing so, they realize the essential

44. Richard Lanham calls this "an odd sentiment to assign to Pyrochles if Sidney meant the scene to be at all serious" (*The Old Arcadia* [New Haven, 1965], p. 284). But Pyrochles does not admire Philoclea's rhetorical skill *per se*; it is the pleasure Philoclea affords him, here rendered through her speech, by which he is momentarily captivated—just as a few moments later, having once again attempted suicide, he finally retires from such attempts with "muche tranquility" because her threats of self-destruction have finally convinced him that lofty stoic principle will achieve nothing for her safety. The point is, the scene *is* comic, but not in the sense that it reveals satirically the shallowness of the lovers. Its comedy is wry: the lovers are young, try to deliberate with serious casuistry, but finally fall back on their love for one another, which decides the question, high-flown arguments aside.

function of fiction, which Sidney describes in the *Apology for Poetry*. There he reminds us, through the mock disputation of the philosopher and the historian, "that one giveth the precept, and the other the example. . . . Now doth the peerlesse Poet performe both."[45] As historian, the poet of the *Arcadia* provides his readers with examples of the amorous and heroic lives through the adventures he recounts; as philosopher, he relates these particulars to significant moral concerns, mainly through dramatized debate. Pyrochles' acquiescence in passion necessitates examination of the provenance and effects of love; Basilius's proposed retreat from Cecropia's castle requires discussion of the duties of king and parent. What we find in these interludes of set argument is the same modulation from actualized event to theoretical discussion that we have already observed in *The Courtier*; in both cases it derives from the Ciceronian admonition that one must seek in each particular case the generic issue in order to understand more clearly the principle at stake.

There is a major difference, however, between the thesis-seeking activity of Sidney's characters and that of Cicero's orator. Cicero never claims that particulars are *reducible* to theses. A man who burns down his city so that the enemy may not enjoy its treasures is not a model patriot; his action may be viewed under the heading of patriotism, since he was motivated by such considerations, but the two are never identical, and the thesis cannot substitute for the more complex hypothesis. Sidney seems to have realized this subtle but crucial distinction, for his *suasoriae* do not simply ground events in general principles; they imitate human beings *attempting* to do so, which is quite another matter. It is one of the continuing ironies of the *Arcadia* that the supremely rational methodology in which Sidney's generation had been schooled—to seek the general principle in the particular case—is often inadequate in the pinch. Ultimately, all theses are simply guides to experience; they help us appraise our situation but, being necessarily reductive, they cannot begin to express the complexity of experience itself. It is this perception that lies behind the broken disputations, and which finally reveals—as we shall see in the trial scene—Sidney's commitment to the particulars that only a mimetic fiction can convey.[46]

45. *Elizabethan Critical Essays*, I. 163–164.
46. In the preceding paragraph, I have normalized the emphasis given the terms

Heuristic exempla and formal debate are Sidney's major instruments of fictional inquiry. But there are others, too. One of these is the creation of a skeptical narrator who, taking on the roles of the many speakers in a dialogue, continually wonders at the provenance of the very things he describes. The text is rich in such speculation, but one or two examples will illustrate the phenomenon. The river Ladon, he tells us, where Philoclea bathed, "ranne upon so fine and delicate a ground, as one could not easily judge, whether the River did more wash the gravell, or the gravell did purifie the River; the River not running forth right, but almost continually winding, as if the lower streams would return to their spring, or that the River had delight to play with it selfe" (1.216). Here, a simple physical description becomes the occasion for speculation upon the relationship of the river bed and its water and also upon the reasons for its irregular flow. When Pyrochles and Philoclea are caught in bed together by Dametas, he wonders why they were sleeping so soundly:

> Who at that tyme, beeying not so muche before the Breake of day (whether yt were, they were so by fore apoyntment surprysed to bringe theyre faulte to open punishment, or that the too hye degree of theyre Joyes had overthrowne the wakefull use of theyre sences, or that theyre sowle lifted up with extremity of Love after mutuall satisfaction had lefte theyre bodyes derely joyned; to unite themselves together, so much more freely as they were freer of that earthly prison, *or what so ever other Cause might be Imagyned of yt*), so yt was, that they were, as then possessed with a mutuall sleepe, yet not forgetting with vyny embrasements to give any eye a perfect model of affection. (4.254, emphasis mine)

Such continual questioning virtually asks the reader to share the burden of interpreting the story, and adds to it yet another layer of complexity.[47]

"thesis" and "hypothesis" because they refer to modes of inquiry rather than to rhetorical exercises in the strict sense. Hereafter this will be the rule, except in cases where additional emphasis seems appropriate.

47. See also the speculations concerning the cause of Pyrochles' awakening a few moments later (4.269); why Pamela kissed Musidorus during their night of captivity in the forest (4.291); and why Pamela and Musidorus are kept as prisoners and not killed by the rebels (4.290). To these may be added the problem arising from the headdresses of the six maidens who entertain the Princesses: "it was doubtful whether the haire drest the garlandes, or the garlandes drest the haire"

A more subtle means of insinuating doubt concerning the significance of facts is seen in the narrator's frequent ironic qualification. It begins almost immediately as the shepherds Claius and Strephon weep the loss of their beloved Urania: "hath not the onely love of her made us (being silly ignorant shepheards) raise up our thoughts above the ordinary levell of the worlde, so as great clearkes do not disdaine our conference?" (1.7). Their account of Urania's pedagogy leads one to believe that they are well on their way up the Neoplatonic ladder, though it is odd to find them so passionately lamenting the absence against which such an ascent is supposed to inure them. It would seem that Sidney is quietly questioning their Neoplatonic presumptuousness. This suspicion is strengthened a few pages later, when Kalander privately praises the great learning of Strephon and Claius, "which all notwithstanding, it is a sporte to heare how they impute to love, which hath endewed their thoughts (saie they) with such a strength" (1.27). Such qualification abounds in the work, affecting our ability to judge not only characters, but also events.[48]

(1.360), and other such instances throughout the book. It is not enough simply to describe these as picturesque *discordiae concordes*; their very conventionality, arising no doubt from the habit of *copia* cultivated by Sidney and other writers, testifies to the thoroughgoing pluralism of the Elizabethan mind. In Sidney's case, it is interesting to note that it is not the blending of opposites, so much as the difficulty of distinguishing adjuncts and contraries, that is emphasized.

48. See, for example, the treatment of the oracle. At the beginning of the story, Philanax, who is introduced as a moral norm, is openly skeptical not only of Basilius's plans but also of the oracle's authority. A second visit, however, upon Anaxius's demand that Pamela marry him, changes his mind. Now he decides it is better not to reason in matters above reason, and devotes himself to the more practical business of building walls. Touching character, the irony is even more pervasive. Pyrochles, disguised as Zelmane, stands at the river Ladon watching with voyeurist rapture the nude Philoclea bathing. Moments later he discovers Amphialus doing the same thing and, outraged, challenges him to combat (1.215–225). Pamela, who through Book 3 insists that her importunate wooers Amphialus and Anaxius obtain her parents' consent before she will wed them, willingly runs off without their consent in Book 4, when Musidorus, the man she loves, proposes the flight. During the trial, Pyrochles, who has apparently embraced the doctrine that the lover desires the good of the beloved, is secretly delighted, when Philoclea is condemned to a life of chastity in a convent, that no one else will enjoy her (4.354).

Still finer instances, revealing the irreducibly problematic character of the experienced life, are also to be found. Early in Book 1, Kalander leads the cousins on a fine morning hunt. Reading the description of this traditional aristocratic pastime we are prepared to forgo whatever modern prejudices spoil our appreciation of the chase, and view it with sixteenth-century eyes. Yet the text forces us to apply reins to this zealous exercise of historical imagination, for we come across such sentences as this:

> The huntsmen were handsomely attired in their greene liveries, as though they were the children of Sommer, with staves in their hands to beat the guiltlesse earth, when the houndes were at a fault, and with hornes about their neckes to sounde an alarum upon a sillie fugitive.

Our enthusiasm is chilled by such words as "beat," "guiltlesse earth," "sillie fugitive." When the stag is finally at bay,

> Kalander (by skill of casting the Countrey) was among the first that came in to the besiged Deere; whom when some of the younger sort would have kiled with their swordes, he would not suffer:

At which point our hopes for the beleaguered animal rise. Then Sidney's prose does an abrupt about face:

> but with a Crossebowe sent a death to the poore beast, who with teares shewed the unkindness he tooke of man's cruelty. (1.60–61)

Whatever Kalander's perception of the pursuit, Sidney's narrator does not permit his audience to escape the awareness that such pleasure is based upon creaturely destruction.[49]

The explorative nature of the *Arcadia* is most fully revealed in its climax. Here, the work that has continually questioned its own premises poses its most overwhelming question: what has it all meant? The question arises because of the apparent murder of Basilius by Gynecia and the

49. The response I suppose is not simply a twentieth-century one. Sidney's passage is a highly refined version of Erasmus's satire of "the fellows who . . . protest they feel an ineffable pleasure in their souls whenever they hear the raucous blast of the horns and the yelping of hounds. . . . Then, with his head bared, on his bended knees, with a knife designed for just this (for it is a sacrilege to use any other), with certain ceremonial gestures he [the gentleman huntsman] cuts just the proper members in the approved order" (*Folly*, pp. 53–54).

suspected complicity of the two sets of lovers—Pamela having eloped with Musidorus and Pyrochles having finally bedded Philoclea.[50] The result is the magnificent trial scene, in which all the major events recorded in the romance—the Princes' advent into Arcadia, their disguises, their services to Basilius, their intimacies with the Princesses, their relationship to Gynecia—are transformed into the givens of a *controversia*, and thoroughly reexamined and reappraised.[51] The scene is a brilliant mimesis of human beings struggling to escape their untenable predicament through the imperfect procedures of rational investigation available to them— and a wry indictment of the inadequacy of precept (this time in the form of statute law) before the complexity of experience.

The warning note is sounded by Philanax when he confronts Pyrochles and Philoclea in what has become their nuptial chamber:

> If your father, Madame, were now to speake unto, truly there should no body be found a more ready advocate for you, then myself. For I would suffer this faulte, thoughe very greate to be blotted oute of my mynde by youre former ledd lyfe, and beeyng Daughter to such a Father: But, synce amonge youre selves yow have taken hym away, in whom was the onely power to have mercy, yow must nowe be cloathed in youre own worcking, and looke for no other then that which Deade pityles Lawes may allott unto you. (4.284)

What he suggests here is that the extenuating circumstances which might prevail with the royal dispenser of law—who alone perceives its intentions—are likely to go unheeded by those who have only the written law to guide them and must frame their judgments of individual actions by drawing them into the context of legislated precepts.[52] Thus there is a

50. Here, of course, we must speak of the issues only in terms of the Old *Arcadia*, since the doctored Books 3, 4, and 5 of the 1593 edition contain inconsistencies that render analysis too problematic. For a full discussion of the issues, see *The Poems of Sir Philip Sidney*, ed. William A. Ringler (Oxford, 1962), pp. 373–379, esp. 378–379.

51. One of Sidney's sources appears to have been Achilles Tatius's romance *Clitophon and Leucippe* (see Wolff, *The Greek Romance*, esp. pp. 314–318). This romance, which also has a climactic trial scene, reveals the influence of Senecan-style *controversiae*.

52. "For the Judges must give sentence according to the Lawe: the King may forgive, as authour of the Lawe, and having power in his hande, may doe as he

chance that justice in the particular case may not be rendered, since the idiosyncratic must be reduced to the generic which it most closely resembles, and cannot be considered on its own terms. The full meaning of this statement gradually begins to unfold as preparations for the trial go forward.[53]

Philanax, in behalf of the Arcadian people, empowers Euarchus to find the guilty, punish them, and restore the state, reserving only "the Righte to Basilius blood, the manner to the auncyent prescribing of theyre Lawes" (4.334). The way therefore seems opened to a fair and impartial settlement, achieved through a rational examination of the facts. Indeed, Euarchus sets the conditions for just such an inquiry in his first address to the Arcadians:

> Remember that I am a Man, that ys to say a Creature, whose reason ys often darkened with error; secondly, that yow will lay youre hartes voyde of foretaken opinyons, else what so ever I doo or say will be measured by a wronge Rule. . . . Thirdly whatsoever Debates have risen among yow may be utterly extinguisshed, Knowing that even among the best men are diversityes of opinyons. . . . Lastly, that yow do not easily judge of youre Judge, but since yow will have mee to Comaunde, thincke yt ys youre parte to obey. (4.338–339)

Here we see the acknowledgment of fallibility (the affairs of men, as Philanax has commented earlier, "receyve not Geometricall certentyes"), the attempt to establish a neutral ground, and the exaction of a promise to adhere to the judgment rendered, that are the essentials of free judicial

shall thinke best" (Thomas Wilson, *The Arte of Rhetorique*, ed. G. H. Mair [Oxford, 1909], p. 98).

53. Cf. Trimpi's discussion of equity as a "negotiation between quantitative [legal] and qualitative [moral] measurement" ("The Quality of Fiction," 23–31, esp. 25): "The quantitative measure, whether it decides the amount of penalty for a legal code or of emotional response for an ethical one, must be 'qualified' with regard to the requirements of the individual case. The quantitative measure is abstract, general, inflexible, and impersonal; the qualitative is 'substantial,' particular, applicable, and casuistic." This casts considerable light on Sidney's rendering of the Arcadian trial. As we shall see, despite Euarchus's reputation for equity —indeed, he warns the Arcadians that reputation may have exceeded reality (4.336, 338)—a "negotiation between quantitative and qualitative measurement" is not achieved.

inquiry. (Lucres set the same conditions.) With all agreed on the proper procedure, and the judge a man of good will, we should expect justice to emerge. But it does not. It fails for two reasons: the judge, "a Creature whose reason ys often darkened with error," is not in possession of all the facts, and the inquiry is not really free—he must decide his case according to the rules of law, judging not Pyrochles and Musidorus as individuals, but "such men" as they are.

The trial is a faithful, if ironic, rendering of the procedures outlined in the rhetoric handbooks. Gynecia, ridden by guilt for her indecorous passion, usurps the role of prosecutor and publicly accuses herself of murder. Given her confession, Euarchus condemns her to be buried alive with her dead husband. There is no reason to inquire further since the first question or conjectural *status* (did she do it?) has been resolved. When the Princes take the stand they challenge the competence of the court to try them, as foreigners and sovereigns, but they are compelled to acknowledge the court's right.[54] Philanax then takes the floor. In his *narratio* he sarcastically summarizes the sojourn of Pyrochles, who "synce beeyng come into this Contry unaccompanyed like a lost Pilgrim, from a Man grewe a woman and from a woman a Ravissher of woemen, thence Prisoner & now a Prince" (4.354). Then he elaborates an entirely new romance, in the manner of the *controversia*, by inferring the moral significance of these events. Having learned of Basilius's retreat, Pyrochles disguised himself as a woman, wormed his way into the chivalrous King's confidence, and soon became Gynecia's confederate: "What ys to bee thoughte passed betwixt two suche vertuous Creatures (whereof the one hath confessed murder and the other Rape) I leave to youre wyse Consideration" (4.360). Having dropped that *color*, he next claims that Pyrochles, pretending devotions to Diana, took up residence in the cave, simply to lure Basilius to his death. Finally, while Musidorus conveyed the King's heir out of the country, Pyrochles seduced Philoclea, "where by the mingling of her shame with his mysdeede he might enforce her to be accessary to her Fathers death" (4.361). It all fits together neatly, as probable a fiction as Sidney himself might have written. To the accusation of murder aforethought, Pyrochles replies with the story as we know it, concealing, however, Gynecia's passion for him and his actual con-

---

54. They are invoking the *status translativa*, considered by some writers to be a subdivision of the *status qualitatis*, and by others to be an independent issue.

summation with Philoclea. Then, coming to the second crime for which he is being tried—the seduction of Philoclea—though he denies he was successful, he pleads the compulsion of love and argues that whatever suspicions of dishonor have been aroused may be remedied by marriage.

Philanax rises again, this time to explicate the role of Musidorus in the conspiracy. His task was "to convey away the Lady of us all: Who (once oute of the Contrye) he knewe, we woulde come with Ollive braunches of intercession unto her, and falle at his feete to beseeche hym, to leave keeping of sheepe and vouchsafe the tyrannising over us" (4.372). He not only accuses Musidorus of complicity in the murder, but also of treason in kidnaping the Princess. Musidorus, of course, denies the first charge, accusing Philanax of ingratitude for their past services which, he argues, prove their dedication to Basilius's safety. As to kidnaping Pamela, he pleads that he was her servant, and in the role of counselor advised her to flee from captivity, compelled thereto by love. Then he makes a direct appeal to Euarchus:

> Therefore (O Judge) which I hope doste know what yt ys to be a Judge, that youre ende ys to preserve & not to destroy mankynde, that Lawes are not made like Lymetwygges or nettes to catch every thinge that tucheth them: But rather lyke sea Marckes to avoyde the Shippwrackes of ignorant passingers synce that oure doynge (in the extreymest interpretation) ys but a humane error. And that of yt you may make a profitable event . . . you will not I trust at the perswasion of this Brabler, burne your house to make yt cleane. . . . (4.375)

It is a plea that Euarchus fashion something positive out of the interpenetration of act and law, and not respond legalistically. But Euarchus does not do this. Hampered by an imperfect understanding of the facts (not only are all the witnesses misleading, but the letters from the Princesses have been suppressed), he is also constrained to draw the details he does know under the rule of the statute and enact justice by precept. He explains this assumption:

> How to Judge well . . . that must undoubtedly bee done, not by a free Discourse of Reason and skill of philosophy, but must be tyed to the Lawes of Greece and municipall statutes of this Kingdome. For allthough oute of them these came and to them must in deed

referr theyr ofspringe, yet by cause Philosophicall discourses stand in the general Consideration of thinges, they leave to every man a scope of his owne interpretacyon. Where the Lawes (applying themselves to the necessary use) foulde us within the Boundes assured, which once broken, mans nature infenitely raungeth. (4.377)

Euarchus is clearly cutting off general speculation into the nature of things—whether, for example, one can resist the power of love, or whether it is right to persuade a daughter to escape the harsh captivity of an unwise parent—as an activity improper to the court of law, where only the precepts society has already agreed upon must govern judgment. To these, all individual acts will be referred. Regarding the accusation of complicity in murder, a question of fact (*an sit?*), he admits that the Princes' stories are as probable as Philanax's, and "as in equallity of conjectures wee are not to take holde of the worste," he will consider them not guilty unless the evidence of the second charge is so strongly negative as to prejudice reasonable doubt of the first.

The second charge, he announces, involves a question of quality (the *status qualitatis*), in which the act is admitted, but its nature must be examined because the defendant pleads extenuating circumstances. Euarchus first defines the crimes—in the one case attempted rape, in the second the ravishment of a child from her father—and declares the punishment which is required by the law. Then he proceeds to examine the qualifying arguments. First is the compulsion of love:

Yf that unbrydeled Desyr which ys intituled Love might purge such a sicknes as this, surely wee shoulde have many Loving excuses of hateful myscheefes: Nay, rather no myscheef shoulde bee committed that shoulde not be vailed under the name of Love. (4.378–379)

He denies that love is an ill-governed passion; it is rather a "sweete and heavenly uniting of the myndes, which . . . hathe no other knott but vertue." How limiting a definition of love this is we know from all we have experienced in Arcadia. The precept has been tried and found wanting. We hope love is *that*, too—but when the compulsive ardor gives the charge, who in Arcadia is to stop the flight of passion? On the basis of idealistic precept, therefore, Euarchus throws out of court the Princes' *purgatio* of Cupid.

To Pyrochles' argument that the fitting remedy to such a situation is marriage, he observes appropriately that justice is not to be confused with expediency. He shall not be married to Philoclea because it will be dangerous

> yf stronge men & riche men shall ever fynde private Conveyences, how to cover such committed disorders, as to the publique shall not onely be inconvenyent but pestilent. This Mariage perchaunce might bee fitt for them, but very unfitt for the state yt were to allowe a Paterne of such procurations of Mariage. . . . (4.379)

It is not Pyrochles the individual who can be considered, but Pyrochles the *general exemplar*. In marrying Philoclea he would be setting a precedent and thus cannot be allowed a union of which he may very well be worthy.

Against Musidorus's argument that he was servant-counselor to the Princess, and thus enjoys the privilege of liberal counsel, Euarchus responds with a legalistic interpretation of both "counselor" and "princess": Pamela was not an effectual sovereign at the time he persuaded her to flee the country, hence no princess; Musidorus was servant to Dametas, hence no counselor. The extenuating circumstances having been denied, Pyrochles is sentenced to be thrown to his death from a high tower, Musidorus to be beheaded. It is all supremely legal, logical, and—from the standpoint of true equity—unfair. And this is so because not all the evidence has been taken into account—some of it having been deliberately concealed from the judge, some necessarily ignored in the reductive application of the law. Only the fortuitous awakening of Basilius prevents the sentences from being carried out, when amid general rejoicing the young couples are promised in marriage and Gynecia extolled as an example of wifely solicitude for all Greece: "So uncerteyne are mortall Judgmentes the same person moste infamus and moste famus and neyther justly" (4.388).

If justice is not to be found in the impartial determinations of a good and wise man like Euarchus, nor in the complacent adulation of the crowd, where is it to be found? Only, Sidney implies, in a complex fiction like the *Arcadia*, where all sides of the question are vividly dramatized, and the reader may respond *continually* with his reason and his emotions to the succession of particular feelings, judgments, and actions that are set before him. In this way he experiences vicariously the fullness of life itself, which is perhaps the best *paideusis* for the judicious mind. It is in this sense that the *Arcadia* fulfills Fulke Greville's famous description:

> In all these creatures of his making, his intent, and scope was, to turn the barren Philosophy precepts into pregnant Images of life; and in them, first on the Monarch's part, lively to represent the growth, state, and declination of Princes, change of Government, and Lawes: vicissitudes of sedition, faction, succession, confederacies, plantations, with all other errors, or alternations in publique affairs. Then again in the subject's case, the state of favor, disfavor, prosperitie, hospitality, travail, and all other moodes of private fortunes or misfortunes. In which traverses (I know) his purpose was to limn out such exact pictures, of every posture in the minde, that any man being forced, in the straines of his life, to pass through any straights, or latitudes of good, or ill fortune might (as in a glass) see how to set a good countenance upon all the discountenances of adversitie, and a stay upon the exorbitant smilings of chance.[55]

The *Arcadia* is instructive not in the manner of a didactic treatise, but as a presentation of the range of moral and practical problems life has to offer, and of the responses that are possible to fallible human beings.[56] For Sidney's fiction, like More's and Castiglione's before him, is an act of pondering, "figured forth." In it characters confront problems, seek ways to resolve them, and try to convince one another that they have resolved them. But they themselves are simply fictional hypotheses that function as the author's instruments of inquiry. They are his means of examining with sensitivity questions that are of continuing concern. And they are also, as Greville suggests, our means as readers. For we are invited to explore in detail the vicissitudes of public and private life and thereafter, with each "posture in the minde," to become the substantial offspring of Sidney's pregnant images. In this way, the seductive fiction of the *Arcadia* functions as something of a pastoral retreat itself, from

55. *Life of Sir Philip Sidney* (Oxford, 1905), pp. 15–16.

56. From a quite different starting point, Walter Davis comes to a similar conclusion, arguing that Sidney's transformation of ideal concept into exemplary image in the *Arcadia* offers the reader opportunities for experimental role playing: "We come to know ourselves by seeing our relation to an image of an Idea of humanity" (*Idea and Act in Elizabethan Fiction* [Princeton, 1969], p. 43).

which we emerge with a fuller understanding of the complexities of our condition and, to that extent, better prepared to meet what life has in store. Erasmus had implied, many years before, that this is the distinctive use of fiction.

The Method Staged: Debate Plays
by Heywood and Rastell

As in fiction, so in drama. One of the early products of the humanist propensity to examine a question *in utramque partem* was the argumentative interlude performed before aristocratic and learned acquaintances of the More circle. These plays reflect that curious amalgam of delight in disputation—in the opportunity to entertain opposing ideas and to discover how they might be defended—and an embracing piety characteristic of a culture that assumes the wide morality of such inquiry. In the aggregate, the plays bear a stronger resemblance to academic disputation than to what we normally think of as drama, for argument far outweighs whatever narrative or theatrical interest they hold. Their nomenclature, in fact, suggests that they were considered games of wit on designated subjects played by the speakers.[1] But in each case the speakers

1. The characteristic formulas are a "play between" or "an interlude of," which suggests that "interlude" carried the force of an acted "interplay" among the speakers. "Of" seems to have meant either "concerning" the subject or "conducted by" the players. The five extant Heywood titles read: *The Playe Called The Four PP: A Newe and a Very Mery Enterlude of A Palmer, A Pardoner, A Potycary, A Pedler; The Play of The Wether: A Newe and a Very Mery Enterlude of All Maner Wethers; A Mery Play Between Johan Johan, The Husbande, Tyb, His Wife, and Syr Johan, The Preest* (see J. Q. Adams, ed., *Chief Pre-Shakespearean Dramas* [Cambridge, Mass., 1924]); *A Mery Play Betwene the pardoner and the frere, the curate and neybour Pratt* (see Rupert de la Bere, *John Heywood, Entertainer* [London, 1937]); *A Play of love, a new and a mery enterlude concerning pleasure and payne in love* (printed by William Rastell, London, 1534, STC 13303). The Rastell title reinforces this

have distinct characters or are recognizable social types, and several of the plays imply place and time. Moreover, in most of them an attempt is made to reconcile the points of view expressed. Therefore they are not really disputations at all, but dramatic hypothesizations that show us Ciceronian debate making the transition to comedy.

John Heywood's *Witty and Witless* is the barest of these plays.[2] It is simply a *thesis* and counter-*thesis* performed, following closely the models in Lorich's Aphthonius. There is no attempt to motivate the action. The only degree of fictionalization is in the flavor given the characters of James and John, who debate one another. James, who defends the proposition "Better ys for man that may be wyttles then wytty," is a skilled disputant, a bit too aware of his own cleverness, while John, who serves as respondent, offers earnest but ill-conceived rebuttal that frequently lands him in trouble. Thus the first half of the play not only proves the *thesis* but also reveals two inadequate human beings engaged in a somewhat superficial kind of argument, as is pointed out by the third character Jerome, who appears later to prove the counter-*thesis*.

The debate of James and John proceeds along announced topics that serve the same function as the marginal glosses in the *Progymnasmata*. It begins under the rubric "temperall welth," with James arguing that the

---

sense: *A Dyaloge Betwen The Marchaunt, The Knyght, and The Plowman, Disputyng Who is a Very Gentylman, and Compiled in Maner of an Enterlude With Divers Toys and Gestis Addyd Thereto To Make Mery Pastime and Disport* (see Kenneth W. Cameron, *Authorship and Source of "Gentleness and Nobility"* [Raleigh, N.C., 1941]).

2. In the following discussion, the order in which the plays are treated does not imply order of composition. It would be gratifying if we could prove that Heywood's gradual hypothesization of debate in his plays was chronological, but the debate fragment "Of the Parts of Man," written between 1545 and 1548, indicates that Heywood never abandoned the more abstract form (see Robert C. Johnson, *John Heywood* [New York, 1970], pp. 87–89). Rather, he seems to have experimented with various combinations of disputation, anecdote, and action, to produce a group of plays in which no two are alike. I have omitted from this discussion *The Pardoner and The Friar* and *Johan*, which, though highly entertaining and nondidactic, are essentially irreverent farces. While by nature they fit into the explorative category, in that they reveal the open-ended battle of wits characteristic of Heywood's other plays, he does not attempt in them that ideological synthesis which suggests that disputation (or marital debacle) is moving toward that realization of an ideal which we may call comic form. On this ground, they are of less immediate interest.

fool (Henry VIII's jester Will Summer is the convenient exemplum) enjoys a secure, carefree living, unlike the witty man who must scrape together his precarious existence. John grants the fool this security, but points out that it is not without discomfort, even for present company:

> Some snap hym some scratch hym
> Some cramp hym some cratch hym
> Some cuff hym some clowt hym
> Some lashe hym some lowte hym
> Some whyske hym some whype hym
> With scharpe naylys some nype hym
> Not evyn mayster somer the kyngs g[r]acys foole
> But tastyth some tyme some nyps of new schoole.
>
> (p. 118)[3]

Thus he introduces the topic "pain," and to the aforementioned occupational hazards he adds the fool's disproportionate joy in trifles and consequent sorrow at their loss. In reply, James vividly recalls the pains of the laborer, which, he insists, are at least as distressing as those of the fool, and adds that the witty man may suffer disappointment at the loss of fortune just as the witless one does. Although he has argued well, James now seems on the defensive, and bluff John cannot help crowing:

> That conclewsyon ys conclewdyd wysely
> Your pryme proposyscyon dyd put presysely
> Better to be wyttles than wytty and now
> As good to be wyttles as wytty sey you
> But that wytt whych putth case in degre comparatyve
> And conclewdyth case in degre posytyve
> Sall not in that case clame degre superlatyve.
>
> (pp. 122–123)[4]

Bridling at this imputation of fallibility, James reminds John that they are yet midway in the debate. Granted that Witty and Witless suffer equal

---

3. Citations refer to pages in de la Bere.

4. Here, as in *Fulgens and Lucres*, notice the expression "put case," the legalism that characterizes the activity of the play: advancing an hypothesis that can be examined on morally neutral territory.

physical pain, he will now prove that Witty's mental distress far outweighs their acknowledged parity of physical pain. To do so, he first inquires whose work is more detrimental to health—the laborer's or the student's. He gets John to concede that physical labor

> purgyth hewmors to mans lyfe and quyckness
> Whyche study bredeyth to mans dethe or sickness.
> . . . .
> Pervert ys your jugment yf ye judge not playne
> That less ys the parell and less is the payne
> The knocyng of knockylls whyche fyngers doth
>   strayne
> Then dyggyng yn the hart or drying of the brayne.
>   (pp. 124–125)

Having established the supremacy of mental distress over physical, he moves swiftly to complete the syllogism that fools are incapable of mental labor, ergo cannot suffer as witty men do. Poor John is nonplussed. And James asks him to concede the game.

John has one more feeble hope, though. Let us determine the issue, he suggests, not on the basis of the greater pain but of the greater pleasure. In this idiotic notion, James is happy to acquiesce, proposing that if one pleasure can be found which outweighs all pains, then he who enjoys it is obviously the winner. The pleasure he postulates is salvation, and he argues that fools, like children, are saved through baptism alone—for "where god gyvyth no dyscernyng god taketh none accownte"—while the witty are saved only if they do well, a big "if":

> That yf leyd for the wytty purposeth a dowte
> But all dowtes in the wytles are scrapt clene out.
>   (p. 129)

This clinches the case. John quietly concedes defeat before the irrefutable certainty of the fool's salvation:

> Off wytty and wyttles I wyshe now rather
> That my chyld may have a fool to hys father

The pyth of your conclewsyons be all so puer
That better be a foole than a wyse man seur.

(p. 131)

The *thesis* is proved.

Or is it? At this point a new character enters, who questions John's last words:

Not so although your fancy do so surmyse
Not better for man to be wytles then wyse
Nor so good to be wyttles as wytty nother
Thus ys your wyt dysseyved in other.

(p. 131)

He is Jerome, and he claims the argument has been conducted improperly. It is not wit that makes a man wise, but wisdom:

Wyt ys the wurker of all persyvyng
And indyfert to good or yll wurking

. . . .

Wysdome governth wytt alwey vertu to use
And all kynds of vys alway to refewse.

(p. 132)

A confusion of terms has cost John the debate.

James is scornful. "Thys ys some yowng schooleman a fresh comonar," he mutters, and stalks out, but John earnestly inquires where he went wrong. Thereupon the counter-*thesis* commences, with the terms somewhat altered. Here, Jerome proves to John that wisdom is preferable to folly, by comparing the relative pleasures of men and beasts. Persuaded that man's physical existence is less burdensome, and his intellectual life richer, John is led to see that if man's rational soul lies unused—as in the fool—then he is no better off than a beast. So much for the rubric "temperall welth." As for the life to come, Jerome reminds John that the wise man who performs good works will merit a higher place in heaven than the disengaged simpleton. And should he sin, he may yet earn salvation through sincere repentance. John is delighted, and declares gratefully that he is more witty for the debate:

111

> Where my mate my lords says that ys gone
> Better be sot somer than sage salamon
> In for sakyng that I woold now rather be
> Sage salamon than sot somer I assewr ye.
>
> (p. 141)

An entertaining piece of repartee even today, this charming play accomplishes several things. Through a fictional hypothesis, it allows the paradox that witless is better than witty to be proved in an exercise of pure wit. Then, on a more serious philosophical level, it adjusts the antithetical vision originally proposed by supplying in the counter-*thesis* the middle term that is missing in the first debate. Jerome's wisdom subsumes the innocence of Witless and the experience of Witty, yet is superior to both. This third term, which unites apparent opposites, is typical of the synthetic vision of these interludes. Lucres's ideal, which combines and transcends Gaius and Cornelius, is one we have already encountered; love of Christ, in *The Play of Love*, is another. The intellectual pattern persists all the way to *Love's Labour's Lost*, where the two alternative ways of life—learning and love—are tested, both found inadequate, and the third term—love through prolonged moral askesis—is the proposed solution. This pattern is apparently the archetype of a comedy derived from dialogic thinking which refuses to abandon either of its original terms, and seeks a *tertium quid* that will fuse and complete them.

The Play of Love, a "newe and a mery enterlude concerning pleasure and payne in love," is a more complex work in several respects, and suggests the variety of pleasures early Tudor audiences looked for in their drama. In its emphasis on disputation, it resembles *Witty*, but in this play Heywood is far more interested in mimesis. The characters deliver first-person *ethopoeiae*, which state their outlook on life, and their behavior reflects their character. The play is given a distinct fictional coloration, that of a legal dispute, becoming, as it were, a comic imitation of a day in court. And action now becomes part of the "proof" in the controversy.

The play opens with the first disputant, Lover Not Loved, stumbling forward through the crowd. Unlike the casual entrances of many characters in Tudor interludes, this one is motivated:

> My maner is to muse and devyse
> So that some tyme my selfe may cary me

> My selfe knoweth not where, and I assure ye
> So hath my selfe done now, for our lorde wot
> Where I am, or what ye be, I know not.
>
> $(10-14)^5$

The reason for his distraction is that he is thinking about his unrequited love, whence he declares:

> Of all payne the most incomparable payne
> Is to be a lover not lovyd agayn.
>
> $(62-63)$

In any other play, such a statement might slip by; in a work by Heywood, it becomes a *positio*, and it is instantly challenged by a lady, Loved Not Loving, who claims that her unwanted lover is causing her far more pain than he suffers from his disdainful lady. Their disputation constitutes the first section of the play, and when it reaches an impasse they go off to seek an impartial judge. For unlike the debaters in *Witty and Witless*, neither will allow the other's arguments.

At this point a new character appears, who delivers a lecture on the necessity for the inward man to manifest his thought in word and deed if society is to rest on a foundation of trust. He is the Lover Loved, and the reason for his excursus becomes clear when he praises the social beneficence of the lover, who can never dissemble his true feelings, and points to himself as the obvious example of the joyful and successful suitor:

> For the hyest pleasure that man may obtayne
> Is to be a lover beloved agayne.
>
> $(300-301)$

"Nowe god you good evyn mayster woodcock," declares a fourth entrant, Neither Lover Nor Loved, designated the Vice in the stage directions. Those who live most pleasantly, he asserts, are not requited lovers but misogynists like himself who enjoy "continuall quyeted rest." The Lover Loved will not believe that anyone who is not a lover can enjoy rest, and so he, too, goes off to find an impartial judge.[6]

---

5. All line references are to Alois Brandl, *Quellen des weltlichen Dramas in England vor Shakespeare* (Strasbourg, 1898).

6. The tendency of staged debate to turn into drama is noted by G. K. Hunter,

Heywood then inserts a miniature novella into the play. It is an amusing set piece on that venerable Latin proverb *moccum moccabitur*, offered by the Vice to reassure those in the audience who doubt his competence to dispute in matters of the heart. It is, in fact, a heuristic exemplum. It tells of his own romantic adventure—an essay in wit in which he had attempted to trap a notorious coquette into falling in love with him, but found himself the victim instead. It runs for nearly 300 lines and obviously was inserted for its own intrinsic interest, but Heywood took pains to make it function as character exposition, further evidence of his concern to give the play fictional depth.

When Lover Beloved returns, whom has he found to judge his dispute but Lover Not Loved and Loved Not Loving! It is here that the debate begins to resemble an action in a law court.[7] For each pair agrees to judge the dispute of the other, and what follows are two sets of fresh arguments that parody the legal procedure of pleading to an issue. In the shadow of realistic law procedure, the play takes on an absurd Alice-in-Wonderland quality. The lady Loved Not Loving begs that her dispute with Lover Not Loved be heard first, "that I may know my payne." When, after more wrangling over distinctions and similarities, each claims that the other willingly remains in torment, the judges split on the decision, and Judge Lover Loved announces:

> Then be we come to a demurrer in law.
> (929)

A demurrer was declared when a case was found not actionable. To settle their dispute, the opponents had to take a new tack and work toward an

---

who makes this observation about *Love*: "What is especially interesting here is the way in which the debate not only creates the plot, but also gives the characters of the play their stances in relation to one another, and (in the context) this means their personalities. Thus the man who rejoices in his negative status (Neither-loving-nor-beloved) is naturally coarser and wilder than the others; he is the 'Vice' of the play; similarly, and just as inevitably, Both-loving-and-beloved is the romantic lead" (*John Lyly: The Humanist as Courtier* [Harvard, 1962], pp. 121–122). One wonders further if the Vice will not tend to be the cynical side-kick of the romantic lead, Mercutio (see n. 16 below).

7. R. J. Schoeck has suggested that it may be a parody of a case in Chancery, reflecting the contemporary feud between Wolsey and the common lawyers. See "Satire of Wolsey in Heywood's Play of Love," *NQ* 201 (1956): 375–376.

issue that *was* actionable.[8] Therefore, Lover Not Loved repeats the argument of Loved Not Loving, and offers a new "entre to answer it."[9] He asks why, if the lady can ease her pain by granting her love to the persistent suitor, she does not do it. Love cannot be forced by an act of will, she replies. Neither can it be stopped at will, he retorts, and declares that seeing his lady is the only medicine that will cure his malady—simultaneous freezings, burnings, drownings, and parchings—whose depredations he describes in detail. At this, the Vice hurries forward to examine the evidence:

> Lo by saynt savour here is a whet ars
> Let me fele your nose, nay fere not man be bold
> Well though this ars be warm and this nose cold
> Yet these twayne by attorney brought in one place
> Are as he seeth cold and whet both in lyk case.
>
> (1020–1024)

This signals a shift from theoretical argumentation to tangible proof, and the lady Loved Not Loving proposes they decide the dispute on a single concrete question. She puts the question in the form of a hypothetical fiction: suppose this man, she says, pointing to one of the judges, loved a woman who fancied him so little that she hid herself from him day and night; then suppose *you* were beloved by a woman so ugly that her kisses disgusted you and her presence was as sweet as . . . "a torde to his nose," supplies the Vice. Which situation is preferable? When her opponent is unable to answer, she explains that this fiction is intended to represent the situations in which they find themselves:

8. "The peculiarity of oral pleading, which was so important in the development of the law, was that it took place in Court before the Judges, who intervened to warn the pleader against an ineffective plea, or settle a point of law in the course of the proceedings. Hence pleaders felt their way toward an issue of fact, first trying one avenue, and if that failed, approaching by yet another" (Harold Potter, *An Historical Introduction to English Law and Its Institutions*, 3rd. ed. [London, 1948], p. 325). Here, of course, the litigants are involved in an issue of quality, to determine comparatively how much pain each suffers. They must "feel their way" toward an adjudicable expression of that issue.

9. Books of "entrees" were records of pleadings. William Rastell compiled such a volume, *A colleccion of entrees, of declaracions, barres, replicacions, rejoinders, issues, verdits, judgements, executions, proces, contynuances, essoynes, & divers other matters*, published by Tottell in 1566.

Fyrst case of these twayne I put for your parte
And by the last case apereth myne owne smart.

(1055–1056)

She goes on to suggest that if he is willing, their controversy may be decided by submitting to the judges the hypothetical case she has just described:

Yf ye now wyll all circumstance eshew
Make this question in these cases our yssew
And the payne of these men to abrevyate
Set all our other matter as frustrate.

(1063–1066)

What she has proposed is that they join issue by means of a fictional *imago* that will substitute for wordish disputation and clarify the principle involved in their disagreement.[10] It is an interesting moment, because it demonstrates in small the process and function of hypothesization that lies behind the entire play. Just as the lady creates a legal fiction in which the principle behind her dispute may be more easily perceived, Heywood has created a dramatic hypothesis that tends to actualize—and therefore enable us to perceive more clearly—the pleasures and pains of love.[11] The lady's

10. She is, in fact, invoking a Ciceronian principle: "there is no reason for not using an imaginary case for illustration [*fictam exempli loco ponere*] in order to make the problem more intelligible" (*De inv.* 2.118, tra ns. H. M. Hubbell, L.C.L. [London, 1949]). The method goes under several names among the rhetoricians. In *De inventione*, Cicero includes among the sources of probability in argument the "comparable," and this has three divisions: *imago, collatio, exemplum. Imago est oratio demonstrans corporum aut naturum similitudinem* (1.49)—a "sketch" revealing similitude of form and quality. (The *collatio* is a simile, while *exemplum* appeals to precedent.) Quintilian recommends the *hypotheses* of the Greeks, which he describes as "the proposition of something which, if true, would either solve a problem or contribute to its solution" (*Inst. or.* 5.10.96 trans. H. E. Butler, L.C.L. [London, 1963]). A similar heuristic aid, according to Erasmus, is the *fictio*, which is a hypothetical situation proposed for comparison, with which one strengthens one's real argument (*Opera omnia* [Leiden, 1703], 1: 86).

11. Sidney explicitly links the art of the poet and that of the jurist when he asks, in the *Apology*, "And doth the Lawyer lye then, when under the names of John a stile and John a noakes hee puts his case? But that is easily answered. Theyr naming of men is but to make theyr picture the more lively, and not to builde any historie; paynting men, they cannot leave men nameless" (*Elizabethan Critical Essays*, ed. G. Gregory Smith [Oxford, 1904], 1. 185–186).

proposal clearly indicates Heywood's consciousness of the distinction between thesis and hypothesis, and functions as an ironic reflection on the play itself. It is a fiction within a fiction which the wittier in Heywood's audience must have relished.

But Heywood experiments further with the process of actualizing a question. He creates a play within a play. Judgment on the first case is deferred until the other two litigants have presented their arguments. Their dispute is based on the question "Who experiences more pleasure—the Lover Beloved or the nonlover?" Lover Beloved sees no pleasure at all in his opponent's situation, while Neither Loving Nor Loved insists that he possesses quietness and contentment. After some preliminary quibbling over whether contentment is really pleasurable (you might be content to ride three nights, Lover Beloved suggests, on an errand for a friend, or find contentment following the death of a child, and still experience no pleasure), Neither Lover Nor Loved gets down to a more generic issue: is love a good? Citing the freezings and burnings of the Lover Not Loved, he argues that it is actually destructive of physical and mental harmony. This debate *a thesi* gets him nowhere, however, before the evidently thriving Lover Beloved, and he suddenly exits, leaving his surprised opponent to boast of his unexpected victory.

But what is about to take place is a little play devised by the Vice to prove his case. For he comes running back, screaming "Fire!" and describes a house, "painted red oker," run "by a broker," that has just burned down, killing the lady who lived within. It is, of course, the Lover's beloved (a courtesan, no less!), and the Lover exits frantically, determined to kill himself if he finds the lady dead. Here, debate has unquestionably turned into drama. For if the most convincing evidence of guilt is the defendant's enactment of the charge against him, then Lover Beloved has just "proved" the Vice's thesis that love is painful, by running off in despair in response to the Vice's enacted argument. It is the final step in the actualization of a question.

Of course the Lover comes back and denies defeat. In a brilliant riposte, he claims his distress was due to his opponent's lie and not to love. Supposing what I claimed were true, suggests the Vice; then Fortune were to blame, answers the Lover, not love. And so the argument returns to the question of contentment versus felt pleasure. The issue they join on is once again a hypothetical case: is it preferable to be a tree (feeling neither

pain nor pleasure) or a horse (experiencing both suffering and enjoyment)? This is the legal fiction imaging their situation which they present
to the judges.

This time each pair of judges is in agreement and declares each case a
draw: the Lover Not Loved suffers as much pain as Beloved Not Loving,
and Lover Beloved enjoys as much pleasure as Neither Loving Nor Loved.
It is perhaps what we expected all along.

But then Heywood does an interesting thing. He begins adjusting his
terms in such a way that contentment and feeling pleasure become aspects
of one another. The litigants announce that they will not contest the ver-
dict. Lover Beloved says that he is content with his lot, and the Vice asserts (somewhat contentiously) that he is just as content. Lover Not Loved,
in his capacity as their judge, then tells them that they should also be content to see each other's contentment, following Christ's admonition:

> Your neyghbour in pleasure lyke your selfe to be
> Gladly to wysh Christes precept doth bynde ye.
> (1542–1543)

Contentment *is* a kind of pleasure after all, and it *is* pleasurable to ride
three days on an errand for a friend. Then, acting in his capacity as judge,
Lover Beloved tells Lover Not Loved and Loved Not Loving that their
contentment to suffer equal pain (like the unfelt pleasure of contentment
at the death of a child) is also a form of grace. Such contentment is, in fact,
the means of achieving feeling pleasure:

> Since such contentacyon may hardely acorde
> In such kynde of love ashere hath ben ment
> Let us seke the love of that lovyng lorde
> Who to suffer passyon for love was content
> Whereby his lovers that love for love assent
> Shal have in fyne above contentacyon
> The felyng pleasure of eternal salvation.
> (1560–1566)

By obeying Christ's injunction to act selflessly on earth, one ultimately
experiences feeling bliss in heaven. Thus the "interlude concerning payne
and pleasure in love"—a Christmas play—finally emerges as a celebration
of the mysterious antinomies of love, and the secular world of contraries

resolves into transcendent unity. It is all an exercise of wit, but of that high order which enables one to envision a point on the mental horizon where parallel lines do, in fact, come together and the tensions of ordinary experience disappear. The vision is comic.

In his other plays, Heywood departs from the verbal intricacies of disputation and explores more broadly the common foibles of humanity. In *The Play of the Four PP* and *The Play of the Weather* he concentrates on the satiric mimesis of social types. While close argumentation is found in these plays, the emphasis is on the juxtaposition of opposing religious and social attitudes rather than chop-wit. Both dramas, however, are still contests fashioned around central questions, suggesting again a game among players.

The Four PP retains the somewhat arbitrary opening of the disputations, but again Heywood is careful to identify the main characters through extended *ethopoeiae*. A Palmer first appears, to give a circumstantial account of his travels, and concludes with a typical declaration of *positio*:

> For be ye sure, I thynke surely
> Who seketh sayntes for Christes sake—
> And namely such as payne do take
> On fote to punysche their frayle body—
> Shall therby meryt more hyely
> Then by anythinge done by man.
>
> (58–63)[12]

His claim is immediately challenged by a Pardoner, who concedes that visiting shrines is a pleasant pastime, but not a particularly efficient means of securing salvation:

> Give me but a peny or two pens,
> And as sone as the soule departeth him
> In halfe an houre—or thre quarter at moste—
> The soul is in heven with the Holy Ghost!
>
> (147–150)

A third entrant challenges them both. He is the Potycary, who insists that no soul gets to heaven without first leaving the body, an operation he is

12. All line references are to J. Q. Adams.

peculiarly equipped to assist. Thus the debate opens on the most certain means of salvation.

It is a question, however, that is not settled by reasoning together. The fourth P, a Pedlar, comes upon the scene and refuses to arbitrate so high a mystery. Instead, he suggests that the matter of *maistrye* be decided by a lying contest. The Palmer agrees, vowing meekly to obey the winner, for "quietnesse In any man is great rychesse" (478–479). But this remark sets off a new contention, as the Pardoner displays his relics as the only true *rychesse*. The Potycary, in turn, denies the Pardoner's definition and empties his bag of medicines, declaring (in parody of the Virgin's womb), "Here lyeth much rychesse in lytell space" (591). Their *disputatiuncula* ends only upon the Pedlar's refusal to be bribed by the Potycary's offer of marmalade, and the opponents then turn back to the contest originally proposed.

Here, Heywood translates into a deceptively informal "proof" the temporal pattern of witty argumentation by which a skilled debater traps his opponent. First, the Potycary tells a tale of his trade, concerning a lady to whom he had administered a clyster, as a result of which she bombarded and destroyed a castle ten miles away. Then the Pardoner describes a trip to hell to reprieve one Marjorie Corson, whom the devils were only too happy to surrender in return for his promise to help keep women out of hell, since they forever wrangle and disturb the peace. The alert Palmer sees his opening. That was a pretty good lie, he admits, but the Pardoner erred in his major premise:

> I never saw, nor knew, in my consyens,
> Any one woman out of paciens.
>
> (1003–1004)

The three others instantly judge this the greatest lie of all, and the Palmer wins the contest and, indirectly, his original thesis.

But it is not to Heywood's purpose to have a final winner, for this would muddy the issue behind the play. And so the Pardoner and Potycary, true to character, refuse to serve the beggarly Palmer.[13] "Now be ye all evyn as ye begoon," the Pedlar concludes. "No man hath lost, nor no

---

13. His attention to ethos is consistent throughout the play. Notice how even the Palmer's winning lie about women is a function of his peaceable character.

man hath won" (1139-1140). If the dramatic reason for this impasse is the pride of the Pardoner and the Potycary, the intellectual reason is that the decision is an impossible one to render. The Pedlar explains:

> Thus every vertue, yf we lyste to scan,
> Is pleasaunt to God and thankful to man;
> And who that by grace of the Holy Goste
> To any one vertue is moved most,
> That man, by that grace, that one apply,
> And therin serve God most plentyfully.
>
> (1173-1178)

Thus Heywood employs the method of examining a question *in utramque partem* in a way that remains true to the question as the humanists of the More circle saw it. They had argued that it is the moral quality of a man's life that determines his salvation, not the specific means he chose to pursue it. Their satire was always aimed at the abuse of respected institutions, not at the institutions themselves, and their essential confidence in the Church permitted Heywood to write a comedy in which salvation is seen as a matter of technology rather than a matter of spirit. Within the technological metaphor, Heywood has composed a serious debate of sustained irony, in which each side is not only equally valid but also equally incomplete because it is devoid of moral feeling. It is the efficacy of technique infused with spirit—the instrumentality of the ideal Church—to which the play points.

In the "enterlude of all maner wethers," he employs the method to hypothesize a political ideal. The play is the most fully mimetic of the debate comedies, representing a day in the King's court. It draws its inspiration from two of Lucian's dialogues, *Icaromenippus* and *The Double Indictment*. In the first piece, Menippus, who has flown to heaven from earth and back again, describes to a friend the scene of Zeus listening to prayers from down below:

From every quarter of earth were coming the most various and contradictory petitions. . . . Of those at sea, one prayed for a north, another for a south wind; the farmer asked for rain, the fuller for sun. Zeus listened, and gave each prayer careful consideration, but without promising to grant them all. . . . In one case I saw him puzzled; two men praying for opposite things and promising the same sacrifice, he could not tell which of them to favor, and experienced a truly Academic suspense of judgment showing a reserve and equilibrium worthy of Pyrrho.[14]

From this suggestion Heywood constructed a lengthy petition scene in which various sectors of English society request from Jupiter (a god come down to earth and thus a figure of Henry VIII) the kind of weather most beneficial to each. Wishing

> to satysfye and content
> All manner people whyche have ben offendyd
> By any wether mete to be amendyd
>
> (87–89)

Jupiter calls for someone to proclaim the opening of his court. He is greeted by a character named Mery-Reporte, who jostles his way through the crowd, and identifies himself as a poor gentleman ready to serve. Jupiter is taken aback by his light behavior and shabby dress: "Thou art no mete man in our bysynes" (113). Mery-Reporte persists in declaring his fitness for the job:

> syns your entent is but for the wethers,
> What skyls our apparell to be fryse or fethers?
> I thynke it wysdome, syns no man for-bad it,
> Wyth thys to spare a better—yf I had it!
> And, for my name: reportyng alwaye trewly
> What hurte to reporte a sad mater merely?
>
> (133–138)

His defense echoes the main theme of *The Double Indictment* that there is a light-hearted, "fictional" way of handling important questions that is distinct from both mellifluous but vapid rhetoric and crabbed but weighty philosophical discourse.[15] It is this way that Heywood—and Mery-Re-

---

14. *The Works of Lucian of Samosata*, trans. H. W. Fowler and F. G. Fowler (Oxford, 1905), 2. 141. Line references in the following discussion refer to Adams.

15. Against the charge of Dialogue that he has debased philosophy, Lucian argues:

> When I first took him in hand, he was regarded by the world at large as one whose interminable discussions had soured his temper and exhausted his vi-

porte, his spokesman—pursues, for weather becomes the central metaphor through which to examine the partial needs of each class of society and to suggest the function of the ruler.[16]

In a special sense, the play might be described as an encomium of the method of arguing *in utramque partem*. For Jupiter and Mery-Reporte preside over a series of one-sided arguments, as in succession there arrive a Gentleman, seeking clear, windless weather for hunting; a Merchant who wants clear weather and moderate trade winds; a Ranger who asks for windstorms to knock down trees so he can gather wood for fuel; a Water Miller who asks for rain without wind; a Wind Miller who wants wind without rain; a Gentlewoman who desires neither wind nor sun so she can promenade without spoiling her beauty; a Launder who needs heat and sun; and finally, a small boy who asks for frost and snow in which to play. The occasion of their petitions becomes a way of arguing their im-

---

tality. His labours entitled him to respect, but he had none of the attractive qualities that could secure him popularity. My first step was to accustom him to walk about the common ground like the rest of mankind; my next to make him presentable, by giving him a good bath and teaching him to smile. Finally, I assigned him Comedy as his yokefellow, thus gaining him the confidence of his hearers, who until then would as soon have thought of picking up a hedgehog as of venturing into the thorny presence of Dialogue (*ibid.*, p. 166).

16. Mery-Reporte is the second character we have encountered in the Heywood canon who is designated a Vice, and like Neither Loving Nor Loved he does not have the "vicious" nature of the morality Vice, though both are amoral. This neutralization of the Vice is the result of a neutralized context, for the plays, as suggested earlier, are not extensions of the actual world but are "liberties" within that world. The Vice, therefore, retains his dramatic function as manipulator, but loses his evil connotation. Mery-Reporte's designation is especially interesting because it suggests a fusion of two traditions. His role is that of Mercury in *Icaromenippus*; thus the morality Vice must have been seen as the appropriate dramatic vehicle for the character of Hermes—trickster, messenger, orator, thief, seducer. We encounter this amoral fun-loving character not only in Mery-Reporte and in that cunning debater Neither Loving Nor Loved, but also in Jack Juggler, the Mercury-turned-Vice in the play of the same name, adapted from Plautus's *Amphytrion*; conflated with the classical parasite in Mathew Merygreke of Udall's *Roister Doister*; in Diccon the Bedlam of *Gammer Gurton's Needle*; and, I suspect, in Shakespeare's Mercutio, whose romance predecessor had none of his cynical wit.

portance to society, and each (the boy excepted) sees his way of life as supremely important.

The effect of all their discourse is to reveal the importance of the mediator, the man who explores the problem from all sides. Jupiter, promising them each a portion of the weather they desire, arranged in such a way that the others will not be inconvenienced, notes the significance of his role:

> Now marke this conclusyon, we charge you arow:
> Myche metter have we now devysed for ye all
> Than ye all can perceyve; or code desyre.
>
> (1182–1184)

In *Weather* the method of arguing *in utramque partem* is seen as a political instrument that can be wielded by a wise ruler for the benefit of all members of society. But true to the Lucianic spirit, Heywood cannot resist a sly dig at the ability of the politician to use circumspection as a device for maintaining the *status quo ante*. Mery-Reporte finally observes:

> Lo, how this is brought to pas!
> Syrs, now shal ye have the wether even as yt was.
>
> (1239–1240)

He anticipates the remark of Elizabeth to Lord Burghley fifty years later.

II

John Rastell's interlude, *Gentleness and Nobility*, is a more serious essay in social speculation. In many ways it resembles More's *Utopia*, not only because it contains similar ideas, but because it uses the stage in the way More uses the printed page—as a privileged sanctuary where heterodoxy may be expressed. It begins with the question we have already encountered in *Fulgens and Lucres*, but rapidly expands, in true dialogue fashion, to cover most of the topics included in *Utopia*.

The play opens with some light skirmishing by the Merchant and the Knight, who touch superficially on the main issues to come. They debate whether commercial or landed wealth entitles one to be called gentle; whether wit determines nobility, and if so, which class is the wittier— artificers who mine and coin gold or aristocrats who end up with it; whether magistrates, generals, and justices have been drawn from the knightly class because of their wisdom or because of the foolish system of inherited office; and whether there is any justification for such a system. At this point, the Plowman enters. He declares the dispute worthless because the Knight and Merchant have cited not their own accomplishments but those of their ancestors. The two attempt to accommodate him, adducing their personal services to the commonwealth, but the Plowman has his own cause to plead. Slyly he asks:

> Is not that the noblyst thyng, indede,
> That of all other thyngs hath lest nede
> As God which reyneth etern in blysse?
> Is not he the noblest thyng that is?
>   (280–283)[17]

When they concede this to be true, he neatly follows up the consequences: that which is most noble is most self-sufficient, that most in need is most wretched. Therefore, since he plows, tills, harvests, nourishes cattle, fowl, and fish, and has everything he needs to survive—while they depend on his supplying these goods—he is most noble, they are wretched. The Merchant is furious:

> Now that is a folysh reason, so God me save,
> For by the same reason thou woldyst have
> Everi best, fyssh, and other foule than
> To be more noble of birth than a man
> For man hath more nede of bodely coveryng
> Than they have for they nede nothinge.
>   (340–345)

In response the Plowman delivers an encomium of man's rational soul, which supplies the defects of his body, but the Merchant declares this a digression, and demands that the Plowman return to the original question.

The first part of the play, then, has very much the flavor of the literary dialogue—"in maner of an interlude." That is, it is delivered standing up, presumably in costume, and with occasional "gestes" (the Plowman tends to beat his adversaries with his whipstock). It airs a variety of definitions, allows leisurely defense, and is more concerned with what can be said on each side than with the strict logic of what is said.

17. All line references are to Cameron.

In the second half of the play the debate on gentleness and nobility develops a more serious tone. Do these qualities consist in birth or "gentle condicyons"? Arguing from man's common ancestry in Adam and Eve, the Plowman refuses to entertain the notion of superior blood—unlike Lucres, who insisted upon honoring Cornelius for his. Accordingly, the Knight argues the gentle conditions of his ancestors, and in doing so proposes a theory of social contract: when the world was new and there were few people, everyone held goods in common. With the increase in population, contention over available goods arose, and his ancestors devised laws to defend those who labored in the soil. In return, the husbandmen gave them a portion of their goods, and later, money:

> So possessyons began and were furst found
> Upon a good and reasonable ground.
>
> (595–596)

The Plowman denies this utterly. "All possessions began furst of tyranny," he declares, and offers an entirely different theory. As society developed, some people began stealing from their more diligent neighbors, who were compelled to give up a portion of their goods on a regular basis in return for their safety, and this extortion was hardened into statutes and perpetuated by laws of inheritance.

This raises the next question: does the system of inheritance have any social value? The Knight insists that land provides an economic basis for learning and good governance, while the Plowman argues that it is the source of economic and legal oppression. The debate expands still further as the Plowman argues that only people who work for the commonwealth should have land to support them during their lives. And he adds:

> Nor I think it not resonable nother
> One man to lyf by labour of an other,
> For ych man is borne to labour truly
> As byrde is to flie naturally.
>
> (793–796)

Thus Rastell is proposing through the Plowman some of the same ideas concerning communal property and the obligation to work that More expounds in *Utopia*. But this is all still within the rules of an exercise of wit. When the Knight tries to defend the custom of inheritance by citing

God's promise to Abraham—*Tibi dabo terram hanc et semini tuo*—the Plowman refuses to allow divine authority to enter a debate conducted by rational argument:

> Thou answerest me now even lyke a fole
> As some of these fond clarkes that go to scole.
> When one putteth to them a subtyll questyon
> Of phylosophy *to be provyde by reason,*
> When they have all theyr wyttes and reason spende
> And can not tell how theyre parte to defende,
> Than they wyll aledge some auctoryte
> Of the lawes or elles of devynite,
> Which in no wyse men may denye.
> And yet ye knowe well that of phylosophy
> The pryncyples oft contrayant be
> Unto the very groundes of devynite.
> > (827–838, emphasis mine)

In a rational exploration of the matter at hand, one must not fall back on divine testimony. When the Plowman reasserts his original thesis, arguing that his virtuous life attests to his gentility, the dialogue reaches an impasse and the Merchant and Knight withdraw. Alone, the Plowman seems suddenly tired. There is no hope in reforming by reason, he says,

> When a man is set in a wyllful credens
> All to fortefye his owne opynyon.
> > (989–990)

He will leave reformation to Princes inspired by God,

> For exortacyon, techyng and prechyng,
> Gestyng and raylyng, mend no thing,
> For the amendment of the world is not in me.
> > (1002–1004)

And he returns to his plow.

His statement echoes Raphael Hythlodaeus's hopelessness about persuading rulers to change their ways when they are fixed in their ideas. As if to underscore this point, the Merchant and Knight reappear for a last word. The Merchant insists that governors need possessions to maintain degree and that the few must drive the multitude to labor, else they will be idle (the argument of *persona* More in *Utopia*). The Knight insists that aristocrats have more "gentle condycyons" than carters who brawl and quarrel over "whych of them, at the skot, shall pay lest," while the gentry "of theyr gentlnes wyll profer to pay"—thereby reducing "gentle condycyons" to a matter of etiquette. As for nobility, rich aristocrats with land and rent are obviously more self-sufficient than "pore people." Indeed, the Merchant concludes it is necessary for some to live in wealth, some in misery:

> For it is Almighty God's purveyance
> Wise men of fools to have the governance;
> And they that rule well I beseech Jesus
> Send them good life and long to continue.
>
> (1093–1096)

The fatuous tone corresponds closely to the final words of the conservative Thomas More in *Utopia*.

There is a final difference, however, that makes Rastell's work a comedy rather than a visionary entertainment. As the contenders retire, a character called the Philosopher comes forward. He proposes that gentle conditions constitute gentilesse, and that nobility does not consist in sufficiency alone, for God is God not only for his sufficiency but for his goodness. Thus beneficent virtue is the basis of both gentleness and nobility, and rulers should come to power because of their virtue and remain in power only so long as it is exercised. But he then goes beyond the theoretical, and offers some practical suggestions for achieving this ideal. Though men must be reasoned with, there are some "blynde bestes" that will not listen to reason, and they must be corrected by law. If present laws are insufficient, princes and governors are bound to make new ones and put just men in authority to execute them. And if, given man's inherent sinfulness, these magistrates are not inclined to do so, laws must be instituted to provide for rotation of office and punishment of offending officials:

> And untyll that such orders be devysyd
> Substauncyally, and put in execycucyon,

    Look never to see the world amended
    Nor of the gret myschefes the reformacyon.
                                    (1160–1163)[18]

In the end, then, he does have a plan for making things better. He does not advocate abolition of inheritance and the public ownership of land, nor does he share the Plowman's pessimism about the use of reason to effect change; yet he has adapted the concepts of rotation of appointed officials and their liability to the public. In effect, he presents a meliorist view of the important positions raised in the dialogue, and thus reveals the progressive aspect of argument *in utramque partem* that is missing in *Utopia*, where More only entertains opposites. In this respect, *Gentleness and Nobility* more closely resembles Starkey's *Dialogue*, where within the safe confines of a speculative artifice, radical ideas are expressed with no expectation that they will be adopted, but the two sides shape together some more immediately realizable goal. The result is twofold: an acceptable *via media* is reached by which the general state of things is improved because the most reasonable elements on both sides are embraced; at the same time, what has been said in behalf of both extremes remains in the mind to stir further thought. In intellectual and political terms, this describes a process of debate and compromise, in which the ideas temporarily discarded are shelved for use at a more appropriate time. In literary terms, it describes an antithetical drama whose contrary elements reach a tentative equilibrium, but are always ready to settle out again.[19] The contrast between this "rational" synthesis and the transcendent resolutions seen in such plays as *Love* and *The Four PP* will also be found in the regular comedies that come to be written in the course of the century. It is to their development that we must now turn.

    18. Notice, he is making the same distinction between the purely intellectual airing of ideas in the play and their "substantial" effects in the actual world that Sidney makes in the *Apology* (*Elizabethan Critical Essays*, 1. 157), indicating that the ultimate value of such "poetic" games of wit is their power to effect change in human behavior.
    19. One thinks of the "reconciliation" of justice and mercy in *The Merchant of Venice* and the "purgation" of self-love in *Twelfth Night*. The realism of these plays lies partly in the tension between the achieved comic solution and the audience's awareness of the impermanence and even of the illusory nature of such wrought harmony.

Terence and the Mimesis of Wit

THE PLAYS OF MEDWALL, HEYWOOD, AND RASTELL ARE RELATIVELY primitive expressions of the impulse to explore questions through mimetic drama. They lack the *mythos* that Aristotle considered the soul of drama, and consist almost wholly of *dianoia* and *lexis*—argumentation and carefully selected diction—with *ethos*, or character, lightly sketched in. They represent but the first stage in the dramatic hypothesization of a question.

We have already seen, however, that the mode of thought which informs a bare debate undergoes a more complicated development in its attempt to better understand the particulars of experience. The inquiring imagination proceeds from thesis to hypothesis, rendering the questions under consideration more specific by visualizing actual persons confronting issues as they arise in their lives. The same intellectual community that had inspired the humanist play of ideas encouraged this movement from thesis to hypothesis in drama through its analysis of a venerable body of ancient mimetic plays—the comedies of Terence. These analyses were accessible in the heavily annotated editions of Terence's work that were produced on the continent and made available in England, but their most direct line of influence was through the grammar school, where Terence was an approved curriculum author. There his work was studied systematically, and in the humanist commentaries future dramatists learned what plays consisted of, and absorbed a way of thinking about drama that was never really lost.

Erasmus, as usual, provides our first set of pedagogical instructions:

You begin by offering an appreciation of the author, and state what is necessary concerning his life and surroundings, his talent, and the characteristics of his style. You next consider comedy as an example of a particular form of literature, and its interest for the student: the origin and meaning of the term itself, the varieties of comedy, and the Terentian prosody. Now you proceed to treat briefly and clearly the argument of the play, taking each situation in due course. Side by side with this you will handle the diction of the writer; noting any conspicuous elegances, or such peculiarities as archaism, novel usage, Graecisms: bringing out any that is involved or obscure in phrases or sentence forms; marking, where necessary, derivations and orthography, metaphors and other rhetorical devices. Parallel passages should next be brought under notice, similarities and contrasts in treatment observed, and direct borrowings traced—no difficult task when we are comparing a Latin poet with his Greek predecessors. The last factor in the lesson consists in the moral applications of what it suggests. . . .[1]

Clearly, Erasmus prescribes a rather thorough treatment of the author. The reasons are many. First, Terence was considered a model of Latin speech. Philip Melanchthon, who builds upon Erasmus's method, makes the point unequivocally:

There is no other writer whatever in the Latin tongue who should be so earnestly studied, learned by heart, and enregistered in the mind as Terence. For since the prime virtue of speech is to speak properly and we do not have a better craftsman of proper speech than Terence, it is wholly fitting that we put a good deal of work and study into learning him thoroughly. And from those who teach boys I earnestly require even a superstitious diligence in the explaining of this author in detail.[2]

In a later passage, he stresses that students especially study the laments, narrations, consultations, and objurgations of the characters. In this way, the drama becomes an important fund of sophistic methodology. It is

1. William Harrison Woodward, *Desiderius Erasmus Concerning the Aim and Method of Education* (New York, 1964), p. 174.
2. Quoted by T. W. Baldwin, *William Shakspere's Five-Act Structure* (Urbana, Ill., 1947), p. 176.

also seen as a source of knowledge about life, in the great sophistic tradition so scorned by Plato in the *Ion*. Concerning the *Andria*, Melanchthon writes:

> Here are depicted the sage old men, the crafty Davus, the young man Pamphilus endowed with an honest and pious mind. Indeed that the disposition of Pamphilus might the more clearly be seen . . . Charinus, very unlike Pamphilus, is contrasted with him: nothing temperate in the former, nothing of counsel: on the contrary, in the other almost all things more moderate than either age demands or love permits.[3]

Here, the drama is viewed as a great anthology, brimful of exempla. These exempla, as we shall see, are usually treated as single frames in a continuous film—each revealing a new facet of the human character as it moves through experience.

Finally, Terence was a source of *moral* instruction. Again, Melanchthon makes the point succinctly:

> All agree that the authors of comedies intended to display examples both of common conditions and of ordinary chances, admonished as it were by which we may judge more prudently of human affairs. . . .[4]

What is particularly interesting here is that moral precepts were extracted from the plays without regard to their dramatic relevance—a striking instance of that search for general principles in the particular which we have observed elsewhere. These lessons are, in fact, designated *theses* or *ethicae*. Their inclusion in Terentian analysis reflects the broad moral assumptions of humanist pedagogy, at one moment focusing upon the techniques of sophistic argumentation, at another seeking appropriately edifying principles. As literary criticism, however, this bifold activity has an odd effect upon the mind of the reader: it suggests to him that the drama may be perceived in two different frames of reference—one particular, qualified, and autonomous, the other reducible to axiomatic moral precept. This shall become clearer as we look into the commentaries themselves.

At the head of the Terentian commentators stands the fourth-century grammarian Aelius Donatus, whose *scholia* provided the foundation upon

3. *Ibid.*, p. 181.
4. *Ibid.*, p. 176.

which later Renaissance critics built. In the prefatory material ascribed to him, he makes an observation about the structure and matter of comedy that was to profoundly influence sixteenth-century playwrights:

> Comedy is divided into four parts: prologue, protasis, epitasis, catastrophe. The prologue is, as it were, a preface to the fable. . . . The protasis is the first act and the beginning of the drama; the epitasis the increase and progression of the agitation, and, as one might say, of the whole knot of errors; the catastrophe is the reversing of affairs toward a happy ending, a recognition having laid open all the action.[5]

Another version went like this:

> Now comedy is divided in four parts: prologue, protasis, epitasis, catastrophe. The prologue is the first speech called by the Greeks πρῶτος λόγος or the discourse preceding the true composition of the fable. . . . The protasis is the first act of the fable, in which part of the argument is unfolded, part withheld in order to maintain the curiosity of the audience; the epitasis is the complication of the plot, exquisitely fitted together; the catastrophe is the unfolding of the fable, through which its outcome is proved acceptable.[6]

Along, then, with the familiar distinctions of person, theme, and mood, comedy is characterized as a three-part fable based on error. From the initial error, there flow a series of mistakings which increase the perturbations of the characters until, in the fifth act, the errors are all revealed, and this brings about a happy ending. In his analysis of the individual plays,

5. comoedia per quattour partes dividitur: prologum, protasin, epitasin, catastrophen. est prologus velut praefatio quaedam fabulae. . . . protasis primus actus initiumque est dramatis; epitasis incrementum processusque turbarum ac totius, ut ita dixerim, nodus erroris; catastrophe conversio rerum ad iucundos exitus patefacta cunctis cognitione gestorum. *Aeli Donati quod fertur commentum Terenti accedunt Eugraphi commentum et scholia Bembina*, ed. Paul Wessner (Leipsig, 1902), I. 22. The passage, though attributed to Donatus, was apparently written by Evanthius, his contemporary.

6. Comoedia autem dividitur in quattour partes: prologum, πρότασιν, ἐπίτασιν, καταστροφήν. prologus est prima dictio, a Graecis dicta πρῶτος λόγος vel antecedens veram fabulae compositionem elocutio. . . . πρότασις est primus actus fabulae, quo pars argumenti explicatur, pars reticetur ad populi exspectationem tenendam; ἐπίτασις involutio argumenti, cuius elegantia conectitur; καταστροφή explicatio fabulae, per quam eventus eius approbatur (*ibid.*, pp. 27–28).

Donatus also applies this concept. Thus in the *Andria*, Davus's advice to Pamphilus that he may safely go along with his father's marriage plans for him "fastens the knot of error of the story and the comic peril."[7] Upon the father's mistaking his son's acquiescence as sincere, the epitasis grows more and more complicated until the fundamental error shared even by the audience—the marriageability of Pamphilus's paramour—is discovered at the end of the play. Similarly, the action of the *Adelphoe* is based upon Demea's mistaken belief that the virtuous Aeschinus has committed the immoral acts of his son Ctesipho; in the *Hecyra*, the fundamental error is the identity of the woman Pamphilus confesses to have seduced; in the *Eunuchus*, the mistaking of Chaerea for a eunuch. The assumption behind this characterization is that in addition to being an *imitatio vitae, speculum consuetudinis, imago veritatis*, comedy shows people moving about in a subjective mist of misapprehension, each groping to achieve his own desires and acting upon very dubious grounds.

How does one find a basis for action immersed in a world of shadowy probabilities? Traditionally, through the arts of rational argument—and the commentators were quick to notice that these dramas of opposing citizens resembled contentions over a central issue, in which secondary questions arising from this issue were treated in a series of subordinate debate scenes linked together by expository material.[8] The *Andria*, the play

7. haec scaena nodum innectit erroris fabulae et periculum comicum (*ibid.*, p. 144).

8. Donatus's own language suggests the resemblance. Notice that in the two definitions quoted above, the terms used to describe the catastrophe have strong legal connotations. A common meaning for the noun *cognitio* (n. 6) is a judicial examination, inquiry, or trial. The use of the verb *approbo* (n. 7) reinforces the sense that the happy ending is the product of a successful application of proofs. Evidently some commentators saw a similarity between the structure of the Terentian plot and that of the judicial oration. The protasis, in which the characters are introduced to inform the audience of preceding events, the current situation, and the intentions of the protagonist and antagonist, is analogous to the exordium, narration, and partition of the oration, in which the speaker gains the good will of the audience, explains the facts leading up to the litigation, and then defines the issue between the contending parties. The epitasis, in which the action grows complicated, bringing the protagonist into greatest danger, as he is forced to respond to the repeated assaults of the enemy, corresponds to the oratorical confirmation and refutation, in which the arguments of plaintiff and defendant are presented. The conclusion of the play is comparable to the peroration in which

usually printed first in the texts, and the most heavily annotated (suggesting that it was the most widely read) will serve as an example. Briefly, the play concerns a conflict between a young man named Pamphilus and his father Simo. Simo has arranged a wedding for Pamphilus with the daughter of his friend Chremes, but the wedding has been called off because Chremes has learned that Pamphilus has been haunting a neighborhood courtesan. To test his son's obedience, Simo pretends that the wedding is still to take place, and informs Pamphilus that he must be married that very afternoon. Pamphilus is despairing because he has already promised to marry the girl he loves—who happens to be living in the courtesan's house and will soon bear his child. His slave Davus, learning of Simo's deception, advises Pamphilus to agree to the imaginary wedding, confident that Chremes will never allow his daughter to marry a notorious frequenter of courtesans. When Pamphilus acquiesces, Simo is convinced his son is reformed and persuades Chremes to reopen the match. The rest of the play is devoted to Davus's anxious attempts to prove to Chremes that Pamphilus is still a brothel haunter, while Simo tries just as hard to see that the marriage takes place. Toward the end of the fourth act, a stranger from Andros named Crito—derived from the act of adjudication, the gloss informs us, because he resolves the controversy— brings news that the girl Pamphilus loves is an Athenian and, in fact, the long-lost daughter of Chremes. Thus Pamphilus gets his girl and Simo his match.

Melanchthon characterizes the play as follows:

> The whole play is similar to speech in the deliberative genre. For old men, youths, and servants reason together in various ways concerning the whole case.[9]

---

the orator clinches his case (see Baldwin, *Five-Act Structure*, pp. 54–55; also Marvin T. Herrick, *Comic Theory in the Sixteenth Century* [Urbana, Ill., 1964], p. 26).

9. Et tota fabula similis est orationi generis suasorii. Nam varie de tota causa consultant senes, adolescentes, ac servi (*Terentius, / in quem triplex edita est P. Antesignani / Rapistagnensis commentatio* [Lyons, 1560], p. 6). In this discussion, I shall be referring to the remarkable *Triple Terence* of 1560 which, along with the great Roigny folio of 1552, may be viewed as a maximal Terence—an index of thought about Terentian comedy in the sixteenth century. Although other editions contain less *scholia*, they are essentially of the same kind. In the *Triple Terence*, each play is preceded by the analyses of Donatus, Muretus, and Melanchthon, and

He is led to this judgment through an analysis of the peril in the play. After praising Terence for his language and comedy for its edifying qualities, he observes:

> Moreover, comedies usually contain a certain danger, for where is the place for counseling, reasoning, and planning if not in doubtful affairs? And indeed comedy is nothing other than a certain picture of human reasoning and its outcome. In the *Andria*, Pamphilus is imperilled in that he must keep faith with Glycerium, after having promised his father in error that he will be under his control and marry the girl his father wishes him to. And this is, as it were, the *status* of the play. All counsels, all complaints, all arguments, must be brought back to this place.[10]

Iodocus Willichius, some twenty years later, comes to the same conclusion. He says that the *Andria*

> is in the deliberative genre and weighs this issue: whether Pamphilus should marry Glycerium. Here on both sides are the persuasions and dissuasions of youths, old men, and servants. In behalf of the son, these indeed are the chief arguments: that he ravished her, that he promised to marry her, that she is an Athenian citizen. Now, on the father's side, these are the main ones: that the son is in the father's keeping; therefore he should submit to him, and should

---

within every play each scene is headed by an argument composed of sentences from Donatus, Barlandus, Muretus, Willichius, Latomus, Hegendomorphinus, and other commentators. The argument includes a plot summary, rhetorical and moral observations, and citations from other authors, in the approved Erasmian manner. In addition, profuse marginal glosses provide further observations about argumentation, style, and character.

10. Fere autem fabulae continent periculum quoddam. nusquam enim consilio locus est, nisi in dubiis rebus. Neq; vero aliud est Comoedia nisi humanorum consiliorum & eventuum imago quaedam. In Andria periclitatur Pamphilus, ut Glycerio fidem promissam praestet, postquam patri per errorem pollicitus est, futurum se in eius potestate, et ducturum quam vellet. Estque haec veluti στασις fabulae. Consilia omnia, querele [sic] omnes, argumenta omnia huc referenda sunt (*ibid.*, p. 6). In translating *consilium*, I have purposely expanded it into the three chief meanings it has in the commentaries, for it is used not only to signify advice, scheme, or plan, but ratiocination in general. (Recall Melanchthon's note that Charinus exhibited "nothing of counsel.")

marry in accordance with his will. . . . . Pamphilus is imperilled not a little by his champion, Davus, by whose counsel and cleverness he is nevertheless delivered. And finally, by unexpected luck, Crito appears, and declares Glycerium to be an Athenian citizen and Chremes' daughter, proving it through circumstantial evidence. Therefore the marriage is certain, confirmed, and legitimate, according to Pamphilus's desires, and thus the catastrophe closes quite cheerfully and the *status* is resolved.[11]

Both commentators are using the language of formal oratory to describe the play. The word *status*, as we have seen, signifies the precise issue over which two parties are at odds, "for this is the place where the defense takes its stand, as it were coming to grips in a counter-attack."[12] Since the question here is "Whether Pamphilus should marry Glycerium," not an issue of fact or definition, it is the *status qualitatis*, concerning right and wrong, that is involved. As in the oration each part—exordium, narration, proofs, and peroration—must relate directly to the issue if the argument is to be presented effectively, so for Melanchthon all the dramatic discourse, both prior and subsequent to the fatal promise, converges upon the *status*. Willichius, too, sees the play as a lengthy deliberation, and uses the language of rhetorical debate to describe it: the verb *censere*, to judge; the Greek κρινόμενον, which Cicero defines as *de re agitur*, the matter in question;[13] and the term *circumstantia*, signifying evidence. For

---

11. Est in genere deliberativo & κρινόμενον censetur. Ducatne in matrimonium Glycerium Pamphilus. Hic sunt utrinque suasiones, dissuasiones, adolescentum, senum, & servorum. Pro filio quidem sunt firmamenta, quia vitiavit, quia promisit se ducturum, quia civis est Attica. Pro patre autum sunt, quia filius est in potestate patris: obsequetur igitur, & pro voluntate patris uxorem ducet. . . . Periclitatur enim non parum Pamphilus Davo authore, cuius tamen consilio & astutia liberatur. Postremo autem casu & insperato Crito advenerat: Glycerium civem, & Chremetis filiam esse exposuit, atque circumstantiis confirmavit. Nuptiae igitur ad Pamphili sententiam certae, firmae, & legitimae sunt, & sic καταστροφή hilarior claudit, & στάσιν complectitur (*ibid.*, p. 7).

12. Cicero, *Top.* 93, trans. H. M. Hubbell (London, 1949). See Ch. III, p. 66 and n. 5.

13. Sed quae ex statu contentio efficitur, eam Graeci κρινόμενον vocant, mihi placet id, quoniam quidem ad te scribo, qua de re agitur vocari (*Top.* 95). Cf. *Ad Her.*: Ex ratione defensionis et ex firmamento accusationis judicii quaestio nascatur oportet, quam nos iudicationem, Graeci crinomenon appellant (1.26).

him this new evidence settles the *status*, for it proves, to everyone's surprise, that it is "right" for Pamphilus to marry Glycerium.[14]

The main reorientation, then, that a modern reader must make to recapture the approach of a Renaissance student of the play is to think of it as a rhetorical construction revolving around a central question which—as we shall see—also contains within it a number of *quaestiunculae* debated along the way. Regarding it in this fashion, we can see that debate thesis has actually emerged as fiction through the full utilization of the minor forms of composition in the imitation of an action. In effect, we are confronting the Aphthonian *thesis* "Shall a man take a wife?"—now travelled the gamut from abstract to concrete in the persons and places of Terence's comedy. That this distinction between thesis and hypothesis was very much alive is indicated by the composite comments of Donatus and Willichius on the second scene of the *Adelphoe*. In the first scene, Micio has come out to explain the difference between his brother's strict way of life and his own. The scene that follows finds both brothers onstage confronting the effects of their tutelage upon the young men they have taken in charge. It is described as

> virtually a model [παράδειγμα] of the previous one. Just as in that scene the two lives are described, as it were, by way of a thesis [θέσει] so here there is a fictionalization [ὑπόθεσις] of both kinds of life, and a figuring forth, by way of an example, where different kinds of men, different fathers, and different pursuits are set before us.[15]

14. Herrick notes that Vincentius Cordatus in his edition of 1570 also analyzed the *Andria* as a disputation between young men and old. The side affirming the young man's right to marry is taken by Pamphilus and Charinus, the negative side, "which denies the right of any young person to marry without the father's consent, is taken by old Simo and Chremes. The stand of the servants in this controversy, according to Cordatus, is 'mixed'" (Comic Theory, p. 179). Not all the plays are characterized so specifically. Of the *Eunuchus*, for example, Melanchthon says only, "In the preceding comedy [the *Andria*], there are many consultations and the whole matter generally rests in the deliberative genre. In this one there is more expostulation, and it is like an accusation and closer to the judicial genre" (*Triple Terence*, p. 202). The *Adelphoe*, too, he notes, containing much accusation and excuse, appears judicial rather than deliberative. But if a statement of the issue is missing from the other plays, the statement of the peril never is, and therefore the *status* is always present (see Baldwin, pp. 184–187).

15. Est haec prioris scenae tanquam παράδειγμα. Sicut illic veluti θέσει duplex

The commentary suggests that simply to talk about an issue is to speak as in a thesis, but to show it is to present an hypothesis. This is precisely what Melanchthon means when he calls comedy *humanorum consiliorum et eventuum imago quaedam.* The play is not simply a debate about ethical or political issues, as in the humanist drama, but a vivid imitation of such debates—and their results—as they are enacted in the course of human life.

Because Terentian comedies are essentially intrigue plays, most of the scenes present the characters either weighing what to do, setting schemes in motion, figuring out the plots of their opponents, or exulting or despairing in the outcome of their own. If they are not literally rhetorical proofs they certainly are pictures of the opponents on both sides of the question working out their strategies and testing them on one another. The critics were alive to this mimesis of *dianoia* in action, and their comments reflect it in various ways.[16] There are, for example, those moments in the play when one side has been stunned by the actions of the other, and a temporary impasse is reached while a character decides what to do next. These are the *quaestiunculae* that sprout from the main trunk of the argument, and they are always pointed out and their questions defined. In 1.3, Davus delivers a perplexed speech, having just been informed by Simo that he is preparing a sudden wedding for Pamphilus:

> If I'm not sharp in looking out, it'll be the ruin of me or else of my young master. And I'm not clear which side to take, whether to help Pamphilus or obey the old man. If I desert Pamphilus, I'm afraid for his life; if I help him, I'm afraid of his father's threats, and he's not an easy man to trick. . . . (206–211)[17]

The argument preceding the scene describes it as a "brief and comic deliberation, evoking with gesture great anticipation of many threatening

---

vita describitur, ita hic utriusque vitae generis est ὑπόθεσις, & quaedam exemplaris repraesentatio: ubi diversi homines, diversi patres, & diversi studia proponuntur (*Triple Terence*, pp. 490–491).

16. I am using the Aristotelian term because it seems best able to express that ongoing process of reasoning and problem-solving which the commentators suggest is the action of comedy.

17. All line references are to *Terence*, trans. John Sargeaunt, L.C.L. (London, 1964).

things. . . ."[18] In other words, it is a dilemma being acted out.

Similarly, when Pamphilus first appears in 1.5, he is incredulous at his father's peremptory behavior and at Chremes' inexplicable reversal. Agonizing over his conflicting duties to father and beloved, he cries out

> My path is blocked with innumerable anxieties, my mind dragged this way and that. There's my passion, my pity for my girl, my worry about the match; on the other side there's my reverence for my father, who has shown me all indulgence up to now and let me follow my bent in everything. Can I oppose a parent like that? Oh, Lord, Lord, I can't tell what to do. (260–264)

Mysis, Glycerium's maid, has been listening, and decides she had better step in and remind Pamphilus of the girl's deserts: "When the mind is in the balance, a straw will turn the scale." The commentary treats the encounter as a *suasoria*:

> In this scene is contained the complaint of Pamphilus against his father and Chremes, the plan for the marriage having been discovered; violently lamenting and overflowing with choler because it is to be solemnized so hastily, he is led by anger into a state of passion. And it is like a deliberative case, in which the two sides are: first, that of the father, and second, that of the beloved. Mysis acts as advocate, to whom he finally promises that he will keep faith utterly with Glycerium, even, should it come to that, against the will of his father.[19]

The most interesting comments, from our point of view, are those that analyze whole scenes or parts of scenes as proofs for one side or the other. In 2.2, Davus enters with exciting news. He has discovered that the proposed marriage is a fake and tells why. Willichius characterizes the scene as one written in the *status coniecturalis*, where the issue is one of fact, for

18. Hic brevis & Comica deliberatio est, magnam expectationem plurimarum rerum imminentium cum motu excitans (*Triple Terence*, p. 58).

19. Continetur hac scena querela Pamphili adversus patrem & Chremetem, cognito nuptiarum consilio; de quibus tam subito celebrandis, vehementer dolens, stomachabundusque atque ira concitus inducitur. et est quasi deliberatio; in qua duae partes sunt: una patris, altera amicem pro suasore Mysis est: cui tandem pollicetur, fidem omnino servaturum se Glycerio, vel invito, si res ita exigat, patre (*ibid.*, p. 65).

the question is whether the marriage is real or fictitious. Davus's proofs are derived from a collection of signs that the marriage will not take place:

Now there are six signs: there is little provision for dinner; Simo seems dejected; Chremes' doorway was empty; no bridal matron either entered or left the house; there was no decoration or excitement; and the slave boy was bringing home to Chremes a bare portion of vegetables and little fish for dinner. From these implications he gathers that the marriage is not to take place.[20]

All these signs, it must be noted, are expounded in very naturalistic discourse.

The above proof is purely discursive. Proofs are also *acted out* onstage. In 3.1, having been persuaded by Davus that Pamphilus has reformed and is eager to marry according to his father's wishes, Simo overhears Mysis telling the midwife of Pamphilus's fidelity to Glycerium, and his promise to acknowledge the expected child as his own. Simo is shocked at this contradictory evidence, and as he is trying to figure out what to make of it he suddenly hears Glycerium, in the throes of childbirth, crying out to Juno Lucina. Simo then smells a rat. Believing Pamphilus could not be so foolish as to get deeply involved with a foreigner, and sensing (incorrectly, as it turns out) that the timing of Mysis's speech and the labor pains is just too pat, he decides that the whole thing is a scenario contrived by Davus and the women to scare off Chremes. Willichius notes:

The scene turns on the conjectural question of whether or not the mistress is pregnant by Pamphilus. In the words of Mysis we see the *intentio* [the charge or accusation], which both the childbirth and the invocation of the woman in labor, functioning as necessary signs, prove. Just so, in Simo, we see a defense against the charge, from the topics *indecorous* and *absurd*.[21]

20. Sunt autem signa sex, quia paululum obsonii adest, quia tristis, quia solitudo ante ostium Chremetis, quia nulla aut introivit aut exivit matrona, quia ibi nullus erat ornatus & tumultus, quia puer Chremeti olera & paucos pisciculos . . . attulit. Ex his coniecturis colligit nuptias non esse futuras (*ibid.*, p. 88). Cf. *Top.* 52: "Circumstances before the event which are looked for are the following: preparations, conversation, the locale, a compact, a banquet . . ."; also *De inv.* 1.37–43 on the proofs drawn from action, cited in Ch. III. Davus is inventing a probable scenario just as an advocate would.

21. Versatur in statu coniecturali, Sitne amica e Pamphilo gravida. In Myside

Some scenes appear to the commentators as miniature trials. Naturally, they are in the judicial genre. In 4.1, for example, Charinus, the young man who is in love with Chremes' daughter, learns that Pamphilus has actually offered to marry her, and charges his friend with treachery. Willichius writes:

> In Charinus we find a lament on the perfidy of man. In Pamphilus is justification via *translatio criminis* [shifting the blame] to Davus. In Davus there is a description of the good servant along with his duties, and then an exculpation of the act perpetrated.[22]

The analysis is technical, and the procedures may be found in the *Ad Herennium, De inventione,* and the *Institutio oratoria.* That he intended the crime of treachery Pamphilus denies by invoking the *status qualitatis,* and pleading extenuating circumstances:

> for he admits indeed that the crime was done, but pleads in excuse and transfers the blame to Davus and the gods. In turn, Davus, having been accused of bad counsel, justifies himself by promising to offer better advice in the future and perform his office assiduously, and by praying for pardon.[23]

---

est intentio, quam & puerperium & invocatio parturientis ceu signa necessaria comprobant. Verum in Simone est depulsio propter indecorum & absurdum (*ibid.,* p. 104). Another funny scene, described as an argument for the protagonist, is 4.4, treated as a *dissuasoria.*

22. In Charino est de perfidia hominum conquestio. In Pamphilo est per translationem criminis in Davum expurgatio. In Davo est descriptio boni servi juxta officium, deinde & purgatio facinoris admissi (*ibid.,* p. 134). The author of the *Ad Herennium* defines *translatio criminis* in a way that further illustrates the frequent cross-referencing between rhetorical argumentation and drama: "A cause rests on the Shifting of the Question of Guilt, when we do not deny our act, but plead that we were driven to it by the crimes of others, as in the case of Orestes when he defended himself by diverting the issue of guilt from himself to his mother" (1.25). *Purgatio,* the author writes, is "the defendant's denial that he acted with intent" (1.24, trans. Harry Caplan [London, 1954]).

23. concedit quidem crimen admissum, sed deprecatur, & in Davum transfert atque deos. Porro Davus accusatus mali consilii, sese expurgat melioris consilii pollicitatione, & sui officii assiduitate, & deprecatione (*ibid.*). *Deprecatio,* according to *Ad Her.,* is a "Plea for Mercy when the defendant confesses the crime and premeditation, yet begs for compassion" (1.24). In this case, of course, premeditation is not identical with motive.

Thus a small scene of accusation and exculpation in the streets of Athens, budding off the main plot, is treated with the subtlety of an actual law case. The deed in question has been committed: Pamphilus *has* expressed a desire to wed Chremes' daughter. But in doing so he did not intend to betray Charinus; he was, in fact, following a plan designed to prevent such an event. The issue is resolved only when fact and intention are distinguished, and Charinus departs reassured in his hopes.[24]

These examples indicate one way in which those who studied Terence were led to think about playwriting. A Terentian comedy was a running controversy waged by characters whose ruminations, inquiries, laments, and rejoicings were imaged responses to the need for proofs required to win the argument. In the *Andria*, Crito is the unexpected proof—whose fortuitous arrival satisfies both parties in such a way that both win. Pamphilus marries the girl he loves and Simo secures the alliance he had sought. Somehow the conflict between romantic love and filial obedience has been resolved in a way that persuades us that opposites can enjoy a kind of idealized coexistence.

Rhetorical analysis is, however, only one concern of the commentators. The other is moral edification, most succinctly expressed in the *theses* or *ethicae* of Iodus Willichius, which were printed again and again in sixteenth- and seventeenth-century editions of Terence. These contain both general observations about human behavior, and strict moral admonitions. As suggested earlier, they are essentially adramatic. A given character will represent different qualities in different scenes. For example, in 2.2, when Davus has concluded that Simo's proposed wedding is a fiction, he reveals "the prudence of a servant in the service of his master";[25] in 2.3, where he persuades Pamphilus to agree to his father's request, he shows us that "servants prevail not by wisdom but by roguery";[26] in 3.2, after Davus, to save his skin, has confirmed Simo's suspicion that Mysis's

---

24. Even more explicit is Chremes' confrontation with Simo in 5.1. Latomus writes: "This scene, is as it were, a legal case: for indeed Simo is the party accused of injustice in the action. He refutes as false what Chremes has proposed through the *status coniecturalis*, arguing that Pamphilus is neither in love, nor has he had a son. And the origin of the dispute is brought forth, when the courtesan is declared to be thoroughly determined to disrupt the nuptials" (*Triple Terence*, p. 169).

25. Hic in Davo est pro hero prudentia servilis. . . . (*ibid.*, p. 84).

26. Servi non sapientia sed malitia vincunt (*ibid.*, p. 90).

praise of Pamphilus and Glycerium's labor pains are a hoax, we learn that "in Davus is the maxim, 'Who is once bad, may be presumed always to be bad.' "[27] What the *theses* do is draw attention to the general principle figured forth in a specific character at a given moment, thus negotiating between the particulars of the action and their underlying meaning, just as Sidney's narrator indicates the significance of his exempla.[28] Implicit in this activity, however—and therefore in the two modes of criticism as well—is a tug of war between the principles of generalization and particularization which becomes apparent when the commentators attempt to reduce whole scenes to *theses*.

One amusing example is found early in the play. 1.4 is described as a scene that is chiefly transitional, functioning for the *oeconomia* of the plot. Here Mysis is on her way to summon the midwife (the following scene is the one in which she exacts Pamphilus's promise to remain faithful to Glycerium) and she delivers this speech:

> I hear, Archilis, I hear: Your orders are to fetch Lesbia. On my word, she's a drunken, reckless creature, not at all a fit person to take charge of a woman in her first labor; am I to fetch her all the same? Just look at the old hag's obstinacy, and all because they're pot companions. Oh heaven, grant my lady a safe delivery, and if the midwife must bungle let it be with others. (228–233)

From this monologue, Willichius draws the following *ethicae*:

1. Deservedly are young women concerned about midwives.
2. In undertaking serious affairs, rashness and drunkenness should not be present.[29]

The most obvious loss is the impromptu tone of the speech, and therefore its status as thought. But also missing is the fussiness of the middle-aged servant, her sense of harrassment, the bustle of the action—in other words,

27. In Davo est γνώμη, Qui semel malus, semper praesumitur malus (*ibid.*, p. 108).

28. Note the ablative construction used in these descriptions (nn. 21, 22, 25, 27). Cf. Sidney's terminology, Ch. III, n. 41.

29. Merito sunt de obstetricibus mulierculae sollicitae. In rebus seriis gerundis, temeritas & ebrietas absint (*ibid.*, pp. 63–64).

the all-important context, which is not even hinted at in the *ethicae*. Similarly, in 4.1, after Charinus bewails the apparent treachery of Pamphilus, complaining that his friend has achieved happiness at his expense, we are told that "They are unjust who join their advantage to the disadvantages of others," and "They are faithless who violate oaths and are forgetful of promises."[30] It matters not in the least that Charinus's accusation is untrue; in formulating the charge he has offered sententious wisdom, and it is this that the moral critic chooses to extract and represent as what we may "learn" from the encounter.

Thus the *moralitas* of Terentian criticism tends to move in a direction contrary to that of the rhetorical criticism. The rhetorical commentary is concerned with particulars—the *oeconomia* of the plot, the ironies of speech in view of past and future events, the necessity for all scenes to relate to the *status*, the invention of proofs, and the subtleties of argumentation and judgment. By contrast, the moral commentary is generalizing and reductive. The fact is, anyone studying Terence through the commentators saw two different things. On the one hand, there was an ongoing debate in which amusing individuals attempted to prove *their* theses (in dramatic terms, to achieve their goals) by inventing arguments and rebutting those of their opponents until the debate was resolved in a way that compromised the principles of neither party. On the other hand, readers found bits of sententious wisdom that rooted the scenes of Terence in conventional moral experience. That both approaches coexist without any apparent awareness of conflict not only testifies to the humanists' faith in the compatibility of sophistic rhetoric and Christian ethics, but also reflects the pedagogue's determination to find "meaning" in fiction— to ground "rhetoric" in "philosophy." This practice will be reflected in the continual reversion to thesis in otherwise nondidactic English plays.

Of particular interest is the *manner* in which the problems of the main characters are resolved. Despite the feverish succession of *consilia* on both sides, involving arguments from contraries, signs, impossibilities, and their companion *topoi*, in nearly all the plays the instrument of denouement is a form of inartificial proof—the foreign witnesses Crito and Chremes in the *Andria* and *Eunuchus*, the nurse Sophrona in *Phormio*, and

30. Iniurii sunt, qui sua commoda ex aliorum incommodis comparant. Perfidi sunt, qui fidem violant, & promissorum immemores sunt (*ibid.*, p. 134).

the ring tokens in *Hecyra* and *Heautontimorumenos*.[31] Traditionally, the use of inartificial testimony is regarded with some scorn by the rhetoricians, because it does not require the orator to search out his own wit in proving his case.[32] The persistent reappearance of this device in the denouement of Terentian comedy, therefore, has the effect of suggesting the *limitations* of rhetoric. The characters who are pitted against one another cannot satisfactorily resolve their mutual problems because they have not been vouchsafed the totality of vision required to perceive all the strands in the knot of errors. Their powers of reasoning are limited to the world of probability; no matter how many ideas they invent to master their situation they are restricted by the epistemological boundaries of their condition and cannot rise above it to see themselves as they really are. It takes some transcendent force—in rhetorical terms, outside testimony; in ontological terms, providential wisdom or fortune—to lay open the truth, whereby the "outcome is proved acceptable." And the truth is that no contention really exists, *sub specie aeternitatis*. For at the heart of things are unsuspected relationships that reason has not even considered. A father discovers that the woman who seemed to stand in the way of the profitable match he had been seeking is his own daughter; a husband learns that the unchaste wife he refuses to acknowledge is the girl he himself had seduced. The implications are disquieting. The joyful celebration of *dianoia* turns out to be also a humble acknowledgement of its ultimate inadequacy. And the final vision, while comic, implies that the desired unity of opposites that is achieved in the perception of relationship—the reconciliation of fathers and sons, the acquisition of both love and money —is a consummation not usually attainable by ordinary human means.

This underlying strain was noted and further cultivated by the English

31. The possible exception is the *Adelphoe*, in which Dromo inadvertently reveals that Ctesipho, not Aeschinus, is enjoying the lute girl.

32. "Of the modes of persuasion some belong strictly to the art of rhetoric and some do not. By the latter I mean such things as are not supplied by the speaker, but are there at the outset—witnesses, evidence given under torture, written contracts, and so on. By the former I mean such as we ourselves construct by means of the principles of rhetoric. The one kind has merely to be used, the other has to be invented" (Aristotle, *Rhet.* 1355b, *The Basic Works*, ed. Richard McKeon [New York, 1941]). In *Poet.* 1454b, (trans. Ingram Bywater, *ibid.*,) Aristotle speaks of the tragic denouement that is effected by signs and tokens—"of which the poets make most use through mere lack of invention"—as the least artistic.

imitators of Latin comedy in the later sixteenth century, achieving perhaps its most moving expression in the early Shakespeare. At the same time, a counter-movement began to develop—naturalizing the transcendent element and thus exalting the power of wit to resolve its own problems. It appears in its most cynical light in Chapman, at its most humane in Ben Jonson.

Inventing Answers in
English Comedy

THE ENGLISH COMEDIES BORN FROM THE LATIN—AND WITH THE PLAYS of Terence we must also include those of Plautus, whose work was analyzed in similar fashion[1]—indicate how unstable was the equilibrium of *moralitas* and wit established by the commentators. In a sense, their great work was itself an extended argument *in utramque partem*. Just as Castiglione's *Courtier* modulated between thesis and hypothesis in order to explore its subject matter as fully as possible, so the commentaries attempted to understand the various ways in which Terence might be an *imitatio vitae*. And even as *The Courtier* was subsequently plundered for doctrine in the courtesy books, so, too, did the Terentian commentaries become all things to all playwrights.

One kind of response is represented by such plays as John Palsgrave's translation of the neo-Latin *Acolastus* (1540), the anonymous *Nice Wanton* (1550), Thomas Engelend's *Disobedient Child* (1560), and the English school play *Misogonus* (1570). These are didactic prodigal son dramas in which such Latin themes as the conflict of youth and age, the contrast in types of young men and servants, and competing methods of education have hardened into moralistic exempla. The opposing sides in the ongoing debate are rigidly dichotomized and the rhetorical devices of Terence assimilated to the spirit of the morality play. *Misogonus* self-con-

1. T. W. Baldwin, *William Shakspere's Five-Act Structure* (Urbana, Ill., 1947), pp. 190–197.

148

sciously offers Terence recollected in the light of the morality. It opens with an apologetic prologue:

> If any ask then why I decke my temples thus with bayse or why this
> garlande her I ware not being Laureat forsooth I come in Homers
> hewe, our historye forth to blase. A[s] custome is & ever was—
> well marke therof the state. . . . (17–20)[2]

The "state" he refers to is, of course, the *status* or issue of contention in the play. But in this curious conflation of the *Adelphoe* and the prodigal son story it is difficult to see what the "state" is, unless it is simply the basic conflict of pious, indulgent father and reprobate son. The author's use of the term suggests that he considered a *status* essential to a legitimate Latinate comedy even though he shows no sensitivity to the dialectical spirit behind it and the way it was traditionally resolved.

Lying in a more liberal area between *moralitas* and wit is Nicholas Udall's *Roister Doister* (1552). This play draws its materials from Terence's *Eunuchus* and Plautus's *Miles Gloriosus*, but suffers a sea change in the course of adaptation. In the Latin comedies the blustering soldier is the antagonist in a story of young love, and it is with the efforts of the lovers to outwit him that we are chiefly concerned. In *Roister Doister*, this figure moves into the foreground to assume the ambiguous role of romantic protagonist comically exploited by the man supposed to be helping him, and so it is his ludicrous wooing of the dignified Christian Custance that chiefly engages our attention.

The reason is not far to seek. In his introduction to the *Eunuchus*, Melanchthon warns:

> Now there is no walk of life where you will not find many Thrasos.
> Nor are there any more pernicious in human affairs than this sort if
> he finds the opportunity to command. Therefore the image of Thra-
> so in this comedy should be studied and contemplated so that you
> may say how absurd these types are, what worthless busybodies. . . .[3]

2. R. W. Bond, *Early Plays from the Italian* (Oxford, 1911), p. 174. For discussion of education drama, see pp. xciii–cix; also F. S. Boas, *University Drama in the Tudor Age* (Oxford, 1914).

3. Nullum autem vitae genus est ubi non plurimum Thrasonum reperias: neque ulli fere rebus humanis perniciosiores sunt, quam id genus, si contingat imperare.

Thus, following the moral commentary, Udall has done Terence one better, bringing the braggart forward as an object of ridicule.[4] The result is a comedy which, while it offers an entertaining object lesson (a desideratum from a schoolmaster's point of view), suffers in consequence a loss of dramatic tension. There are *consilia* aplenty as Mathew Merrygreke counsels Roister Doister in his wooing,[5] but to all of Ralph's enacted "proofs"—serenades, letter, token, Petrarchan wooing, and pretended indifference—Dame Christian simply says no. For Ralph is a grotesque among more realistic comic figures and cannot be taken seriously.

The legal cast of Terentian comedy remains, however, though it is turned to novel use. In Terence's play the major peril is Thraso's according to Melanchthon, because his affair with Thais is threatened by his rival, young Phaedria. Translated into Udall's terms, the *status* therefore is whether Roister Doister or Gawain Goodluck shall wed Christian Custance. The focus changes in the fourth act, however, because of Udall's stronger moral concern. Christian's credit with the returning Gawain has been called into question by Roister Doister's persistent courtship. As Ralph prepares to assault her house—having failed at every other means of persuasion—Dame Custance sends for Tristram Trusty, a town officer. "What is your *cause*?" he asks, and she explains the danger to which she has been exposed by Ralph's importunities:

> Wherefore, I beseech you, with me to be a *witnesse*,
> That in all my lyfe I never intended thing lesse.

... Quare diligenter est intuenda, contemplandaque Thrasonis imago in hac fabula, ut dicas, quam sint inepti, quam nihili ardeliones isti ... (Terentius, in quem triplex edita est P. Antesignani Rapistagnensis commentatio [Lyons, 1560], p. 203).

4. Cf. his own prologue:

> Our comedie, or enterlude, which we intende to play
> In named "Roister Doister," in-deede,
> Which against the vayne-glorious doth invey,
> Whose humour the roysting sort continually doth feede.

(J.Q. Adams, ed., *Chief Pre-Shakespearean Dramas* [Cambridge, Mass., 1924], Prol. 22–25.) All citations refer to this edition.

5. The words "counsel" and "counselor" occur frequently enough to suggest Udall's familiarity with Melanchthon's definition.

And what a brainsicke foole Ralph Roister Doister is
Your-selfe know well enough.

(4.5.43–46)

When Ralph appears for battle, Trusty tries to ascertain *his* cause:

TRUSTY: Is hir *offence* so sore?
MATHEW: And he were a loute, she could have done no
more.
She hath calde him foole, and dressed him like a foole,
Mocked hym lyke a foole, used him like a foole.
TRUSTY: Well, yet the sheriffe, the justice, or constable,
Hir *misdemeanour* to punishe might be able.
RALPH: No, sir! I mine owne selfe will in this present
cause
Be sheriffe, and justice, and whole judge of the lawes.

(4.7.82–89)

When Trusty fails to persuade Roister Doister to take the law, the great
kitchen battle ensues, and of course Christian and her knightesses beat
back the cowardly aggressors. Then she turns to Tristram:

CHRISTIAN: Friend Tristram, I pray you, be a *witnesse*
with me.
TRUSTY: Dame Custance, I shall *depose* for your hon-
estie.

(4.8.58–59)[6]

Thus the Thrasonic battle that settles the original conjectural *status* becomes a qualitative proof—a demonstration of Christian's honesty before an outside witness who will testify in her behalf. With this testimony,
Christian Custance clinches her case with Gawain Goodluck.[7]

The *status* is not fully resolved, however, until the last act. In Terence's
play the braggart, though defeated, is invited to share Thais's favors with
Phaedria for the very practical reason that he can keep her in her accustomed style and the young man cannot. Lacking Terence's wry means of

6. I have emphasized the legal terms in which Udall couches the incident.
"Cause" is the English equivalent of *causa*, the common term for law case.

7. Here Udall may have picked up a hint from Terence's own text. In the
Eunuchus, the newly discovered brother of Thais's slave girl attempts rather timo-
rously to secure *advocatos* at the time of the battle (764).

accommodation, Udall concludes his play in precisely the way we might have anticipated. Roister Doister reenters the social order because Christian Custance submits to Gawain's demand for Christian forgiveness. Though there is much twitting when he returns, this is the message behind their final exchange:

> GAWAIN: I pray you, sweete Custance, let him to us
> resort.
> CHRISTIAN: To your will I assent.
>
> (5.5.18–19)

It is a rather slack resolution, compared to the irony of the original, but in context quite appropriate. In the end, it is *moralitas*, not wit, that triumphs.

Many English comedies, however, more strongly reveal both the form and spirit of argument *in utramque partem*, as it is manifested in Terence's plays. These share a common interest in observing the mind at work—inventing, planning, moving toward a solution—rather than in the enunciation of moral doctrine—though in the better plays, as in Terence, moral considerations always underlie the action. In this, they reflect the need of rhetoric itself to remain rooted in broad human concerns lest it become an empty (and dangerous) exercise of wit.[8]

The most delightful of these early plays is *Gammer Gurton's Needle* (1553). A marvel of intrigue structure, it adumbrates several of the concerns we have already observed in the Latin tradition. Since it is a university play, its author was certain to be familiar with the Terentian commentaries, and a more apt translation into English terms of Donatus's formulation of comedy as a series of plots and errors would be hard to find. The play is constructed around the question "Who's got the needle?", and Diccon the Bedlam orchestrates the search into a series of confrontations between town and country that begins with a conjuration

8. This was a possibility of which the rhetoricians themselves were acutely aware. "Wisdom without eloquence does little for the good of states," Cicero writes; "eloquence without wisdom is generally highly disadvantageous and is never helpful." Indeed, the orator who simply cultivates technique acquires "something useless to himself and harmful to his country" (*De inv.* I.1). It was for this reason that rhetoricians insisted upon their right to discuss general questions, resisting the attempts of philosophers to confine the discipline to legalistic argument and occasional oratory.

and ends with a formal legal inquiry. Gammer Gurton has lost her most precious possession—her "neele"—and no one knows where to find it. Having learned of this domestic casualty (charmingly conceived as heroic), Diccon insinuates himself into the situation. He tells Dame Chat, proprietress of the local tavern, that Gammer Gurton has accused her of stealing her fair red cock. Enraged by the charge, Dame Chat eagerly prepares to face down her accuser, but Diccon advises watchful waiting instead. Then he tells Gammer Gurton that Dame Chat found her needle and took it home with her. Off goes Gammer. After she and her man Hodge come off the worse in a violent battle with the tavern keeper, the heroic lady decides to call in the curate, Doctor Rat, to settle the issue. But now Diccon refuses to swear that Dame Chat stole the needle—for politic reasons, he assures them—and promises to supply a better proof. On this pretext he goes off to visit Dame Chat. He warns her to guard the hole in her wall because Hodge is planning to come through it and steal her chickens in revenge. Then, returning blithely to the curate, he informs him that he has just seen Chat sewing with Gammer's needle. "O Diccon, that I was not there then in they steade!" laments Doctor Rat (4.4.23). Whereupon Diccon tells him he can see for himself if he just creeps into that little hole in Dame Chat's wall. . . .

The pattern is one of beautiful and self-sustaining symmetry. Diccon sets up two adversaries and they go to their confrontation. The defeated side then brings in a third party to judge the dispute. He then becomes an adversary in a new confrontation. When he, too, is victimized, he calls in a fourth party to settle his dispute. Thus a complex knot of errors has been woven in the manner of the classical epitasis, and virtually all of Act 5 is devoted to de-knotting these mistaken assumptions in the time-honored fashion: through a trial presided over by the Bailly, the Crito of this piece.

The scene is a funny parody of what must have frequently gone on in Tudor litigation. The *status* is conjectural. Doctor Rat, suffering from contusions acquired while breaking into Chat's house, accuses Dame Chat of attempted murder. Dame Chat denies the charge flatly, claiming that she has not even seen the curate in seven weeks—he has been too busy with his minions, she adds spitefully. He offers his wounded head in evidence. She insists rightfully that it does not prove it was she who hit him. The Bailly then attempts to fix the time of the alleged injury: two hours since. Someone did try to enter at that time, Chat admits, but it was not Rat. Who? asks the Bailly. Rat cries out in despair:

> Alas! sir, aske you that?
> Is it not made plain inough by the owne mouth of
>   Dame Chat?
> The time agreeth, my head is broken, her tong can
>   not lye;
> Onely upon a bare nay she saith it was not I.
>   (5.2.39–42)[9]

His argument via the topics of conjecture forces Chat to reveal that she had beaten Hodge while he was trying to steal her chickens. The Bailly is filled with indignation:

> Call me the knave hether. He shal sure kysse the
>   stockes.
> I shall teach him a lesson for filching hens or cocks.
>   (54–55)

The case is altered, quoth Plowden, and the Bailly is now off pursuing a new charge, much to the curate's despair. Hodge, of course, denies the accusation, displaying his unharmed head in evidence, and, furious that Dame Chat has impugned his honesty, accuses her of stealing Gammer's "wisshimacal." Whereupon Gammer enters a third charge into the proceedings, that of needle theft. Chat is newly outraged:

> Thy nedle, old witch? How so? It were almes thy scul
>   to knock!
> So didst thou say the other day that I had stolne thy
>   cock,
> And rosted him to my breakfast—which shal not be
>   forgotten.   (126–128)

The poor Bailly is now totally confused. He tries hard to bring the dispute to an issue:

> BAILLY: This is the case: you lost your nedle about the
>   dores,

9. Citations refer to Adams.

> And she answeres againe she hase no cocke of yours;
> Thus, in you[r] talke and action, from that you do in-
>   tend [accuse]
> She is whole five mile wide from that she doth defend.
> Will you saie she hath your cocke?
> GAMMER: No, mary, sir, that chil not!
> BAILLY: Will you confesse her neele?
> CHAT: Will I? no, sir, will I not!
> BAILLY: [with a sigh] Then there lieth all the matter.
>   (5.2.156–162)

Without agreeing on the accusation, they cannot join on an issue. After further questioning, however, it becomes apparent that all their errors arise from the same source—Diccon—who is arraigned by the Bailly and confesses his lies. The Bailly, wishing to end this comedy of errors on a mirthful note, mitigates the punishment demanded by Rat and sentences Diccon to take an oath on Hodge's leather breech. Diccon accomplishes this with a "good blow on the buttock" that produces a sharp pain for Hodge and, of course, discovers the needle, which has been lodged there all the time. Thus Diccon emerges the hero, for "springing the game."

But "hero" does not adequately express his larger symbolic function in the play. A conflation of two familiar literary figures, the Vice and the Fool—with perhaps a touch of the Parasite added—he exercises a pervasive influence upon the goings-on of the other characters that probably stems from his morality origins.[10] In the morally neutral atmosphere of *Gammer Gurton's Needle*, the "viciousness" of the morality Vice—who recognizes no decorum, no self-limitation (hence his evil)—becomes secularized as the folly of Diccon the Bedlam, who exists day by day without plan or direction:

> Now were he a wyse man by cunnynge cold defyne
> Which way my journey lyeth, or where Dyccon will
>   dyne,
> But one good turne I have: be it by nyght, or daye,

10. On his relations to the Vice, see Bernard Spivack, *Shakespeare and the Allegory of Evil* (New York, 1958), pp. 322–327.

South, east, north, or west, I am never out of my
waye.   (2.1.7-10)[11]

Since Diccon is the manipulating force in the play, the plot, so to speak,
is an actualization of his mind. He insinuates ideas into the other characters, and motivated by his folly they launch their misconceived attempts to find the needle. Thus the action is a mimesis of human beings
released from the world of reasonable limits into a world of pure delusion, personified and called into being by the Bedlam. In this it is a re-
creation *ad absurdum* of the subjective world of Latin comedy.

The epistemological predicament is given dramatic emphasis by the
fact that much of the action takes place in the dark. In 1.4, a great deal
of time is devoted to the problem of obtaining a light with which to look
for the lost needle. Gammer orders her boy Cock to light an inch of tal-
low from the fireplace, but there is not enough fire to do even this. In
the following scene, the pursuit of light leads Hodge on a merry chase
after Gib the black cat, whose eyes, he believes, are sparks that he can
blow into flame. The attempt finally ends in hopelessness:

Our candle is at an ende: let us all in quight,
And come another tyme, when we have more
lyght!   (1.5.56-57)

The metaphor of darkness is developed even more fully in Doctor Rat's
invasion of Chat's house, where he suffers contusions because he is mistaken for a thief:

RAT: I am no theefe sir, but an honest, learned clarke.
BAILLY: Yea, but who knoweth that when he meets you
        in the darke.
I am sure your learning shines not out at your nose
. . . .
RAT: [showing his head] Is not this evill ynough, I
        pray you, as you thinke?
BAILLY: Yea, but a man in the darke, if chaunces do
        wincke,

11. Cf. the characterization of Folly in Erasmus, and the fool in *Antonio's Revenge*, Ch. IX, p. 298.

As soone he smites his father, as any other man,
Because for lacke of light discerne him he ne can.

(5.1.14–17, 21–24)

In the context of Terentian comedy, this statement has added resonance. There, as we have seen, nonrecognition of relationship—suggesting the submergence of natural feeling—is a prominent feature. Now both literally and actually "in the dark," neighbors do not recognize one another.

Gammer Gurton's Needle is thus a play about the folly of *consilia*. If it contains any message, it is this, for it delights in the intricate mental engineering that goes into the weaving of pointless schemes, the predicaments of self-deceiving victims deluded by false suppositions, and the frustrated attempt of the judge to de-knot the perplexed action through rational procedures. There is a certain madness in Gammer Gurton reviling Dame Chat for the theft of a needle, while Dame Chat is defending herself against the charge of chicken-stealing. It is only the madness of ignorance, but somehow it epitomizes the condition of mystery which these comedies of error assert is man's usual mode of existence. Diccon makes this explicit when he is arraigned before the Bailly for having duped Doctor Rat:

God's bread! hath not such an olde foole wit to save
  his eares?
He showeth himselfe herein, ye see, so very a coxe,
The cat was not so madly alured by the foxe
To run into the snares set for him, doubtlesse;
For he leapt in for myce, and this sir John for madnes.

(5.2.229–233)

Against the force of such delusion, ordinary prudence—let alone jurisprudence—can hardly function. Only with great difficulty does the Bailly unravel the tangle of accusation and counter-accusation with which he is presented. And significantly, his powers of ratiocination avail not at all in the task of finding the needle. Only his act of good will, as Diccon thumps Hodge on the backside, answers the original question.

Direct evidence of this interest in subjective rationalization as a matter for mimesis is offered by the 1575 edition of Gascoigne's *Supposes* (1566). Here, whether at the author's instigation or the printer's, we find twenty-five marginal comments on the plots and errors of the play.[12] All are sub-instances of the title itself, which is glossed in Gascoigne's prologue:

> But understand, this our Suppose is nothing else but a mystaking or imagination of one thing for another. For you shall see the master supposed for the servant, the servant for the master: the freeman for a slave, and the bondslave for a freeman: the stranger for a well knowen friend, and the familiar for a stranger.[13]

Thus the term "supposes" seems to signify errors relating to mistaken identity. As one goes on to examine the glosses, however, it becomes clear that it is better translated as "conjectures," or even "theses," since it is applied not only to beliefs about people, but also more generally to a given character's assessment of his situation. In this light, the play looks more like an imitation of intellectual management and mismanagement —precisely that mimesis of *dianoia* we have seen in Terence.

The play opens with a *consultatio* between the heroine Polynesta and her nurse Balia, which serves as the narration of the argument. Polynesta explains that the servant Dulipo, with whom she is having a love affair, is really a Sicilian gentleman named Erostrato, and that the Erostrato who comes to court her is really his servant Dulipo, whose suit has been devised to keep her father from marrying her to the old advocate Clean-der. The speech is glossed "The first suppose and grownd of all the sup-poses" (p. 5)—that is, the fundamental error. In the following scene, Cleander, the rival suitor, reveals to his parasite that he lost his only son many years ago at the siege of Otranto: "An other suppose," for the son will turn out to be in Ferrara under his very nose. The third scene por-trays the anxiety of the young lover, and reveals the *status* of the play: Polynesta's father Damon is losing interest in the suit of the false Erostrato since his family is unknown, and is about to accept Cleander's offer; how, therefore, may the real Erostrato prevent this marriage without reveal-ing his true identity, thereby antagonizing his father, who thinks he is pursuing the life of a student in Ferrara?

But there is a *consilium* afoot. In the second act we learn that his servant has persuaded a Sienese traveler to pose as Erostrato's father Philogano,

---

12. These are not in Ariosto's originals, nor in the undated first edition.

13. Bond, *Early Plays*, p. 12. All subsequent line references are to this edition.

on the pretext that the Ferrarese are confiscating the goods of all Sienese who enter the city. When shortly afterward we meet this gentleman, he is puzzled at the strange turn of events:

He that travaileth in the worlde passeth by many perilles.

To which his servant replies:

You say true, sir, if the boate had bene a little more laden this morning at the ferrie, we had bene all drowned, for I thinke, there are none of us that could have swomme.

The Sienese snaps:

I speake not of that. (2.2.1–5)

The servant's reply, quoted above, is glossed "An other suppose," indicating that verbal misconstruction is one form of erroneous affirmation depicted in the play. A different form follows immediately—character assessment. The Sienese reflects:

God reward the gentle yong man that we mette, for else we had bene in a wise case by this time. (2.2.14–15)

Which is glossed, uncharitably, "A doltish suppose."

These glosses appear throughout the text as casual observations pointing up a variety of misapprehensions. When in Act 3 Polynesta's father discovers her affair with the supposed servant Dulipo, he sends his man Nevola to secure a pair of fetters from the jailor. Nevola sagaciously wags his head over Dulipo's evident turn of fortune:

Fye upon the Devill, it is a thing almost unpossible for a man nowe a dayes to handle money, but the mettal will sticke on his fingers: I marvelled alway at this fellowe of mine Dulipo, that of the wages he received he could maintaine himselfe so bravely apparelled, but nowe I perceive the cause, he had the disbursing and receit of all my masters affaires. . . . (3.4.10–16)

"An other suppose." For, of course, "Dulipo" is not being imprisoned for stealing money at all.

In Act 4, the real Philogano turns up in Ferrara and goes to the house of the purported Erostrato. He is refused admittance because, he is told, Erostrato is inside entertaining his father, one Philogano from Cathanea in Sicily. He is bewildered at this palpable impossibility, but his servant Litio offers some help in the matter:

> I cannot tell you what I shoulde say sir, the worlde is large and long, there maye be moe Philoganos and moe Erostratos than one, yea and moe Ferraras, moe Sicilias, and moe Cathaneas: peradventure this is not that Ferrara whiche you sent your sonne unto. (4.4.43-46)

"Another suppose," perhaps the maddest of them all. Elsewhere we find "A shameless suppose," "A needlese suppose," "A shrewd suppose," "A pleasant suppose," all indicating misconceptions of one kind or another. On the other hand, toward the end of the play, these conjectures begin to resemble truth, and are labelled "A gentle suppose," "A crafty suppose," "A right suppose." These labels themselves suggest the rhythm of the plot as it progresses from the darkness of entanglement to enlightened denouement.

As in many of the Terentian models, the original controversy ultimately dissolves. Once again a legal consultation is the medium of resolution. Philogano, convinced by Dulipo's refusal to acknowledge him that his own son has met foul play, engages Cleander as his counsel. He offers to send to Sicily for witnesses of his identity, and then, to fill in the picture for the advocate, he tells how Dulipo came to be his servant. It is through this narrative of fact that Cleander discovers Dulipo is his lost son, and having recovered his heir, he no longer desires to marry. Philogano, on his part, is anxious to make amends to Damon for his daughter's injury, and offers his lands in dower to Polynesta. Thus Erostrato gets his girl, Damon his match, Cleander his issue, and everyone is accommodated in the traditional Terentian fashion.

But in an important way, this ending is different from the expected judicial resolution. Near the conclusion of the play, Cleander remarks to Philogano:

> And you Philogano, *may thinke*, that god in heaven above, hath ordained your coming hither at this present, to the end I might recover my lost sonne, whom by no other means I could ever have found out.

To which Philogano replies:

Surely I *think* no less, for I *think* that not so much as a leafe falleth from the tree, without the ordinance of God.

(5.8.9–15, emphases mine)

In one sense, the exchange is simply another instance of that mimesis of *dianoia* which comedy presents—in this case the effort of two old men to place their experience in a context they can understand. But in a play that traces a curve of such suppositions from the false to the true, the implication is that these are "right supposes." The fathers are acknowledging that the rational procedure available to them—legal consultation— was rendered effective only by the aid of divine providence. In so doing, they place in proper perspective the frantic and often erroneous *consilia* that inform the action, confessing their inability to penetrate beyond the world of probability and their dependence upon a beneficent God to reveal the truth. It is the very gesture we might expect in the Ciceronian tradition of argument *in utramque partem*, and an appropriate thesis upon which to end the play.

II

Other imitations of Latin comedy in England to the time of Shakespeare reflect the same interest in the invention of ideas and the management of a cause through wit. The tendency in this period is to create more complicated plots, which become triumphs of intellectual juggling. One early effort, *July and Julian* (1560?),[14] was apparently written for young schoolboys, to be presented following the learned exercises of their elders. It is an original English comedy filled with intrigue and *ethicae* in classical balance. July is a young man secretly in love with Julian, his mother's gentlewoman in waiting. The action concerns his attempt to woo and marry her, aided by his servant Wilkin, who is an endless source of clever *consilia*. Just as their plot seems to be bearing fruit, a Brabant merchant claims Julian (an anachronistic reminder of her courtesan origins) and, paying 300 marks for the girl, leads her off to captivity. Once again a device is invented, this time for liberating the girl and getting back the money:

14. Although Harbage gives 1570 as the date of this play, the editor of the Malone Society edition (Malone Society Reprints, Oxford, 1955) offers evidence that suggests it may have been written as early as 1559. Citations are to this edition.

> yt is hard, but I dispeare not, if thou wilt do thi dili-
> gence.
> but we shall nycke the marchaunt man with sume
> pretence.   (722–723)

When their scheme succeeds, the conspirators ply Chremes, July's father, with drink, and disguise Julian as a rich heiress. Always on the lookout for a profitable match, Chremes insists his son propose to her, and thus July and Julian are betrothed. So pleased is the old man with this bit of good fortune that he promises to grant whatever petitions are presented to him. The servants request their freedom and July asks pardon for past misdeeds. This granted, he reveals the identity of his bride,

> whom by honest crafte
> I won to my wife and the merchant hath leaste
> With owt any distaynyne of your honestye.
>   (1229–1231)

Chremes is not only forgiving but intrigued by the whole plot:

> Come all in and tell me who labered the best
> to morowe ys the marriage lett them come to the
> fest.   (1243–1244)

Here, in a very early Terentian imitation, we find not only the repeated emphasis on counsel and devices that we have noted in the originals, but also the emergence of rational wit as a positive value. Chremes hints of Judge Clement and Lovewit to come.

   The Bugbears (1564), an adaptation of Antonfrancesco Grazzini's *La Spiritata*, portrays the fortunes of two sets of lovers and the elaborate apparatus of deception employed to bring about their happiness. Formosus has been secretly married to Rosimunda for one year and now she is pregnant. He sues for her hand in marriage, but his own father, a miser named Amadeus, demands 3,000 crowns in dowry, which the girl's father cannot afford. Meanwhile, Cantalupo, a venereal old man, is so madly in love with Rosimunda himself that he offers his own daughter Iphigenia to Amadeus with 3,000 crowns, just to get rid of Formosus as a rival. Although Iphigenia is in love with another man named Manutius, the bargain is accepted.

The *status* of the play is clear: Formosus must confess his first marriage because he cannot marry two women, but if he does, he will lose his father's love and his inheritance. How can he keep his wife and his patrimony? The *consilium* devised by the servant Biondello is simplicity itself. They will arrange for Rosimunda's uncle Donatus to offer 3,000 crowns as her dowry. These will be obtained from Amadeus's own coffer. To accomplish this they will pretend the house is haunted by ghosts, which will drive the old miser away, and while he is gone the "ghosts" will steal the money, to be re-presented to him later by Donatus. The plot works smoothly, indeed too smoothly. It is Terence slicked up, for it contains none of the overcalculation and subsequent minor crises that are among the joys of the Roman plays. Like these ancient models, however, it is a play about counsel. Not only does Formosus seek counsel, but more interestingly, Amadeus, plagued by the ghosts in his house, does so too. His friend Cantalupo is too hotly in love to be of any help, and his confessor is of no more use when he tells him the spirits are God's punishment for covetousness. So he turns to the "astronomer" recommended by Formosus, who supplies him with certain charms and, after the robbery, tells him that he lost his money because of his avarice. Here again the playwright is interested in imitating the affirmations we make to explain the things that happen to us; in this case, the explanations are patently false; nonetheless Amadeus believes them, and it is on the basis of this belief that he accommodates himself to the marriage of his son to Rosimunda. Formosus, in turn, can now afford to conform:

I yeld my full consent yf my father say ye. . . . (5.9.72)[15]

Thus both parties find satisfaction. Amadeus retains his dignity and exacts his original demand for the dowry, while Formosus remains obedient son and faithful lover. The *status* that seemed hopelessly insoluble is mastered by the mutual exercise of wit on the part of deceiver and deceived.

Mother Bombie (1589), John Lyly's only Terentian play, demonstrates a third variation of emergent wit comedy. In this play, the taste for complication brings together four fathers, one mother, four servant-schemers, and six lovers. The occasion for the play is really display of the verbal and mental agility of the four boys. Each of the two leading boys, Dromio and Risio, is given the task of arranging a marriage between his master's

15. Bond, *Early Plays.*

child and the child of his friend's master, without disclosing that his master's child is a simpleton. In this way the two fathers, Memphio and Stellio, hope to secure good marriage settlements for their undesirable offspring. All this while, two other fathers, Sperantus and Prisius, are trying to discourage the love affair of their children, in the hope of making a better match, and determine to wed them to the children of Memphio and Stellio. When the boys of all four fathers get together, they go to a tavern *ad deliberandum* and hatch a plot whereby the two fools will marry each other and the young lovers will marry with their fathers' blessings. Thus far the plot elements are resolvable, but not without some unhappiness on the part of the fools' parents. And so a final pair of lovers is introduced in the third act. They are apparently brother and sister, chastely resisting what they believe is an unnatural love. With their appearance, the elements are now present for an idyllic resolution, since they are the real children of Memphio and Stellio.

This resolution is achieved, though, only partly through the wit of the boys. The true lovers are married and accepted by their parents, who rationalize that it is better thus than for their children to be married to fools. With their secret out, even Memphio and Stellio are appeased, each resigned to marry his child to a fool, since no other match is now possible. But then an unexpected intervention occurs. It takes place through the agency of Mother Bombie, a character who sits at the epistemological navel of the play, and whose sole function has been to utter cryptic oracular pronouncements to the lovers and plotters who have sought her aid. "In deed," remarks Memphio, "she is cunning and wise, never doing harm, but still practicing good" (5.3.330).[16] Plainly, she is the figure of beneficent fate or providence whose truth, presented in riddles, is beyond the grasp of those immersed in private intrigue. To only one person does she speak directly, and that is Vicinia, a poor woman who visits her because she is troubled by the rumor of marriages abroad. She is urged to come forward and confess that she had exchanged Stellio and Memphio's children for her own while wetnursing them years ago. The fools are in fact *her* children, and the "incestuous" brother and sister the marriageable heirs of the plotting fathers. The inspired testimony of Vicinia (*peregrinus* denizenized) serves the same function as that

16. *The Complete Works of John Lyly*, ed. R. W. Bond, 3 vols. (Oxford, 1902).

of the Terentian Crito: it lays bare the whole truth, removes all dissatisfaction, and opens the way to the ritual that celebrates the comic fulfillment of desire. And significantly, it is an "inartificial proof"—suggesting, in this highly witty play, that wit is not all.

These dramas are efficient pieces of entertainment, but it is not until the nineties that the implications of intrigue comedy are seriously explored. The three strains we have noticed in *Mother Bombie*, *The Bugbears*, and *July and Julian*—which may be called the providential, cynical, and festive views of human wit—are developed with considerably greater interest in three important works of the decade—Shakespeare's *Comedy of Errors*, Chapman's *All Fools*, and Jonson's *Every Man in His Humour*.

III

The Comedy of Errors differs from the Latinate plays we have been considering in that it contains no motivating intrigue. Shakespeare has provided some of the pressure of intrigue by framing the Plautine story with the plight of Aegeon, doomed to die at sundown, but since neither he nor anyone else is active in his behalf, his presence must be accounted for in another way.[17] Essentially, *The Comedy of Errors* is an extension of the theme we have already encountered in *The Supposes* and which, I have suggested, lies behind the fascination of *Gammer Gurton's Needle*. Gascoigne was concerned to point out the various conjectures his characters made about their situations in the light of imperfect knowledge. Thus an important object of his play was to imitate the intellectual affirmations with which human beings construct a reasonable world for themselves. *The Comedy of Errors* examines this phenomenon in a form so concentrated as to be virtually a symbolic distillation of the theme. For here, *with no attempt at deception*, the plot is a congeries of "supposes" based on appearances that pass for realities. It is a sustained plot only because these conjectures—arising from the single presupposition that there can be only one Antipholus and one Dromio in Ephesus—generate conflict and a subsequent dialectic of action and reaction that substitutes for the plan-counter-plan pattern of normal intrigue comedy.

Shakespeare, therefore, has created a play that has no other object of imitation than the conjectures and affirmations upon which people act.

17. Aegeon's predicament derives from none of the known sources. See R. A. Foakes, ed., The Arden Shakespeare (London, 1962), pp. xiv–xxxiv.

Why? It was his common practice, even in early work, to examine the serious implications of his sources. And it appears from his completed play that the original Donatan concept of comedy arising from a basic error, supplemented by Lambinus's enumeration of errors in the *Menaechmi*,[18] and perhaps Gascoigne's notes, stimulated him to think about the moral significance of error. For here is a play about two young men looking for their twin brothers who cannot recognize their traces when they see them; about a wife who preaches mutuality between lovers, yet jealously catechizes her husband in bed, at board, alone, and in company; a husband who lightly substitutes the companionship of a courtesan for that of his young wife; a spinster, fearful of the "troubles of the marriage bed," who exhorts her sister to wifely obedience. All habitually think of themselves in relation to their fellows, but actually draw a narrow perimeter around themselves that prevents community. In these circumstances, it is little wonder that they err. Their errors, it would seem, are a metaphor for their essential egoism, and the plot is a function of their characters.[19]

In Shakespeare's hands, the Plautine comedy of errors becomes something of an exercise in defining the self: *quid sit?* Each of the major characters contributes toward this definition. Antipholus of Syracuse, the most sympathetic, is perhaps the most self-aware. Even though he is anxious to find his mother and brother, he is frightened at the possible loss of integrity that is threatened by his search:

> I to the world am like a drop of water
> That in the ocean seeks another drop,

18. Lambinus, *Plautus* (1576), cited by Baldwin, pp. 691–694. These may well have been inspired by the enumeration of the "supposes" in Gascoigne's play, printed a year earlier.

19. Willichius etymologizes the name Antipho, which is the apparent source of Shakespeare's Antipholus, as follows: Αντίφων *reluctans & renitens, semper contrarius, ab* ἀντὶ & φάων (*Terence* [1567], cited by Baldwin, p. 696). Baldwin does not believe this is the source, arguing that it derives from *Antiphila*, "one who returns love," but this does not characterize the behavior of the brothers, which is *reluctans* and *renitens*. Geoffrey Bullough suggests the name may, in fact, be taken from the unloving Antiphilus of Sidney's *Arcadia* (*Narrative and Dramatic Sources of Shakespeare* [London, 1957], 1. 9).

Who, falling there to find his fellow forth,
(Unseen, inquisitive) confounds himself.

$$(1.2.35-38)^{20}$$

The immediate occasion for this sentiment is his enforced loss of identity as he is warned by the Ephesian merchant to pretend that he is from Epidamnum because of the present danger to all Syracusans:

This very day a Syracusian merchant
Is apprehended for arrival here,
And, not being able to buy out his life,
According to the statute of the town
Dies ere the weary sun set in the west.

$$(1.2.3-7)$$

Antipholus's response to this news is odd. Though rueful about having to "lose himself," he shows no interest whatever in the fate of his fellow citizen, even when handed the money needed to "buy out his life." It is an early sign of his instinctual insularity. This becomes a recognizable character trait when, after wooing and offering himself to Luciana, he draws back in fear and repents falling in love:

She that doth call me husband, even my soul
Doth for a wife abhor. But her fair sister,
Possess'd with such a gentle sovereign grace,
Of such enchanting presence and discourse,
Hath almost made me traitor to myself;
But, lest myself be guilty to self-wrong,
I'll stop mine ears against the mermaid's song.

$$(3.2.157-163)$$

Ironically, it is just this loss of self that Adriana describes to the puzzled Syracusan as the fulfillment of self:

Ah, do not tear away thyself from me;
For know, my love, as easy mayst thou fall
A drop of water in the breaking gulf,

20. Citations refer to Foakes's edition.

And take unmingled thence that drop again
Without addition or diminishing,
As take from me thyself, and not me too.
                                    (2.2.124–129)

This is a theoretical *positio* in the continuing discourse that is perhaps as insufficient as Antipholus's defensive individualism, for it certainly is not working for Adriana. She is urging this ideal mingling of souls upon a stranger—one whom she takes to be her husband on the basis of sense alone. Her real husband, we soon find out, is a man who would not understand her philosophy anyway. Although different in personality from his more romantic brother—a soldier and man about town—he is like him in his solitude of spirit. This is suggested not only in the neglect of his wife, but in the little debate he conducts with his guest Balthazar on the respective merits of food and conviviality:

> ANTIPHOLUS: You're sad, signior Balthazar; pray God
>   our cheer
>   May answer my good will and your good welcome
>   here.
> BALTHAZAR: I hold your dainties cheap, sir, and your
>   welcome dear.
> ANTIPHOLUS: O signior Balthazar, either at flesh or fish,
>   A table full of welcome makes scarce one dainty dish.
> BALTHAZAR: Good meat, sir, is common; that every
>   churl affords.
> ANTIPHOLUS: And welcome more common, for that's
>   nothing but words.
> BALTHAZAR: Small cheer and great welcome makes a
>   merry feast.
> ANTIPHOLUS: Ay, to a niggardly host and more sparing
>   guest;
>   But though my cates be mean, take them in good
>   part;
>   Better cheer may you have, but not with better heart.
>   (3.1.19–29)

It is a commonplace *disputatiuncula* on spirit vs. matter, but Shakespeare has skillfully used Antipholus's position in the colloquy, as he had Adriana's speech, as an index of his character, which tends to be materialistic and lacking in charity. This is amplified a few moments later when, enraged by his wife's innocent refusal to let him in (Antipholus of Syracuse is dining upstairs), he threatens to break down the door with a crowbar until Balthazar persuades him that to do so might permanently damage his reputation. Balthazar's words and Antipholus's response are significant. After citing the danger to reputation, Balthazar offers an additional argument:

> Once this,—your long experience of her wisdom,
> Her sober virtue, years and modesty,
> Plead on her part some cause to you unknown;
> And doubt not, sir, but she will well excuse
> Why at this time the doors are made against you.
>
> (3.1.89–93)

He is invoking the topics of equity here.[21] Do not get angry just because the door is barred, he advises; consider who she is and what circumstances might justify her action. But Antipholus will have none of this. Instead of patiently going off to the Tiger, as Balthazar suggests, to await an explanation from his wife, he invites his guests to the Porpentine, where the courtesan resides, and presents her with the golden chain intended for Adriana. He is a petty and legalistic man, who sees a wife merely as a mindless instrument of his own comfort.[22]

The fourth position in this discourse on self and other is that of Luciana, the spinster who commends the behavior of Grissel to her fretting sister:

21. Cf. Ch. III, p. 67.

22. Antipholus's legalism reflects that of Ephesus in general. The town is a commercial center, populated by merchants, goldsmiths, and businessmen, and its normal activities consist in trading, manufacturing, issuing loans, and—as this scene suggests—holding business lunches. More importantly, it exists in a *world* of accounts receivable: when its "well-dealing countrymen," unable to buy their way out of Syracuse, are executed by the neighboring city, Ephesus passes a retaliatory law which requires any captured Syracusan to pay 1,000 marks in exchange for his life. This is the context of Aegeon's predicament. Though he explains that he finds himself in it "by nature, not by vile offense" (1.1.34)—because, that is, of the very human need to recover his family, and not through a desire to violate Ephesian law—Duke Solinus remains fixed in his determination to follow the statute to the letter. For quantity, not quality, is the measure of human life in Ephesus, and Aegeon's appeal to the *status qualitatis* fails as does Balthazar's after him. How this standard changes is seen in the denouement.

> There's nothing situate under heaven's eye
> But hath his bound in earth, in sea, in sky.
> The beasts, the fishes, and the winged fowls
> Are their males' subjects, and at their controls;
> Man, more divine, the master of all these,
> Lord of the wide world and wild wat'ry seas,
> Indued with intellectual sense and souls,
> Of more pre-eminence than fish and fowls,
> Are masters to their females and their lords;
> Then let your will attend on their accords.
>
> (2.1.16–25)

This is the reasoned hierarchical view, but it illustrates the reductiveness of argument *a thesi*, for it provides but cold comfort before the particulars of Adriana's experience. It is even more ironic, however, in its relation to Luciana. She is totally unseasoned in matters of domestic relations, and moments later confesses a fear of the marriage bed; though decorously virginal, the confession suggests her own reluctance to undergo precisely the submission she urges upon her sister, and Adriana is quick to challenge her:

> So thou, that has no unkind mate to grieve thee,
> With urging helpless patience would relieve me;
> But if thou live to see like right bereft,
> This fool-begged patience in thee will be left.

Luciana replies:

> Well, I will marry one day, but to try.
>
> (2.1.38–42)

The debate ends unresolved, as do the other positions expressed in the play—which only emphasizes the fact that each character "understands" his situation in his own way and will not be moved to change.

Indeed, no one in the play ever seriously doubts his own presuppositions. This attitude is well expressed in Ephesian Dromio's "Say what you will, sir, but I know what I know" (3.1.11)—for no one ever dreams that what he knows may be an inadequate basis for judgment. The Syracusan Antipholus blames all the day's peculiarities on sorcery. Adriana is convinced that Antipholus is mad. And when Aegeon himself, that dedicated searcher of sons, finally confronts the Antipholus who never saw him and therefore cannot possibly recognize him, does he consider that this might be the son he lost as an infant? He does not. His response is totally egoistic. Assuming that it is the Syracusan Antipholus who denies him, he delivers a lengthy apostrophe to Time, whose ravages must have altered *his* face and *his* voice beyond recognition. It is, in the long line of supposes, perhaps the funniest of them all—final evidence, that in spite of their interest in lost relations, the people gathered at Ephesus tend to look inward, not outward.[23]

As we might expect, no rational investigation yields the truth about the self. Antipholus of Syracuse tries to pursue it on his own, immediately after Adriana and Luciana have mistaken him for his brother:

> What error drives our eyes and ears amiss?
> Until I know this sure uncertainty,
> I'll entertain the offer'd fallacy.
>
> (2.2.180–182)

But first-hand examination only gets him further knotted in error. This epistemological entanglement comes to crisis in the final trial scene. The Duke's position—"Why, what an intricate impeach is this!"—is the predicament of Gammer Gurton's Bailly writ large. He is offered two opposing accounts of the day's events by Adriana and Antipholus of Ephesus, plus witnesses who will support one side in some arguments and the other in some, but neither *in toto*. It is a unique legal proceeding because both parties are, in fact, speaking the truth, yet the whole truth is the sum of their partial statements and can be seen only when Antipholus of Syracuse is led forth from the Priory. It is at this point that so many of the haunting strains that have sounded fitfully through the drama coalesce in an atmosphere of preternatural denouement.

> Am I in earth, in heaven, or hell?
> Sleeping or waking? mad or well-advised?
> Known unto these, and to myself disguised!
>
> (2.2.208–210)

23. Alexander Leggatt has made this point with some force. He argues that not only do the characters not know each other, but they "seem at times to inhabit different worlds, different orders of experience," which is reflected in the stylistic contrasts of their speech (*Shakespeare's Comedy of Love* [London, 1974], pp. 1–19).

Antipholus of Syracuse had asked earlier. Taken literally, the question must be answered in the negative, for he was always in Ephesus, and neither asleep, mad, nor enchanted. But in another sense he was all these, and has undergone transformation, along with the rest of his family. No one actually attributes it to Providence, yet the language of the play insists that something beyond reason has occurred. All during the action, Ephesus has been described as a "fairyland," "a town . . . full of cozenage," where "none but witches do inhabit." Antipholus has feared it as a haven of sin, where the mind is altered and the body deformed by evil spirits, and twice has sought release from its enchantments. When Luciana admonishes him for neglecting her sister, he replies in wonder and new-felt passion:

> Teach me, dear creature, how to think and speak.
> Lay open to my earthy gross conceit,
> Smoth'red in errors, feeble, shallow, weak,
> The folded meaning of your words' deceit.
> Against my soul's pure truth why labour you,
> To make it wander in an unknown field?
> Are you a god? Would you create me new?
> Transform me then, and to your pow'r I'll yield.
>
> (3.2.33–40)

It is both a courtly wooing speech and a real plea for enlightenment, but Luciana is not a goddess, and although she winds about his soul's pure truth the darker strands of her own, she cannot show him how they relate to one another. Again he calls for help when, after a particularly frustrating exchange with the wrong Dromio, he exclaims:

> This fellow is distract, and so am I,
> And here we wander in illusions.
> Some blessed power deliver us from hence!
>
> (4.3.37–39)

His prayer is answered in the fifth act. The port of deliverance is, of course, the Priory, where he had sought sanctuary, and the agent is the Abbess, his mother. Deliverance from sinful illusion turns out to be, as he had hinted unwittingly in his plea to Luciana, deliverance from earthly unconsciousness. More specifically, it is a birth into warm human so-

ciety, as the Abbess suggests when she invites the company to a gossips'
feast:

> Thirty three years have I but gone on travail
> Of you, my sons, and till this present hour
> My heavy burden ne'er delivered.
>
> (5.1.399–401)

Time, which had seemed to be so insistently conducting Aegeon to
death, and the Antipholi only to confusion at the Phoenix, the road, the
mart, and the Courtesan's, has actually been labouring toward this moment of epiphany. "There's a time for all things," Antipholus of Syracuse tells his Dromio, in an unsuspected pun.[24]

It is not surprising that the *cognitio* takes place only after Antipholus
gives up his attempt to decipher the puzzle on his own, throwing himself instead upon the mercies of a divine agency. We have had intimations
of this gesture before, although it has never been so fully dramatized. It
acknowledges the final inability of human wit to extricate itself from the
condition of mystery in which it is implicated, and its need for some transcendent power to reveal the truth. In *The Comedy of Errors*, this condition is seen as a destructive egoism, which makes Antipholus of Syracuse
afraid to stain his "soul's pure truth," his brother harsh and insensitive to
his wife's needs, Adriana jealous and possessive, Luciana fearful of the
submission she extols, and Aegeon blind to the discovery of his long-lost
son. Each is, in fact, to himself disguised.

And this, it would appear, is the larger reason for the presence of
Aegeon and Aemelia in the city. All the elements in the pattern have
been there all along—father, mother, wife, sister, twin sons, twin slaves
—but no one of them has been able to see the pattern until Antipholus
has humbled himself in the sanctuary. Their ignorance is due not simply

24. The scene is a linguistic debouchment, bringing into unity much of the
verbal music we have attended through the action. Aegeon's *travel*, for example,
is now seen to have been *travail* (1.1.130, 139), as were Luciana's romantic attractions *labour* (3.2.37). Pinch's attempt to establish Antipholus of Ephesus "in his
true sense again" (4.4.44) is a rehearsal for the success of the Abbess in bringing
his brother "to his wits again" (5.1.96); and Syracusan Antipholus promises to
make good in reality his dreamlike courtship of Luciana, "if this be not a dream
I see and hear" (5.1.376).

to a lack of omniscience—which is, after all, a common human failing; rather it symbolizes the moral inadequacy of the centripetal lives they all lead. For as each individual's practical understanding increases through the collective testimony of the trial, so also does his concept of self, seen now in all its relations. The result is that he remains himself and yet is also a function of other selves, as Dromio of Ephesus tells his newfound twin:

> Methinks you are my glass, and not my brother:
> I see by you that I am a sweet-faced youth.
>
> (5.1.418–419)

It is in reflection that the self is completed, and it is this totality that finally walks offstage in the new-baptized twins:

> We came into the world like brother and brother;
> And now let's go hand in hand, not one before the
> other. (5.1.425–426)

Self and reflection—subject and object—each walking on his own two feet, not one before the other, seems to be Shakespeare's final suggestion toward a solution of the question of human identity. It is a new relationship, one not perceived earlier, and offers a fine comic image toward which to strive.[25]

If *The Comedy of Errors* gently suggests that error is moral shortcoming, Chapman's *All Fools* (1598) reveals it to be a necessary mode of human accommodation.[26] The play makes explicit what the Terentian com-

25. This discovery of relationship also accounts for Duke Solinus's unexplained act of magnanimity in the last few moments of the play. Up until the "intricate impeach" of Adriana and Ephesian Antipholus, he has insisted that Aegeon fulfill the law by submitting to death or paying 1,000 marks. After the denouement, he abrogates the law by setting Aegeon free without payment of any ransom whatever (5.1.390). His gesture acknowledges that the force of statute law dissolves in the full comprehension of motive and circumstances, and is replaced by the law of equity. For the moment at least, the value system in Ephesus has changed, through the instrument of the *cognitio*, from a quantitative one to a qualitative one.

26. The dating of the play is problematic. Although the quarto appeared in 1605, an entry in Henslowe's *Diary* suggests that it was being composed early in 1598, and its most recent editor argues that it was probably played by the Admiral's Company soon after completion. See Frank Manley's introduction to the Regents Renaissance Drama edition (Lincoln, Neb., 1968), pp. xvii–xviii. All citations refer to this edition.

mentators had always argued—that comedy shows the mind mastering reality by means of *consilia*—but regards the phenomenon with an irony that the commentators had never expressed. Donatus and his successors had emphasized the mistakings, the plots that grew out of them, and the ultimate explication by means of which the final state of affairs was proved acceptable to all parties. Implicit in their commentaries was a fundamental delight in the wit that can, with the best of intentions, become hopelessly entangled and then extricate itself when all chance of happiness seems lost—and admiration for sheer technical achievement, above and beyond the moral quality of the result. We have already encountered an early consequence of this attitude in *The Bugbears*. It is far more explicitly developed in Chapman's play, which celebrates the capacity of wit to fulfill its desire, even at the cost of truth.

The work is an adaptation of Terence's *Heautontimorumenos* and *Adelphoe*. Its *status* is expressly described at the outset by Rinaldo, the chief plotter:

> Alas sir, where can he bestow
> This poor gentlewoman he hath made his wife,
> But his inquisitive father will hear of it?
> (1.1.163–165)

The "he" referred to is the young rake Valerio, who must prevent his rustic father Gostanzo from learning that he has not only turned city gallant but has also taken an unauthorized, undowered wife. This seems to be the traditional dilemma of the young man torn between romantic love and filial duty, but unlike the Terentian predicaments, it contains no moral element. Valerio's problem is not to integrate filial piety and passion but simply to secure his patrimony. He and his friends are essentially brash, unlovable wits pitted against a harsh old fool who fancies himself a cunning machiavel. Thus the *status* is not qualitative—"Should Valerio remain true to his wife or his father?"—but simply conjectural: "How may he have both the girl and the money?" This emphasis on sheer brain power is underscored by the translation of the youth's traditional ally, the scheming servant, into a figure who personifies his function, for Rinaldo is a scholar from Padua, and it is his "learning" that he ostentatiously places at the service of his friend. With the rustic machiavel set against the university wit, the *dianoia* which in the Latin plays was the means of working out the larger issue begins to emerge more clearly as the *subject* of the play: whose wit is superior—scholarly wit or "politic" wit or, later, "jealous" wit?

The play opens with a traditional disputation—a thesis and counter-thesis on the nature of love, argued by contemporary versions of Lover Loved, Lover Not Loved, and Neither Loved Nor Loving. Valerio is the joyful lover, having married Gratiana unbeknownst to his father, while his friend Fortunio is miserable because he cannot get near Bellanora, Valerio's closely guarded sister. Rinaldo himself is a disappointed lover who delivers a lengthy vituperation of love, beauty, and women. This tripartite set piece is used to accomplish the initial exposition of the argument. Rinaldo then devises a scheme whereby both lovers may have safe access to their ladies. He pretends to Valerio's father that Gratiana is not Valerio's wife but his brother Fortunio's, and asks his help in pacifying their father, Marc Antonio, who has not consented to the betrothal. Gostanzo, however, is an inveterate meddler and, instead, persuades Marc Antonio (the Micio of the piece) to denounce his son; then, to show him the correct way to bring up children, he takes Fortunio and his "wife" into his own home, where by virtue of his counsel and the example of his prudent son Valerio he plans to reform them. When Rinaldo returns with the news that Valerio and Fortunio are to live under one roof with their ladies, they are filled with admiration at his wit. But he silences them:

> Peace, be rul'd by me,
> And you shall see to what a perfect shape
> I'll bring this rude plot, which blind Chance (the ape
> Of counsel and advice) hath brought forth blind.
> (1.2.121–124)

His language reveals his *servus* origins, yet he goes a step further than his forbears in overtly trumpeting the faculty that can master unexpected situations. And having ensconced Valerio and Fortunio in Gostanzo's house with Gratiana and Bellanora, he turns his brain to new *consilia*.

Plot then follows upon plot. Determined to "vary the pleasures of our wits," Rinaldo and Valerio look for mischief in the household of the jealous Cornelio. When Cornelio and his courtier friend Dariotto trick Valerio into demonstrating his (non-existent) courtly accomplishments, the young man gains revenge by spreading rumors that Dariotto has cuckolded Cornelio. Thereupon Cornelio stabs Dariotto and initiates divorce proceedings against his wife Gazetta. Meanwhile, at home, Gostanzo overhears Valerio wooing Gratiana, and, fearing that his virtuous son is about to cuckold Fortunio, he decides to get rid of her. Rinaldo, however, persuades him to send the girl to Marc Antonio for safekeeping and to pretend that she is in fact *Valerio's* unauthorized wife, proclaimed Fortunio's only to test Marc Antonio. To "prove" this great hoax, Rinaldo stages a trial scene before Marc Antonio in which Valerio confesses his guilt to Gostanzo, pleads the external pressure of Gratiana's beauty *(translatio criminis)*, and wins his father to bless what he supposes is a fictional marriage. Thus Rinaldo fulfills his vow to bring the plot to "perfect shape."[27]

But the design has an unexpected tail. When Cornelio learns that his jealousy was deliberately aroused by Valerio, he ends the game by exposing the young man's charade to his father. Rinaldo is gulled into leading Gostanzo to a tavern where Valerio is found indulging his newly acquired tastes for drinking, dicing, and wenching. One gambit of wit has succeeded another, and the jealous wit outwits the "shallow scholar," whose chief gull, the "politic wit," finally has his wit cleared. How, then, is the *status* finally resolved? The Latin plays end with an accommodation of opposing parties through the presentation of a "proof" that each can accept: in the *Andria*, Glycerium is found to be an eminently marriageable Athenian citizen, and Pamphilus's deceits are conveniently forgotten; in the *Eunuchus*, one plot provides the restoration of the slave girl to her family and marriage with Chaerea, the younger brother, while the other provides a practical sharing of Thais by Thraso and Phaedria. Opposition dissolves with the discovery of the happy truth and through genial accommodation to reality. Here, opposition dissolves not through the discovery of truth, which is hardly comforting, but through a sudden and expedient belief in the propriety of the deception. When Gostanzo learns the truth about his son, he instantly disinherits him and declares his daughter his heir. But Fortunio has in the meantime married the daughter, and

27. The many references to counsel, persuasion, and devices throughout the play—and the use of specific legal terminology and procedures—testify to Chapman's familiarity with the Terentian commentaries. They also suggest somewhere in the play's history an Inns of Court audience. See esp. 2. 1. 310–335, 4.1.224–346.

when this is revealed, Gostanzo is stymied. All he can do is accept the trap that has been laid for him, and he does so by consciously converting wrath into admiration:

> Now all my choler fly out in your wits.
> Good tricks of youth, i'faith, no indecorum.
>
> (5.2.153–154)

Persuading himself that such deception is appropriate behavior in young men, he accepts both unions, declaring "marriage is destiny." Notice that he is not changing character; rather, he is changing the character of the act he must deal with. His method of accommodation is illuminated by that of Cornelio, which follows.

When fathers and sons have reconciled, only Cornelio stands out in disharmony. Rinaldo urges Gostanzo to exercise his rhetorical faculty to assuage the jealous husband:

> Now here all are pleas'd,
> Only but Cornelio, who lacks but persuasion
> To reconcile himself to his fair wife.
> Good sir, will you (of all men our best speaker)
> Persuade him to receive her into grace?
>
> (5.2.158–162)

Gostanzo then tells Cornelio how his father, who was Gostanzo's friend, dealt with his mother's infidelities. She was an honest enough woman, he tells him, but "she would tickle Dob now and then, as well as the best on 'em." So

> when he saw 'twas but her humor (for his own quietness' sake) he made a back-door to his house for convenience, and got a bell to his fore-door, and had an odd fashion in ringing, by which she and her maid knew him, and would stand talking to his next neighbor to prolong time, that all things might be rid cleanly out o'the way before he came, for the credit of his wife. This was wisdom now, for a man's own quiet. (5.2.196–202)

Cornelio listens for a moment, then exclaims:

> Why, hark you, you two knights. Do you think I will forsake Gazetta?

To which Gostanzo replies:

And will you not?

Cornelio:

Why, there's your wisdom. Why did I make show of divorce, think you?

And he quickly explains that he had only intended the bill of divorcement as a warning to bridle Gazetta's wanton tendencies. To find occasion for it, he had lured Dariotto into his house, given him opportunities with his wife, winked at his indiscretions. "And now," he declares, "shall the world see I am as wise as my father" (5.2.207–211).

It is a charming demonstration of *dianoia* triumphing in the most adverse circumstances. Taking the hint, Cornelio has decided to ignore the disquieting indications of Gazetta's infidelity and fashion a scenario that will allow him to live comfortably with an unpleasant reality. Valerio is amazed:

Is't come to this? Then will I make a speech in praise of this reconcilement, including therein the praise and honor of the most fashionable and authentical HORN. (5.2.231–233)

And he delivers an encomium of cuckoldry that is a rhetorical dilation of the reasoning that has just transpired in Cornelio's head. It is a fitting ending to a play that celebrates the capacity of wit to gull others and the self.

IV

In such plays as *Gammer Gurton's Needle*, *The Supposes*, *Mother Bombie*, and *The Comedy of Errors*, we have witnessed a developing acknowledgment that human wit, for all its inventive power, has its limitations. In *July and Julian*, *The Bugbears*, and *All Fools*, the emphasis is just the reverse; here, there is a tendency to celebrate wit for its sheer virtuosity and, in Chapman especially, a danger (always implicit in the cultivation of rhetoric) that wit will become detached from its moral base. Ben Jonson discriminates the matter more finely. For him, the inventive faculty is both an instrument of knowledge and of morality, and consequently the "supposes" arrived at through the exercise of invention are neither comic manifestations of epistemological limitation nor ironic, though satisfactory, accommodations to unpleasant reality. The validity of a "suppose" lies entirely in its relation to *reasonable* truth. This is because Jonson's dramas are concerned with the secular world of probability, and in the Ciceronian tradition assume that a well-reasoned view of truth is an adequate guide to the moral life. Jonson's concern with the relation of invention to truth was lifelong; in *Every Man in His Humour* (1598), he examines the problem carefully for the first time, drawing upon both the Latin and native traditions to create a comedy with a new humanistic standard.

Not unexpectedly, the central question of the play is formulated in self-consciously literary terms. Which is the more valuable in the education of a young man, Jonson asks, poetry or experience? It is a typical school question, but a matter neither trifling nor irrelevant to a journeyman playwright who was already taking his art seriously. It is sounded in the very first scene, when Lorenzo Senior is discovered shaking his head over the course of his son's studies:

> Myself was once a student, and indeed
> Fed with the self-same humour he is now,
> Dreaming on naught but idle poetry;
> But since, experience hath awak'd my spirits,
> And reason taught them how to comprehend
> The sovereign use of study.
>
> (1.1.16–21)[28]

Dreaming and poetry, reason and experience. These are the initial antitheses upon which the inquiry is based.

The intrigue plot snaps into action directly from this clash of values. "What wind hath blown thee hither in this shape?" Lorenzo Junior asks Musco when he appears in Florence disguised as a soldier. "Your easterly wind, sir," Musco replies, "the same that blew your father hither" (2.3.190–191). In fact, it is the same wind that blew Lorenzo Junior himself to Florence (as Jonson points out in his revised version)—the inspiration of Prospero's letter.[29] This is the letter in which young Lorenzo is

28. All line references are to the parallel text edition of the 1601 Quarto and the 1616 Folio, ed. J. W. Lever (Lincoln, Neb., 1971).

29. "The breath o' your letter, sir, this morning: the same that blew you to the Windmill, and your father after you" (F 3.1.208–209).

urged to come to town so that Prospero may show him "two of the
most perfect, rare, and absolute true gulls that ever thou saw'st" (1.1.149–
150). The letter is written in so swaggering a manner ("'Sblood, invent
some famous memorable lie or other, to flap thy father in the mouth
withal; thou hast been father of a thousand in thy days, thou couldst be
no poet else"), and contains such dark hints of mutual wantonness
("Lorenzo, I conjure thee. By what? Let me see: by the depth of our love,
by all the strange sights we have seen in our days—ay, or nights, either—
to come to me to Florence this day") that the old man, who has inter-
cepted it, is horrified:

> Is this the man my son so oft hath prais'd
> To be the happiest and most precious wit
> That ever was familiar with the art?
> Now, by our Lady's blessed Son, I swear
> I think him most unfortunate
> In the possession of such holy gifts
> Being the master of so loose a spirit.
> (1.1.169–175)

Since this may well be the only extant Renaissance play in which an
epistolary style launches the major intrigue (one hesitates to be categorical) Prospero's manner of composition must be regarded as an important
clue to Jonson's intention in the action that follows. The letter is composed in the *genus floridum*, a mode whose rhetorical aim is to delight,
and thus allows full indulgence of one's inventive faculties to create a
loose and whimsical fabric of figure and metaphor.[30] Its risks are obvious

30. In the Folio, young Lorenzo explicitly designates it "your flourishing style"
(F 3.1.43). Cicero distinguishes the *genus floridum* from the *genus subtile*, whose
function is to reason (*probare*), and the *genus vehemens*, whose office is to move
(*flectere*). The function of the middle style is to delight (*delectare*). It is "a brilliant
and florid, highly coloured and polished style in which all the charms of language
and thought are intertwined." (*Or.* 69, 96, trans. H. M. Hubbell, L.C.L. [London,
1939]). The familiar epistle, however, was traditionally a plain style genre, and its
aim was to convey lucidly and subtly the thought of the writer. Lorenzo's wry
comparison of Prospero's "rare letter" with those of Pliny, who was praised in
the company of Plautus and Terence for cultivation of the direct style, suggests
how far it was from this ideal (2.3.26–30). For discussion of the epistolary tradition
and Jonson's criticism of the middle style, see Wesley Trimpi, *Ben Jonson's Poems:*

from the context. It does not plainly convey its message—emphasizing pleasure rather than instruction—and therefore the intentions of the writer cannot be completely understood unless the recipient is familiar with his *ethos*. Unfortunately, Lorenzo Senior prizes bluntness. "Nay, never look at me, it's *I* that speak," he tells Stephano; "Take't as you will, I'll not flatter you" (1.1.47–48). As one who believes that men speak as they are, he takes Prospero's suggestive *copia verborum ac rerum* for the man himself, and determines at once to follow his son to Florence and wean him from so pernicious an influence. Out of this mischievous disjunction between matter and form begins the war of experience and poetry.[31]

But Prospero's invitation to Lorenzo Junior is less insidious than his manner implies. He has no intention of seducing his friend into the ways of town gallants; he really wants to *show* him Bobadilla and Matheo—to whom Lorenzo adds Stephano for his host's benefit—and later, when Doctor Clement's name comes up, he reminds his visitor that "I showed him to you the other day" (3.2.46). Prospero's insistence upon their *seeing* the more absurd types of Florentine society suggests that Lorenzo's sojourn in town will be an experience rather like attending a comedy, "wherein the common vices of men and women are apparently de-

---

A Study of the Plain Style (Stanford, 1962), esp. pp. 60–75, 104–114. For references to Pliny in the anti-Ciceronian movement, see George Williamson, *The Senecan Amble* (London, 1951), *passim*.

31. Apparently Prospero is a young man in search of a distinctive manner who does not yet know the power of words. His apprenticeship is given a sharp jolt late in the play when, attempting to reassure Biancha and Thorello that no harm has come of inviting the gallants to their home, he inadvertently sets the match to Thorello's twice-dried tinder:

> BIANCHA: But what harm might have come of it!
> PROSPERO: Might? So might the good warm clothes your husband wears be poisoned, for anything he knows, or the wholesome wine he drunk even now at the table.
>
> (4.3.14–17)

Instantly, Thorello begins to burn and gag, as Prospero looks on in amazement: "What, will he be poison'd with a simile?" Precisely, Jonson implies, which is why one must always "speake to the capacity of his hearers" (*Ben Jonson*, ed. C. H. Herford and Percy and Evelyn Simpson [Oxford, 1925–1952], 8.587).

clared in personages."[32] And this is precisely what it turns out to be—with the major modification that in Jonson's expanding metaphor the spectators, too, become players.

More specifically, Prospero and Lorenzo enter into *humanorum consiliorum et eventuum imago quaedam*, for their adventure in Florence is an extended essay in the uses people make of wit in order to achieve their desires. The common expedient appears to be the creation of fictional *personae*. Bobadilla, a descendant of Terence's Thraso and Plautus's Pyrgopolynices, possesses an imaginative gift that is employed chiefly in the creation of a *Bobadilla eroica*. Using his inventive faculty to draw suitable theses from the *topoi* of person and action, he transforms his mean chamber at the house of Cob the watercarrier into the symbol of a rare and private nature. He lives thus, he informs Matheo, "in regard I would not be so popular and general as some be" (1.4.114–115). It is for the same reason that he refuses to frequent the schools of fencing, although upon occasion he does invite some select gentlemen to his quarters for lessons in the fine art of the *stoccado* and the *passado*. His lexical fastidiousness is another aspect of the same transmuting process. Unlike Giuliano, that Coridon of gentlemen who mistakes cudgel for *bastinado*, Bobadilla chooses his words with care to ensure that his *persona* corresponds precisely to that inward idea of the self he would be. His ethopoetic program is, in fact, not unlike that of Castiglione's Courtier, who also faced the problem of decorously manifesting his nature. The essential difference between them, of course, is that, theoretically, no incongruity existed between the spiritual *areté* and the outward appearance of the perfect Courtier. In Bobadilla's case, it is revealed every time he is called upon to put his judgment or physical prowess to the test. But with blessed lack of awareness, he is able to extract from each situation the most favorable reading. When, for example, he is finally cornered and cudgeled indeed by Giuliano, he immediately knows how the encounter must be interpreted by right-minded persons:

A rude part, a touch with soft wood, a kind of gross battery used, laid on strongly, borne most patiently; and that's all. (4.4.6–7)

32. Sir Thomas Eliot, *Biblioteca Eliotae* (1548), cited by Madeline Doran, *Endeavours of Art* (Madison, 1954), p. 382.

Such carefully wrought fictions are seen by all but the greatest gulls to be simply elaborate excuses. But they are more than that. Created virtually *ex tempore*, they reflect a habit of mind in which the imagination automatically detaches itself from reality under "the imposition of the heart," as one of Jonson's characters remarks on another occasion, and instantly creates the appropriate delusion.[33]

Matheo is a more explicit example of this tendency to assume a character not one's own, since he is an outright plagiarist. Jonson reveals his inauthenticity through his characteristic vice. He steals indiscriminately from both Daniel and Marlowe, and gives first place to one of the most artificially rhetorical passages of the past decade—Hieronimo's "Oh eyes, no eyes, but fountains fraught with tears"—replete with the *correctio*, *paroemion*, and *antithesis* which to a later generation bespoke calculated sentiment. Stephano, the least presumptuous of the gulls, lacks even the technical skill needed to construct his desired self-image, and requires coaching:

> Come, come, for shame: do not wrong the quality of your desert in so poor a kind, but let the idea of what you are be portrayed in your aspect, that men may read in your looks: "Here, within this place, is to be seen the most admirable, rare, and accomplish'd work of Nature." (1.2.98–103)

In this passage, Lorenzo Junior facetiously urges him to play out his "fore-conceit" and become a vivid dramatic exemplum such as Sidney had described. His failure to realize the melancholy gallant—even superficially—is foreshadowed in his reply to Marina's declaration of love:

> STEPHANO: *The deeper, the sweeter,*
> *I'll be judged by Saint Peter.*
> LORENZO: How, by Saint Peter? I do not conceive that.
> STEPHANO: Marry, Saint Peter, to make up the meter.
> (2.1.39–42)

33. Jonas Barish, analyzing the sentence immediately following the one quoted, comments that "the parisonic members, hardened by alliteration, set up a kind of incantation which permits Bobadilla to forget his recent humiliation and triumph once more in fantasy. . . . Years of poring over books on the duello have ended in his being able to mesmerize not only Matheo and Stephano but himself into a belief in his own valor" (*Ben Jonson and the Language of Prose Comedy* [Cambridge, Mass., 1960], pp. 102–103).

Such poesy, Jonson was to argue elsewhere, "expresseth but by fits, True Conceipt," and neatly epitomizes Stephano's radical insincerity.[34]

The most complex exemplum encountered by Prospero and Lorenzo is Thorello, the would-be cuckold. What makes him especially interesting is the coexistence within his soul of an awareness that his fiction-making is a malady, along with a corresponding inability to stop himself from indulging in it. He is an incorrigible hypothesizer. Jonson offers a detailed anatomy of Thorello's flawed *inventio* in his agonized auto-*consultationes*. Notice how, in the following passage, he creates a false scenario by proceeding from the actual circumstance—the physical proximity of the gallants and his wife—and uses the commonplace that beauty wars against chastity to transform that proximity into a proof of potential cuckoldry. Then, assuming the *truth* of this potentiality—that his wife and the gallants share a mutual desire for one another—he reasons that all they lack is time and opportunity, which he vows not to allow them:

> Why, 't cannot be, where there is such resort
> Of wanton gallants and young revelers,
> That any woman should be honest long.
> Is't like that factious beauty will preserve
> The sovereign state of chastity unscarr'd,
> When such strong motives muster and make head
> Against her single peace? No, no. Beware
> When mutual pleasure sways the appetite,
> And spirits of one kind and quality
> Do meet to parley in the pride of blood.
> Well, to be plain, if I but thought the time
> Had answer'd their affections, all the world
> Should not persuade me but I were a cuckold.
> Marry, I hope they have not got that start;
> For opportunity hath balk'd them yet,

34. *A Fit of Rime Against Rime*. In *Discoveries*, Jonson scornfully refers to "Rayling and tinckling *Rimers*, whose Writings the vulgar more greedily read" (*H&S*, 8. 572). His impatience with mere rhymers stems from that same concern to make expression match matter which led him to prefer the couplet to the stanza in his own verse: "The couplet does not commit him to any more lines than his subject demands, and in stanzas the form rather than the subject matter in many cases determines how long a given statement must be" (Trimpi, p. 106).

And shall do still, while I have eyes and ears
To attend the imposition of my heart.
My presence shall be as an iron bar
'Twixt the conspiring motions of desire;
Yea, every look or glance mine eye objects
Shall check occasion, as one doth his slave,
When he forgets the limits of prescription.

(1.4.157–178)

In this soliloquy, the familiar forensic technique of adducing probable proof from place, person, motive, commonplace, time, and occasion— and of imposing a certain *color* over the whole—has been transformed into a subtle instrument for the portrayal of character. Jonson shows us not only the mind drawing elements of proof from both actuality and its own storehouse of sententious truths, but also the leaps it must take under the compulsion to confirm such proof. This compulsion is rendered the more vivid by the *color* Thorello unconsciously uses—the transparent imagery of frustrated sexual desire through which he expresses his intention to prevent the realization of his own scenario. The speech is a devastating exposé of false rhetoric, in which the advocate reveals himself more than he knows.

The gulls whom Prospero and Lorenzo encounter, then, are not merely *exempla* engaged in comic *consilia*, but more particularly, creators of bad fictions. Their fictions are bad because their inventive faculty serves their passions, and thus is out of touch with the facts that reason might reveal—in particular, those facts pertaining to themselves.[35] In the light of their behavior, Lorenzo Senior's assumption that poetry is divorced from experience appears to be true. But theirs is not the complete proof.

---

35. This is probably the deeper significance of *humours* in this very literary play. In *Discoveries*, Jonson defines poesy as the "skill, or Crafte of making: the very Fiction it selfe, the reason, or forme of the worke . . . the habit, or the Art" (*H & S*, 8. 636). It is an apt description of the febrile activity of the gulls in *EMI*, and at the end of the play, when Doctor Clement replies to young Lorenzo's praise of poetry as a way of setting forth truth, he explicitly connects the two: "Ah Lorenzo; but election is now govern'd altogether by the influence of humour; which, instead of those holy flames that should direct and light the soul to eternity, hurls forth nothing but smoke and congested vapors" (5.3.326–329). Bad poetry is created by bad-humoured men.

In direct contrast to them, Jonson develops the figures of Prospero, Lorenzo Junior, and Musco. They belong to a different fraternity of inventors, and their common note is an unfailing self-awareness in whatever character they fashion for themselves. The clearest expression of this trait is found in Musco's *apologia* when he dons the guise of an old veteran in order to waylay Lorenzo Senior en route to Florence:

> 'Sblood, I cannot choose but laugh to see myself translated thus, from a poor creature to a creator; for now must I create an intolerable sort of lies, or else my profession loses his grace. . . . Oh, sir, it holds for good policy to have that outwardly in vilest estimation that is most dear to us. So much for my borrowed shape. (2.1.1–7)

In this complicated little passage, he is punning on his metamorphosis from servant to soldier, a type notorious for lying. But at the same time he reassures the audience that in playing the outward liar he retains reverence for truth within. And the nature of this truth? It is simply a clear-eyed understanding of who one is, as he suggests a moment later when he explains that he has disguised himself "the rather to insinuate with my young master—for so must we that are blue-waiters, or men of service, do, or else perhaps we may wear motley at the year's end" (2.1.10–12).

For Musco, the exercise of poesis, in alliance with his master's heir, is a way to insure the future. Its function for Prospero is less immediately apparent. At first it simply appears to be an experiment in a style of living. Prospero (*It.* "well-disposed," "growing," "flourishing") is a youth trying on the mask of gallant for the possible pleasure it may afford. But in doing so he, too, never forgets who he really is, as he hints parenthetically in his original letter to young Lorenzo:

> Sirrah, how if thy father should see this now? What would he think of me? Well, however I write to thee, I reverence him in my soul for the general good all Florence delivers of him. (1.1.157–159)[36]

"However I write to thee. . . ." It is precisely the sentiment expressed by Musco concerning his disguise. When we examine Prospero more closely, therefore, we discover that beneath the flourishing style is an au-

---

36. That a significant change in Prospero's behavior has taken place is confirmed in the complaint of Thorello to Giuliano (1.4.24–55).

thentic self whose fiction-making is a productive form of play that enables him to draw out truths that would be otherwise unavailable. He cultivates Bobadilla and Matheo so that they may lay themselves patent. He deliberately provokes his brother in order to bring out his hidden nature:

> A tall man is never his own man, till he be angry. To keep his valor in obscurity is to keep himself, as it were, in a cloak bag. What's a musician, unless he play? What's a tall man, unless he fight?
>
> (4.3.8–11)

His final act is to dispose appropriately his virtuous sister—a maid of good ornament and much modesty—which he accomplishes by introducing Lorenzo into Thorello's house in the company of the gallants, where he and Hesperida silently view, then like, one another.

Lorenzo is a still more shadowy figure. He, too, assumes the role of gallant, but rather than encourage the folly of the gulls, more often he warns them about it—when, for example, Stephano insists upon buying the "Toledo" sword, or takes Giuliano's cloak for himself, or when Bobadilla excuses his cowardice by pleading that he is bound to the peace. His role seems to be more the prudent observer than the expositor of folly.

The larger function of *ethopoeia* for the conspirators should now be apparent. Unlike the gulls, it allows them *to remain in touch with reality*. By means of their various roles, Musco may follow his private good, Prospero reveal the decorous norm, and Lorenzo perceive it. There is nothing moralistic in this program; its morality lies solely in its allegiance to reasonable truth. Invention employed in the service of truth, Jonson implies—whether that be fidelity to one's best interest, the scourging of others' pretensions, or the discovery of an appropriate mode of conduct—is wit well used. Hence the paradox that one can be disguised and yet remain honest.[37]

37. It is illuminating to compare the assumption of fictional *personae* by the characters in *EMI* with Jonson's famous remark in *Discoveries*: "I have considered, our whole life is like a *Play*: wherein every man, forgetfull of himselfe, is in travaile with expression of another. Nay, we so insist in imitating others, as wee cannot (when it is necessary) returne to our selves; like Children, that imitate the vices of Stammerers so long, till at last they become such; and make the habit to another nature, as it is never forgotten" (*H & S*, 8.597). On the face of it, this statement implies an antitheatricalism strangely at odds with his profession—a

Comparison of the two kinds of poesis suggests that Jonson is treating his proposed question as a qualitative one. From the original opposition of poetry and experience, he has inquired into the uses of fiction, and has distinguished the kind of fiction which is created to satisfy the passions from that which functions as a medium for seeking truth in harmony with reason. But what of experience? How is its value measured? There are two characters whose bluntness of manner indicates that they meet life directly, without the mediation of poetic invention. One is Giuliano, whose angry humor is congenital and not an affectation (he becomes Downright in the Folio). An indomitable literalist, he is unable to detect Thorello's heavy-handed subterfuge when asked to rebuke Prospero for bringing gallants into the house; he watches with mounting fury the patently unreal wooing of the ladies by the gulls; and in his earnestness, is easily duped by the conspirators into a wild-goose chase at the end of the play. Lacking imaginative capacity, he cannot suppose himself in another's place, and therefore cannot perceive others' motivations. He testifies to the triumph of true wit over experience. But perhaps this is "realism" in the service of passion, for Giuliano is a man of ill will. Jonson also investigates what the direct approach accomplishes in a rational, benevolent nature such as old Lorenzo's. The results are the same. Initially he misinterprets Prospero's letter and goes on a foolish errand to Florence. A second mistaking of appearances leads him, on the highest moral impulses, to take the conniving Musco into his service. Finally he is duped into accepting his new servant's word at face value, and disgraces himself outside Cob's house. So much, says Jonson, for the old man's "experience"; thrice he has been taken in by appearances, and if the "poetry" of the gulls is unrelated to reality, the experiential judgment of Lorenzo Senior proves to be no more so. We recall the Sileni of Alcibiades.

This process of examination would be schematic indeed if not for

---

theme developed by Barish, "Jonson and the Loathed Stage," *A Celebration of Ben Jonson*, ed. William Blisset, Julian Patrick, and R. W. Van Fossen (Toronto, 1973), pp. 27–53. But, as we can see in *EMI*, it also implies a Jonsonian ideal—the human being whose play is an instrument of understanding and who therefore is not "forgetfull of himselfe." Jonson's motto, "Tamquam explorator," succinctly expresses this ideal. See Thomas M. Greene, "Ben Jonson and the Centered Self," *SEL* 10 (1970): 325–348.

Jonson's skill in developing his rhetorical inquiry as a credible mimetic action. The scandalous letter sets the intrigue in motion, Musco's instinct of self-preservation engenders the first disguise, and Lorenzo Senior's misplaced benevolence leads to the major complication. In the remainder of the play, too, occasion ostensibly shapes the plot; but when we examine events more closely we discover that once again the mimetic is in the service of the rhetorical.

With Musco a confidant of old Lorenzo, opportunity has been established for mischievous plotting against the father in behalf of the son. But Jonson does not seem anxious to develop the intrigue he has so carefully set up. Only after Prospero and Lorenzo have had time to observe the gulls plying their music does Musco appear to let them know that the old man is fast on their trail. And even then, Prospero is in no hurry to react. Instead, he asks Musco to come along with them to Thorello's and tries to cheer his worried friend:

> I pray thee, good rascal, droop not; 'sheart, an' our wits be so gouty
> that one old plodding brain can outstrip us all, Lord, I beseech thee,
> may they lie and starve in some miserable spital, where they may
> never see the face of any true spirit again. . . . (2.2.209–213)

This speech invokes the familiar Latin contest of age and youth, but oddly enough offers no specific *consilium*. Even more anomalous is Prospero's insistence that Musco accompany them: to what end is not at all clear. The reason does not emerge, in fact, until several scenes later, when he asks Lorenzo:

> But tell me zealously, dost thou affect my sister Hesperida, as thou
> pretendest? (3.6.15–16)

It is here that the full outline of Jonson's dramatic design becomes evident. Behind Prospero's original invitation to Lorenzo, it would seem, was an unstated determination to introduce him not only to the counterfeit gallant and the poetaster, but also to the virtuous virgin. Although there is no hint of this in the letter of the Quarto version, there is in that of the Folio, where Lorenzo is urged to "change an old shirt for a whole smock with us" (F 1.1.154–155)—to leave his father, that is, and seek a wife. It is less likely that this revision represents a change of intention than that it is simply another instance of the sharpening that much Quarto material undergoes in the Folio. For it now becomes apparent that Jonson has been silently drawing upon yet another dramatic tradition to render his matter in its appropriate form—that of the native *Wit* interludes. These were themselves adaptations to the morality pattern of the venerable material treating the marriage of Mercury and Philology—wit and learning.[38] In these plays, the *Wit* hero, having been nurtured by Father Reason, seeks the hand of Lady Science, and must overcome such perils as Tediousness, Idleness, and Ignorance in the course of a romantic journey to her abode. Prospero's invitation to Lorenzo to leave his supremely rational father and sojourn with him in the town of gulls, though strongly colored by its Latin overlay, clearly reflects this pattern. And the modest Hesperida, guarded by the dragon Thorello, is surely meant to suggest just such a treasure as Lady Science.[39]

38. The plays are *Wit and Science* (1539), *The Marriage of Wit and Science* (1568), *The Marriage between Wit and Wisdom* (1579). The *De nuptiis Philologiae et Mercurii* of Martianus Capella (c. 410–439) was an influential document in transmitting to the Middle Ages and the Renaissance the Ciceronian ideal of a rhetoric dealing with broad ethical issues. It appeared in eight editions between 1499 and 1599. See Ernst Curtius, *European Literature and the Latin Middle Ages* (New York, 1963), pp. 38–39, and *passim*. The relationship of its theme and that of the *Wit* interludes to *EMI* has apparently not been noticed before.

39. Thorello himself makes the connection, while jealously ruminating on his dilemma:

> What earthy spirit but will attempt
> To taste the fruit of beauty's golden tree
> When leaden sleep seels up the dragon's eyes?
> (3.1.18–20)

Here, Hesperida is depicted as a kind of ideal beauty, guarded by one who cannot see her, and therefore can make no use of her. During the Renaissance, the apples of the Hesperides were associated with abundance of knowledge, and Hercules' theft was allegorized as the acquisition of the power to speak wisely. Cf. this verse in Alciati's 137th emblem, *Invehit in patriam externis bona plurima ab oris*, explicated as follows by Claudius Minois: *Undecimo aurea mala Hesperidum, occiso prius dracone pervigili, sustulit, quod est referendum ad illam, qua docti & sapientes homines abundant, insignem rerum copiam, qua eos sua fortuna vitaeque conditio beat* (*Emblemata* [Leiden, 1608], p. 511). If, as it appears, Hesperida's beauty is meant to function symbolically as learning, then it is clear that she will not be perceived by Thorello,

It is toward the securing of this union that Musco's wit has been reserved by Prospero. During the latter half of the play we are offered visible proof of how valuable poetry is in the education of a young man, as a knot of error is drawn about Lorenzo Senior, Doctor Clement, Thorello, Biancha, Giuliano, Cob, and Tib, to effect Hesperida's flight with young Lorenzo. The instigating agent is Prospero, but Musco takes his rude plan and hammers it into shape on the forge of his invention. As the old *Disparview* he lures Lorenzo Senior to Cob's house, to get him off his son's trail; then, entering a tavern with Peto, Clement's man, he plies him with drink, strips him, and in his clothes summons Thorello to Clement's house so that Hesperida may get away. It is only when he attempts to extend the game gratuitously—disguising himself as a varlet to pick up some small change from Bobadilla and Matheo—that, in his own words, he makes "a fair mash of it," and is compelled by Giuliano to lead Stephano before the magistrate.[40]

Jonson's denouement explicates both the errors of the play and the implications of a dramatic tradition. Upon hearing the complaint of the company who had been lured to Cob's house, Doctor Clement, that merry Crito, deduces that they have all been gulled by a mischievous device. But he unties the knot no further. It takes Musco to reveal the whole truth. His confession comes about in a fashion delightfully true to the premises of the play. Clement, a mad stickler for decorum who dons armor to parley with a soldier, is outraged at the way Musco, disguised as a varlet, has apprehended Giuliano: he had said to him "I must arrest you," instead of "I do arrest you," thereby creating a discrepancy

whose imagination is perverted to the service of his passions (hence his sterile *fictiones*), but that she is the proper object for the poet who seeks truth.

40. The fact that this is a piece of gratuitous acting is significant. Musco seems to have lost sight of his reason for role-playing (helping his young master to a wife, and thereby pursuing his own self-interest), and is simply enjoying his own virtuosity. But this is not reason enough, and accordingly his wit is self-defeating. His temporary loss of contact with himself is a forecast of the far more frightening situation of Volpone, whose exercise of wit becomes a substitute for a real self that seems to have disappeared. For an illuminating discussion of the ramifications of this theme, see Stephen J. Greenblatt, "The False Ending in *Volpone*," *JEGP* 75 (1976): 90–104.

between intention and act. For this breach of decorum he is ordered to prison and the action seems destined to close, just as it opened, in stylistic controversy.

The controversy is resolved, however, as Musco unmasks, revealing himself *in propria persona*: "An' I be committed, it shall be for the comitting of more villainies than this; hang me, an' I lose the least grain of my fame" (5.3.118–120). His words reflect the pride of an artist,[41] and he recounts in minute detail the tricks performed throughout the day in behalf of his young master. Doctor Clement's reaction to his tale is illuminating. He does not merely acknowledge that Musco's wit does indeed deserve his countenance; he expands the tenor of Musco's own claim:

> *Pro superi! ingenium magnum quis nosset Homerum, Ilias aeternum si latuisset opus?* [Gods above! Who would have known the great genius Homer, if he had concealed that immortal work the *Iliad*?]
> (5.3.197–198)

The comparison, of course, is as absurd as Clement himself, but through the words of the eccentric magistrate Jonson is reminding us that Musco has been the chief author of an elaborate fictional scenario, in which he never forgot (until the very end) who he was and what cause he served.

The final cause, it would seem, is the marriage of Mercury and Philology. This is the end of the plot—young Lorenzo weds Hesperida—and it is also the subject of the young man's defense of his vocation, after poetry is attacked once more by his father:

> Indeed, if you will look on Poesy
> As she appears in many, poor and lame,
> Patch'd up in remnants and old worn rags,
> Half-starved for want of her peculiar food,
> Sacred invention, then I must confirm
> Both your conceit and censure of her merit;
> But view her in her glorious ornaments,
> Attired in the majesty of art,
> Set high in spirit with the precious taste
> Of sweet philosophy, and, which is most,

41. He is specifically designated an "architect" in the Folio (3.2.231).

Crown'd with the rich traditions of a soul
That hates to have her dignity profan'd
With any relish of an earthly thought:
O, then how proud a presence doth she bear!
Then is she like herself, fit to be seen
Of none but grave and consecrated eyes.

(5.3.300–315)[42]

It is a lofty encomium, delivered in a style foreign to the rest of the play, but quite appropriate as the formal graduation exercise of a very earnest young scholar. Lorenzo is offering for the edification of his friends the broad thesis toward which the argument *in utramque partem* has been moving. Neither false fictions nor nearsighted experience are of value in the education of a young man, but a poetry that truthfully reveals the effects of both *is*. The complex fabric of *Every Man in His Humour* is such a poetry. It functions to draw out the truth in each of its component parts. Its *mythos* exhibits the pattern of one young man's journey to understanding through the medium of comic fiction. Its *ethos* presents the wide variety of human society he encounters and his response to the experience. Its *dianoia* lies in the proofs the gulls find to justify the impositions of the heart and which the true wits employ to secure their authentic good. Its *lexis* is the touchstone of truth. Lorenzo is at once part of the fiction and its beneficiary, for through its instrumentality he joins wisdom to wit.

His achievement is symbolized a few moments later on a more broadly comic level, which brings us happily down to earth. Doctor Clement, having reconciled all outstanding parties (save Bobadilla and Matheo), embraces Musco and invites the company to be his guests this evening, where they will laugh and

carouse to the health of this heroic spirit, whom, to honor the more, I do invest in my own robes. (5.3.424–426)

And he places his cloak upon Musco's shoulders. It is a gesture that we have been awaiting a long time. In a single comic emblem, it marks

42. Notice the same cluster of images used earlier by Thorello in connection with the beauty he guards: taste, earthy spirit, eyes that cannot see. Although he is praising poetry, Lorenzo Junior is also describing his own marriage to Hesperida—the maid of "good ornament and much modesty" (*F* 4.4.18–19).

the emergence of a new hero—the humane wit—capable of supposing himself other than he is in order to judge more equitably the problems of our common life. Given Jonson's high aims for his art, it is perhaps not surprising that this hero in whom moral philosophy and sophistic rhetoric are united should turn out to be a comic playwright.[43]

43. In the Folio, their union is verbalized more explicitly. Judge Clement orders Ed Knowell to initiate the festivities:

Master Bridegroom, take your bride and lead; everyone a fellow. Here is my mistress—Brainworm! To whom all my addresses of courtship shall have reference. (*F* 5.1.278–281)

Quaestiones Copiosae:
Pastoral and Courtly in John Lyly

IF ONE WAY IN WHICH A QUESTION MAY BE REALIZED THROUGH FICTION lies in the direction of realism—by imitating an action engendered by the problem or troubled by it—another way leads toward enriched significance. In this case the writer will not be concerned to trace the temporal sequence of events out of which the question arises—thus rendering ethopoetically the continuing mental responses of protagonist and antagonist to the issue—but rather he will tend to expand his frame of reference and probe the implications of the question metaphorically, in a wider spectrum of experience. The great poetic dramatists, of course, do both. But some extraordinary illuminations can be effected by a playwright without Aristotelian ambitions, who prefers to hypothesize his *quaestiones* by means of loosely connected deliberations and disputations which are developed through a variety of exemplary proofs. Preeminently in our period this is the method of John Lyly.

Lyly has been aptly described by G.K. Hunter as a spiritual descendant of the early humanist playwrights and their drama of ideas.[1] Like them, he is concerned primarily to stimulate the intellect, and his plays frequently reveal their affinities to the "Dyalogue ... compiled in maner of an interlude with divers toys and gests added thereto to make mery pastime and disport." But of course they are very different. Some of that difference lies in Lyly himself, but a great deal is to be attributed to the fortunes of humanism in the preceding fifty years. Hunter's argument concerning

1. *John Lyly: The Humanist as Courtier* (London, 1962).

the decline of the humanist from educator to entertainer need not be repeated here.[2] What ought to be emphasized, however, is the positive result of that unrealized ideal: if the humanist did not emerge as royal pedagogue shaping policy for an adoring queen, he did become a witty and perceptive poet who performed an important service by exercising the awareness of the Elizabethan court with close-packed argument and enticing spectacle. Without the humanist program of education there could not have been a John Lyly, nor the continual reminders of life's complexity that fill his plays.

These plays differ from their forbears in several respects. Most obviously, they are not bare debates, but *theses* figured forth through all the rhetorical devices available to a writer intent upon engaging the imagination of a learned though not necessarily scholarly audience. Again, they contain none of the radical political speculation and religious satire that was permissible in the relative freedom of pre-Reformation days. Instead they are fashioned around the traditional questions and oppositions that had become standard courtly themes: the nature of sovereignty; the place of love in the life of a public person; the relationship between courtier and monarch; the character of woman; the rival claims of love and friendship, of passion and chastity. They are, in one sense, emasculated "problem plays," destined to flatter the Queen and her court by rehearsing for them the *topoi* that constituted the basic education of those who made their lives at the center of power. But it is in the treatment of these *topoi* that Lyly shows himself to be a poet and *psychogogue* rather than merely a royal entertainer. For he uses them as points of departure to consider some of the more covert implications of courtly idealism. In his hands, the familiar litany of courtesy begins to resume the grandeur and significance so frequently masked by its own clichés—suggesting, in terms designed to capture and hold the attention of a sophisticated audience, that issues of great moment are concealed in the daily conversation and social ritual of the royal establishment. How this comes about is our present concern.

It has been recognized for some time that Lyly's Euphuism is not simply a decorative style, employing antitheses, balanced clauses, and matching parts of speech for euphonic pleasure alone. It is a style of inquiry and analysis, through which Lyly examines experience as a dialectical rhetori-

2. *Ibid.*, pp. 1–35.

cian, always holding any given perception up to the light of other possibilities; characteristically he "lays phrases and clauses side by side, instead of subordinating them," thereby forcing continual awareness of contrary or different viewpoints.[3] Recently, Peter Saccio has argued that the investigative mode of Euphuism informs plot structure itself in *Campaspe*, Lyly's first play.[4] He describes its "plot" as a methodical search for social decorum, and characterizes its dramaturgy as "situational": characters and roles are defined by juxtaposing them in a variety of discrete arrangements throughout the play. The problem raised by his essay is where such a drama might have come from. Our study of the *quaestio* argued *in utramque partem*, which permeates so much sixteenth-century fiction, suggests the answer. It is the hypothesized question— whether in the form of speculative *thesis, deliberatio, suasoria,* or *querela*— that constitutes the basic scenic unit of *Campaspe*. And it is the *quaestiuncula*—in the shape of flyting, amorous witplay, or dialogic commentary on the main action—that informs most of the connecting scenes.[5]

3. Jonas Barish, "The Prose Style of John Lyly," *ELH* 23 (1956): 28n.
4. *The Court Comedies of John Lyly* (Princeton, 1969).
5. This explanation goes far toward providing a literary basis for Wilson Knight's acute comparison of Lyly's characters with the figures of a morality play:

> Those started with a rigid abstraction: poverty, good-deeds, or such like, and set it walking in human form. The resulting personality either outgrows the conception and general plan, or stays severely limited. The Elizabethan recognizes the complexity and contradictions and dramatic oppositions *within* the single personality and the baffling indecisiveness of all moral categories. So he starts with a concrete, often mythical or pseudo-historical, figure and lets his abstract thinking play around and into its growth ("Lyly," *RES* 15 [1939]: 149-150).

Precisely. As we have seen, such pluralistic thinking was inculcated primarily *through* fiction: supposing this person or that was in such-and-such a situation. This is the method of the *ethopoeia,* the *suasoria,* and other *progymnasmata* which trained the mind to perceive characters and ideas problematically. So strong was this habit that when Lyly came to Plutarch's life of Alexander, he saw the episodes he chose to dramatize as controversial subjects. Examples in the play of speculative *theses* are the Parmenio-Timoclea debate on conquest (1.1.41–47) and the comical catechism of the philosophers (1.3.81–98); *deliberatio* opens the play as Parmenio and Clitus weigh which of Alexander's virtues ought to be more highly praised (1.1.1–13), and informs the soliloquy in which Apelles determines

A close examination of the text reveals that familiar "naturalization" of abstract inquiry which we have noticed in other sixteenth-century fictions. But it also reveals a difference between Lyly's plays and the open-ended *quaestio* that we have come to associate with distinctly comic forms—that passage through exploration to some kind of tentative proposition based on a fuller apprehension of the facts. Here, for example, is the initial encounter between Parmenio and Clitus, Alexander's lieutenants, and Timoclea, his royal Theban captive:

> PARMENIO: Madame, you neede not doubt, it is *Alexander*, that is the conqueror.
> TIMOCLEA: *Alex.* hath overcome, not conquered.
> PARMENIO: To bring under his subjection is to conquer.
> TIMOCLEA: He cannot subdue that which is divine.
> PARMENIO: Thebes was not.
> TIMOCLEA: Virtue is.
> CLITUS: *Alexander*, as he tendreth vertue, so he will you; he drinks not bloud, but thirsteth after honor, he is greedy of victory, but never satisfied with mercy. In fight terrible, as becometh a captain; in conqueste milde, as beseemeth a king. In all things, then which nothing can be greater, he is *Alexander*. (1.1.41–52)[6]

The first thing we notice in this passage is that, as in the early humanist play, a conversational gambit instantly becomes a *positio*. This *positio* is then subjected to examination through debate. The debate is carried on by means of two inductive analyses rendered as dialogue:

> A. Alexander has conquered you.
> To conquer is to bring all under subjection.
> All of Thebes (including you) is brought under subjection.

---

to blemish Campaspe's picture (3.5.13–61); *dissuasoria* is used in Hephaestion's counsel against love (2.2.29–76); *querelae* are found in Campaspe's soliloquies (4.2.1–17, 4.4.18–33). For flyting, see any scene with the Pages (e.g., 1.2); for amorous witplay, the introductory scenes between Apelles and Campaspe (3.3, 4.2); for dialogic commentary, the worried exchanges between Parmenio and Clitus (3.4, 4.4).

6. All citations from Lyly's plays refer to *The Complete Works*, ed. R. Warwick Bond, 3 vols. (Oxford, 1902), with "v" and "j" normalized.

B. Alexander has not conquered me.
   One cannot conquer, but only physically over-
   come the divine.
   Virtue (my essence) is divine.

Here the debate stops, having discovered the concealed premises behind the two claims—and thereby the problematic nature of Alexander's power. In strict logic the debate must end here, for the respective theses have been reached. But Clitus resolves the impasse by showing the relationship between Alexander and Timoclea's final term. He deduces three species of the genus *virtue* (love of honor, victory, and mercy) and generates a new Alexander who encompasses all these qualities.[7] The result is that the original, limited assertion (Alexander conquers) *and* the counter-assertion (Alexander overcomes) are subsumed in a fuller generalization that transcends both (Alexander exercises virtue). This intellectual process characterizes the entire action of the play. In pursuing the arts of peace, Alexander plans to become a philosopher king, but in dialogue with the philosophers he recalls that political action and scholars' arguments do not mix happily. Therefore he determines instead to be a king who will make politic use of philosophers. Similarly, in his sally into the visual arts, he discovers through experiment that he will make a better patron than a painter and, as a man who appreciates beauty but cannot create it, he may more satisfactorily pursue higher culture by employing the services of an accomplished artist than by trying to become one. In the major crisis of the play, his love for Campaspe, he concludes after passionate debate with himself and Hephaestion that there is a place for love in his life, but that it must come after conquest, and in the meantime he may best honor it by uniting the lovers in his own court. In each case—as in the interview with Timoclea—Lyly sets up an assertion (or pair of assertions) about Alexander that is analyzed, found insufficient, and then reformulated as a more comprehensive proposition that pays due regard to the new-found complexity. It is the traditional procedure for arguing a question *in utramque partem*.[8]

7. The progression is from the specific enumeration ("he drinks not . . . mercy") to the more general statement ("In fight . . . king") to the final proposition ("In all . . . *Alexander*").

8. In his discussion, Saccio argues that the main logical concern in the play is definition, but this disregards the larger and more significant process of general-

In both its local argumentation, then, and its larger outlines, *Campaspe*
is designed to lead an audience to examine the concealed implications
of assertions, to weigh the alternative meanings and values discovered
through analysis, and to reassemble the distinctive—if sometimes antithetical—qualities perceived into some kind of harmonious order. The
play functions very much as an exercise in invention,[9] conducted with
charm and grace, to be sure, but relying for its effectiveness upon the
auditor's willingness to allow his wit to be worked.

II

In *Campaspe* this wit is engaged and directed primarily by means of
explicit statement. Experiencing the play is therefore rather like being
argued at; there is little opportunity for the awakening of that wonder
which is stimulated obliquely, allusively, to perceive complexity, note
differences, and speculate upon the relations of things. This may well be
why Lyly, who conceived of drama as a speaking picture that exercised
the wit, soon abandoned the discursive mode of *Campaspe*, and began to
experiment with allegory. Through allegory he could pursue his questions with even greater vividness, and engage more spontaneously and
intensively the inventive faculty of his audience. A great deal has been
written about Lyly's allegory, usually in an attempt to decipher specific
plays, but very little about its nature, and perhaps nothing about its
origins.[10] In this respect, our approach to *Campaspe* may be of some help.
If, as it appears, the play is designed, from periodic structure through
plot resolution, to stimulate the wit to new inferences and more complex

---

ization that takes place. Definition is only an intermediate stage, prior to the
discovery of a broader thesis.

9. Cf. Thomas Wilson's discussion of inference, Ch. II, pp. 51-52.

10. The major essays in historical allegory concern *Endimion*, and are by N. J,
Halpin, *Oberon's Vision* (London, 1843); R. W. Bond, *The Works*, 3. 81-103;.
J. W. Bennett, "Oxford and *Endimion*," *PMLA* 62 (1942): 354-369. Moral alle-
gory has been discussed in detail by Percy W. Long, "The Purport of Lyly's
Endimion," *PMLA* 24 (1909): 164-184; Bernard Huppé, "Allegory of Love in
Lyly's Court Comedies," *ELH* 14 (1947): 93-113; Paul E. Parnell, "Moral Alle-
gory in Lyly's *Love's Metamorphosis*," *SP* 52 (1955): 1-16. The most suggestive
descriptions of Lyly's manner are by Wilson Knight, "Lyly"; J. A. Bryant, Jr.,
"The Nature of the Allegory in Lyly's *Endimion*," *RenP* (1956): 4-11; Saccio
Court Comedies.

perceptions, then the seeds of Lyly's allegory may lie in the images he uses there. Barish has pointed out that the examples from nature that Lyly's characters invoke in their dialogue function in ways parallel to the analytic periods themselves—revealing dual potentiality, multiplicity, and paradox in the natural world, which correspond to the human behavior under examination.[11] This is only to say, of course, that they are *functional* analogies, not merely *bizarreries* inserted for their exotic flavor, but it is an important point, for it implies that the auditor's wit is being exercised vertically, as well as laterally, up and down the chain of being, as a given argument is pursued. Let us look closely at the effects of such peripatetic proof in an oft-quoted passage from the second act (divided here for convenience of discussion):

> Bewty is like the blackberry, which seemeth red, when it is not ripe, resembling pretious stones that are polished with honny, which the smother they look, the sooner they breake.

> It is thought wonderful among the seamen, that Mugil, of all fishes the swiftest, is found in the belly of the Bret, of all the slowest: And shall it not seeme monstrous to wisemen, that the hearte of the greatest conquerour of the worlde, should be found in the handes of the weakest creature of nature? of a woman? of a captive?

> Hermyns have faire skinnes, but fowle livers; Sepulchres fresh colours, but rotten bones, women faire faces, but false heartes.

> Remember *Alexander*, thou hast a campe to governe, not a chamber; fall not from the armour of *Mars* to the armes of *Venus*, from the fiery assaults of war, to the maidenly skirmishes of love, from displaying the Eagle in thine ensigne, to set down the sparow.
>
> (2.2.48–61)

The context is Hephaestion's *dissuasoria*, in which he counsels Alexander to resist his love for Campaspe. His first argument concerns beauty, and it takes the form of two similes: "Bewty is like the blackberry . . . resembling pretious stones." The proofs adduced against beauty, via the similes, are that when it appears to promise sweet enjoyment, in experience it "tastes" sour; when it seems the more flawless, it is the more brittle. The logical predicaments, *substance* and *quality*, inform both proofs,

11. "Prose Style," p. 23.

but they are drawn from two different levels of creation, vegetable and mineral, and involve two different characteristics, sweetness and durability. Thus four quite distinct categories have been invoked to exemplify the disadvantage of pursuing beauty, and we are asked to acknowledge that a likeness exists between attractive but ultimately unsatisfying beauty *and* delicious-looking but sour berries *and* apparently strong but fragile gems. This is considerable mental activity for two short sentences, but it is not all we are asked to do. As the similes are developed, they begin to function as allegory or extended metaphor, because we must infer the specific experience of beauty to which they refer: presumably, in the figure of fruit and taste, the bathos of sexual pleasure; in stone and hardness, the tenuousness of good faith. The connecting lines are not drawn for us, as they are in the similes most frequently cited by the rhetoricians, and part of the pleasure they afford lies in discovering the exact point of similarity between the comparison and the compared.[12]

In the second argument, two social levels are joined—those of seamen and wisemen—and their respective concerns—fish and great leaders. Here the comparison adduced is expressed first, and it is simply the marvel, reported by ordinary seamen, that the swiftest fish is consumed by the slowest. Then Hephaestion employs a *collatio*, or direct comparison, to indicate his real concern—the paradox that the heart of the strongest man should be captured by the weakest of creatures, a woman. The translation of "wonderful" to "monstrous" signals a shift from the neutral context of the animal world to the moral context of the human. The movements within the parable are therefore complex. For the argument to work, we must accept as comparable relationships the activities of fish and men, the qualities swiftness-slowness and strength-weakness, the functions of belly and hands, and natural and moral phenomena.

In the third argument, three antitheses are juxtaposed, united by the common disparity between their outer covering and inner content. The first contrast is aesthetic, the second chronological, the third moral. Although this last is presumably the base upon which the others form vari-

12. See, for example, George Puttenham, *The Arte of English Poesie,* ed. Gladys D. Willcock and Alice Walker (Cambridge, 1936), pp. 240–246, and Erasmus, *De copia verborum ac rerum,* "Tertius modus locupletandi exempla," and "De parabola" (*Opera omnia,* 1. 92–95 [Leiden, 1703]); also his *Parabolae sive similia* (*ibid.,* 1. 561–624).

ations, syntactically it is simply one of a series drawn from natural, architectural, and human contexts—all of which perform the same function of transmitting the argument.

The final plea urges the impropriety of a soldier in love. In the first clause, Hephaestion employs the synechdoche of camp and chamber to carry his meaning, thereby indicating the alternative environments in which Alexander may spend his life; in the second, the same point is made through the more vivid metonymy of Mars's armor and Venus's arms; in the third, contrasting epithets and nouns state directly what he will be about; in the fourth, the ridiculous spectacle of a maidenly tournament is evoked by the periphrasis of a champion displaying his impresa.

Some useful observations may be drawn from all this. First, a given argument in Lyly may be exemplified anywhere on the chain of being (and here I would include a link for such fictive emanations from the mind of man as Mars and Venus). Second, the specific characteristics of the exempla adduced in any single argument need not be analogous to one another, so long as their larger conceptual identity with their referent is maintained.[13] Third, through sheer abundance of matter, the distinction between tenor and vehicle is often blurred, and turns out to be not really important, since the point comes across anyway. As a result, the argument seems to be carried successively by different areas of experience, each reinforcing the central point, but also adding its own distinctive insight to the original problem.

The ideal informing this style of reasoning is *copia*. Principally, it is embodied in the tenth and eleventh methods of enriching an argument which are described by Erasmus in *De copia verborum ac rerum*—varying by proposition and by exemplum. We have noted the former before; it consists in propounding different arguments in support of a single thesis, along with proofs of those arguments. In Hephaestion's speech, the aim is dissuasion from love, and appropriate arguments are offered against

13. Rosemund Tuve makes precisely this point in her discussion of the logical predicaments and Elizabethan imagery: "the majority of images using trope would be covered formally by the definition: two things seen to be in parallel predicaments or 'places'" (*Elizabethan and Metaphysical Imagery* [Chicago, 1947], p. 286). Although she is warning us against reading undue significance into the sensuous accidents of such imagery, I am more interested in the way those accidents create a wider range of reference for any given concept.

beauty, uxoriousness, women, and impropriety. The proofs, as we have seen, are largely exemplary. The usefulness of such exempla in illuminating and strengthening an argument is stressed again and again by every rhetorician in the sixteenth century. "For furnishing *copia*," Erasmus writes, "exempla hold the first place, whether you may be deliberating, exhorting, consoling, praising, or vilifying. In sum, whether you wish to induce belief, or move, or delight."[14] Although these exempla are to be employed judiciously, the emphasis on their suasive powers and the illusion they provide of commanding a vast range of knowledge destined them for wide rather than restrained usage. Reading through Erasmus's book, one can recapture momentarily the excitement that a man like John Lyly must have experienced in drawing together his own *silva*, with potential proofs gathered under such headings as "Beneficence," "Treachery," "Gratitude," "Fidelity." Just look at the matter that Erasmus suggests might be placed under the heading "Inconstancy": from the poets, *fabulae* about Mercury, that cunning disguiser; exempla of Proteus, Morpheus, and Circe; the personification Opportunity; anecdotes about the hero Ulysses, always adapting himself to circumstances; from natural history, *similitudines* of the circling moon and of the changing autumn sky; a *collocatio* of the ebbing and flowing sea; from moral philosophy, exempla of the whims of childhood, the fickleness of women, the uncertainty of the multitude; from the arts, the *descriptio* of a shifting weather vane and of delicately balanced scales; from ingenium, a *comparatio* of the inconstant mind of man and a glittering mirror that hangs in a busy forum reflecting the movements of the crowd below; from history, the elusive nature of Cataline and the inconstancy of the Greeks; from comedy, the uncertainty of the lover Phaedria; from tragedy, the varying moods of Phaedra. The list goes on and on.[15] What is particularly suggestive about it—and Erasmus's work is only one of many such compendia in the period—is that an imaginative mind, contemplating the shifting forms of "Inconstancy," might easily take these exempla intended to

14. Ad parandam copiam, exempla primas tenent, sive delibeves, sive exhorteris, sive consoleris, sive laudes, sive vituperes. Et ut summatim dicam, sive fidem facere studeas, sive movere, sive delectare (*Opera omnia*, 1. 89). For a detailed discussion of the pursuit of *copia*, see William Garrett Crane, *Wit and Rhetoric in the Renaissance* (New York, 1937).

15. *Opera omnia*, 1. 103–105.

illustrate an argument and make them the *substance* of an argument—
thereby transforming it into a poetic declamation or the plot of a play.
Such a plot would slip lightly in and out of naturalistic and metaphoric
exposition, invoking a wide range of experience to carry its thesis forward, and create a continuous play of wit among its auditors. The dis-
tances between simile, metaphor, and allegory are short in Renaissance
poetics. And they share the common aim of arousing the wit to new apprehensions. "Allegory not infrequently results in enigma," observes
Erasmus. "Nor will that be unfortunate, if you are speaking to the learned,
or if you are writing. . . . For things should not be so written that everyone perceives everything, but rather so that they are compelled to investigate certain things, and learn."[16]

It is precisely this activity that is enjoined upon us by Lyly's characteristic medium—the elegant, allegorical court play. And if we approach it
in the terms outlined above, it becomes apparent that its plot, arising
from a *quaestio*, is often really a pair of *theses* argued copiously, now
through one order of the cosmos, now through another, until the whole
universe seems caught up in the strife. And like the argument of Hephaestion, when even one order finds accommodation, the rest seem to
resolve into new harmony. The most interesting examples of this delicate and witty kind of dramaturgy, it seems to me, are two of the middle
plays—*Gallathea* and *Endimion*—although the others also share its char-

16. Allegoria nonnumquam exit in aenigma. Neque id erit vitiosum, si doctis
vel loquaris vel scribas. . . . Neque enim ita scribendum, ut omnes omnia intelli-
gant, sed ut quaedam etiam vestigare ac discere cogantur (*ibid.*, 1. 19). That allegory is extended metaphor is a rhetorical commonplace of the period. In their
analysis of metaphor, the rhetoricians frequently discussed its cognitive function:
"the hearer is ledde by cogitation uppon rehearsall of a Metaphore, and thinketh
more by remembraunce of a worde translated, then is there expressly spoken"
(Thomas Wilson, *The Art of Rhetorique*, ed. G. H. Mair [Oxford, 1909], p. 171);
"they are requisite to match the compassing sweetness of men's minds, that are
not content to fix themselves upon one thing but they must wander into the confines. . . . Besides, a metaphor is pleasant because it enricheth our knowledge with
two things at once, with the truth and with the similitude" (John Hoskyns, *Directions for Speech and Style*, ed. H. H. Hudson [Princeton, 1935], p. 8). Metaphor is
not merely decorative, but an instrument for exercising the wit. This is, of course,
a main theme in Tuve.

acteristics.[17] Since they are generally considered to be the most provocative—and perplexing—plays in the Lyly canon, it might be profitable to examine them closely in the light of the *quaestio copiosa* and see if their peculiarities become more comprehensible.

III

Gallathea appears at first glance to be an oddly asymmetrical play. It begins with an exciting enough romance dilemma: in revenge for the destruction of his temple by the invading Danes, Neptune had flooded Lincolnshire, withdrawing only on the condition that every fifth year the most beautiful virgin in the country be sacrificed to the monster Agar as he swims up the Humber to fetch her. The year has rolled round once more and Tyterus, believing his daughter Gallathea to be the fairest, has disguised her as a boy, determined "to prevent (if it be possible) thy constellation by my craft" (1.1.65). Gallathea heroically argues that "Destiny may be deferred, not prevented," but nonetheless accedes to his wishes that she hide herself during the time of trial. What seems to emerge from the scene is a charming aetiological tale about the tidal bore or "eagre" that periodically floods the Humber and a good debate thesis turned dramatic cliffhanger: can the wiles of mortal shepherd evade divine destiny?

Two scenes later, the *quaestio* is complicated by the appearance of another father and daughter doing the same thing. "Everie one thinketh his own childe faire," Melebeus tells Phillida, "but I know that which I most desire and would least have, that thou art fairest" (1.3.4–6). Lest he allow her "to perrish by a fond desire, whom I may preserve by a sure deceipt," he persuades her to circumvent the custom of the country by hiding in the woods disguised as a boy "till the time be past, and *Neptune* pleased." Phillida consents reluctantly, not because she believes it futile or dishonorable, but simply because what her father asks is indecorous— man's apparel "will neither become my bodie, nor my minde." There is something highly comical, of course, in the spectacle of a second pair preparing to ward off the same unique fate—Neptune, after all, has called

17. It gets off to an uncertain start in *Sapho and Phao*, which is pitched between the discursive and allegorical modes, but is quite apparent in *Love's Metamorphosis*, *Midas*, and *The Woman in the Moon*.

for the "beautifullest virgin," not a brace of them—which immediately suggests that at least one of the shepherds is reading the divine intention in the light of the paternal eye. But more important is the drop in heroic tone that characterizes Melebeus's assessment of the situation, for it raises the possibility that what the shepherds are confronting is not destiny at all, but the whim of a lascivious god indulging his "fond desire." The question hangs in abeyance as we are soon absorbed by two new and unexpected developments.

One is the relationship of the now disguised girls, who meet in the woods and, each taking the other for a boy, fall in love. The growing seriousness of their piquant flirtation, as they begin to recognize their predicament, is traced delicately through the second, third, and fourth acts. Parallel to their growing dilemma, a conflict among the gods begins to take shape. Cupid, escaped from Venus, is loose in the woods. He encounters a nymph of Diana, who boasts to him that "there is none of *Dianaes* trayne that any can traine, either out of their waie, or out of their wits" (1.2.6–7), whereupon he instantly determines to prove his deity. He finds his opportunity when the two "boys," who have interrupted Diana's chase, are enlisted in her hunting party. He wounds the nymphs with desire for them, and giving up their chase they fall to sighs and jealous wrangling. Diana furiously chides such unaccustomed wantonness, and seizing Cupid asleep in the woods, she binds him and sets him to work pricking out all the amorous fables embroidered in her tapestry. Now it is Cupid's turn to threaten, and he does so in terms we have heard before: "*Diana* shall yeeld, she cannot conquer destenie" (4.3.89). A second fatality takes its place beside the first.

Meanwhile, a substitute virgin has been located by the shepherds, offered to Neptune, found wanting, and rejected. Enraged that men "dote so much on their daughters, that they stick not to dallie with our deities," Neptune vows that "the inhabitants [shall] see that destiny cannot be prevented by craft"—and then, oddly enough, threatens not simply to heap destruction upon the mortal shepherds but to wreak havoc on Diana's nymphs as well, and so to stain his temple with maidens' blood that "there shall be nothing more vile than to be a virgin" (4.3.11ff.). Whereupon Diana enters with her nymphs, pleading with Neptune not to forsake her, and Venus follows hard upon, demanding the release of Cupid. Suddenly—and rather comically—the bellicose Neptune finds himself the arbiter of a full-scale *altercatio* between the goddesses of love and chastity. *"Diana* I must honor," he concludes, "her vertue deserveth no lesse; but Venus I must love, I must confesse so much" (5.3.66–67). To resolve the dispute he agrees permanently to revoke the sacrifice of virgins if Diana will restore Cupid to Venus.

At this point the guilty fathers arrive, confessing their intrigue, and Neptune tells them—huffily, if rather anticlimactically—"Well, your deserts have not gotten pardon, but these Goddesses jarres." Gallathea and Phillida come forward and express their love for one another, dismaying everyone until Venus, convinced that their love is "unspotted, begunne with trueth, continued wyth constancie, and not to be altered tyll death," solves their problem by transforming one of them into a man (5.3.133–135). Which one we are not shown, but the heroic and feminine natures the girls displayed in the first act suggest the ultimate disposition of the sexes.

A happy ending for a comedy, but strangely off the point, it would seem. What has happened to the initial conflict of mortal and deity? And to Neptune's and Cupid's "destiny"? The fathers have successfully defied the sacrifice, but they really have not earned their victory since the ritual was cancelled to end the conflict of Venus and Diana. Besides, in seeking to preserve their daughters, they have lost them to a strange metamorphosis. Has Lyly, perhaps, begun with one story, only to wander into another? The play begins to attain clarity only when we recognize Lyly's peculiarly fluid method of developing his argument, and that we have begun by asking the wrong question. To ask the right one (or ones), we have to understand the way in which the initial situation is propounded, and then we will see that he has not lost track of his argument at all; he has simply made it manifest in different kinds of events as the play develops.

Lyly begins, as we have noted, with an aetiology of the Humber bore. But this involves several peculiarities which would not escape the attention of his audience. They would notice first that the setting is paradoxical. In characteristic fashion, Lyly has drawn together two distant worlds and treated the union as quite normal. The effect is palimpsestic. The action takes place at home—in England—and also in the classical pastoral world; thus the problems are simultaneously English and Arcadian, historic and eternal. It is an ideal medium in which to examine ethical questions of present concern, while enjoying the reassurance that they are only literary, after all.

Once alerted to the doubleness of vision required by Lyly's exposition, the audience can concentrate on the moral problem suggested by his allegorization of a familiar natural phenomenon. A powerful god has been insulted by the Danes and, in the form of the sea, has flooded the land in revenge. But not content with this, he has institutionalized vengeance among the present inhabitants by means of Agar's quinquennial assaults upon a chaste virgin. Concerning her fate all they can say is, "Whether she be devoured of him or conveied to Neptune or drowned between both, it is not permitted to knowe, and encurreth danger to conjecture" (1.1.54–56). It becomes clear in the course of Tyterus's *narratio* that while there is a certain justice in the god's action, his revenge is grown out of proportion and smacks of tyranny. In addition, there is more than a hint of sexual assault in the account of Neptune's doings. It is suggested in Melebeus's reference to the sacrifice as a means of satisfying the god's "fond desire," and in Tyterus's remark to Gallathea that "it is better to use an unlawfull means (your honour preserved) than intollerable greefe (both life and honor hazarded)" when he persuades her to hide in the woods (1.1.63–64). But beyond this is a mythic resonance that reinforces the ambivalence. In creating his initial situation, Lyly has conflated the myths of Galatea and Hesione. Galatea was traditionally associated with whiteness, purity, beauty (in Lyly she is at one point identified as a figure dressed in white), and her pursuer the cyclops Polyphemus, a son of Neptune, was identified with brutish concupiscence.[18] The sacrifice of Hesione, on the other hand, demanded by Neptune because her father Laomedon did not properly acknowledge his help in building the walls of Troy, was most frequently interpreted as a warning to give the gods their due.[19] Lyly's choice of name for his heroine, his characterization of

18. Telusa describes her as "the faire boy in the white coate" (3.1.43). George Sandys, the translator and popularizer, provides a typical reading of the moral allegory: "By the huge proportion of Polyphemus, the Physiologists present wrath, violence, and dissolute appetite. . . . His violent love to Galatea, no other then brutish concupiscence; of whom he is hated. For Galatea, begot by Nereus on Doris, to express her divine original, signifies beauty: and what sympathy hath beauty with deformity, be it either in person or manners?" (*Ovid's Metamorphoses Englished, Mythologized, and Represented in Figures. . . .* [Oxford, 1632], p. 453).

19. "From hence we may produce this allegory; that no common wealth or

Neptune as willful and peremptory—indeed, he is a caricature of the Calvinist deity—and his repeated hints that the sacrifice is a ritual deflowering, suggest that he wishes his audience to read the event in the light of the Galatea myth. But there is just enough hedging, in the repeated references to destiny, to raise prudent doubts about the wisdom of such defiance.[20]

As a result, the original dilemma we perceived—the opposition of human will to divine destiny—takes on much greater complexity. It becomes a matter of "should," not simply of "can." As the Terentian commentators might say, on the side of the fathers there is the extreme penalty exacted from them for a Danish crime, their fears for their daughters' honors, and the resonance of the Galatea myth; on the side of the god, there is the historic insult he has suffered, the sovereignty of divinity over human life, and the moral of the Hesione myth. This *status* is argued by adducing proofs from quite different contexts: "historic" exemplum (Tyterus's *narratio*), moral commonplace ("better to use an unlawfull means, your honour preserved, then intollerable greefe, your honor hazarded" vs. "destiny may be deferred, not prevented"), and mythic fable. It is not enough, therefore, to see the contention solely in terms of crafty mortals trying to cheat a god of his rights;[21] it involves just as deeply the question whether chastity can (or should) overcome lust, whether natural feeling and the rule of law are antithetical to one another, and whether private and public goods may be accommodated. These are all

---

Citty can be raised but by the devine assistance; or continue without religion, justice, and performance of promise; which violated, is the cause if not of utter ruine of infinite calamities" (*ibid.*, p. 391). In the *fabulosa exempla* of Marcus Antonius Tritonius, published with Conti's *Mythologiae*, Laomedon makes his appearance in no less than three vicious categories: *Avari, Ingrati,* and *Perfidi* (*Natalis Comitis / Mythologiae / sive explicationis fabularum / libri decem.* . . . [Padua, 1616]).

20. Neptune's determination to "marke all" and in the end "marre all" (2.2.24) seems childishly vindictive, as does his plan to "shew as great crueltie as they have doone craft" (4.3.5–6). But the Calvinist cast of his relationship to the shepherds is most explicit in the Augur's stern admonition: "If you imagine *Neptune* pittilesse to desire such a pray, confesse your selves perverse to deserve such a punishment" (4.1.5–7). The shepherds, however, have done nothing; they are merely being punished for the Danes' original sin.

21. This is the crucial flaw in Saccio's frequently illuminating discussion of the play (*Court Comedies*, pp. 114–129).

matters of concern to Lyly's audience, and they are shown in the play as aspects of one another, so that it becomes apparent that small, individual actions may have the widest of consequences.

Just as the problem is initially propounded through different kinds of proof, so it is carried forward on different levels of argumentation. As the plot progresses, the conflict of parents and god recedes from view and no longer bears the burden of the argument. Instead, Lyly develops the growing friendship of Gallathea and Phillida, attempting via romantic fable to examine the relationship of physical desire and chastity, will and destiny, feeling and order—and to seek some resolution of the common problem. The heroines appear intermittently to reveal the change they are undergoing. They are at first attracted by one another's beauty (2.1); then begin to feel the effects of passion (2.4, 5); then become dismayed as they suspect that they are of the same sex (3.2); finally, they agree to play lover and mistress despite what they know about one another (4.4). They are, in fact, making the passage from virginity through desire to love— as Gallathea herself implies when, lamenting her enslavement to Cupid, she decides nonetheless to follow Phillida into the woods, praying, "And thou, sweet *Venus*, be my guide" (2.3.12–13).[22]

While this steady moral progression is taking place as naturalistic exemplum (the *character* Cupid is not involved in their love affair), the inquiry is carried forward on another level in the mythic fable of Cupid and Diana. Their conflict is not physically separated from the story of Gallathea and Phillida, for traditionally in pastoral mortals and gods share the same terrain, but they are a different breed of dramatic character and in them the issues take on lighter, more broadly comic outlines.[23] In this opposition, there is no stern, frightening god pitted against a humble, if comically doting, set of parents, but rather a mischievous imp set loose amongst a petulant spinster and her bevy of young wards. As the battleground for Cupid and Diana, the nymphs are relatively multidimensional figures, but the champions themselves are virtually emblematic. Diana is the embodiment of strict chastity, who sees only the

22. It is essential to notice that Venus and Cupid are not identical in this play.

23. The fulsome use of simile, employed throughout *Campaspe*, is largely confined in this play to the fruity dialogue of the Cupid-Venus plot. Lyly seems to be making a conscious effort to differentiate his styles and thus the respective tones of his analogues.

painful, superficial aspects of love. "You should think love like Homer's moly," she counsels her nymphs, "a white leaf and a black root, a fair show and a bitter taste" (3.4.23–25). Having no patience with play, she consistently personifies virginity, industry, and—somewhat oddly, considering her myopic point of view—reason. Set against her notion of destiny is Cupid's physical desire, idle contemplation, and irrational impulse:

> A heate full of coldnesse, a sweet full of bitternesse, a paine full of pleasantnesse; which maketh thoughts have eyes, and harts eares; bred by desire, nursed by delight, weaned by jelousie, kild by dissembling, buried by ingratitude; and this is love! fayre Lady, wil you any? (1.2.16–20)

As *emblemata*, Cupid and Venus sometimes function as objective dramatic characters, sometimes as moral allegories. In his capacity as dramatic character, Cupid plots and attacks Diana's nymphs, and is captured by them. But as he is set to the ignominious task of untying love knots, he finds that he cannot do it, for "it goeth against my mind to make them loose" (4.2.31). Thus, even when the nymphs, restored to Diana's rule, capture and torment him, he is still exerting his innate force upon all that he touches. Lyly cleverly exploits this duality to bring about the denouement. When Diana vows to keep Cupid prisoner so she may punish him for leaving scars in her virgins' hearts, Venus replies:

> Scarres, *Diana*, call you them that I know to be bleeding woundes? Alas! weake deitie, it stretcheth not so farre, both to abate the sharpness of his Arrowes and to heale the hurts. No! Loves woundes when they seeme green, rankle; and having a smoothe skinne without, fester to the death within. (5.3.45–49)

Thus virgins, though they desire to be chaste, may still suffer the pangs of desire. In the face of this stalemate, Venus demands judgment of Neptune: "let either *Diana* bring her Virgins to a continuall massacre or release *Cupid* of his martyrdome" (5.3.51–52).

It is here that the most revealing modulation of all occurs. For the "massacre" that Venus refers to is the devastation Cupid continues to wreak on the wounded nymphs; but Neptune immediately translates it into the ritual "massacre" he has himself been leading against the shepherds' daughters. He settles the debate by restating Venus's proposal in his own terms: "*Diana*, restore *Cupid* to *Venus*, and I will for ever release the sacrifice of Virgins" (5.3.68–69). This can only mean—simultaneously—"*your* virgins will no longer be tormented by Cupid" and "the mortal virgins I have pursued will no longer be ravished by me." The conflation demonstrates that the theomachy of Cupid and Diana and the debate confrontation in which Venus appears as Cupid's advocate are simply analogues to the sacrifice of the virgins demanded by Neptune: as Cupid ravishes his victims with desire, sacrificing their spiritual virginity, so does Agar physically rape them. But they are not analogues in the way subplot is analogous to main plot. They are all coordinate vehicles for transmitting a single dramatic argument. It is because the question *can* be argued in different contexts that Neptune, responding to an ostensibly different "event," is able to settle the original problem—thereby altering the state of affairs from continual strife between lust and chastity to accommodation in chaste love. It is a peculiar dramatic method, but a not unexpected result of arguing copiously on both sides of the question.

The other issues that have appeared from time to time as aspects of the conflict between chastity and lust are also brought to resolution here. In accepting Venus's plea, Neptune remarks, "It were unreasonable that I shold not yeeld," and then urges Diana to do her part by releasing Cupid, "if therefore you love your Nimphes as shee doth her son, or preferre not a private grudge before a common griefe" (5.3.68–71). Reason, in the context of community obligation, has been opposed to personal feeling several times in the play. It is acknowledged in Tyterus's decision, quoted above, "to use an unlawful means rather than suffer intollerable greefe," and it is stated explicitly in the augur's warning to the recalcitrant fathers, "If you think it against nature to sacrifice your children, thinke it also against sence to destroy your country" (4.1.4–5).[24] Throughout the play it is apparent that a civic crisis has been precipitated by Neptune's demand, and the conflict between natural, creaturely feeling and communal duty seems irreconcilable. But this opposition, too, simply

24. Neptune echoes the sentiment when he declares that "so over carefull are Fathers to their children, that they forgette the safetie of their Country, & fearing to become unnatural, become unreasonable" (4.3.3–5); and poor Hebe, the substitute virgin, implies the same antithesis when she complains, "Shall it onely be lawfull amongst us in the prime of youth and pride of beautie, to destroy both youth and beautie?" (5.3.21–22).

melts away as Neptune acquiesces before Venus. The problem, it would seem, obtains only when the ruler is a cupidinous despot; when he abdicates his sceptre to the conciliatory goddess of love, feeling and law are wedded.

This is most clearly revealed when the lovers emerge once again into the foreground and actualize the ideological and mythic accommodations that have taken place. Hearing their story, Venus offers to complete their joy in each other instantly by turning one of them into a man, for "What is to Love or the Mistrisse of Love unpossible?" (5.3.142). In this act, all oppositions are disposed harmoniously. The girls are chaste, and yet love. Feeling and order coalesce. Private good becomes public good. And destiny has been fulfilled. But that destiny is Venus—not Neptune, or Cupid, or Diana, or even parental domination.

At this point Lyly's English boys—Rafe, Robin, and Dick—who have up to now also been unsuccessful in attempting to scrutinize the divine intention—come trooping out and find their vocation as choristers at Gallathea's wedding. They have put in an appearance every third scene or so, reminding us through their adventures with the mariner, alchemist, and astronomer that the pastoral adventure is, after all, taking place at home.[25] Now, for the first time, they join the Arcadian shepherds and the classical deities, as Lyly brings his audience back to England with the implied *collatio* that here, too, Neptunes and Cupids, Dianas and meddlesome fathers, may assert their partial ways, but social content and moral satisfaction may be found only in the ardent constancy of Venus. In a court dominated by an autocratic Queen, who nonetheless desired both social harmony and the adoration of her subjects, the point would not be missed. But the point is neither simply to flatter nor admonish the Queen and her courtiers. It is rather to lead them, lightly and gracefully, to consider the ramifications of the familiar questions concerning love,

---

25. Saccio interprets their running adventure as a critical comment on the desire of men to usurp the functions of the deity, and therefore sees it as an analogue of the main plot, in which the shepherds defy Neptune. But if my argument is correct that Neptune is an unjust, partial god—as are Cupid and Diana—then the professionals in this analogue represent on the human level the same myopic view of power, which is suggested in their idiosyncratic jargon. The satire is directed not against men who try to ape the gods, but against those who follow blind gods.

obedience to a ruler, private and public obligations that fill their literature and conversation—and to perceive that here, at the hub of empire, these inevitably interweave. A compassionate ruler, and subjects who manage to forge moral relationships among themselves and with their sovereign, need not experience the wrenching conflict between personal and public loyalties that tears so many societies apart. "Yeeld to love," Gallathea urges the ladies in the audience, as she delivers her epilogue. Should that ideal be achieved, Lyly suggests, perhaps even the Humber will cease to flood its banks.

IV

Gallathea is an outrageous piece of playwriting. To figure forth his question, Lyly invokes landscapes from England and the Aegean, tragic and domestic psychologies, human shepherd figures and emblematic deities, mythic allusion, disputation, romantic exemplum—creating an imaginative world in which each level of experience may participate at one time or another in the fundamental strife and ultimate reconciliation. In *Endimion*, he attempts a variation on this form that is at once more complex and more controlled. Now, instead of dilating a central question by projecting it in a dramatic argument that is enacted successively by different characters who represent its various ontological manifestations, he constructs a fable out of three related issues that are considered separately—all of which, however, involve a *single* set of characters who, without changing their names, continually shift their significances. The questions are traditional: What kind of relationsh˙p must the Courtier have with his sovereign? Should love or friendship bear the greater sway in determining men's actions? What constitutes royal justice? Each of them provides a distinct area of exploration that enables the plot to proceed to the next stage and ultimately to its conclusion. The result is a subtle critique of court life which, unlike *Gallathea* (in this respect, more closely resembling *Sapho and Phao*), suggests that in the achievement of general harmony there can be real personal loss.

The play opens upon Endimion's passionate declaration of love for Cynthia. His speech represents one side of that familiar Renaissance controversy, whether the life of the Courtier should be devoted to arms or the lady. Eumenides' reply represents the other side:

If you be enamored of any thing above the Moone, your thoughts are ridiculous, for that thinges immortall are not subject to affections; if allured or enchaunted with these transitory things under the Moone, you shew your selfe senceless, to attribute such lofty tytles, to such lowe tryfles. (1.1.7–11)

Whether ethereal or sublunary, Eumenides argues, love is equally nonsensical. It is important that we notice the debate substructure of this first scene because it provides the proper perspective for viewing the ensuing action, in which Endimion is conceived as a Courtier at the crossroads. If his dilemma is to be resolved, both elements in his life—the amorous and the honorable—must be appropriately disposed so that he can function as an integral human being. The problem has obvious relevance to members of Elizabeth's court, and they would follow the plot with interest to see how this ideal might be achieved.

Whatever his ultimate vocation, Endimion is already an accomplished wit. Seizing Eumenides' universal condemnation of love as a happy opening, he adroitly discloses the exact nature of his own. It is placed neither above the moon, nor below it, but in the moon itself. To his friend's horror, he then delivers an encomium of the beloved planet, which Eumenides interprets literally, believing him mad. Endimion, however, hints to the audience that he has, in fact, been expounding the virtues of his lady through an extended *allegoria*:

Vaine *Eumenides*, whose thoughts never grow higher then the crowne of thy head. Why troublest thou me, *having neither heade to conceive the cause of my love, or a hart to receive the impressions*: followe thou thine own fortunes, which creepe on the earth, & suffer me to flye to mine, whose fall though it be desperate, yet shall it come by daring. (1.1.70–75, emphasis mine)

With this speech, Endimion begins to suggest some of the more profound implications of the traditional love-honor conflict upon which one may feed one's wit. The significant word pairs are *creep-earth* and *fly-daring*. They are amplified in the scene immediately following. Just after the two friends depart, Tellus comes onstage to revile Endimion for betraying her. In her first speech she speaks as an injured Court Lady abandoned by her "servant." But when Floscula, her companion, re-

217

minds her that Cynthia's state being so high above her own, she ought
rather to admire Endimion's exalted thoughts than condemn them, she
answers:

> Is not my beauty divine, whose body is decked with faire flowers,
> and vaines are Vines, yeelding sweet liquor to the dullest spirits,
> whose eares are Corne, to bring strength, and whose heares are
> grasse, to bring abundance? Doth not Frankinsence & Myrrhe
> breath out of my nostrils, and all the sacrifice of the Gods breede in
> my bowels? Infinite are my creatures, without which neyther thou,
> nor *Endimion*, nor any could love, or live. (1.2.19–26)

Here, Tellus abruptly modulates from Court Lady to a figure of the
earth itself, providing sustenance for its creatures. In this context, Endimion's desire to fly above the earth, expressed earlier, seems daring
indeed—in fact, unnatural and unhealthy—while Eumenides' propensity
to creep seems an appropriate mode of conduct for a man. Lyly has used
the physical allegory to provide another view of Endimion's aspiration,
which shadows a desire to abandon his creatureliness. When we recall,
however, that in their original terms, to "fly" meant to pursue the life
of love and to "creep" meant to pursue the life of honor, a third pair of
alternative impulses becomes apparent—the desire for immortality (his
"imaginations," Floscula observes, "are immortal") opposed to the desire for (mere) earthly honor.[26] Endimion's conflict has therefore been
presented successively as a choice between love and honor, the Queen
and her Gentlewoman, creaturely suicide and nurture, and immortal
longings and domestic fame. The original question, examined in different
contexts, has rapidly expanded to suggest the full resonances of the
Courtier's choice of life at the hub of Eliza's symbolic universe. Again
the approach is sophistic, and derives from the ideal of copious argumentation. The death of Socrates, Erasmus observes, may be used as an exemplary proof that death should not be feared by the good man, that
virtue is never safe from envy, that the study of philosophy leads one to
a bad end, that judges always respect aristocracy before merit. The image

26. The antithesis recalls Octavius's later remark in *Antony and Cleopatra:* "No
grave upon the earth shall clip in it A pair so famous" (5.2.355–356). There, of
course, the conflict assumes tragic proportions, but the terms remain the same:
"Kingdoms are clay . . . the nobleness of life Is to do thus" (1.1.35–37).

remains the same; only its significance shifts.[27] Through a similar exercise in invention, the courtly audience now begins to perceive that within that staple of polite conversation—the conventional love-honor question—other, more deeply existential conflicts lie enfolded.

All this has been suggested within only two scenes. But there is even more before we get much further into the play. Following hard upon her rich physical allegory as symbol of fecundity, Tellus begins to talk like Mundus in a morality play:

> I will entangle him such in a sweet nette, that he shall neither find the means to come out, nor desire it. All allurements of pleasure will I cast before his eyes, insomuch that he shall slake that love which he now voweth to *Cynthia*, and burne in mine, of which he seemeth carelesse. . . . All his vertues will I shadow with vices; his person (ah sweet person) shall he decke with such rich Roabes, as he shall forget it is his own person; his sharp wit (ah wit too sharpe, that hath cut off all my joyes) shall he use, in flattering of my face, and devising Sonnets in my favour. (1.2.41–45, 54–58)

Here Lyly again complicates the Cynthia-Tellus opposition, by switching to a *moral* allegory that suggests not the dangers of abandoning creatureliness but those that inhere in allegiance to the too-much-loved earth. This transition to yet another rhetorical vantage point has misled many commentators into assuming that Endimion's sleep represents a lapse into sensuality, from which he can be aroused only by the spiritual invigoration of Cynthia's kiss. But it would appear from his own lamentation to Cynthia shortly before he is put to sleep that he has resisted such temptation:

> Whom have I wondered at but thee? Nay, whom have I not contemned for thee? Have I not crept to those on whom I might have trodden, only because thou didst shine upon them? . . . With *Tellus*, fair *Tellus*, have I dissembled, using her but as a cloak for mine affections, that others seeing my mangled mind, might think it were for one that loveth me, not for *Cynthia*, whose perfection alloweth no companion nor comparison. (2.1.16–19, 22–26)

Here it becomes clear that Endimion has survived Tellus's designs upon his character. But ironically, he has become subject to her in another way.

27. *Opera omnia*, I. 102.

He has "crept"—he has, that is, courted worldly favor—which is precisely what Tellus wanted. "It shall suffice me," she tells Floscula, "if the world talk that I am favored of Endimion" (1.2.73–74). Thus Tellus now emerges as that aspect of earth which was suggested before: earthly fame, with all its vicissitudes. It is Endimion's honor, not his character, that she has been able to debase.[28] That she is indeed Rumor, Full of Tongues, is suggested in her exchange with Cynthia, following the discovery of Endimion's enchantment. Regretfully, Cynthia expresses her forlorn hope that Endimion's maturity might have amended his wayward youth. Tellus replies spitefully:

> But timely, madam, crooks that tree that will be a cammock, and young it pricks that will be a thorn; and therefore he that began without care to settle his life, it is a sign without amendment he will end it. (3.1.36–39)

For this malicious slander Cynthia banishes her to the desert castle, there to work tapestries of histories and poetry, "for she shall find examples infinite in either what punishment long tongues have."[29]

Clearly, Lyly is unfolding his fable in the most oblique manner imaginable, and has woven the whole first section of the plot—up to Endimion's enchantment—out of different refractions emitted by the Courtier's problematic relationship to royal power. But if the enchantment itself is not meant to suggest acquiescence in sensuality (and Dipsas's remark as she casts her spell confirms this[30]), what are we to make of it? Tellus's vengeance appears to be the vehicle for a more serious psychological process occurring within Endimion. A clue to its nature is found in Endimion's acknowledgement, quoted above, that Cynthia's perfection "alloweth no companion nor comparison." This is an admission of his failure to gain his suit. Having no hope of possessing her, and with his

28. Tellus is frequently linked with fortune in the play, and the lover's fortunes contrasted with his fidelity. Thus earthly fame influences one's fortune despite desert. See 1.2.85–86; 2.1.6; 2.3.2–3.

29. Her chastisement seems to work, for when she returns to testify at the end of the play, it is repeatedly emphasized that now she speaks the truth. Cf. 5.3.55, 136, 157.

30. "Hadst thou placed thy heart as lowe in love, as thy head lieth now in sleepe, thou mightest have commanded *Tellus* whom nowe in stead of a Mistris, thou shalt finde a tombe" (2.3.25–27).

thoughts nonetheless "stitched to the stars," he now tends to isolate himself and withdraw from all action. "I would die with wondering," he says to Tellus (1.4.100); "I will see if I can beguile myself with sleep," he tells himself later, "and if no slumber will take hold in my eyes, yet I will embrace the golden thoughts in my head and wish to melt by musing" (2.3.4–7). His obsession with the unattainable ideal draws him toward self-annihilation, and in this respect his slumber upon the bank of lunary symbolizes the inertia brought about by the growing hostility of Cynthia under the influence of Tellus's rumors.[31]

That he suffers a kind of spiritual sloth is revealed by the dream he has immediately after falling asleep. In his first vision, he sees himself subjected to judgment, which suggests that he feels guilt for some offense.[32] The second vision indicates the content of this guilt. As he describes it later, an old man presents him with a book of three leaves. The first and second, containing "counsels" and "policies," he rejects, to the outrage of the bearded elder. The third he accepts, and is horrified to find portrayed upon it the vivid image of a court intrigue directed at Cynthia's life. The scenario warns him that in removing himself from the round of activities that constitutes the courtier's proper function—offering advice and planning policy—he has abandoned his sovereign to the drones and beetles who will suck her life blood. Ironically, this has come about from worshipping her too well.

Endimion's sleep is a dramatic event and also a rhetorical impasse. To resolve it, Lyly launches the second movement of the play, centered this time on Eumenides.[33] En route to Thessaly for a cure, Eumenides comes upon Geron[34] at a magic fountain that grants the wish of any true lover

---

31. The word "melt" and its cognates are used several times in the play to signify moral dissolution, e.g. 3.4.2, 74; 4.3.122; and, in parody, 3.3.62.

32. In the dumb show, the Endimion figure will show signs of fright corresponding to Endimion's later testimony: "I started in my sleepe, feeling my verie veines to swell, and my sinewes to stretch with feare, and such a colde sweate bedewed all my bodie, that death it selfe could not be so terrible as the vision" (5.1. 90–93).

33. The "benevolent one," but also a play on *menoides*, the new moon.

34. An old man, but also (L. *geranitis*) a precious stone which owes its name to the crane's neck (Pliny, *Naturalis historia*, 37.187). See Cynthia's reference to Dipsas's habit of collecting "stones agreeable to thine Arte" (5.3.29). It would seem that Pliny is also the source of the "rough hewne," "tough and unsmoothed"

who weeps into its waters. He begins to tremble at this news, for he has secretly adored Semele[35] these many years, and now fears that perhaps his motive has been lust and not true love. Whereupon he begins to weep copiously and the water clears, disclosing a message at the bottom of the fountain. It is here that Lyly's concern to air the complexity of a courtly issue takes a rather waggish turn. Given the opportunity to obtain one wish, Eumenides suddenly—if not unexpectedly—decides to ask for Semele. But just as he is about to do so, he remembers his mission. With that, he enters upon a classic *deliberatio*, weighing the remote dangers of Endimion's slumber against the immediate pleasures of sleeping with Semele, the loss of a friend against the loss of his beloved, the value of enticing beauty against that of rare fidelity, and so on.[36] The full irony toward which this debate is heading does not become apparent until Eumenides, unable to resolve his dilemma, asks Geron's advice. After another lengthy *comparatio*, the old man counsels him to honor eternal friendship before ephemeral physical love. Eumenides acquiesces in this argument, declaring that "Vertue shall subdue affections, wisdom lust, friendship beauty" (3.4.143–144), and begs the fountain for the secret of Endimion's cure. What has been entirely forgotten in their extended contemplation of the opposing claims of love and friendship is that Eumenides has been recognized by the fountain as a true lover—not a luster after the flesh. Thus, while the "decision" gets the plot moving again, it by no means concludes the inquiry. Tacitly, at least, Lyly is commenting on the artificiality of such categorization, and is, in fact, suggesting that only a true lover can be a true friend.[37]

Corsites (L. *corsoides*), a stone, Pliny remarks, that reminds us of gray hair (*ibid.*, 37.153).

35. Perhaps *simila*, fine wheat flour, in the physical allegory. But morally, accord—ing to Conti, the etymology of the name Semele is *membra concutiens* [sic], from σειεν (*concutere*) and μελες (*membrum*) (*Mythologia sive explicationum fabularum / libri decem* . . . [Venice, 1568] p. 339b). Hence, a disturbing member of the court.

36. Lyly is pursuing here, in the more explicit form of debate, the same kind of inquiry that he had wrought so much more artfully *through plot* in the first two acts. There is a consequent falling-off in imaginative impact, but what we are experiencing is simply a less fully hypothesized version of the same expository impulse we enjoyed earlier. Such are the pleasures of allusive fiction over those of direct argumentation.

37. This truth is later made explicit by Geron when he exonerates Eumenides

The final question to be considered—the nature of royal justice—is occasioned by Bagoa's betrayal of the plot against Endimion after he has been cured by Cynthia's kiss. Cynthia presides at the trial of Dipsas, Tellus, and—since he is a material witness—of Endimion himself. Her actions in this scene culminate a long and subtle process of development. It begins in the first part of Endimion's frightening dream. There, a lady who holds a knife and a mirror is accompanied by two other female figures who seem to represent revenge and mercy. The former urges her to stab Endimion, while the latter bewails his misfortune but does nothing to prevent it. After some hesitation, the first lady gazes into her mirror, and casts down her knife. The figure holding the knife is apparently some kind of executive power, for the others wield no weapons but merely influence her. Revenge, or strict justice, urges the death of Endimion— as it should, for in the paradoxical terminology of Elizabethan psychology, revenge is an active passion. Mercy, being meek, only "wrings her hands, lamenteth, offering still to prevent it, but dares not" (2.2.s.d.). The identity of the central figure is indicated by the instruments she holds. She can, incited by revenge, summarily execute; or, heeding the plea of mercy, seek out the truth of the matter (symbolized by the *speculum sapientiae*) and forgive, if the truth warrants forgiveness. This central lady, therefore, suggests a distinctly civic virtue—the pursuit of equity. And the dumb show adumbrates, very early in the plot, the final *quaestio* through which the denouement will be effected: how is the just ruler to respond to the evils that are generated by Court life?

But it is still only a dumb show, placed in the second act to figure forth Endimion's sense of guilt. Its larger public significance does not become evident until the fifth act, when Endimion describes his dream to the Court. In his account, the central lady is flanked, as before, by two contrasting figures, but now their ontological separation from her is made clear:

> After long debating *with her selfe*, mercie overcame anger; and there appeared in her heavenlie face such a divine Majestie, mingled with a sweete mildnesse, that I was ravished with the sight above measure. (5.1.96–99, emphasis mine)

---

of Semele's accusation that he preferred his friend to his beloved (5.3.224-225). Thus the irony is deliberate.

With these words, Endimion explicates the allegory: mercy and revenge represent qualities within the central lady, and as they work upon her she is transfigured into a symbol of *maiestas* and *misericordia*—sovereign power infused with grace. By contrast, her companions remain unchanged, for "the one retained still an unmoveable crueltie, the other a constant pittie" (101–102). They are personifications, while she is the symbol of a *process*.

In the course of his narration, however, all three abstractions take on more particular qualities. The central lady, who appears at first to be "passing faire, but very mischeevous," brings to mind Cynthia, whose hostility caused Endimion's despair, and with whom alone majesty has been associated.[38] Similarly, the second figure is characterized as a lady "with a settled malice engraven in her eyes," and the word "malice" has been attached repeatedly to Tellus.[39] The third figure, whom Endimion portrays as one who lamented his fortune but could do nothing about it, recalls Floscula, who has remained strangely quiescent, but deeply sympathetic to him from the beginning.[40] Lyly's point in suggesting these associations is not to make us believe that Cynthia *is* equity, Tellus revenge, and Floscula mercy—any more than we were to believe they were moon, earth, and flowers in the first act—but rather once again to expand the specific human actions in the play to reveal the wider moral concerns behind them.[41]

38. "Thy Majestie *Cynthia* al the world knoweth and wondereth at, but not one in the world that can immitate it, or comprehend it" (2.1.16–18). Cf. Tellus's later remark (5.3.145–149).

39. 1.2.52; 2.3.36; 4.1.9; 4.3.145; 5.3.4, 64.

40. See esp. 1.4.5–6. Here, as Tellus determines to execute her malice through the agency of Dipsas's magic, Floscula mysteriously withdraws from further action with the words, "Use your discretion: I will in this case neither give counsell or consent." It is the reticence of mercy that she is figuring, though in a context that does not allow us to dwell upon it. Perhaps her words (and those of Tellus) are accompanied by gestures that are repeated in the pantomime of the dumb show to cause a flicker of recognition.

41. The relationship between the characters in the play and the figures in the dream allegory has been a matter of some speculation among recent critics. Huppé, Bryant, and Saccio regard the dream as a version of the traditional allegory of the Four Daughters of God—despite the numerical discrepancy—and the various Daughters have been both summed up in Cynthia and attached to other characters. The most detailed argument is Saccio's: since, in the final scene, Cynthia

As the trial opens, then, we are well prepared to perceive the general issue that underlies the particular judgment of Dipsas, Tellus, and Endimion. We know that in considering each case, Cynthia shall "heare of it in justice, and then judge of it in mercy" (5.3.10–11). But how this will come about remains a mystery. It is the final exercise in invention to which our wits are lured.

As ever, Lyly is full of surprises. The trial opens not upon the spectacle of Astrea returned to earth, but in the English Court, here and now. For he modulates his metaphor once again to point up the relevance of this fictional issue to the present concerns of his audience. As Cynthia arraigns Dipsas, she becomes more explicitly than ever England's Virgin Queen confronting an old enemy who has for "almost these fifty years practiced that detested wickedness of witchcraft" (21–22). The reference to Dipsas's facility with wonder-working simples and stones of secret virtue gathered from the earth—associating her with a long line of experimenting *religieux*—deftly draws into view Elizabeth's problems with the perennially scheming Roman Church. The allegory need extend no farther than this speech to serve its purpose, which is to light up yet another sphere of courtly concern, deeply involving the question of royal justice.[42] But within this extended metaphor, Cynthia employs the tra-

---

threatens revenge, seeks truth, extends mercy, and establishes peace in her Court, she represents the divine attributes in God's vice-gerant. But since Tellus speaks only truth, Dipsas demands justice upon herself, and Semele is pacified after her early contentiousness, the Court Ladies *also* figure three of the Daughters, while in this configuration Cynthia figures mercy. Although the first part of this argument is perhaps plausible, the confusion engendered by the latter (Cynthia is simultaneously all four Daughters and *also* mercy) renders it a highly improbable method of exposition, even for Lyly. But the greatest objection remains, surely, the implausible stretching of the three figures into four.

42. The twice-repeated period of fifty years of mischief obviously refers to the upheaval of the thirties, when Henry VIII was excommunicated and the foundations laid for a permanent break with Rome. But if the play was written prior to 1587, Dipsas may be figuring Mary Stuart (b. 1542), with whom, for all Lyly knew, there was still hope of reconciliation. My aim is not to urge any specific reading—the precise allusion is probably no longer retrievable—but merely to point out that the allusion *is* religious, and that it is perfectly in keeping with Lyly's use of allegory that he touch lightly on a contemporary issue to suggest the wider relevance of the matter at hand.

ditional legal procedures through which one may arrive at the truth and judge in knowledge.

She begins her examination of Dipsas by delineating the full scope of her offense, and Dipsas responds by admitting everything. Thus the first *status* of the judicial cause—*an sit?*—is resolved. Though Dipsas, whether in the character of the Church or *in propria persona*—seems penitent, Cynthia is not disposed to offer mercy. She threatens instead to send her "into the Desertte amongst wilde beastes, and try whether you can cast Lyons, Tygars, Bores, and Beares into as deade a sleep as you did Endimion" (66–68). Only when the sorceress has passed through all three stages of Christian repentance—confession, contrition, and amendment of purpose—does Cynthia relinquish revenge and respond with forgiveness.[43] As foreshadowed in the dumb show, mercy is not vouchsafed gratuitously; it is an achieved response, and the vehicles of that achievement are rhetorical structures designed to ascertain factual and moral truth. Through them, the first reconciliation of revenge and mercy is effected.

In dealing with Tellus, Cynthia begins in exactly the same mood of revenge. At first she threatens a punishment commensurate to the crime; then, in the spirit of honest inquiry, she demands to know the reason for such aberrant behavior:

> But tell me *Tellus*, what was the cause of this cruel part, farre unfitting thy sexe, in which nothing should be but simplenes; and much disagreeing from thy face, in which nothing seemed to bee but softnes. . . . Say on, *Tellus*: I cannot imagine anie thing that can colour such a crueltie. (69–72, 79–80)

Although angry, she extends an invitation to Tellus to employ the *status qualitatis* in her defense, that mode of argument which allows for exami-

43. The steps are clearly marked in the dialogue: "Madame, thinges past may be repented, not recalled: there is nothing so wicked that I have not doone, nor anything so wished for as death" (5.4.39–41); "Yet among al the things that I committed there is nothing so much tormenteth my rented and ransackt thoughts, as that in the prime of my husbands youth I divorced him by my divillish Arte" (41–44); "Madame, I renounce both substance and shadow of that most horrible and hateful trade; vowing to the Gods continuall penaunce, and to your highnes obedience" (262–264). What Lyly has done is graft onto the *an sit* argument the traditional Christian procedure for discovering the truth and securing equity, thereby subtly extending the religious allegory.

nation of motive and circumstances, and thus for an equitable judgment. Tellus proclaims the truth, pleading the *purgatio cupidinis*—the constraints of love—and unfolds the whole history of her passion for Endimion, his treachery, and her subsequent desperation. It is evident here that Lyly has adapted to court comedy the Latin judgment scene which serves both as epistemological denouement and moral solvent. For Cynthia seems genuinely distressed to discover that Endimion has despised his life and sought death because of his love for her, and the inquiry now proceeds to him:

> Was there such a time when as for my love thou didst vow thy selfe to death, and in respect of it loth'd thy life? speake, *Endimion*, I will not revenge it with hate. (159–160)

With this question, the action reaches a critical point, for the Courtier cannot publicly declare his passion for the Queen without forever compromising their relationship.

And so Endimion does the next best thing, in their mutual interest. He invokes the third procedure traditionally used to arrive at a just assessment of the issue—the *status definitivus: quid sit?* That he has honored Cynthia above all the world he readily admits, "but to stretch it so far as to call it love I never durst" (163–164). And he goes on to acknowledge that their stations being so far apart, his relationship to her must be compounded only of duty, loyalty, and reverence. But then, the public voice suddenly fades, and a strange lyric note creeps in:

> with imagination of which, I will spend my spirits, and to my selfe that no creature may heare, softlie call it love. And if any urge to utter what I whisper, then will I name it honor. (173–175)

It is an intimate message to Cynthia, informing her that he has not really rooted his passion for her from his heart; he has only learned to control it more discreetly.

But Cynthia in her wisdom absorbs this oblique declaration of personal devotion into the larger covenant through which she relates to all her subjects, and transforms Endimion's message into a practical public understanding:

> Endimion, this honorable respect of thine, shalbe christned love in thee, & my reward for it favor. Persever *Endimion* in loving me, & I

account more strength in a true hart, then in a walled Cittie. I have
laboured to win all, and studie to keepe such as I have wonne. . . .
 (179–182)

She, too, can make use of the *status definitivus*. Let us indeed, she declares,
call your respect for me "love," and in this game my largesse will be considered a lady's "favor." Slowly, through her speech, the ardent and romantic Endimion recedes from view and becomes just another faithful
courtier, offering the appropriate response. Which is all that Cynthia
really needs. The resolution of the play is thus highly witty and not a
little disturbing. Cynthia has settled the intrigues of her Court by hearing each case through the traditional procedures of justice and judging
each in mercy—thereby realizing a truly humanistic approach to creaturely evil.[44] And Endimion has come to understand the necessity of re-
disposing his desires so that he may fulfill his proper function as a citizen
of Cynthia's commonwealth. But the inner conflict he felt at the beginning he still feels, and—for all we can tell—will go on feeling. Lyly seems
to offer no solution for the individual who aspires to excellence in a rigidly hierarchical system—which is just the insight we might expect of
the playwright who exercised his wit for the Queen all his professional
life and was never granted the distinction he sought. In the epilogue, the
allegory modulates one final time to include a troubled court maker:

> Dread Soveraigne, the malicious that seeke to overthrowe us with
> threats, do but stiffen our thoughts, and make them sturdier in
> stormes: but if your Highnes vouchsafe with your favorable beames
> to glaunce upon us, we shall not onlie stoope, but with all humilitie,
> lay both our handes and heartes at your Majesties feet.

It is a plea that for him, too, Cynthia reconcile justice with mercy.

44. Notice that she is speaking as queen here and not as divinity. She makes it
clear that her jurisprudence has limitations, beyond which the problem of evil
lies in the hands of supernatural powers: "I have laboured to win all, and studie
to keepe such as I have wonne; but those that neither my favour can moove to continue constant, nor my offered benefits gette to be faithfull, the Gods shal eyther
reduce to trueth, or revenge their trecheries with justice" (182–186).

VIII

Seneca and the Declamatory Structure of Tragedy

In STUDYING THE DEVELOPMENT OF EXPLORATIVE COMEDY, WE DISCOVERED
that the form reflects the rhetorical structure and aim of argument *in
utramque partem*. The play is fashioned around a central question or questions, and the plot constitutes proof and counter-proof in a progressive
movement toward a solution. The agents in this quest are the characters
themselves, who present for the audience's delight different perspectives
upon the problem and try to master it in a variety of ways.[1] Much of the
pleasure that is provided by these comedies lies in watching the characters exert their inventive powers, though the notion of invention shifts
in the course of the century from the distinctly ratiocinative activities
of Terence's schemers to the qualities of imagination explored by Shakespeare and Jonson. Ultimately these dramas move toward an accommodation achieved either through the revelation of a truth that dissolves
apparent oppositions or through the discovery of a reasonable ideal that
embraces them. In general, they tend to look benignly upon human wit,
reflecting the Elizabethans' boundless enthusiasm for attacking a problem from all sides and—in many of the plays, at least—their confidence
in the capacity of wit to master its difficulties.

The explorative tragedies that emerge during this period are of a somewhat different character. Most obviously, they are not well-made plays,

1. In a special sense, this is true of Lyly's plays, too, where inquiry progresses
toward understanding through allegorical variation as well as explicit rhetorical
proof.

like those stemming from the Terentian model. Usually there is no intrigue through which opponents conduct a continuing battle of wits in an attempt to resolve their conflict.[2] Rather, they are assemblages of scenes—each focusing upon a particular moment in the progressing *mythos*—arguing, deliberating, describing, and often lamenting the course of events. This composite structure makes them appear literally more "artificial" than their comic analogues. There is another significant difference between them. Although the tragedies share the same interest in rhetoric—emphasizing scenes of persuasion, consultation, and analysis—they take a much dimmer view of the efficacy of such activity. In this they reflect the darker strain of comedy, wryly remarked by Melanchthon. "Varia finguntur consilia," he observes, "in quibus alia fallunt, alia felicia sunt. Saepe casus potest, quam ratio."[3] Invention, too, has its limits. In the tragedies, these limits are seen primarily in two ways: invention fails, as in comedy, because it cannot transcend man's epistemological condition and attain to truth—and it fails because it deals with a world in which will, not reason, determines human actions. This strange confluence of interest in rhetoric and pessimism regarding its worth produces a paradoxical drama. Although the audience is granted a wide and generous view of the tragic plight—which is examined from many perspectives—it does not learn how the resolution of the conflict may be attained. The best it can achieve is an equitable judgment of the hero, who is compelled by the demands of his own nature and the force of circumstances to do evil. Thus, despite the most arduous exercise of invention, both auditor and hero remain confined to their little state of man.

The seeds for this drama are to be found not only in Latinate comedy, but more immediately in the work of Seneca. Although it is no longer a critical axiom that Seneca was "responsible" for Elizabethan tragedy, it seems evident that in one respect, at least, his influence was profound.[4]

---

2. When this does occur, as in *The Spanish Tragedy* and *Hamlet*, the influence is comic. See Ch. IX, p. 277 and n. 39.

3. *Terentius, / in quem triplex editia est P. Antesignani / Rapistagnensis commentatio* (Lyons, 1560), p. 202.

4. On the influence of the domestic narrative tradition, the morality play, Ovidian and heroic poetry, and the Italian novella, see Willard Farnham, *The Medieval Heritage of Elizabethan Tragedy* (Berkeley, 1936); Howard Baker, *In-*

Seneca was the only tragic dramatist most Elizabethans knew, and he presented as a model of *bona fide* tragedy a play in which the central problem was treated from distinctly different viewpoints, inviting, in effect, a "circumstantial" approach to the nature of evil and suffering. This is because a Senecan drama, while deeply concerned with the moral life, is not, strictly speaking, a didactic work—as is the negative morality play or *de casibus* tragedy. It is a sophistic construction, carefully designed to evoke a wide range of intellectual and emotional responses to the action as it unfolds. Indeed, it most closely resembles the dramatized declamation, a literary form artfully "composed" of elaborate *descriptiones*, exempla, witty *sententiae, ethopoeiae, loci communes*, and other rhetorical elements—all joined together to provide an exciting and varied entertainment rather than a steady, consistent argument.[5]

Medea will serve as a convenient illustration. The play opens directly upon a distraught *pathopoeia*, in which the heroine, invoking both the gods of Olympus and the infernal deities, calls down curses upon Creon and Creusa, reserving to Jason a life of homeless wandering. Then she snatches vaguely at further vengeance. "And may his children be like their sire, and like their mother," she cries:

---

duction to Tragedy (Baton Rouge, 1939); David Bevington, *From Mankind to Marlowe* (Cambridge, Mass., 1962); Fredson Bowers, *Elizabethan Revenge Tragedy* (Princeton, 1940); Marvin T. Herrick, "Senecan Influence in *Gorboduc*," *Studies in Speech and Drama in Honor of A. M. Drummond* (Ithaca, 1944); G. K. Hunter, "Seneca and the Elizabethans: A Case Study in Influence," *SS* 20 (1967): 17–26. For a recent survey of the problem of Senecan influence, see Anna Lydia Motto and John R. Clark, "Senecan Tragedy: A Review of Scholarly Trends," *RenD* n.s. 6 (Evanston, 1973): 219–235.

5. The composite structure of declamation is discussed in detail by S. F. Bonner, *Roman Declamation in the Late Republic and Early Empire* (Liverpool, 1949), pp. 51–70. A comprehensive analysis of the corresponding elements in the plays is provided by H. V. Canter, "Rhetorical Elements in the Tragedies of Seneca," *U. of Ill. Studies in Language and Literature* 10 (1925): 1–86. Social and literary backgrounds are reviewed by C. W. Mendell, *Our Seneca* (New Haven, 1941), pp. 22–63. Evidently the plays were written for the same kind of audience that attended the declamations in Nero's Rome. Like the declamations, they were probably delivered "ethicos"—in character—even though they were not actually staged, and they were fragmented into a wide variety of "interest centers."

parta iam, parta ultio est:
peperi.

$$(25-26)^6$$

A common Renaissance gloss on these lines is that she asks that the children be *perfidos*, like Jason, and *venificos*, *crudeles*, like herself, and thus repay their father in kind.[7] The passage lucidly reveals Seneca's method and intention. Unlike Euripides, who opens his play with a conventional exposition that explicitly foreshadows the infanticide,[8] Seneca thrusts forward his enraged heroine without explanation, at a stage when her response to Jason's treachery is still inchoate, allowing his audience to infer the significance of words which she herself does not yet understand. He does this because he is not really interested in imitating an action in the logical, Aristotelian sense. He *is* interested in displaying the turnings of a mind in anguish and in stimulating the audience to perceive the connection between unconscious life and objective event. His technique is invariably allusive, forcing the listener to piece together the bloody events of the past and to weigh their import for the present, as the impious deeds of Colchis are juxtaposed to the chilling maternal irony:

> Away with womanish fears, clothe thy heart with unfeeling Caucasus. Whatever horror Pontus has beheld, or Phasis, Isthmus shall behold. Wild deeds, unheard-of, horrible, calamities at which heaven

6. "Already borne, borne is my vengeance! I have borne children!" All citations from Seneca's tragedies in this chapter refer to the Loeb edition, 2 vols., trans. Frank Justus Miller (London, 1917).

7. *L. Annaei / Senecae / tragoediae / cum exquisitis / variorum / observationibus / et nova / recensione / Antonii / Thysii jcti* (Leiden, 1651), p. 40. The gloss is that of Georgius Fabricius, whose commentary on Seneca was first published in 1566.

8. The Nurse briefly recounts the events that led Medea to Corinth and reveals her desertion by Jason. She is then joined by the children's Attendant, who brings news that Creon has just decreed her banishment. Fearfully, the Nurse instructs the Attendant to get the children out of the way:

> But thou, keep these apart to the uttermost:
> Bring them not nigh their mother angry-souled.
> For late I saw her glare, as glares a bull,
> On these, as 'twere for mischief. . . .

(*Euripides*, trans. Arthur S. Way, L.C.L. [London, 1919], 4.90–93).

and earth alike shall tremble, my heart deep within is planning—
wounds, slaughter, death, creeping from limb to limb. Ah, too trivial the deeds I have rehearsed; these things I did in girlhood. Let my
grief rise to more deadly strength; greater crimes become me, now
that I am a mother. (42–50)

What is most striking about this prologue is its vagueness. It reveals
nothing of the circumstances surrounding Jason's desertion, the justice or
injustice of Medea's plight—which is not the case in Euripides. Instead,
it has been fashioned in the most compact manner to portray the violence
of Medea's fury, to suggest her instinctive, though unformulated, recourse
to the children as instruments of vengeance, and to generate in the audience a state of dreadful surmise.

In the sharpest contrast to this mood, the Chorus next sings a glowing
epithalamion for Jason and Creusa, praising the perfection of their match:

So, so, ye heaven-dwellers, I pray you, let this bride surpass brides,
this husband far excel husbands. When she has taken her stand midst
her train of maidens, her one beauty shines more brightly than all.
So does starlight splendour wane with the coming of the sun, and
the huddled flock of the pleiades vanish away when Phoebe, shining
with borrowed light, with encircling horns encloses her full-orbed
disk. While on such beauty the young lover gazes, see, her cheeks
are suddenly covered with rosy blushes. So snowy wool, dipped in
purple dye, doth redden; so shines the sun when the shepherd at
dawn wet with the dew, beholds it. (93–101)

The juxtaposition is disorienting. It is not the kind of ironic conjunction
we find, for example, in the fourth act of *Romeo and Juliet*, where Juliet
lies drugged in her chamber while the family bustles unsuspectingly below preparing for the wedding. There, we watch the doomed proceedings with one eye on the reality upstairs; here the transition to idyll is
complete, and we are thoroughly captivated by the voice of the Chorus.
The ode celebrates light, beauty, natural harmony—and the gods who
were previously enjoined to behold Jason's treachery are here invoked
as witnesses of the new marriage. Twice it is emphasized that it is *lawful*
wedlock that shall be solemnized—"Let *her* pass in silent gloom who steals
away to wed with a foreign husband"— and our sympathies are engaged,
both by the attractive pastoral images associated with Creusa and by the
sense of order restored, on the side of the royal pair.

But we are not permitted to dwell in this atmosphere for long. Abruptly following the choral ode, we are wrenched back to Medea's reality. She has heard the epithalamion and is literally beside herself: "Perplexed, witless, with mind scarce sane, I am tossed to every side" (123–124). At first she fulminates against Jason, attempting to find some object with which to revenge herself—a brother, his new wife (notice, no children are mentioned here). She recounts the crimes she has committed for his sake, and offers a defense: it was not wrath but *infelix amor* that moved her to commit such deeds. Then suddenly she begins to defend *Jason*:

> But what else could Jason have done, once made subject to another's will and power? He should have bared his breast unto the sword— nay, ah, nay, mad grief, say not so! If possible, may he live and, mindful of me, keep unharmed the gift I gave. The fault is Creon's, all, who with unbridled sway dissolves marriages, tears mothers from their children, and breaks pledges bound by straitest oath; on him be my attack, let him alone pay the penalties which he owes. (137–147)

The focus in this impassioned *deliberatio* is Medea's internal dianoia; Seneca wants to show her still-potent love for Jason struggling with an abandonment that she cannot accept. She justifies Jason (thereby preserving the illusion that he still loves her) by fixing the blame on Creon. The depth of her feeling for him, her intense desire to save her marriage, are un-Euripidean, and are designed to enlist our emotional allegiance.

This forceful soliloquy, however, is interrupted by the Nurse, who counsels her to silence, and their exchange quickly falls into stichomythic debate on the subject of bearing misfortune with patience. Here the brevity of speech creates a crisp, sharp tone:

> NURSE: The king is to be feared.
> MEDEA: My father was a king.
> NURSE: Fearest thou not arms?
> MEDEA: Not though they were sprung from earth.
> NURSE: Thou'lt die.
> MEDEA: I wish it.
> NURSE: Flee!
> MEDEA: Of flight I have repented.

NURSE: Medea,
MEDEA: I will be.
NURSE: Thou art a mother.
MEDEA: By whom, thou seest.
(168-171)

The transition warrants notice. From the brooding, intense, psycho-machic speaker of a moment ago, Medea becomes an ironic, tightly controlled disputant. To the first two objections put forth by the Nurse, she retorts with oblique reminders of her past successes against kings and earth-sprung soldiers. In the fourth, she alludes sardonically to her misbegotten flight from Colchis; in the fifth, she wrests the argument from the Nurse to assert her integrity; in the sixth, she wryly negates the moderating influence of maternity by reminding the Nurse of its source. The excitement of the scene has been greatly stepped up, but it is now of a different order. It is mixed with delight and admiration at the skill with which she converts the Nurse's arguments into their antitheses—a reaction, we shall see, which was recorded by Renaissance commentators. As a result, the emotional engagement that we felt in the preceding monologue evaporates, and we find ourselves participating in a new kind of entertainment.

But this, too, is terminated abruptly, as Creon enters to see that Medea leaves his territory immediately. The scene then modulates into a mock trial, as Creon allows Medea to plead her cause before him. In the *narratio* of her argument, she recalls her royal ancestry, her illustrious suitors, her heroic rescue of the Argonauts, her acceptance of exile for Jason's sake. Then she announces her plea. She will not deny her evil deeds, "but as for crimes, this only can be charged, the rescue of the Argo" (237-238). What others call crime must be reckoned by Creon, the beneficiary, as achievement. Here, Seneca is exploiting the *status* system of judicial oratory, and his interest is in how Medea can turn Creon's own charge against him by employing the *status definitivus*, and later, in how she can exculpate herself via *translatio criminis*. The emphasis on legal argument enables us to see how the nefarious acts of Medea's life might well be excused, and provides further insight into her case.

The second chorus, which follows, has a quite different function than the first. It is essentially adramatic and seems to be spoken from a point in time long after the events at Corinth.[9] It uses material of the Medea legend—the conquest of the sea by the Argonaut pilot Tiphys, the terrors of the voyage through the Symplegades, and the passage of Medea to Corinth—to point an unexpected moral:

> The lands, well separated before by nature's laws, the Thessalian ship made one, bade the deep suffer blows, and the sequestered sea become part of our human fear. (335-339)

Historically, the voyage of the Argos has ended the golden age, when men remained within the confines of their countries, lived artlessly, and did not pervert nature. Now, with all boundaries removed, the Chorus looks forward apprehensively to the day when the sea will release its binding force (*Oceanus vincula rerum laxet*) and the whole earth will lie revealed. It is not the expectation of a brave new world that is suggested but rather a loss of order, and the conviction that human evil has irremediably ruptured the stability of the macrocosm.[10] Thus the entire episode of the Golden Fleece takes on a new and troubling meaning. From the particulars of the Argonaut voyage and whatever questions of individual justice Medea has just debated with Creon, Seneca has educed a proposition to make us consider the more disturbing implications that underlie the story. Hypothesis has modulated to thesis.

The third act is composed of three different perspectives upon Medea's predicament. Medea comes forth once again inveighing against Jason—this time arguing against her last position. He could not have married Creusa for fear of Creon or Acastus, she reasons, as love knows no fear; but even if he had surrendered in fear, he might at least have come to explain, to bid her farewell. This, however, he was afraid to do. Here Seneca is internalizing *within character* the venerable method of varying an argument through propositions, as Medea sets forth the case against Jason. So far, however, we know nothing of Jason beside the fact of his desertion and his mediation with Creon to prevent her death (183-186).

Jason then enters and in soliloquy reveals that fear was indeed his reason

---

9. See 364-374. There is a similar passage at 622-624, which Fabricius points out as an anachronism (*L. Annaei Senecae*, p. 85).

10. C. J. Herrington remarks that human evil inevitably contaminates the natural world in Seneca, for he draws "little or no distinction between spiritual, moral and material realities" ("Senecan Tragedy," *Arion* 5 [1966]: 434).

for remarriage; not fear for himself, but for his sons, who would surely have died with him had he refused Creusa. He has had to choose whether to be faithful to Medea, as she deserves, and die at Creon's hands, or to break faith and thereby save himself and his children. His conclusion: "the sons have prevailed upon the sire" (441). Unlike Euripides, Seneca does not present Jason as a sophist; he is clearly a good man, motivated solely by love for his children.

When he goes to confront Medea, however, no mention is made of this motivation for his remarriage. Instead, Medea greets him in high irony and recites in detail each act of violence that she has performed for his benefit, causing her name to be hated and feared throughout the world:

> Shall I seek Phasis and the Colchians, my father's kingdom, the fields drenched with my brother's blood? What lands dost thou bid me seek? What waters dost show to me? The jaws of the Pontic sea through which I brought back the noble band of princes, following thee, thou wanton, through the Clashing Rocks? Is it little Iolcos or Thessalian Tempe I shall seek? All the ways which I have opened for thee I have closed upon myself. (451–458)

To her perfectly justified accusation of ingratitude he merely reiterates that he has intervened with Creon to save her life, and urges her to escape the king's wrath while she has the chance. When she suggests that he shares her guilt—"who profits by a sin has done the sin"—he blandly waves off the charge. Obviously the perspective has shifted drastically again, for Jason now emerges heartless and immoral. And this would seem to be because Seneca is interested—despite his emphases elsewhere upon Jason's nobility—in the actual rights of Medea's case, which are brought forth most clearly against an obdurate adversary.

Having won Jason's consent to see the children once more, Medea calls for the robe she will present to Creusa, and the third chorus opens, appropriately enough, warning of the dangers of a woman scorned. But quickly the subject shifts. Medea's vengeance becomes the occasion to dilate upon the cruel fate of all the Argonauts who—like Jason—violated the sea. The ode thus turns out to be a lengthy argument, piling up "historical" examples in proof, that the sea takes vengeance upon those who explore her secrets. While in the drama proper, Jason's danger comes from

Medea, in the chorus it is now seen, from quite another point of view, as the consequence of his trespassing upon Neptune's domain. It is yet another instance of drawing from the particulars of a case a thesis suggesting a quite different causality.[11]

In the fourth act, Medea is once again the frightening witch of the prologue. But the emphasis is not the same. There, her ravings were vague, allusive. This scene opens with the Nurse's vivid description of the deadly concoction Medea is preparing for Creusa:

> supplicating the grim altar with her left hand, she summons destructive agencies, whatever burning Libya's sands produce, what Taurus, stiff with arctic cold, holds fast in his ever-lasting snows, and all monstrous things. Drawn by her magic incantations, the scaly brood leave their lairs and come to her. Here a savage serpent drags its huge length along, darts out its forked tongue, and seeks against whom it is to come death dealing; hearing her incantation, it stops in amaze, knots its swollen body into writhing folds, and settles them into coils. . . . She seizes death-dealing herbs, squeezes out serpents' venom, and with these mingles unclean birds, the heart of a boding owl, and a hoarse screech-owl's vitals cut out alive. . . .
>
> (680–690, 731–734)

The piece is a *demonstratio*, one of the figures of thought recommended for courtroom use to vividly set forth an action proceeding in time. It is a familiar form in Seneca,[12] and it originated in the orator's attempt to secure conviction by appealing to the visual imagination of his hearers: "for oratory fails of its full effect, and does not assert itself as it should, if its appeal is merely to the hearing, and if the judge merely feels that the acts on which he has to give his decision are being narrated to him, and not displayed in their living truth to the eyes of the mind."[13] Ob-

11. The method by which this argument is dilated is one used by the declaimers, who support a commonplace (*implere locum*) by citing historical examples that illustrate it. See Bonner, pp. 61–62.

12. The Messenger's account of Atreus's sacrifice in the subterranean grove of his palace (*Thyestes*, 682–788) and Creon's description of Tiresias's invocation of Laius (*Oedipus*, 548–658) are notable instances.

13. *Inst. or.* 8.3.62. Quintilian treats the figure as *enargeia* (but cf. *Ad Her.* 4.68). Significantly, he comments that modern authors, "more especially the declaimers, are bolder" in the use of the figure; "indeed they show the utmost animation in

viously it is a form made to order for declamatory drama, and in the sequence that immediately follows, the incantatory rite is "acted out" by Medea herself. In this scene, Seneca's aim is, literally, sensationalism. He wants to draw before his auditors, "not merely on broad general lines, but in full detail,"[14] the appearance, sound, texture, and temperature of Medea's evil rite, and make them experience it. For this cultivation of the senses is one of the functions of tragedy, even though the result is a reaction quite different from that elicited by the scenes of judicial debate, gnomic witplay, and choral moralizing.

In the final act, Medea receives the news that Corinth is ablaze. Here, the tone is quieter, the focus once again internal. She had thought briefly of using the children as a means of revenge following her colloquy with Jason in Act 3, when he had refused to let them go into exile with her because he loved them so (550). But that idea, like the reference in the Prologue, was vague and unformulated. Now Seneca traces Medea's discovery of the unrealized impulse that has been lurking in her mind all the while:

> Whither, then, wrath, art tending, or what weapons art thou aiming at the forsworn foe? A dark purpose my fierce spirit hath resolved within me, and dares not yet acknowledge to itself. Fool! Fool! I have gone too fast—would that mine enemy had children by his paramour! (*She pauses and then addresses herself.*) All offspring that thou hast by him are Creusa's brood. Resolved is this way of vengeance, rightly resolved; for a last deed of guilt, I see it now, must my soul make ready. Children that once were mine, do you pay penalty for your father's crimes. (916–927)

But even then, the emotional see-saw begins again, as she reveals the animadversions of a soul that wishes to prove the children worthy of death even though the mother's heart shrinks from the deed:

> What sin will the poor boys atone? Their sin is that Jason is their father, and greater sin, that Medea is their mother. Let them die, they are none of mine; let them be lost—they are my own. (932–935)

---

giving reign to their imagination," and he cites an example from a *controversia* recorded by the Elder Seneca. He goes on to note that this figure "is too dramatic: for the story seems to be acted, not narrated" (9.2.42–43, trans H. E. Butler [London, 1920]).

14. *Ibid.*, 9.2.40.

At last Medea's sense of guilt for the atrocities that have filled her life produces reasoning that dooms the children on either side of the question. And still she cannot kill her first-born but as expiation for the brother she murdered, and spares the second until she spies the hated Jason watching her below. As she ascends the air borne by serpents, and casts the dead children at his feet, he cries after her in anguish, "Go on through the lofty spaces of high heaven and bear witness, where thou ridest, that there are no gods!" (1026–1027). It is as problematic an ending, considering the wavering moral status of the speaker, as one could wish.

I have taken the liberty of analyzing *Medea* at such length because it is essential not to be reductive in approaching Seneca; rather, we must examine the many movements of his drama if we are to understand the aesthetic that informs it. It should be apparent from the foregoing that the play, unlike the Euripidean version, does not present a consistent argument on one side of the issue or the other. In Euripides, there is no doubt that Jason is a scoundrel and that Medea is driven by his particular outrage against her, and by her limited status as a woman, to commit the ultimate unnatural act. Nor does Seneca's play suggest a conflict of two goods, in the sense, let us say, that Sophocles' *Antigone* does. Instead, within the broad outlines of the Medea myth, each situation is examined and exploited for its own intellectual and emotional interest. We must accept as dramatic fact that at one moment Jason's motives are impeccable, and at the next he is callous and morally irresponsible; that no sooner are we drawn into the pathos of Medea's agony than we must abruptly step back and admire her wit. This is merely to acknowledge that *Medea* is quintessentially sophistic drama. If we follow Seneca's discourse sympathetically, we shall find that our attention is continually being diverted from one focus of interest to another, and that our various preoccupations never coalesce into a unified response. The play is simply not constructed in a manner that allows us to do so. Rather it encourages the most widely differentiated kinds of reaction—horror, compassion, nostalgia, fear, admiration, even wry amusement—in what seems to be a deliberate attempt to keep us continually responding anew to the material. As in sophistic declamation, there is never a perspective into which one can settle comfortably. Each scene exists as an epicycle in the larger movement of the tragedy.[15]

15. E. M. Waith has observed the same pattern of multiple focus in the pseudo-

At least one aim of this aesthetic is to exercise the inventive faculty of the audience. An insight into Seneca's method may be gained by closely examining his scenes of argumentation. These are extremely important in laying bare the fundamental conflicts on which the action is based. Each play has at least one scene containing a lengthy *suasoria* and a reply to the course of action proposed. These tend to focus on the central ethical issue of the tragedy. In *Hippolytus*, for example, Phaedra's Nurse urges her mistress to drive away her illicit passion, offering proof after proof of the dangers of her course: though Phaedra thinks that her husband Theseus, still in the Underworld, cannot see her action, she is not safe from the judgment of Minos, her father; if he does not see it, she will be detected by her grandfather, the sun; even supposing that the gods do not abhor incest, still she will be conscience stricken herself, and find no peace of soul. The method of argument is by now familiar. Phaedra's reply is that she is compelled by Amor, whereupon the Nurse declares the divinity a fiction created by those who seek liberty for their lusts. Later in the same play, however, the Nurse reverses herself and, employing her rhetorical powers in Phaedra's behalf, she urges Hippolytus to abandon the secluded life and enjoy his youth in the haunts of men. The scene is developed as thesis and counter-thesis on the merits of the pastoral life. While the Nurse cites its hardships, loneliness, and chaste barrenness, Hippolytus replies in defense of its freedom, innocence, and peace—delivering a lengthy condemnation of civilization and its crimes, fostered chiefly, of course, by women. What is especially odd about these

---

Senecan *Hercules Oetaeus:* "The dramatic portrait which finally emerges is made up of five different portraits, one superimposed upon another. They are: Hercules the benefactor, the lustful Hercules, Hercules transformed by suffering, Hercules the man of Stoic endurance, and Hercules the god" (*The Herculean Hero in Marlowe, Shakespeare, Chapman, and Dryden* [New York, 1962], p. 35). This is not to assert that Senecan tragedy is shapeless. Herrington (p. 449) has shown that Seneca followed a characteristic pattern whose three stages he designates "The Cloud of Evil" (the opening atmosphere of guilt and fearful foreboding); "The Defeat of Reason by Passion" (signified by the second act colloquy between the protagonist and an attendant); and "The Explosion of Evil" (the results of this defeat). With this pattern, however, the dramatic *membra* are sharply differentiated, and appeal to quite different interests. Mendell's useful, though unsympathetic comparative analysis of the Senecan and Sophoclean *Oedipus* (pp. 3–21) supports this contention.

scenes of argumentation is that they seem dramatically unnecessary, for they do not really influence the course of the action. Everyone has already made up his mind—at least for the duration of a given debate—and no one persuades anyone.

There are possibly two reasons for this. First, the issues are considered interesting and important in themselves, and Seneca, the former advocate, wishes to air them by showing how the various positions can be defended—regardless of their effect upon the action. This is a desideratum of declamatory drama, and from what we can infer about Seneca's audience such argumentative display was a major attraction. But perhaps, more profoundly, Seneca is suggesting the ineffectiveness of rhetorical argument before such figures as the stoic Hippolytus, who has no need of arguing both sides of the question, and the passionate Phaedra, with whom no argument can prevail. He remarks in Epistle 88 that the Academy—which he links to Protagoras, who "declares that one can take either side in any question and debate it with equal success"—is a useless school of philosophy because it teaches non-knowledge. "If I cleave to Protagoras, there is nothing in the scheme of nature that is not doubtful," he complains. "What are we, then? What becomes of all these things that surround us, support us, sustain us? The whole universe is then a vain or deceptive shadow."[16] Haunted by the fear of uncertainty, he rejects all skeptical doctrines because they do not provide a basis for action. This may explain why, although arguments on both sides of the question are so plentifully invented and so liberally expressed in the plays, they almost invariably have no effect upon the behavior of the characters. In the last analysis, it is will and not discursive reasoning, with its elusive equivocations, that is the motivating force.

The lengthy *suasoriae* are usually followed by a second kind of argumentation. This is that stichomythic dialogue we noted in *Medea*, during which the opponents suddenly step up the pace of their dispute. The effect of these exchanges on an audience is described by Martinus Delrius, an important sixteenth-century editor of Seneca:

16. *Ad Lucilium epistulae morales* 88.43, 45, 46, trans. Richard M. Gummere, L.C.L. (London, 1920). Trimpi observes similar Stoic attitudes toward argument *in utramque partem* in the contemporary Philo Judaeus and later in St. Augustine ("The Quality of Fiction," *Traditio* [1974]: 47 n. 55).

How excellent are closely packed dialogue, frequent and rapid conversations, of either single verses or half lines, in seizing the audience's attention. Moreover, those dialogues are best which contain sharp and animated *sententiae*, especially if they seem opposed to each other: which our poet uses in *Hercules Furens*, when Lycus and Megara speak; in *Oedipus*, between Oedipus and Creon; in *Thyestes*, between Atreus and the servant; in *Octavia*, where Nero and Seneca dispute in this fashion.[17]

Sharp and animated sententiae, especially if they seem opposed to each other. Delrius's remark suggests that excitement is effected not only by an accelerated delivery (if, indeed, delivery was a real consideration), but, more importantly, by the antithetical nature of the lines. *Sententiae*, as we learned from Aphthonius, are universal "proofs" used in exhorting and dissuading. Specifically, they are the premises and conclusions of enthymemes, or rhetorical syllogisms, and Delrius defines them as such, quoting Minturno, who in turn quotes Aristotle. A sentence is a brief speech

> in which a serious person, experienced in the things about which he speaks, pronounces upon not any subject he wishes, but on what ought to be pursued as the more excellent, and what should be shunned as the worse. . . . Sentences are either subjoined to premises, or have reasons subjoined to them, or are taken for granted, with-

17. Quantum attentioni parandae praestent, crebra diverbia, frequentes & incitatae collocutiones, quae vel singulis versibus, vel dimidiatis constent. excellent autem illa diverbia, quae sententiae continent acutas & erectas, maxime si repugnantes esse videantur: quibus noster utitur, in *Hercule Furente*, ubi Lycus & Megara; in *Oedipo*, ubi Oedipodes & Creon; in *Thyeste*, ubi Atreus & servus; in *Octavia*, ubi Nero & Seneca sic altercantur (*Martini / Antonii Delrii / ex societate Jesu / syntagma / tragoediae Latinae*. . . . [Paris, 1620], pp. 4–5). This book provides valuable documentation of the reconciliation between Aristotelian, Horatian, and "Terentian" criticism that took place in the latter part of the sixteenth century. The Aristotelian qualitative and quantitative analyses are related to the Horatian concept of five acts and the Donatan prologue, protasis, epitasis, and catastrophe. So, too, the qualitative part *ethos* is treated as the demonstration of *mores*, in the manner of the Terentian commentators, and the argumentative element *dianoia* becomes *sententia*. For an account of these changes, see Marvin T. Herrick, *The Fusion of Horation and Aristotelian Literary Criticism* (Urbana, Ill., 1946), and his *Comic Theory in the Sixteenth Century* (Urbana, Ill., 1964).

out supporting propositions, when they are simple and credible in themselves.[18]

When we realize that Seneca's *sententiae* were considered abbreviated enthymemes, it becomes evident that he is deliberately increasing the tension of the disputation by creating the most concise kind of argument possible, in which each character is forced to search his wits for the aphorism that will best prove his case.

This exercise of the wit is brilliantly illustrated in a scene from the *Troades*, when Pyrrhus demands from Agamemnon the sacrifice of Polyxena, as ordered by Achilles' ghost, while Agamemnon contends that the Greeks' revenge has gone far enough. Beginning with lengthy *suasoriae*, their dispute spreads to mutual recrimination for past actions, including Pyrrhus's sparing of Priam when the latter came to request Hector's body Pyrrhus replies majestically to Agamemnon's charge of negligence:

> PYRRHUS: 'Tis a high, a kingly act, to give life to a king.
> AGAMEMNON: Why then from a king did thy right hand take life?
> PYRRHUS: The merciful will oft give death instead of life.
> AGAMEMNON: And is it now in mercy thou seekest a maiden for the tomb?
> PYRRHUS: So *now* thou deemst the sacrifice of maids a crime?
> AGAMEMNON: To put country before children befits a king.
>
> (327–332)

Here, a very complicated history is evoked in six brief lines. Agamemnon counters Pyrrhus's lofty gnome with a witty antithesis (Pyrrhus did, after all, end up slaughtering Priam), the reply to which is another fine aphorism on the mercifulness of death. When Agamemnon sarcastically tests Pyrrhus's sentiment against the present circumstance, Pyrrhus con-

18. Sententiam ex Aristotle . . . describit, qua vir gravis, earumque rerum de quibus agit peritus, non quod lubeat, sed quod sequendum sit, ut praestantius, & quod deterius fugiendum . . . pronunciat. hae vel rationi subiunguntur, vel subiunctam habent rationem; vel solae sine ulla ratione summuntur, qui simplices sunt, & cuius credibilis (*Delrius.*, p. 12).

futes him by recalling his own sacrifice of Iphigenia, which Agamemnon quickly answers with yet another sentence invoking his statesmanship. Not only is the wit of the speakers sharp indeed, but the activity of inference demanded of the audience is also extraordinary. Such passages were clearly aimed at listeners who relished a rapid play of wit and exercised their own by supplying the missing terms of arguments conducted in "shorthand."[19]

In Renaissance editions, *sententiae* were frequently printed in distinctive type for the convenience of the reader who wished to garner a store of such aphorisms for his own use. (We recall that they were among the important elements of the declaimers' speeches preserved by the Elder Seneca.) They were, of course, more than instruments of rhetorical witplay. They also added *gravitas* to discourse, as the critics continually pointed out. Petrus Crinitus praises Seneca "propter sublimitatem carminis, gravitatemque sententiarum," and Bartholomeus Riccius asks his readers, "Whose work is more tightly compacted of *sententiae* than the unique Seneca's? Whose more weighty? . . . In so many lines, almost as many vehement *sententiae* may be counted"—and this standard of value is reflected in Sidney's commendation of *Gorboduc* for its "stately speeches and well sounding Phrases, clyming to the height of Seneca his stile."[20]

19. The potential danger of such an exercise is indicated in Thomas Newton's reply to moralistic critics of Seneca in 1581:

> And whereas it is by some squeymish Areopagites surmyzed, that the readinge of these Tragedies, being enterlarded with many Phrases and sentences, literally tending (at the first sight) sometime to the prayse of Ambition, sometyme to the mayntenaunce of cruelty, now and then to the approbation of incontinencie, and here and there to the ratification of tyranny, cannot be digested without great dauger [sic] of infection; to omit all other reasons, if it might please them with no forestalled judgment, to mark, and consider the circumstaunces, why, where, and by what manner of persons such sentences are pronounced, they cannot in any equity otherwise choose, but find good cause ynough to lead them to a more favourable and milde resolution (*Seneca His Tenne Tragedies* [Bloomington, Ind., 1968], pp. 4-5).

Notice how "circumstantial" reading is equivalent to equitable judgment.

20. Quis autem unico Seneca in sententiis est crebrior? quis etiam gravior? . . . in eo quot versus, tot pene gravissimae sententiae numerentur. . . . (Delrius, p. 70). For Sidney, see *Elizabethan Critical Essays*, ed. G. Gregory Smith (Oxford, 1904), i. 196–197. Not everyone, however, was as enthusiastic as Riccius and Sid-

Two features of Senecan drama, then, which would encourage an explorative English tragedy are its variety of set pieces, eliciting different and often contradictory emotional responses, and its scenes of disputation, where a given issue is examined *in utramque partem*. But of equal significance is the relationship of the chorus in its ethical capacity to the events of the action proper. As we have observed in *Medea*, the chorus frequently disengages itself from the particulars of the plot to adduce theses that offer new perspectives on the action. Sometimes, however, these odes are not simply contrastive, but actually run counter to the events in the play. In *Thyestes*, for example, after Atreus lays plans to entice his brother to a false reconciliation, the Chorus, innocent of his motives, rejoices at the coming reunion. It is an occasion to argue the Stoic theme that kingship lies not in riches and power, but in peace of mind, and concludes with the famous passage imitated by Thomas Wyatt and others:

> Let him stand who will, in pride of power, on empire's slippery height; let me be filled with sweet repose, in humble station fixed. . . .
>
> (391–393)

Then, following the supposed reconciliation, the Chorus celebrates the triumph of love over strife, affirming the rule of mutability. This suggests in turn a political warning to rulers, via a sentence quoted again and again in Elizabethan tragedy:

---

ney. Justus Lipsius, in his *Animadversiones* of 1588 complained that Seneca's *sententiae* "were not torches, but sparks; not strong and true blows, but as in a dream, puny and fruitless efforts—which nonetheless he packs together too closely and almost to the point of surfeit. Nor does he invent them but rather appropriates them—perhaps not so much his fault as that of his age, to which this sort of thing, belonging to rhetoricians and declaimers, was so welcome" (*L. Annaeus / Seneca / tragicus; / ex recensione & museo / Petri Scriverii.* . . . [Leiden, 1621], Part 2, p. 7). He goes on to quote Quintilian, never a great admirer of Seneca, who was obviously unimpressed by this kind of witplay. The latter remarks that the old tragedians and writers of comedy were "more careful about dramatic structure [*oeconomia*] than the majority of moderns, who regard epigram [*sententia*] as the sole merit of every kind of literary work" (*Inst. or.* 1.8.8–9). Both commentaries indicate that there existed within the rhetorical tradition a more balanced view of structure to curb Senecan excesses, which emerged in England after the first round of Inns of Court drama.

quem dies vidit veniens superbum
hunc dies vidit fugiens iacentem.

(613-614)

Neither of these odes has any *dramatic* connection with the situations in
the play, for they comment upon events that have not taken place. Nor
can they be read ironically, since their great length vitiates whatever
ironic effect they might have. Seneca is pursuing not irony here, but
morality, and it is apparently unimportant to him that it have dramatic
relevance. Just as the declaimers adduce *loci communes* in order to relate
their arguments to broader moral concerns, so the particulars of the tragic
plot must be drawn into a general ethical context.[21]

A more extreme example of this dissociation between *moralitas* and
plot is seen in the *Troades*. Here, at the beginning of Act 2, Talthybius re-
ports seeing the ghost of Achilles, who has demanded the sacrifice of his
intended bride Polyxena as revenge for his own death. The tragic pathos
of the play, as well as its central disputation, depends upon this event. At
the end of the act, however, the Chorus asks whether it is really true that
souls live after death, or whether this is simply a tale. It then argues at
length that the soul dies with the body, and

> Taenarus and the cruel tyrant's kingdom and Cerberus, guarding
> the portal of no easy passage—all are but idle rumors, empty words,
> a tale light as a troubled dream. Dost ask where thou shalt be when
> death has claimed thee? Where they lie who were never born.
>
> (402-408)

The introduction of such a speech might suggest that the Greek demand
for the sacrifice is a hoax, and thus raise a whole new issue, but this is
never hinted at in what follows. Again, the speech is simply occasioned
by an event in the play—the reported appearance of Achilles' ghost—
which licenses a thesis questioning the existence of an afterlife. That the
speech potentially undermines the whole action is simply not noticed,

21. The *topoi* are frequently identical: the fickleness of fortune, the degener-
acy of the age, the advantages of the humble life, the evils of envy, adultery,
profligacy (see Bonner, pp. 60-61). The advantage of these commonplaces, as
Cicero and others observed, was that they could be applied to any number of
situations.

which once more attests to the fact that the plays were not viewed as unified entities, but were enjoyed for the intellectual and emotional pleasures provided by their separate parts.

This attitude carries right over to the Elizabethans. Jasper Heywood, the most accomplished of the translators, actually improves upon Seneca in this respect. In his preface to the *Troades*, he apologizes for certain changes he has made, especially in the chorus. In the first act, he has supplied a chorus where there was none—an exhortation to heed the fate of Troy, adapted from the political chorus in *Thyestes*; to the chorus questioning the afterlife in Act 2, he has added three stanzas of lamentation for Andromache whose son must also be sacrificed; and he has eliminated completely the chorus in the third act, which contains a catalogue of ancient localities, substituting instead a chorus questioning God's providence adapted from *Hippolytus*. "Which alteration," he remarks, "may be borne withall, seynge that chorus is no part of the substance of the matter."[22] Although *that* chorus may not be especially germane to the action, Heywood's free way with the other choruses as well suggests that they all seemed easily interchangeable to the sixteenth-century reader, who required a certain measure of moral reflection in his tragedy, but was not too particular about where it was placed.

The most telling piece of evidence, however, is the entirely new episode Heywood creates for the *Troades*. Instead of simply having Talthybius report the appearance of Achilles' spirit, Heywood inserts a scene at the beginning of the second act in which the ghost itself appears and demands Polyxena. The addition attests to his desire to enliven the action, but in the process he renders the chorus that questions the existence of such spirits absurd, for now we have seen one for ourselves.[23] Like Seneca, he has no over-all view of the play, for tragedy is a loose collocation of sophistic forms, in which each section casts its distinctive light upon the subject at hand, and encourages only local judgments. Developing these into a wider, equitable response is one of the major achievements of the later Elizabethans.

22. *Seneca His Tenne Tragedies*, Book 2, p. 4.
23. This may shed some light on why Hamlet talks of an "undiscovered country, from whose bourne No traveler returns," after he has already seen his father's ghost. Shakespeare is not above creating an independent thesis.

Tragic Perspectives Among
the Elizabethans

THE INFLUENCE OF THE SENECAN MODEL IS READILY DISCERNIBLE IN *Gorboduc*, the first English "classical" tragedy.[1] Within the framework of this apparently didactic play lurk several odd ambivalences. They are not due to its dual authorship, for they exist within single scenes and even within single speeches.[2] As in Seneca, one is tempted to look for ironic intention but, also as in Seneca, one is reduced to the conclusion that the authors are interested in pursuing a number of different ideas, whose potential conflict is simply not a matter of concern to them, because each

1. In this discussion I shall follow the venerable tradition, which began with Sidney, that *Gorboduc* is "Senecan," even though it is clear that in some aspects, e.g., its chronological plot, its lack of stichomythia, and its bluntly homiletic choruses, the play departs from the Senecan practice. This is not, of course, to deny its native sources.

2. The traditional division of labor, based upon the authority of the first quarto, ascribes the first three acts to Norton, the last two to Sackville. Howard Baker deduced from the divergent political sympathies of Sackville and Norton, and from certain differences in style, that Sackville wrote 1.1, in which Videna warns Ferrex of his coming disinheritance, all of Act 4, but only 5.1, which stresses absolute obedience to the monarch; while Norton wrote 5.2, emphasizing parliamentary prerogative, and the rest of the play (*Induction to Tragedy* [Baton Rouge, 1939], pp. 15–47). Mortimer Levine, *The Early Elizabethan Succession Question* (Stanford, 1966), pp. 30–44, has since shown that the positions of the two men were not so far apart as Baker had assumed, an argument amplified by Ernest W. Talbert, "The Political Import and the First Two Audiences of *Gorboduc*," *Studies in Honor of De Witt T. Starnes* (Austin, Texas, 1967), pp. 89–115.

possesses its distinct value. These ambivalences lie in the authors' treatment of primogeniture, their concept of nature, and their view of tragedy itself.

Gorboduc is a play that purports to demonstrate the dangers that ensue when a king will "change the course of his descending crown" and when "no certain heir remains" after his death. These are, in fact, two different issues, tied together because the play was apparently the initial sally in a Protestant campaign to pressure Elizabeth into designating Lady Catherine Gray next in succession, in accordance with Henry VIII's will, and into publicly declaring that her father's choice was also her own. The double proposition would account for the fact that the play really falls into two parts: Gorboduc's decision to divide the realm, contrary to custom (presumably Henry's will), which results in the progressive slaughter of the royal family through Act 4; and the faction among the nobility when there is no heir designate, which leads to civil war, in Act 5. This would not violate any concept of tragic structure likely to be held by Sackville and Norton. As far as they were concerned, a tragedy was a five-act play that begins in calm and ends in storms, involves death, and contains a certain number of passionate speeches, debates, descriptions, and moralizing choruses. One tragedy, Seneca had shown, could easily preach two morals, and Sackville and Norton succeeded remarkably well in putting together a single story that did just that.[3]

Geoffrey of Monmouth says nothing about Gorboduc's division of the kingdom—merely that a contention arose between the sons Ferrex and Porrex over the succession as their father approached senility. To demonstrate what happens when due order is breached and the legal heir is not

3. In the past, critics have been hard pressed, because of this structure, to designate a hero for the play, so that by default England has become the real protagonist, as in the morality *Respublica*. See Willard Farnham, *The Medieval Heritage of Elizabethan Tragedy* (Berkeley, 1936), p. 353; Baker, pp. 39–40; Irving Ribner, *The English History Play in the Age of Shakespeare*, rev. ed. (London, 1965), p. 45. This gives the play a comfortable unity, but it also stretches the truth, for the widow Respublica, the real *and* nominal hero of her own play, does not disappear in the fourth act to become a vague patriotic entity; she is there, a personification to the end. Gorboduc, however, is killed, as he must be, along with his family, so that the second admonition may be educed from the action. It is probably a mistake to ascribe a concern for Aristotelian unities to Sackville and Norton, writing a full generation before Sidney.

allowed to succeed to the throne, Sackville and Norton make the division of the kingdom dependent upon Gorboduc's choice. They devote, in fact, a whole scene to this decision, although we know from the Queen's earlier remark that Gorboduc has already made up his mind. Perforce, the consultation scene consists of wholly gratuitous speeches. Although it has frequently been likened to analogues in the morality plays,[4] the scene is really quite different, and much more closely related to the Senecan type. Gorboduc himself, a man bent on action, resembles not the pliable morality hero, but the obdurate character who engages discussion in Seneca's consultation scenes. His advisors, Arostus, Philander, and Eubulus, do not function as good and evil angels—as do the counselors of Ferrex and Porrex. Throughout the play they act as responsible statesmen. Furthermore, neither the dumb show nor the chorus in Act 1—which serve to explicate the action—is concerned with good and evil counsel (as are their counterparts in Act 2), but rather with changing traditional procedure and dividing the realm. The scene therefore serves simply to demonstrate the king's willful choice and—a function of signal importance —to argue several points of view.[5]

This is readily apparent from the division of the speeches. Arostus is wholly in accord with Gorboduc's plan, Philander approves half of it, and Eubulus approves none of it. Arostus speaks not as a flatterer, but gives good ethical reasons for supporting Gorboduc's proposal. His response is divided into two major arguments: that Gorboduc will personally be relieved of burdens too great for his age and more suitably borne by his sons, and that the sons will benefit from his tutelage during their years of fledgling statesmanship, when they are most susceptible to corruption by flatterers. His argument looks to the profit of the king, his sons, and the state, and, so far as it goes, makes sense.

---

4. The idea apparently stems from J. C. Cunliffe, *Early English Classical Tragedies* (Oxford, 1912), p. 302.

5. Wolfgang Clemen observes, with some exasperation, that "these three speeches, for all their length and detail, do not in any way advance the action of the play. The 'case' is considered from various theoretical standpoints, yet Gorboduc's closing speech shows that he has not changed his own. . . ." (*English Tragedy Before Shakespeare* [London, 1961], p. 64). This is surely a departure from morality "persuasion"—though Clemen does not suggest either the intellectual function of the colloquy or the Senecan pessimism that may underlie the result.

Philander explores the proposal more deeply, though still idealistically. He is in favor of dividing the kingdom because the smaller the realm, "the nearer justice to the wronged poor," and a state so divided between brothers is "not as two but one of double force." Then he adds:

> And such an egalness hath nature made
> Between the brethren of one father's seed
> As an unkindly wrong it seems to be
> To throw the brother subject under feet
> Of him whose peer he is by course of kind.
> (1.2.181–185)[6]

Philander is supporting his position by probing beneath the immediate issue to the general consideration, and, in accordance with his method, the remainder of his speech *in favor of the proposal* is devoted to examining the propriety of primogeniture.[7] It is, he argues, "unkindly," that is, unnatural, for mere chronology to take precedence over consanguinity. Furthermore,

> nature, that did make this egalness,
> Oft so repineth at so great a wrong
> That oft she raiseth up a grudging grief
> In younger brethren at the elder's state,
> Whereby both towns and kingdoms have been razed
> And famous stocks of royal blood destroyed.
> (1.2.186–191)

Students of *Gorboduc* have usually ignored this embarrassing speech, delivered by a patently virtuous counselor, probably because it strongly contradicts the "moral" of the play, which is that by right and custom the throne should have descended to Ferrex alone. But the authors are clearly interested in investigating the case against primogeniture, and they support it with a definition of "kind" that does not correspond to the rational principle of hierarchical order—*nomos*—by which it is defined most frequently in the play. Here the meaning is closer to the simpler *physis*

6. All references are to Irby B. Cauthen's edition (Lincoln, Neb., 1970).

7. In this case, the recourse to thesis may have direct political overtones, since Lady Catherine Gray was descended from Henry VIII's younger sister, while her strongest rival, Mary Stuart, was descended from Henry's elder sister.

that signifies the passionate principle—natural force, instinct, blood affinity.[8] Philander argues that the same "kind" that makes the brothers equal will in fact rebel against the imposition of an *artificial* hierarchical order and raise a "grudging grief" in the son whose natural equality is so abridged.

Things become even more complicated when the same speaker then goes on to consider the second half of Gorboduc's proposal: to abdicate now in favor of his sons. Philander argues against immediate division of the kingdom because

> the head to stoop beneath them both [the sons]
> Ne kind, ne reason, ne good order bears.
>
> (1.2.203–204)

He urges Gorboduc not to pervert nature's course by changing roles with his sons, and is somewhat apologetic for intimating that this particular father and these sons might be derelict in their offices:

> Only I mean to show, by certain rules
> Which kind hath graft within the mind of man,
> That nature hath her order and her course,
> Which (being broken) doth corrupt the state
> Of minds and things, even in the best of all.
>
> (1.2.218–222)

Now let us observe what has happened. Where earlier, Philander had argued against primogeniture because it violated "kind"—*physis*, or equality of blood—by imposing unnatural hierarchical order, here he argues against the king's resignation of power to his sons because it violates "kind"—*nomos*, or natural hierarchical order. It is really impossible to reconcile the two arguments, until one recognizes that they are just that—two distinct arguments, each of which has its separate function: the first, to support division of the kingdom, the second, to dissuade the king from

---

8. The distinction is treated extensively in A. O. Lovejoy and G. Boas, *Primitivism and Related Ideas in Antiquity* (New York, 1965). Fundamentally, *physis* seems to have been associated with the innate, the objectively true, *nomos* with custom and subjectivity. The more familiar distinction between *physis* as instinct and *nomos* as the rational principle is discussed by Hiram Haydn, *The Counter Renaissance* (New York, 1950), pp. 468ff.

immediate abdication. When viewed on its own terms, each argument is cogent and effective; viewed together they make no sense.[9]

Eubulus's speech, which follows, moves in yet another direction. It attempts to set the two concepts of nature into a comprehensive relationship. He argues that

> Such is in man the greedy mind to reign,
> So great is his desire to climb aloft,
> In worldly stage the stateliest parts to bear,
> That faith and justice and all kindly love
> Do yield unto desire of sovereignty,
> Where egal state doth raise an egal hope
> To win the thing that either would obtain.
>
> (1.2.262–268)

Here he suggests that man's characteristic impulse is ambition, which violates ties of "kindly love"—the natural bond that Philander has invoked. His speech, though it has roots in Seneca,[10] probably reflects Norton's Calvinism. For Eubulus implies that there is a strain of pride in man that opposes and can defeat the ideal godly order of "kind"—and therefore it is necessary to impose hierarchical order upon him if anarchy is not to result. He is actually invoking the distinction between pre- and post-lapsarian nature that was argued by Reformist political writers in their justification of government. Thus, he offers a formulation of "kind" that transcends the earlier definitions and incorporates them in a new theory of *realpolitik*.[11] In doing so, Eubulus goes beyond the merely dis-

9. That this is a "consultation" scene is indicated by the fact that Philander's first argument, against primogeniture, is never refuted, as is Tyndar's advocacy of despotism in 2.2 which is in a "morality" scene.

10. Marvin T. Herrick, "Senecan Influence in *Gorboduc*," *Studies in Speech and Drama in Honor of A. M. Drummond* (Ithaca, 1944), pp. 82–83.

11. In the *Institutes*, Calvin describes the function of moral law: "This constrained and forced righteousness is necessary for the public community of men, for whose tranquility the Lord herein provided when he took care that everything be not tumultuously confounded. This would happen if everything were permitted to all men." Now, "hindered by fright or shame, they dare neither execute what they have conceived in their minds, nor openly breathe forth the rage of their lust" (Bk. 2, Ch. 7, Sec. 10, trans. F. L. Battles [Philadelphia, 1906]).

putative virtue of his colleagues and achieves a Ciceronian resolution.

Events, of course, bear out his argument, but that is not our immediate concern. What is our concern is that Sackville and Norton have constructed a scene that derives not from the morality play but from the tradition of arguing *in utramque partem*. In the movement of its argument toward synthesis, it echoes the dialogue of Pole and Lupset on similar matters,[12] but as a dramatic unit it is inspired by Seneca. Clearly there is real interest in giving each position its due—even, as we have seen, if it contradicts the dominant moral of the play or exhibits only local coherence. This is because Sackville and Norton were using the drama as neutral ground for the examination of complex problems, and wanted to explore the ways in which one could argue the "case" presented by Gorboduc—a desire undoubtedly shared by their Inner Temple audience, who must have heard the scene with the same enjoyment they experienced at a declamation or a mooting.

The antithetical use of the term "kind" does not end with Eubulus's resolution. It appears prominently in the fourth act, when Gorboduc confronts Porrex following the murder of his brother (4.2.15–27), and reappears in a slightly different form later in the same scene, when Arostus counsels Gorboduc to conquer the despair that has overtaken him:

> neither should nature's power
> In other sort against your heart prevail,
> Than as the naked hand whose stroke assays
> The armed breast where force doth light in vain.
> (4.2.155–158)

Here, "nature's power" seems to signify either the random force of an external, capricious nature or the power of passion that now wells up in Gorboduc and leads him to despair. In either case, the term definitely suggests *physis* and not *nomos*. Gorboduc replies to this stoic counsel in similar language:

John Ponet, in his *Shorte Treatise of Politicke Power* (1559), argued that after the flood man was too far corrupted to rule himself by reason, and therefore God instituted government to supply its place lest man swerve from the law of nature. See W. S. Hudson, *John Ponet (1516–1556)* (Chicago, 1942).

12. See Ch. II, pp. 36–38.

> Many can yield right sage and grave advice
> Of patient sprite to others wrapped in woe
> And can in speech both rule and conquer kind,
> Who, if by proof they might feel nature's force
> Would show themselves men as they are indeed,
> Which now will needs be gods.
>
> (4.2.159–164)

In this speech, "kind" clearly means passion and not the rational principle, while "nature's force" again shares the ambiguous suggestion of random external power or the impulse of passion.

The ambivalent use of the terms "nature" and "kind" and their cognates is too frequent to be accidental, and must be viewed as a deliberate form of wit.[13] It is explorative in impulse, clearly an attempt to make the mind shift back and forth between the two primary significations and their various nuances. We have seen as early as Heywood's *Witty and Witless* and Erasmus's *Folly* that the juxtaposition of several meanings of a term is a way of enlarging the understanding, of moving toward truth. It is apparent that this same practice has so penetrated the didactic purposes of *Gorboduc* that the play harbors sedition within its piously sententious framework.

The final ambivalence, and perhaps the most significant, is in the concept of tragedy that informs *Gorboduc*. A dramatized mirror for magistrates, the work has long been celebrated as a play in which the hero clearly is responsible for the evil he brings upon himself—a rational development of the older fortuitous *de casibus* tradition.[14] The Chorus makes that much clear at the end of Act 1:

> And this great king, that doth divide his land
> And change the course of his descending crown
> And yields the reign into his children's hand,

13. Cauthen remarks that *kind* and its variants appear thirty-seven times, and *nature* and *unnatural* appear twenty times in the text. But he has apparently not noticed their variant meanings, since he defines them simply as signifying "sound principles or commonsense actions" (pp. xxi).

14. See Farnham, pp. 353, 355; Ribner, p. 46; E. M. W. Tillyard, *Shakespeare's History Plays* (London, 1944), p. 96.

From blissful state of joy and great renown,
A mirror shall become to princes all
To learn to shun the cause of such a fall.

(1.2.388–393)

A more explicitly didactic exemplum could not be wished. This lesson
is reiterated both by the Chorus and Eubulus throughout the play. Everyone seems to be aware of why the tragedy is taking place; everyone, that
is, except Gorboduc. He has an entirely different view of the matter.
When he enters in Act 3 (his first appearance since the council scene) with
Dordan's letter concerning Ferrex's preparation for war, he offers no acknowledgment that he is personally responsible for the growing conflict.
Instead, he sees himself as part of the long line of Trojan victims still pursued by vengeful gods:

> O cruel fates, O mindful wrath of gods,
> Whose vengeance neither Simois' stained streams
> Flowing with blood of Trojan princes slain,
> Nor Phrygian fields made rank with corpses dead
> Of Asian kings and lords can yet appease;
> Ne slaughter of unhappy Priam's race,
> Nor Ilion's fall made level with the soil
> Can yet suffice; but still continued rage
> Pursues our lives and from the farthest seas
> Doth chase the issues of destroyed Troy.

(3.1.1–10)

This is a view of the evil befalling him that is radically different from
that of Eubulus and the Chorus, and casts the tragedy into a new mold—
that of the dynastic curse, which makes it deterministic and not a tragedy
of moral choice at all. The passage is not merely atmospheric decoration,
either. For when, shortly afterward, Philander pleads with Gorboduc to
"employ your wisdom and your force" to prevent bloodshed between
the brothers, he fatalistically declines to act—"Their death and mine must
'pease the angry gods"—and Philander must convince him that the fates
have not conspired against him, but rather have preserved him to heal
the hatred between the brothers. To make sure that no one misses the
significance of the crisis, Eubulus then states the official reading:

257

> Lo, here the peril that was erst foreseen
> When you, O king, did first divide your land
> And yield your present reign unto your sons.
>
> (3.1.134–136)

Gorboduc never reacts to this. Instead, receiving word that Ferrex has been killed, he again calls down heaven's wrath upon "the traitor son and the wretched sire," in a speech that suggests no awareness of responsibility but only that the gods must somehow be avenged. His final words on the matter, which follow his interview with Porrex in Act 4, show that his vision of his predicament has in fact undergone no change at all:

> What cruel destiny,
> What froward fate hath sorted us this chance,
> That even in those where we should comfort find,
> Where our delight now in our aged days
> Should rest and be, even there our only grief
> And deepest sorrows to abridge our life,
> Most pining cares and deadly thoughts do grow?
>
> (4.2.142–148)

Once and for all, he sees himself as the victim of fate. To appreciate fully the idiosyncratic nature of his interpretation it is only necessary to recall Eubulus's final words, which summarize the dominant point of view:

> Hereto it comes when kings will not consent
> To grave advice but follow wilful will.
>
> (5.2.234–235)

What all this adds up to is that Sackville and Norton have actually written two tragedies—a demonstrative tragedy of moral error, which is the tragedy Eubulus, the Chorus, and the nobles see unfolding, and a tragedy of fate perceived only by the hero.[15] They probably did so because both ideas were important to them—the moral tragedy for its crucial political lesson, the fatalistic tragedy for its patriotic (and melodramatic) Trojan theme, which, they discovered, could be sounded by a hero

15. And, just briefly, Philander (2.2.75–79) and Chorus 3 (182–185). For variations on the dominant theme of tragic error leading to retribution, however, see Dordan (2.1.193), Philander (2.2.75), Chorus 2, Chorus 4, and especially Eubulus (5.2.234–245).

who sees his doom in the light of an ancient curse. As in Seneca, there is no hint of irony in this juxtaposition, no awareness that the concepts conflict. Both are simply "entertained," for they offer thought-provoking glimpses of a tragic fall.

The explorative tendencies we see in *Gorboduc* are also found in various forms in the other Inns of Court tragedies. In *Gismond of Salerne* (1567), there is a wide discrepancy between the play's purported function as a mirror against unchaste love—the theme expressed by the Chorus—and the characters of the lovers, who are presented between choruses as noble and innocent. As a result, the play is marked by striking affective and intellectual disjunctions. The story concerns a young widow named Gismond who falls in love with her father's courtier, but is prevented from marrying him by the old man's jealousy. After much argument and subterfuge, the father, Tancred, discovers them together, executes the lover, and presents his heart to Gismond. Despairing, she commits suicide, and the old man is not slow to follow.

As the plot unfolds, however, two quite different movements take place. The action is introduced as an instance of Cupid's revenge. The god descends in prologue, complains that his deity is neglected, and vows to demonstrate his power by raising "much ruth and woe" in fair Gismond. At the beginning of the third act he returns, and reveals that it was he who had inspired Tancred with jealousy and inflamed the hearts of Gismond and her courtier. In between these appearances, though, the Chorus has commented on Gismond's behavior by praising the chaste women of antiquity—Penelope, Lucres, Portia—and rebuking those modern females who cannot follow their example. In Act 3, after Gismond's servant has sympathetically described her mistress's struggle with divided loyalties, the Chorus offers a lecture on keeping busy, "for love assaults none but the idle heart," and exhorts the audience to resist Cupid. In the fourth act, after Gismond's courtier has apologized to Tancred for causing him grief, and pleads the irresistible power of Cupid, the Chorus preaches that "the end of wicked love is blood," and cites the case of Paris and Helen. Obviously, there are two *Gismond of Salernes*—a romantic one and a moral one—and they exist side by side. In the romantic play, Gismond and her lover are courteous, sensitive creatures who are meant to engage our sympathy by their very human responses to adverse circumstances; in the moral play, they are sinners and cautionary exempla whom we must shun. One cannot respond to them in a coherent way. To this ambivalence of feeling must be added an ambiguity of reasoning: the action of the play shows that Cupid's assaults cannot be resisted, while the Chorus preaches that they must be resisted. These disjunctions between the action and its choral frame reflect the Elizabethans' interest in seeking useful theses beneath the particulars of human action, and their amazing ability to respond on very different levels to the same story. Evidently it did not matter to them that their emotional and moral allegiances might draw them in opposite directions. Nurtured in the sophistic tradition, they were content to acknowledge the validity of both truths.

A somewhat more complex dramatic work is Gascoigne and Kinwelmarshe's *Jocasta* (1566), which offers further insight into mid-sixteenth century notions of tragedy. A translation of Ludovico Dolce's Italian adaptation of Euripides' *Phoenissae*, the play is presented as a mirror against political ambition.[16] It is an interpretation to which Euripides' play easily lends itself. As heirs of Oedipus, Eteocles and Polynices had agreed to share the throne in annual succession. Once Eteocles had gained power, however, he had refused to relinquish it, whereupon Polynices recruited a vast army of foreign allies and attacked Thebes. The deaths of the brothers at one another's hands leaves the kingdom in possession of Creon, who upon the advice of Tiresias sends Oedipus into exile, accompanied by Antigone.

To emphasize their admonitory reading, Dolce-Gascoigne make the wronged Polynices a more sympathetic figure than he is in Euripides— chiefly through the devotion of Antigone[17]—and cast Creon as a "type of tyranny."[18] But the subject matter of the play is actually more problematic than the moral overlay suggests, and the authors seem to be aware of this, too. While neither Euripides nor Dolce-Gascoigne leave any doubt that Polynices is theoretically in the right, the actual circumstances in which the brothers confront one another render their contention

16. See 1.1.160–170; 1.2.76–84; Chorus 1; 2.1.603–615; Chorus 5; Epilogus. Citations are from Cunliffe, *Classical Tragedies*.

17. See 1.2.28–40, 62–71, 88–104; 4.1.193–202; 5.3.22–26.

18. P. 67. The designation is apparently derived from his inflexible determination to banish Oedipus.

less clear-cut. For if Eteocles has committed evil in usurping power, so has Polynices in leading a foreign army against his own country.

Jocasta makes this abundantly clear in her attempt to reconcile her sons. She denounces not only Eteocles' usurpation of the crown but also Polynices' relentless pursuit of his legal right, and in the course of her exposition reveals the full implications of their actions. Against Eteocles' ambition, she adduces the moral blindness, the fears, the inevitable loss of worldly goods, and the widespread suffering that accompany the pursuit of power; against Polynices' legalism, the prospect of either an inglorious victory over his own kinsmen or disgrace and vilification should he bring defeat upon his allies. The effect of her two speeches is to shift much of the guilt onto Polynices, for the multiple commonplaces she has adduced against both sides transform the "bare was" of their conflict into a complicated issue that will not yield an easy solution. The complement of intellectual illumination is dramatic impasse. Eteocles articulates the Senecan pessimism underlying this situation as he remarks:

> The question that betwixt us two is growen
> Believe me mother, can not ende with words.
>
> (2.1.510–511)

Will, not reason, shall determine the issue.

The connection between tragedy and the faltering human *logos* becomes even more apparent when we examine Eteocles' words in their full context. Although drawn from Euripides, these lines are cast against a background that is Senecan rather than Euripidean. The presuppositions of Euripides' play are fundamentally rational. The fate of Oedipus and his family is specifically traced to his father's crime against the gods.[19] Similarly, when toward the end of the play it becomes necessary to sacrifice Creon's son Meneucus in order to save Thebes, Euripides provides an historical explanation for the act.[20] Both family tragedies are seen with-

19. Consulting Apollo's oracle about his prospects for an heir, the childless Laius was ordered not to beget children. Afterwards, in a fit of drunken lust, he sired Oedipus. Because of his disobedience, the remainder of the oracle—that the son would slay his father and marry his mother—was fulfilled in divine retribution (*Phoenissae*, ll. 13–22).

20. It is necessary to propitiate Ares, whose dragon was slain by Cadmus when he founded the city (*ibid.*, ll. 930–950).

in a rational pattern which, if cruel, has at least the virtue of logical causality, and is therefore comprehensible. In the Dolce-Gascoigne version, this rational element is absent. No mention is made of Laius's disobedience to the gods. Rather he is described as one

> desirous still to searche
> The hidden secrets of supernall powers. . . .
> (1.1.37–38)

While the oracle's prediction and his attempt to evade it are recounted, there is no intimation that he had ever had a choice. Even the manner of his death has undergone a change. In Euripides' play, he is killed at a crossroads in Phocis, when Oedipus in his pride refuses to step aside at the charioteer's command. In Dolce-Gascoigne, father and son chance to be fighting on opposite sides in a Phocian civil war when Oedipus, "with murdering blade unawares his father slewe" (1.1.105). Repeatedly, the play presents human beings ignorantly acting out their destinies before an arbitrary, inscrutable cosmos.[21]

In the corresponding Meneucus sequence, the sense of man's helplessness is intensified. The explanation for the sacrifice is omitted, and instead an exotic and mysterious augury scene is adapted from Seneca.[22] Then an entirely new exchange is added between Creon and Meneucus. In Euripides' play, Creon refuses to allow Meneucus to offer himself to the god, and Meneucus readily complies—only to assert his intention to sacrifice himself after his father has gone. Dolce-Gascoigne insert a typically Senecan debate, composed of *suasoriae* and stichomythia, on the merits of sacrificing one's self for one's country (3.2.1–92). Again the desire to debate the issue has moved to the forefront. But in spite of Creon's impressive arguments, Meneucus remains the obdurate Senecan figure, as we discover a few scenes later, when his death is announced by a messenger.

The revision of Euripides has moved, therefore, in two contrary directions. On the one hand, his action has been moralized, in a rather clumsy and superficial fashion, to provide the desired *ethicae*. But much more

21. Oedipus's innocence is reiterated at 1.1.133–134; 5.4.18–21; 5.5.192–196.

22. The scene recalls the Manto-Tiresias episode in Seneca's *Oedipus*, and Cunliffe points out the similarity of 3.1.118–120 to ll. 211–224 of that play (*Classical Tragedies*, p. 311).

subtly the tragedy has come to be connected with the failure of human *consilia* to circumvent a tragic destiny—a theme reflected not only in the scenes of unsuccessful suasion, but in the many suggestions of cosmic opacity that are scattered through the play. On this matter, Oedipus has the last word:

> to this heinous crime and filthy facte
> The heavens have from highe enforced me,
> Agains't whose doome no counsell can prevayle.
>
> (5.5.34–36)

Perhaps the most interesting Inns of Court play is Thomas Hughes's *Misfortunes of Arthur* (1588), which reveals in its stiff, academic fashion so many of the ways in which the study of Roman drama influenced English tragedy early in Marlowe's career and on the eve of Shakespeare's. The work is an exotic gallimaufry of Seneca, Geoffrey of Monmouth, and Malory. It concerns the return of Arthur to his wife Guenevora after nine years' war in France and his conflict with Mordred (now Guenevora's lover), which leads to civil war and the deaths of both men. In Hughes's play, this material is given a Senecan revenge frame that provides a nominal unity to the work: the tragedy is seen as retribution for Uther Pendragon's adultery with Gorlois's wife, which produced Arthur, and Arthur's incest with his sister Anne, which resulted in the birth of Mordred. Thus the play is a mirror against lust, and a generally consistent one, too.[23]

But within this neat framework is a sophist's delight. More than any of the other Inns of Court tragedies, *The Misfortunes of Arthur* may well be described as "an image of human reasoning and its outcome," for the consultation scenes so far outnumber any in Seneca that one suspects Hughes's early training in Terence was put to use.[24] Many of these con-

23. See 3.4.18–27; 5.1.119–121. Citations are from Cunliffe.
24. The *argumenta* to three of the four scenes in Act 1 will suggest some of this flavor:

In the second scene, *Guenevora* hearing that *Arthur* was on the Seas returning, desperately manaceth his death, from which intent she is diswaded by *Fronia*, a Lady of her Court & privie to her secrets.

In the third scene *Guenevora* perplexedly mindeth her owne death, whence being diswaded by her sister she resolveth to enter into Religion.

tain the conventional set debates that we have already seen in *Gorboduc* and *Jocasta*. Some, however, are conceived dramatically, to suggest a mind anxiously seeking the proper course of action. The second and third scenes of Act 1, for example, carefully trace Guenevora's decision to enter a religious house. This is accomplished by means of an extended debate with two different interlocutors. Through continuous argument with her maid and sister, she moves from a desire to revenge Arthur's desertion, to remorse for her adultery, to a wish for death, and finally to a fixed resolve to expiate her sin. In this sequence, Hughes makes a significant advance on his predecessors, for he utilizes the debate mechanism to express the progressive dianoia of a character in a dramatic situation. It is yet stilted speech, with clumsy transitions, but in its shiftings from one issue to another it successfully mirrors a mind coming to grips with a complex problem.

The device is used for even more effective characterization in Act 3, where Arthur debates with his followers Howell and Cador whether or not to fight Mordred. The topic itself is that of a deliberative oration, but the familiar technique of arguing by means of varying propositions is used here to suggest Arthur's basic repugnance at the prospect of facing his son in civil war. He is at first inclined to let heaven revenge his wrong, and admits that his natural love for Mordred makes such a conflict abhorrent to him:

> Whereof who knows which were the greater guilt,
> The sire to slai the sonne or sonne the sire.
>
> (3.1.56–57)

Cador advises him to leave it up to "Lawe" and "let him die that deserves," cautioning Arthur that there is "no worse a vice then lenitie in Kings." This leads to an extended debate *a thesi* on the merits of justice and mercy in kingship. Cador argues that rigor is the only cure for unlawful rebellion, Arthur that compassion best befits a father and a king:

In the fourth scene *Mordred* goeth about to perswade *Guenevora* to persist in her love, but misseth thereof; And then is exhorted by Conan (a noble man of Brytain) to reconcile himselfe to his Father at his comming, but refuseth so to doe and resolveth to keepe him from landing by battaile. (Cunliffe, p. 26. See also the *argumenta* to 2.2, 2.3, 3.1, 4.1, and 4.3.)

Law must not lowre. Rule oft admitteth ruth.

(86)

When Cador warns him to "beware a reconciled foe," Arthur changes propositions and argues his case for acquiescence on the *topos* of *contemptus mundi*. The Senecan manner of *gnomic* argumentation is evident in these hemistiches on the dubious value of kingship:

CADOR: To rule is much.
ARTHUR: Small if we covet naught.
CADOR: Who covets not a Crowne.
ARTHUR: He that discernes
The swoord aloft.
CADOR: That hangeth fast.
ARTHUR: But by
A haire.
CADOR: Right holds it up.
ARTHUR: Wrong puls it downe.
CADOR: The Commons helpe the King.
ARTHUR: They sometimes hurt.
CADOR: At least the Peeres.
ARTHUR: Sield, if allegeance want.
CADOR: Yet Soveraigntie.
ARTHUR: Not, if allegeance faile.

(3.1.153–158)

This approach proving unsuccessful, Cador then tries to rouse Arthur with the prospect of glory, but the old king is impervious to that argument, too:

Fame's but a blast that sounds a while,
And quickely stints, and then is quite forgot.

(178–179)

Unconvinced by Arthur's stoicism, Cador suggests that the real reason for Arthur's reluctance is simply his blind affection for Mordred, since for a lesser insult he led thirteen kings into France against the Romans. This provides Arthur with the opening for his final argument: he has expended enough of his countrymen's blood in foreign brawls, and will not now inflict civil war upon them.

The scene ends with Arthur still unpersuaded to go to war, but differs from the similarly unproductive counsel scene in *Gorboduc* in that the protagonist has argued his own case and revealed all his rationalizations for acting as he does. Hughes has, in fact, written two *suasoriae*—pro and con—in the form of a colloquy in which the interlocutors feed one another arguments. In this way he has provided both a broad exposition of the issue and a recognizable character for Arthur, who makes us feel that he is compassionate, humble, and more than a little weary. He comes closer to being a complex character than any other figure in these Inns of Court plays, simply by virtue of Hughes's obsessive rehearsal of all possible proofs for his case. It is an amusing demonstration of the legal-rhetorical principle that the more circumstances one adduces in the consideration of an issue the nearer one comes to recreating reality itself.

Unlike Guenevora's debates in Act 1, the political discussions that focus on the major issue of the play—the conflict between Mordred and Arthur —resolve nothing. This is true not only of the colloquy between Arthur and his counselors, but also of those between Mordred and his. It is not rhetorical *inventio* that leads to action in these instances, but, in the case of Mordred his will to power, and in Arthur's case Mordred's threat to destroy him unless he fights. Thus the basic Senecan disjunction between action and argument prevails. More important, the tragic outcome is attributed largely to the ineffectiveness of counsel. Conan, Mordred's advisor, takes a rather philosophic view of his impotence. Even men in the greatest favor with their king, he remarks,

> Can worke by fit persuasion sometimes much:
> But sometimes lesse: and sometimes nought at all.
>
> (4.1.32–33)

But Mordred, the object of his unsuccessful ministrations, provides the darker reason for this failure, after arguing with Gawain earlier in the play:

> Since then the sagest counsailes are but strifes.
> Where equall wits may wreast each side alike,
> Let counsaile go: my purpose must proceede:
> Each likes his course, mine owne doth like me best.
>
> (2.3.135–138)

In Mordred's cynical disbelief in the capacity of rhetoric to lead to any constructive solution, we find a dim portent of that moment when an anguished Hamlet cries out in bewilderment that God could not have given us such large discourse, "looking before and after," to fust in us unused—and vows his thoughts will now be bloody or be nothing worth. The theme is pervasive, and grows stronger.

II

Viewed against the Inns of Court plays—which as avant-garde drama must have been familiar to ambitious young dramatists—both the peculiarities and considerable achievements of *The Spanish Tragedy* (1587–1589) may be more clearly understood. The chief problem the play has presented to modern readers is the moral discrepancy between its dramatized frame and action proper. Stated briefly, the difficulty is this. Kyd created a Senecan frame in which a restless ghost, Don Andrea, returns to the scene of his mortality with Revenge, who promises that he shall witness the death of Balthazar, the Portuguese prince who killed him in battle. This implies a pagan ethic of simple retributive justice. The ethic seems to materialize in the action proper as Bel-imperia, revenging Balthazar's defeat of Andrea, refuses his suit and takes Horatio as her lover; in return, Balthazar, incited by Lorenzo, slays Horatio; and in the major action, Hieronimo requites this murder with the assistance of Bel-imperia. Thus Andrea's death is avenged.

But as the plot unfolds, a certain moral thickening occurs. Hieronimo is a good man—by profession, a man of law—and is deeply concerned with principles of justice. Although driven by the desire to revenge his son's murder, he awaits corroborative evidence of Lorenzo's and Balthazar's guilt, and even then determines to act legally by presenting his case to the King. When he is unable to gain the King's ear, he debates with himself the next step—whether to follow Christian orthodoxy and leave revenge to God, or to take matters into his own hands. He concludes upon a personal—and stealthy—vengeance. Feigning friendship for his enemies, he devises a cunning strategem and stages a spectacular revenge upon all the accessories to his grief. As a result, the gratified ghost of Andrea promises at the end of the play to intercede with Proserpine so that his friends Hieronimo, Horatio, Bel-imperia, and Isabella may spend eternity in the Elysian Fields, while his enemies (and theirs) will be consigned to the legendary tortures of deepest hell.

The problems raised by a play whose action is predicated on revenge, then questions the morality of revenge, and finally rewards revenge, are obvious. First, is Kyd simply being careless? If not, is he actually suggesting to his Christian audience that such moral scruples as Hieronimo's are gratuitous, since the universe is deterministic anyway? So the character Revenge implies, when he assures Andrea that though he appears to have done nothing, his "mood" has been working upon the Spanish courtiers:

> Behold, Andrea, for an instance, how
> Revenge hath slept, and then imagine thou
> What 'tis to be subject to destiny.
>
> (3.15.25–27)[25]

On the other hand, if Kyd is not predicating a determinist universe, what is the function of the frame, and how are we to regard the hero, who abandons Christian ethics, deliberately adopts the machiavellian tactics of his enemies, and is responsible for the deaths of five people, including his own?[26] Finally, how are we meant to respond to Andrea's simplistic disposition of good and evil after being made aware that the question of revenge is more complex than the frame suggests?

These problems can be at least partially resolved if we think about *The Spanish Tragedy* in terms of its Senecan legacy. Seneca's plays do not purport to be extensions of the actual world—certainly the philosopher would never have endorsed the moral determinism his plays, viewed as

25. The "instance" referred to is the bloody marriage masque presented by Revenge to show Andrea that the forthcoming nuptials between Bel-imperia and Balthazar will not take place. Citations are from Philip Edwards's edition, *The Revels Plays* (London, 1959).

26. This has probably been the central question in the criticism of the play. Fredson Bowers, *Elizabethan Revenge Tragedy*, argues that we are meant to condemn Hieronimo for assuming the divine prerogative, and he has recently been seconded by Eleanor Prosser, *Hamlet and Revenge* (Stanford, 1967). Ernst de Chickera, "Divine Justice and Private Revenge in 'The Spanish Tragedy,'" *MLR* 67 (1962): 228–232, takes a more moderate position. For justifications of Hieronimo, see John Ratliff, "Hieronimo Explains Himself," *SP* 54 (1957): 112–118; Einar Jensen, "Kyd's *Spanish Tragedy*: The Play Explains Itself," *JEGP* 64 (1965): 7–16; David Laird, "Hieronimo's Dilemma," *SP* 62 (1965): 137–146.

mirrors, imply. Rather they are "liberties" within the actual world—neutral places in which to arouse emotions, ask certain broad philosophical questions, and expound a variety of attitudes toward the tragic story being unfolded. The structure most amenable to this function is a loose collocation of sophistic forms. The prologue serves as something of a poetic *thesis*—indicating in a general way what the action is to be, and suggesting its underlying causality. But as we observed in *Medea,* there is a sharp contrast between the generic vagueness of the prologue and the particular mental events that actually determine the shape of the action. This often leads—especially in the plays with supernatural prologues—to an apparent discrepancy between the determinism assumed initially and the autonomy suggested by the extended dianoia of the major characters.[27] Their demonstrations of moral responsibility would be totally gratuitous if the psychology implied in Seneca's frames was extended with any consistency into the action proper. But it is not. And this is because the prologues are rhetorical rather than strictly conceptual instruments. They postulate causality, arouse dread, and prepare us for the tragic catastrophe; in the realization of that catastrophe, however, other motivations and moralities are frequently countenanced in the lengthy ruminations of the principal characters and the Chorus.[28]

In Seneca's Elizabethan imitators, as we have seen, the relationship between action and frame becomes less subtle. In their search for theses, they tend to elaborate their dramatic frames, even as they entertain assumptions within the work that are not compatible with the dominant

27. Witness the indecisiveness of the returning Thyestes, "fated" by Tantalus and the Fury to suffer Atreus's revenge, and the psychomachic struggle of shame, adulterous love, and hatred within Clytemnestra, who is "condemned" by the ghost of Thyestes to be the murderer of Agamemnon.

28. Even in *Hercules Furens,* Seneca's most "determinist" play, Hercules' profound sense of guilt following the slaughter of his wife and children is at odds with the fact that as Juno's unwitting instrument, he is not responsible for their deaths. Yet he insists: "As for my glorious deeds, at others' hest I did them; this alone is mine" (*Seneca's Tragedies,* trans. Frank Justus Miller [London, 1917], 1. 1268). And he is not proved to be wrong. This suggests that attention has been displaced from acceptance of the frame's fatalism to inquiry into other possibilities and temporary acquiescence in the notion that a man is responsibile for his deeds and must therefore bear their consequences. Given Seneca's sophistic mode of composition, this is perhaps better described as a change in focus than in conception.

thesis. This dual tendency clearly informs the composition of *The Spanish Tragedy*; for, no doubt about it, Kyd did create a play with a frame that points in one direction and an action that points in another. But like Seneca's prologues, this frame, too, is a rhetorical rather than a conceptual instrument. It invites us "to imagine . . . what 'tis to be subject to destiny," detaching us from the world of moral complexity and drawing us instead into a mysterious, mechanical world of a divinely sanctioned *lex talionis*. Here we may enjoy the luxury of watching a predetermined pattern unfold, and taste the rough justice of revenge, without having to make fine moral distinctions—for such matters as motive, character, and circumstance are of no concern.[29] It is an intellectually comforting and an emotionally stimulating environment, but it is perfectly consonant with sophistic practice that we do not remain in it long. For, having established this unifying frame, Kyd then leads us to examine his proposed matter more closely, through a densely packed human action in which several complicated issues are raised, concerning the nature of love, justice, knowledge. And as we view this action, released for large gaps of time from the tutelage of Revenge and Andrea, we come to judge it in quite a different way. We do so because Kyd modulates from thesis to hypothesis (from "what" happens to "how" it happens) within the play proper, adducing in his exposition of Hieronimo's revenge a wide range of qualifying circumstances that enable the theatre audience to comprehend the action more fully than the Plutonian spirits, in their simpler generic world, seem capable of doing.[30] As a result, the play invites us to respond in several different ways: to enjoy the visceral pleasures of a well-deserved blood revenge, to ponder more carefully the

29. Barry B. Adams, "The Audiences of *The Spanish Tragedy*," *JEGP* 68 (1969), observes that "Revenge is guiding Andrea and the theatre audience toward a formalistic or aesthetic interpretation" of the play (p. 230).

30. An example of the simplistic perspective of the supernatural world is the debate between Aeacus and Rhadamanthus over Andrea's disposition in the Underworld, recounted in the first scene. Aeacus wishes to send him to "our fields of love" because he "both liv'd and died in love," but Rhadamanthus argues "it were not well with loving souls to place a martialist," and demands that Andrea be sent to scour the plains with Achilles and his Myrmidons (1.1.32–49). While the infernal judges insist upon dichotomizing human life, the action proper just as insistently unites love and war, most explicitly in the sexual battle of Belimperia and Horatio (2.3.34–52).

problematic situation of the man who would be just, *and to reflect upon the simplistic judgment of the frame as an aspect of his problem.* The first two affective imperatives are familiar enough from our experience with the digressive plays of Kyd's predecessors. But the last is original. Evidently sporting Kyd, assiduously studying English Seneca by candlelight, discovered what earlier playwrights had failed to see: that the contrasting perspectives of frame and action proper might be made to reflect ironically upon one another. This means, in effect, that for the first time an English dramatist succeeded in drawing the centrifugal elements of the Senecan tradition into a comprehensive tragic statement.

Before we examine the nature of this statement and how it is made, it will be useful to trace Kyd's declension from thesis to hypothesis in more detail. His interest in developing a simple action, bearing its own crude ethic, into a more circumstantial and therefore problematic situation, is most clearly seen in the three accounts of Andrea's death that are offered in Act 1. The first of these, delivered by the Ghost himself, describes the event only in the most general terms:

> For in the late conflict with Portingale
> My valour drew me into danger's mouth,
> Till life to death made passage through my wounds.
> (1.1.15–17)

Nothing here about the man who killed him, or the peculiar circumstances of his death. When in the next scene the victorious Spanish general makes his report to the King, he adds some important details. After three hours of steady fighting between the Spanish and the Portuguese, "The victory to neither part inclined." Then Andrea bravely led his lancers forward and made so great a breach in the enemy's ranks that they retired in confusion.

> But Balthazar, the Portingale's young prince,
> Brought rescue and encouraged them to stay;
> Here-hence the fight was eagerly renew'd,
> And in that conflict was Andrea slain—
> Brave man at arms, but weak to Balthazar.
> (1.2.68–72)

Here, significant elements begin to fill in the original outline—the equality of the rival armies, Andrea's great courage and initial success, his defeat by Balthazar, Balthazar's apparently superior prowess. From bare fact, Kyd has sketched in a real episode, shaded by the qualities of the men involved.

The final account is presented by Horatio, entreated by Bel-imperia "to relate The circumstance of Don Andrea's death." Now we learn, *in the fullest circumstantiality*, that a fresh supply of Portuguese halberdiers had attacked Andrea in his moment of triumph, stabbed his horse, and knocked him to the ground, where

> young Don Balthazar with ruthless rage
> Taking advantage of his foe's distress,
> Did finish what his halberdiers begun,
> And left not till Andrea's life was done.
>
> (1.4.23–26)

Here, a moral act further qualifies the situation, and for the first time we discover the motive for revenging Andrea's death—

> For what was't else but murd'rous cowardice,
> So many to oppress one valiant knight,
> Without respect of honor in the fight?
>
> (73–75)

What originally appeared to be a mechanical, mindless revenge is now seen as a process of stern, but real justice.

These three accounts are not simply different views of the same event that invite skepticism concerning the truth;[31] they do not conflict with one another, but differ in a *descending order of particularity*, proceeding

---

31. Though, for a contrary view, see Peter B. Murray, *Thomas Kyd* (New York, 1969), pp. 46–48. Murray argues that Horatio deliberately colors his account to gain Bel-imperia's favor. The problem with this reading is that there are no cues anywhere to suggest that Horatio is being deceptive; certainly Balthazar's jealous complaint that Horatio is filling Bel-imperia's ears with "sly deceits" (2.2.127) is too vague to be taken as anything but a reference to love-talk, and Lorenzo's vicious observation that the "ambitious proud" Horatio now hangs high (2.4.60) simply reflects his anger that yet another man of "not ignoble" descent has caught his sister's fancy.

from a blunt representation of a fact to a detailed analysis which transforms the nature of that fact. The procedure is investigative in the strict
forensic sense of examining a given in the light of attendant circumstances
so that its significance may be assessed with a subtlety otherwise unattainable. It is to just this process of more and more finely discriminating
the matter of revenge that the action proper draws us, as we view the
predicament of the hero. Kyd is very careful to specify Hieronimo's distinguishing qualities, making use of such analytic *topoi* as those which
Castiglione employed in fashioning his Courtier. Hieronimo is a virtuous
and loyal old man (the *topos* is *natura*), a magistrate who has manifested
a lifelong concern for equity (*victus*).[32] He is beloved in the state (*fortuna*).[33] When he discovers Horatio's body, he goes about as cautiously
as possible to gather evidence on which to act (*studium*).[34] Since his first
response upon receiving Pedringano's letter is to "go plain me to my
lord the king," we may assume that his natural inclination is to obtain
justice through the traditional procedures of law (*habitus*). His situation is made especially burdensome because his official duties continually
remind him of his own failure to secure justice;[35] as a result, his suppressed
emotions erupt under the strain, and he lapses into periodic fits of madness
(*affectio*). Finally, his major debate with himself (the "Vindicta mihi"
consilium) indicates his awareness of the moral issue, and comes at a time
—after he has secured the necessary evidence and has been circumvented
in his attempt to reach the King—when his reasoning *away* from Christian patience is supported by all we have learned of his situation.[36] In
short, Hieronimo's predicament, drawn through the heuristic of judicial

32. "There's not any advocate in Spain That can prevail, or will take half the
pain That he will, in pursuit of equity" (3.13.52–54). The *topoi* listed here are
drawn from *De inv.* 1.34–36.

33. "Lorenzo, know'st thou not the common love And kindness that Hieronimo hath won By his deserts within the court of Spain?" (3.14.61–63).

34. "I therefore will by circumstances try What I can gather to confirm this
writ" (3.2.48–49).

35. "Thus must we toil in other men's extremes, That know not how to remedy
our own" (3.6.1–2).

36. Indeed, Scott McMillan, examining the issue with great subtlety, argues
that Hieronimo's apparently distorted quotations from Seneca reveal his awareness that the aggression forced upon him must lead to his own destruction ("The
Book of Seneca in *The Spanish Tragedy*," *SEL* 14 [1974]: 201–208).

examination, has been deliberately given a complex reality that makes it impossible to judge it at the level of precept; it must be judged equitably, in the light of all the circumstances. Then, his decline into machiavellianism is seen to be neither wicked, as some modern literary censors have contended, nor triumphant, as those contemporary critics, Revenge and Andrea, so blandly proclaim—but tragic.[37]

If Kyd had been content simply to contrast the levels of realism in frame and action proper, his play would still remain an outstanding example of Elizabethan multiple-view drama in the Senecan tradition.[38] But evidently he saw in the contrast itself a certain tragic implication which he took pains to develop. For the discrepancy between the ethical complexity of frame and action opens up the larger question of what is involved in any act of adjudication—what procedures, what variables, what chances there are for an equitable issue: judgment based upon understanding. The problem must have been of considerable interest to him, for he made it the most important object of mimesis in the play.

What, Kyd asks repeatedly, constitutes an act of judgment? One begins with an event—a fact outside one's self—then seeks to comprehend it by gathering qualifying details which give that event a certain ethical shape in relation to the perceiver. Then one acts upon one's sense of its meaning. The most perspicuous instance of this process is found in the frame itself. For four acts, Andrea and Revenge sit observing the behavior of the Spanish Court. During the first, second, and third intervals, Andrea, who has watched the action closely but does not understand how it will further his vengeance, demands explanation of his companion. Revenge assures him each time that what he has seen is but a step in the larger design over which he has been sent to preside. It is only when the particular image perceived by Andrea has been related to his involuntary

37. The above enumeration of *topoi* does not, of course, constitute a full portrait of Hieronimo, but is meant to indicate how such a character is fleshed out and how certain salient features are highlighted to affect our judgment of him.

38. Two other plays written at about the same time reveal the same interest in contrasting thesis and hypothesis. The anonymous *Rare Triumphs of Love and Fortune* (1584) is a romantic comedy framed by a debate between Love and Fortune, who dispute each other's influence on the action proper; in its mirror image, *Soliman and Perseda* (1590), Death, Love, and Fortune argue in somewhat simpleminded fashion who had the greatest influence on the tragedy. This play is usually attributed to Kyd.

journey to the Plutonian Underworld and Proserpine's command that it becomes meaningful to him, for, as Cicero reminds us, particulars cannot be properly understood without their underlying theses. Ultimately Andrea will "understand" the entire action of the play in terms of Revenge's thesis, and thus in good conscience consort his friends in Elysium and doom his foes to Hell. It is an appropriate judgment within the abstract and ethically simple world he and his mentor inhabit.

The scenario rehearsed by Andrea and Revenge suggests a serious problem, though. While theoretically the reason acts upon the particulars of visual and aural evidence to arrive at a just disposition based upon an understanding of their wider meaning, in fact judgment is more likely to be shaped by the context in which the perceiver "understands" the case. This phenomenon may be observed quite early in the play proper when the King of Spain stands overlooking his victorious troops—come "to show themselves" and "by demonstration" prove that only a small number have perished. Seeing below him a foreign dignitary flanked on one side by his nephew Lorenzo and on the other by a stranger, he asks their identity, and is told the foreigner is Balthazar and the stranger Horatio. Knowing nothing yet of Lorenzo's role in the capture of Balthazar, and having heard of Horatio's heroism from the General, he congratulates Hieronimo:

> Hieronimo, it greatly pleaseth us,
> That in our victory thou have a share,
> By virtue of thy worthy son's exploit.
> (1.2.124–126)

Moments later, however, he is confronted by the same trio and learns that while Horatio had forced Balthazar to yield, Lorenzo had seized his arms. This additional evidence changes the "picture," and as the young men contend politely but firmly, the King's assessment begins subtly to shift. To Hieronimo's gentle reminder of true right in the matter ("He hunted well that was a lion's death, Not he that in a garment wore his skin"), the King replies, in a direct reversal of his earlier statement,

> Content thee, Marshal, thou shalt have no wrong,
> And for thy sake thy son shall want no right.
> (172–173)

What has happened is that the King's blood relationship has been called into the question; he is no longer simply a monarch honoring a hero, but also an uncle making sure his nephew gets part of the spoils. Right has been transformed into a matter of politic accommodation, and Horatio and Lorenzo must divide the reward.

The scene suggests not only how greater circumstantiality changes the meaning of an image, but also how self-interest may work upon the more complicated image to produce the subjectively most meaningful interpretation. The pattern is repeated more explicitly in the dumb show presented for the entertainment of the Portuguese Ambassador. Here, the image seen is that of three knights defeating three kings, and Hieronimo is called upon to supply the clarifying circumstances:

> Hieronimo, this masque contents mine eye,
> Although I sound not well the mystery.
>
> (1.4.138–139)

Hieronimo explains that the first two knights were Englishmen who conquered the Portuguese, whereupon the King puts the evidence together and draws the appropriate thesis:

> That Portingale may deign to bear our yoke
> When it by little England hath been yoked.
>
> (159–160)

The third knightly encounter, however, represents John of Gaunt's defeat of Castile, and the Portuguese Ambassador explains that *it* warns Spain not to be arrogant in its present conquest. Having understood the details of the images and adduced their moral significance, the King and the Ambassador are content:

> Hieronimo, I drink to thee for this device,
> Which hath pleas'd both the Ambassador and me.
>
> (172–173)

Hieronimo's pageants are calculated to invite these judgments, but *visibilia* are not always so easily interpreted. Coming upon Horatio's body hanging in the arbor, the old Knight Marshall exclaims:

> But stay, what murd'rous spectacle is this?
>
> (2.5.9)

It is another dumb show, and his first response to it is gross, subjective apprehension: it is simply a "man" hanged in his garden to place the blame on him. As a jurist, this is what he naturally thinks of first. When he discovers it is Horatio, though, the context changes, and he responds as a father, asking heaven why night was created to cover such sin, earth why it did not devour the murderer. But these impassioned questions cannot help him to understand the meaning of the horrifying image he sees—or enable him to act upon it—and so he forces himself to resume the circumspection necessary to discover the facts and judge the case. His awareness of the necessity to do so distinguishes him from every other character in the play, and provides the locus for the tragic irony that finally envelops him.

It is at this point that *The Spanish Tragedy* most clearly departs from the Senecan model and follows instead the pattern of Latin comedy.[39] The *status* is conjectural—who committed the crime?—and the first piece of evidence Hieronimo comes upon (*invenit*) is Bel-imperia's letter:

> What means this unexpected miracle?
> My son slain by Lorenzo and the prince!
> What cause had they Horatio to malign?
> Or what might move thee, Bel-imperia,
> To accuse thy brother, had he been the mean?
>
> (3.2.32–36)

Such suspect evidence is itself in need of explanation:

> I therefore will by circumstances try
> What I can gather to confirm this writ.
>
> (48–49)

Search for additional facts leads first to an encounter with Lorenzo, where Hieronimo presents such a suspect picture himself that Lorenzo infers his

39. The comic origin of Kyd's plot has been noted by Alfred Harbage in "Intrigue in Elizabethan Tragedy," *Essays on Shakespeare and Elizabethan Drama*, ed. Richard Hosley (Columbia, Mo., 1962), pp. 37–44, though he does not discuss its cognitive function.

secret is known and attempts to cover his tracks by executing the witnesses Serberine and Pedringano. This episode, in turn, provides Hieronimo with new testimony, in the form of Pedringano's letter. But he is unable to use it because of his increasing emotional instability. When he appears before the King to demand justice, shaking with fear and anger, all the King sees is a furious man:

> What means this outrage?
> (3.12.79)

Explication is conveniently provided by Lorenzo, and the King, having no evidence to the contrary, accepts it. This destroys all chance that Hieronimo will ever obtain legal justice.

This pattern of proof-counter-proof informs most of the third act, as Hieronimo plays *senex* to Balthazar's *adulescens*, aided and abetted by the *servus-cum-vice* Lorenzo. When finally thwarted in his attempts to obtain redress in the legal way, he pauses to deliberate on the next move. The question is no longer conjectural, but qualitative: should Hieronimo take vengeance upon the murderers of his son, even though he is bound to observe the law? Adducing the testimony of St. Paul on one side and Seneca on the other, he persuades himself that awaiting heaven's justice will only endanger his own life and that he must act. But he does so in a way that remains true to the magistrate within him.

In the Latin plays, the *status* is resolved by the presentation of a proof that satisfies the interests of both sides. Thus Crito appears in the *Andria* as a witness that Glycerium is Chremes' long-lost daughter, and Pamphilus may therefore marry her with her father's approval. In *The Spanish Tragedy* this final proof is the play of Soliman and Perseda, designed by Hieronimo as the instrument by which the *status* can be answered. He will revenge his son, but he will also reveal that the act is just. His comment to Balthazar as they plan the production indicates its Terentian origin:

> BALTHAZAR: But this will be a mere confusion,
>   And hardly shall we all be understood.
> HIERONIMO: It must be so, for the conclusion
>   Shall prove the invention and all was good.
>   And I myself in an oration,
>   And with a strange and wondrous show beside,

That I will have there behind a curtain,
Assure yourselves shall make the matter known.
(4.1.182–187)

In words echoing Donatus's remark that "the catastrophe is the unfolding of the fable, through which the outcome is proved acceptable," he is saying that the *status* shall finally be resolved through an indisputable proof of his own invention. He will punish Lorenzo and Balthazar unhindered, and then, playing his own Crito, enter to justify the *status quo* by publishing the motives behind the bloody spectacle through speech and tokens.[40]

As an instrument of public justice, however, *The Tragedy of Soliman and Perseda* is a terrible failure. Hieronimo effects his revenge, to be sure, but no one in his audience seems to understand why:

> KING: Speak, traitor: damned, bloody murderer,
> speak!
> For now I have thee I will make thee speak:
> Why hast thou done this undeserving deed?
> VICEROY: Why hast thou murdered my Balthazar?
> CASTILE: Why hast thou butcher'd both my children
> thus?   (4.4.163–167)

These questions are asked *after* Hieronimo, stepping out of his role as Bashaw, has fully explicated the play in the vulgar tongue. There is no logical reason for his audience's continued ignorance,[41] and so explanation must be sought in the nature of the proof Hieronimo has presented and in his audience's manner of perceiving it. The vehicle he has chosen is a rhetorical *imago* or similitude to the action at issue. Even as Lorenzo planned and executed the death of Horatio, Balthazar's rival, for the love of Bel-imperia, so the Bashaw slays Erasto, Soliman's rival, for the love of Perseda. As a heuristic device the play is perfectly conventional, and one that might be expected of a legal advocate.[42] But Hieronimo is

40. The latter are, of course, the body of Horatio and the bloody handkerchief.
41. M. D. Faber and Colin Skinner have argued, not very convincingly, that the audience believes Hieromino is still acting while delivering his explication ("*The Spanish Tragedy*: Act IV," *PQ* 44 [1970]: 454–457).
42. We have already encountered one in *The Play of Love*. See Ch. IV, p. 116, and n. 10.

no longer a conventional advocate. Whatever his justification, he has become a private revenger, and so the device is subtly distorted in his hands.

The logical way to present such an *imago* would be to have the actors of the original crime play the analogous roles in the tragedy—Hieronimo playing Erasto, the image of Horatio, to Balthazar's Soliman and Lorenzo's Bashaw. In this way, Lorenzo and Balthazar would visibly reenact their crimes. But since he is using the play as an instrument of punishment and not simply one of revelation, Hieronimo is forced to obscure the parallel by assuming Lorenzo's original role. It is a sign of his degeneration from just magistrate to bedevilled revenger that he enacts the murderer's part and thus blurs the image he has invented to clarify the issue. But he does more. His decision to play the tragedy in foreign tongues—a bitter gesture to symbolize the futility of reason in the Spanish Court—effectively reduces the play to a dumb show. (We recall Balthazar's warning.) Offered a dumb show, all the audience can do is concentrate on the particulars of the image—not its meaning. This interest is registered in their comments on the actors:

> KING: See, Viceroy, that is Balthazar your son
> That represents the emperor Soliman:
> How well he acts his amorous passion.
> VICEROY: Ay, Bel-imperia hath taught him that.
> CASTILE: That's because his mind runs all on Bel-
> imperia. (4.4.20–24)

This is not an audience absorbed in a play. Their attention fixes itself on the surface—on the actual identities of the performers, their technique, and the real-life sources of their inspiration. That they are not following the dialogue is made absolutely clear by the King's comment when Erasto enters. The character Soliman has just said:

> But let my friend, the Rhodian knight, come forth,
> Erasto, dearer than my life to me,
> That he may see Perseda, my beloved.
>
> (30–32)

The stage direction then reads "Enter Erasto," and the King remarks:

> Here comes Lorenzo; look upon the plot,
> And tell me brother, what part plays he?
>
> (33–34)

He has obviously not understood a word of what has just passed, and is simply pleased to see his nephew on the stage.[43] Such attention to the players is not surprising, given the nature of the presentation. Like late arrivals at an unfamiliar opera performed by well-known stars, all this audience can perceive are the familiar figures, costumed, gesturing broadly, making emotional utterances. Deprived of clarifying dialogue, they do not follow the import of the plot, cannot draw its particulars into a generic significance—which is required for any analogy—and therefore can respond only with vague admiration for superficial details. Having never entered into the play's meaning, they then fail to see any relationship between the murder of their children onstage and Hieronimo's tale of a hanged son. To the obsessed Hieronimo, the significance of the action is perfectly clear; to an audience prepared for a dynastic celebration, it simply spells political catastrophe—the assassination of the heirs apparent by the traitorous Knight Marshall:

> What age hath ever heard such monstrous deeds?
> My brother, and the whole succeeding hope
> That Spain expected after my decease!
>
> (4.4.202–204)

The tragedy of *The Spanish Tragedy* consists most profoundly, then, in Hieronimo's failure to "make the matter known." His long and frustrating search for legal justice has resulted in his unconscious transformation into the very murderer he seeks to punish, and this subtly distorts his ability to present his case in a way that his audience can understand. Deprived of the appropriate cues, they can only respond with gross, subjective apprehension. Thus he is prevented from obtaining the only justice he cares about: judgment in understanding.[44] The fact is, his experience can only be understood by the theatre audience who have witnessed *Kyd's* play and learned why he acted as he did. They, it may be

---

43. This fact has not been pointed out, so far as I know, in the controversy over whether the play was actually performed in sundry languages. It strongly supports the contention that it was, and suggests that the English translator did his work rather carefully.

44. Notice that it is justice and not acquittal that he seeks, for he is prepared to pay for revenge with his life (4.4.146–152).

hoped, will judge him in the light of all the circumstances, and while acknowledging his guilt, show compassion for the cause.

In this light, the final scene between Andrea and the Ghost is especially ironic. Like Hieronimo's courtly audience, Andrea sums up the events as he sees them:

> Horatio murder'd in his father's bower,
> Vild Serberine by Pedringano slain,
> False Pedringano hang'd by quaint device,
> Fair Isabell by herself misdone,
> Prince Balthazar by Bel-imperia stabb'd,
> The Duke of Castile and his wicked son
> Both done to death by old Hieronimo,
> My Bel-imperia fall'n as Dido fell,
> And good Hieronimo slain by himself:
> Ay, these were spectacles to please my soul.
>
> (4.5.3–12)

Perceiving only the simplest meaning of the image, he then promises to lead the passionate Bel-imperia to the abode of vestal virgins and ensure that Hieronimo, the tragic hero, shall attend the muse with Orpheus—who, like himself, was a most accomplished showman. In his infernal innocence, the misunderstanding is complete.

III

The subtle dramaturgy of *The Spanish Tragedy*—conflating so brilliantly the traditions of Seneca and Terence—is not seen again for several years. But over the next decade, the sophistic practice of evoking a wide variety of attitudes toward a single action is found in a number of plays, and the tragic view of rhetorical invention is manifested in interesting new forms. Audiences to these plays are invited to contemplate—often quite adramatically—certain experiences of abiding human concern: what it feels like to be exiled from one's homeland, or to lose a child; how a man reacts to newly acquired power; how one can rise to nobility in the face of failure; how the human imagination deals with a difficult reality. The result is a kind of play in which, at its worst, interest is simply fragmented into many discrete moments, and nothing approaching tragic perception emerges. In the hands of more skillful dramatists, however, the practice succeeds in shaping a genuinely humanistic response to men and women who find themselves—despite good intentions—enmeshed in evil, and then it achieves the equity of tragedy.[45]

The gradual emergence of this more refined dramaturgy may be illustrated by three plays of our period that were produced under quite different auspices—Thomas Lodge's *Wounds of Civil War*, Samuel Daniel's *Cleopatra*, and John Marston's *Antonio's Revenge*. *The Wounds of Civil War, as lively set forth in the true Tragedies of Marius and Scilla,* was apparently in the repertory of the Admiral's Men around 1589.[46] It is largely a condensation of Appian's *Bellum Civile,* and traces the conflict of the rival leaders, from Marius's assumption of Sulla's command against Mithridates in 89 B.C. to Sulla's death in the year 78. Its theme is the horror of civil discord, but against this background Lodge so frequently shifts characterization of the two men for special effects that it is impossible to ascribe responsibility for the disaster or to sympathize with either party for longer than two or three consecutive scenes.

Sulla begins as the villain of the piece, as he leads an army against the Senate after having lost his command to Marius. Lodge develops his despotic bent in two important speeches—one in which the play's moral touchstone, the optimate consul Mark Antony, pleads with Sulla not to pursue personal honor in defiance of Roman law, and the other in which Sulla glories in the lust for conquest. In contrast, Marius is portrayed as a noble refugee, seeking asylum from uncertain allies. But Lodge then tampers with these sympathies by examining the seditious activities of the Marian forces at home. Their leader Cinna is a firebrand, intent upon giving the "young" citizens sovereignty over the "old,"[47] and in this

---

45. This does not mean that more crudely sophistic drama disappeared (cf. Greene's *Selimus,* or the academic *Tragedy of Caesar and Pompey*), nor that the more craftsmanlike plays later in the period were not anticipated earlier. But the process of sophistic refinement, as a phenomenon of the nineties, is a genuine *development,* representing a substantial advance upon the dramaturgy of the previous decade.

46. The problem of dating is discussed by Joseph W. Houppert in his edition of the play (Lincoln, Neb., 1969), pp. xii–xiv. All citations in the text are from this edition.

47. Lodge is curiously literal here, suggesting an overthrow of political order by youthful rebels, not the enfranchisement of the "new" Italian citizens. Whether he understood the issue is not clear.

struggle it is the Marians who are impiously defying the Senate, as Antony observes:

> Why then the Senate's name, whose reverent rule
> Hath blaz'd our virtues 'midst the Western Isle,
> Must be obscur'd by Cinna's forced power.
>
> (3.1.18–20)

A battle is about to break out between both sides when ominous thunder is heard. Interpreting it as a sign of the gods' displeasure, the optimate consul Octavius obediently retires. Cinna, on the other hand, mutters:

> High Jove, himself, hath done too much for thee,
> Else should this blade abate thy royalty—
>
> (81–82)

and promises vengefully that Marius is at hand to maintain the rights of the "young Italian citizens." The Marian cause now appears dangerous and innovative.

Yet following this disquieting scene, we find Marius in Minturnum, portrayed as a Stoic hero. Here Lodge is concerned to show the plight of the political exile, and so Marius engages in stichomythic debate with his jailor on the deceptive blessings of fortune and then delivers an encomium of the humble life, in the course of which his virtue is reasserted. By the time he has wandered in hunger across the African desert, rejoined his son, and departed with him for Rome and Cinna, we are once again won over to the side of the Marians.

Early in the next act, however, Lodge redirects our sympathies once more. The consul Octavius, accompanied by Antony and the grave senators, has sought refuge in the Janiculum:

> You see how Cinna, that should succor Rome,
> Hath levied arms to bring a traitor [Marius] in.
>
> (4.1.3–4)

Bravely he waits to confront Marius,

> Hoping that Consul's name and fear of laws
> Shall justify my conscience and my cause,
>
> (25–26)

but his hopes are instantly disappointed when Marius enters, for he is stabbed to death preventing Cinna from assuming his consul's chair. Within moments, however, we are offered a new portrait of Marius: Marius the gallant. Lightly teasing the captive wife and daughter of Sulla, he pretends to be arranging their deaths when he is actually ordering that treasures be brought them:

> Virtue, sweet ladies, is of more regard
> In Marius' mind where honor is enthron'd
> Than Rome or rule of Roman Empery.
>
> (390–392)

And off they go in triumph to his adversary.

Similar turnabouts are found in the presentation of Sulla. By the final act, Marius is dead. Having reestablished his power in Rome, Sulla blames the wavering multitude for the bloodshed of civil war:

> The reasons of this ruthful wrack
> Are your seditious innovations,
> Your fickle minds inclin'd to foolish change.
>
> (5.1.8–10)

His impeccable Tudor conservatism vanishes, however, in his mass proscription, and statesmanship shades quickly into despotism again. His behavior is contrasted with that of young Marius, now besieged in Praeneste, who leads a wholesale suicide of his followers to avoid capture. Sulla hears of this heroic gesture at the moment of his greatest glory—as he is declared perpetual dictator—and is so impressed by Marius's constancy that he undergoes a sudden change of heart. He does not repent; he simply renounces fortune's gifts, and—after much debate with his followers—resigns his office. Moments later he dies, a hero to family and city.

Obviously, *The Wounds of Civil War* is a crude play. But it is symptomatic. It exhibits, at large, the Elizabethans' intense interest in observing the responses of men to the changes of fortune, their desire to argue the commonplaces (Antony's dubious defense of the "law," for example, in Act 1, and Sulla's speech against innovation in Act 5), and their satisfaction with short-term moralizing. The play cannot be said to portray the conflict between Marius and Sulla problematically, since Lodge's frequent shifts in characterization are calculated not to trouble the audience's preconceptions but rather to focus attention upon certain piquant situations. The pluralistic impulse is there, but neither the critical mind nor the dramaturgic skill to exploit it for tragic effect.

Of special interest, though, is the view of rhetoric found in the play. The true hero of the piece is Antony, consul, moralist, and singularly unsuccessful orator. His early attempt to persuade Sulla to give up his ambition ends in utter failure:

> Enough, my Anthony, for thy honied tongue,
> Wash'd in a syrup of sweet conservatives,
> Driveth confused thoughts through Scilla's mind.
>
> (1.1.282–284)

And when he pleads for his own life before Marius's soldiers, he is rewarded with a fatal stabbing. Significantly, his inability to persuade is conceived not so much as the failure of *reasoning*, as in the earlier neo-Senecan plays, as the failure of *imaginative language*. Repeatedly, his speech is characterized as "honeyed," "cunning," "enchanting." At his death, his assassins eulogize him thus:

> Even in this head did all the Muses dwell;
> The bees that sat upon the Grecian's lips
> Distill'd their honey on his temper'd tongue.
> The crystal dew of fair Castalian springs,
> With gentle floatings trickled on his brains.
> The Graces kiss'd his kind and courteous brows,
> Apollo gave the beauties of his harp
> And melodies unto his pliant speech.
>
> (4.2.154–161)

It comes as something of a shock to recall that it is one of the interlocutors of *De oratore* whom Lodge is comparing to Homer, until we realize that his words reflect the assimilation of rhetoric by poetic as the final decade of the sixteenth century was approaching.[48] In this play, the stern moral

---

48. Cf. Sidney on the poet-civilizers, who drew "with their charming sweetnes the wild untamed wits to an admiration of knowledge" (*Elizabethan Critical Essays*, ed. G. Gregory Smith [Oxford, 1904] 1. 151). Or George Puttenham's contention that "the Poet is of all other the most auncient Orator . . . that by

counselor of the neo-Senecans has been reimagined as a poet-orator, and his "tragedy," such as it is, is closely connected with the inadequacy of his "terms of art" in the face of political reality.

A similar evaluation of rhetoric, this time in the light of moral reality, is reflected in Sulla's speech of triumph in Act 2:

> You Roman soldiers, fellow mates in arms,
> The blindfold mistress of incertain chance
> Hath turn'd these traitorous climbers from the top
> And seated Scilla in the chieftest place,
> The place beseeming Scilla and his mind.
> For were the throne where matchless glory sits
> Impal'd with furies threat'ning blood and death,
> Begirt with famine and those fatal fears
> That dwell below amidst the dreadful vast,
> Tut, Scilla's sparkling eyes should dim with clear
> The burning brands of their consuming light,
> And master fancy with a forward mind,
> And mask repining fear with awful power.
> For men of baser metal and conceit
> Cannot conceive the beauty of my thought.
>
> (2.1.1–15)

Here, Lodge's gaudy recollections of *Tamburlaine* specify as the source of human power a mind that can overcome external obstacles through the exercise of "conceit"—imagination. Again, the passage reflects a disjunction between the real—in this case, the ethical norm—and the invented —here expressed as "the beauty of my thought"—that is located in the very quality of Sulla's speech. To poetize thus is to tyrannize over reality, as Sulla acknowledges at the end of the play, when he considers the psychological effects of power:

> Can he remain secure that wields a charge?
> Or think of wit when flatt'rers do commend?

---

good and pleasant perswasions first reduced the wilde and beastly people into publicke societies and civilitie of life" (*The Arte of English Poesie* [Cambridge, 1936], p. 196). This is precisely the role ascribed to the orator in the Preface to Thomas Wilson's *Art of Rhetorique*, ed. G. H. Mair (Oxford, 1909).

Or be advis'd that careless runs at large?
No, Pompey, honey words make foolish minds,
And power the greatest wit with error blinds.

(5.5.124–128)

Here the conventional Senecan *topos* of regal instability is linked directly
to the improper use of wit, which has been manifested chiefly in Sulla's
exaggerated Marlovian rhetoric. The appropriate condition of the mind,
the scene tells us, is humble, firmly bound to a pastoral existence. Imagination is dangerous.[49]

This idea emerges more explicitly in Samuel Daniel's *Cleopatra* (1593),
a coterie play which, unlike Lodge's work, does seem designed to forge
a complex response to its protagonist. Early in the first act, Cleopatra,
now a prisoner of Caesar, sounds a familiar *de casibus* note as she compares
her former glory to her present state:

> Am I the woman whose inventive pride,
> Adorn'd like *Isis*, scorn'd mortality?
> Is't I would have my frailety so belide,
> That flattery could perswade I was not I?
> Well, now I see, they but delude that praise us
> Greatnesse is mockt, prosperity betrayes us.
> And we are but our selves, although the cloud
> Of interposed smoake makes us seems more.

(33–40)[50]

The speech recalls Sulla's bitter reflections upon the vanity of earthly
ambition, but here the illusion of power is expressly attributed to the inventive faculty. It is "inventive pride" that makes us feel we are more
than mortal and tempts us to a self-assertion that cannot be sustained.
The opposition between the ethical norm and invention is clear. But
even as she admits the falsity of that invention, Cleopatra begins to lament the fact that she has been reserved to grace Octavius's triumph at-

49. Cf. Jonson's view of wit in *Every Man in His Humour*. As in comedy invention detached from reality becomes ridiculous, so in tragedy it is potentially evil
and vulnerable to reaction from the ethical norm. The theme is developed further by Marlowe, as we shall see in the next chapter.

50. Citations are from *The Complete Works*, ed. Alexander B. Grosart (1885,
rpt. New York, 1963).

tended by only a brace of servants, and her will stiffens. Within minutes
she is once again asserting a determination to control her own fate:

> Thinke, *Caesar*, that I liv'd and raign'd a Queene.
>
> . . . .
>
> No, I disdaine that head which wore a crowne,
> Should stoope to take up that which others give.
>
> (64, 71–72)

The reversal is complete. Having just vilified the pride of princes, Cleopatra now exhibits the very weakness she claims to despise. And this, it
would seem, is because Daniel wishes us to realize that "inventive pride"
is also the source of her greatness. She is constitutionally incapable of remaining a *de casibus* mirror, and instinctively reverts to *ethopoeia* as a way
of mastering an untenable reality—in this instance, by envisioning the
greater nobility to be attained through an honorable death.[51]

This double view of invention reflects Daniel's generally more purposeful use of the prismatic approach to his subject matter. Each act of
the play, separated by a moralizing chorus that adduces another thesis to
explain the fall of Egypt, presents a different glimpse of Cleopatra. In

---

51. This theme is amplified by the Chorus in its fourth-act ode against Opinion:

> O malecontent seducing guest, —
> Contriver of our greatest woes:
> Which borne of winde, and fed with showes,
> Doost nurse thy selfe in thine unrest,
> Judging ungotten things the best,
> Or what thou in conceit design'st;
> And all things in the world doest deeme,
> Not as they are, but as they seeme.
>
> (417–424)

Here, Opinion does not simply mean popular errors. The term was associated
with wit in the sixteenth century, and among writers affected by the neo-Stoic
revival was frequently used in a pejorative sense to designate the Platonic *doxa*:
illusion. See Peter Ure, "A Note on 'Opinion' in Daniel, Greville and Chapman,"
MLR 46 (1951): 331–338. This seems to be Daniel's intention here, for the Chorus
not only blames Opinion for Cleopatra's lust and Antony's ambition, but also
for Cleopatra's present conviction that she will gain honor by death—implying
that even her final heroic gesture is an imaginative bubble.

Act 2, her "inventive pride" is indirectly praised, as Caesar complains
that he has won victory over his rival, acquired territory and treasure,
but

> Onely this Queene, that hath lost all this all,
> To whom is nothing left except a minde:
> Cannot into a thought of yeelding fall,
> To be dispoz'd as Chaunce hath her assign'd.
> (276–279)

Shortly afterwards, it is her vulnerability that is stressed. Proculeius
describes her response to Caesar's offer of lenity:

> With that (as all amaz'd) she held her still,
> Twixt majestie confuz'd and miserie.
> Her proud griev'd eyes, held sorrow and disdaine,
> State and distresse warring within her soule:
> Dying ambition dispossest her raigne,
> So base affliction seemed to controule.
> Like as a burning Lampe, whose liquor spent
> With intermitted flames, when dead you deeme it,
> Sends forth a dying flash, as discontent,
> That so the matter failes that should redeeme it:
> So she (in spight to see her low-brought state,
> When all her hopes were now consum'd to noght)
> Scornes yet to make an abject league with Fate,
> Or once descend into a servile thought:
> Th'imperious tongue unused to beseech,
> Authoritie confounds with prayers, so
> Words of command conjoyn'd with humble speech,
> Shew'd she would like, yet scorn'd to pray her foe.
> (312–329)

Here we are meant to contemplate, through the extended simile of the
dying lamp, the reaction of a woman attempting to remain a queen
even in defeat. The portrait is tender and sympathetic. It matters not that
we know Cleopatra is faking (she has long since determined to die); the
elaborate description is meant to create compassion for her generic plight,
and that is enough to enlist our sympathies for *her*.

In Act 3, it is the clever Cleopatra whom we meet, as she temporizes with Caesar. We can fully enjoy her skill in manipulating Octavius because Daniel provides her with just such arguments as she had earlier conjectured she might use in such a situation. When Seleucus accuses her of withholding certain treasures for herself, it is clear (as it is not in Shakespeare) that she has employed the device simply to deceive her enemy, "seeming to sute my mind unto my fortune" (190), and we delight in her wit. In Act 4, she is a maternal Cleopatra. Here, Rodon tells Seleucus how she had commissioned him to escape with Caesario to India, and describes in exhaustive detail her tearful farewell to her son. Daniel now focuses upon the mother's struggle to part from the thing she loves best in the world, adding to the portrait a quality not often associated with the serpent of old Nile.

The final view of Cleopatra is provided by a Nuntius. This man is her old attendant, who had disguised himself as a clown that he might as a final service bring to his mistress the instruments of her liberation. The essence of his message is the *wonder* of his mistress's act:

> Must I the lamentable wonder shew,
> Which all the world must grieve and marvell at?
> The rarest forme of death in earth below,
> That ever pitty, glory, wonder gat.
>
> (1391–1394)

He describes Cleopatra furnished as she had first met Mark Antony upon the river Cydnus. She greets the aspics, woos and worships them, hesitates as a tournament between Life and Honour plays forth in her imagination; and having concluded,

> so receives the deadly poys'ning tuch;
> That touch that tride the gold of her love, pure,
> And hath confirm'd her honour to be such,
> As must a wonder to all worlds endure.
>
> (1611–1614)

This is the last word on Cleopatra. She dies beautifully—a sight to arouse *admiratio* that such nobility and devotion can exist in the world. And her death seems to affect even the Chorus's moral perspective, for its final lines reflect a new awareness of value:

Is greatnesse of this sort,
That greatnesse greatnesse marres,
And wrackes it selfe, selfe-driven
On rocks of her own might?
Doth order order so
Disorder's overthrow?

(1776–1781)

In these last questions, the pieces of Daniel's mosaic suddenly come together, and we can see that he has been attempting to create a complex
character, not simply discrete vignettes. The multiple views of Cleopatra
are intended to qualify her case in our eyes and evoke tragic understanding.

Of an altogether different shape and feeling is John Marston's *Antonio's
Revenge*, written in 1599. Traditionally a play lightly regarded because
of its dropsical bloodthirstiness and lack of any overt moral standard, it
is one of the most interesting and complex of the sophistic tragedies of
the nineties. Here we find the two strains observed in earlier tragedies—
the theme of invention's claim upon reality and the technique of the
shifting perspective—realized in particularly imaginative ways. Let us
examine the theme first.

Because *Antonio's Revenge* is a self-consciously theatrical play, it is difficult to discover precisely where its serious values lie.[52] It is compounded
of grotesquely heightened speeches of vengeance, overstated declara-

52. Modern criticism on the whole has been hard put to find any. Harbage
frequently cites the play as an example of amoral coterie drama (*Shakespeare and
the Rival Traditions* [New York, 1952]); Robert Ornstein considers Marston a
dramatic opportunist whose moral concerns are peripheral (*The Moral Vision of
Jacobean Tragedy* [Madison, 1960], p. 155); Eleanor Prosser describes the final scene
as a "moral never-never-land" (*Hamlet and Revenge*, p. 61); Bowers, who admires
the play, is nonetheless dismayed at the ending, and writes "that Marston continued
to treat Antonio as a guiltless hero, must be laid to the obvious influence which
the morality of Seneca exercises in the play" (*Elizabethan Revenge Tragedy*, p.
124). The reference to Seneca here is significant, as we shall see, but that this
means Antonio is considered guiltless is simply not true. For a defense of the play's
seriousness, see Anthony Caputi, *John Marston, Satirist* (Ithaca, 1961), who also
concedes that it is not very successful, and J. W. Lever, *The Tragedy of State*
(London, 1971), who offers a judicious interpretation of its comic and tragic
elements.

tions of stoic imperturbability, ritualized murders, and an elaborately
developed pattern of stage metaphor that is reminiscent of Kyd, yet is
more flexible and varied.[53] Indeed, the most puzzling feature of the play
is the heavy theatricalism of the major characters. In Kyd's play we are
aware of an audience framing an action in which the participants themselves function as players and spectators to one another, but there is never
any suggestion that the characters have actually assumed theatrical roles.
Here, Piero, Antonio, and Pandulpho play out most of the action in what
appear to be consciously assumed literary personalities. This is apparent
from the very first entrance of Piero, poniard in hand and smeared with
blood:

> Ho, Gaspar Strotzo, bind Feliche's trunk
> Unto the panting side of Mellida.
> 'Tis yet dead night, yet all the earth is clutch'd
> In the dull leaden hand of snoring sleep;
> No breath disturbs the quiet of the air,
> No spirit moves upon the breast of earth,
> Save howling dogs, nightcrows, and screeching owls,
> Save meager ghosts, Piero, and black thoughts.
> One. Two. Lord, in two hours what a topless mount
> Of unpeer'd mischief have these hands cast up!
> I can scarce coop triumphing vengeance up
> From bursting forth in braggart passion.
>
> (1.1.1–12)[54]

One moment later, however, he does burst forth in braggart passion to
detail the grounds for his murder of Andrugio and Feliche, and so relishes
each of the maneuvers leading to the consummation of his scheme that
his accomplice Strotzo, burning with important news, finds it impossible

53. Characters invoke the applause of unseen spectators; they function as audience to their own shows; they refer frequently to play acting, scenes, and plots;
there is even a Kydian ghost who sits in on the finale to applaud the hero's revenge;
and in the epilogue, the characters come forward to express the hope that a tragedy might some day be written about their experience. The work is obviously directed to an audience that relishes play of wit and is familiar with the popular
stage tradition inaugurated by Kyd.
54. Citations are from G. K. Hunter's edition (Lincoln, Neb., 1965).

to interject a word. Finally, he gives up, and simply offers monosyllabic assent to Piero's self-congratulation. This enrages Piero:

> No! Yes! Nothing but *no* and *yes*, dull lump?
> Canst thou not honey me with fluent speech
> And even adore my topless villainy?
> Will I not blast my own blood for revenge,
> Must not thou straight be perjur'd for revenge,
> And yet no creature dream 'tis my revenge?
> Will I not turn a glorious bridal morn,
> Unto a Stygian night? Yet naught but *no* and *yes*?
>
> (83–90)

Piero sounds as though he has done a comparative analysis of Senecan atrocities (English and Latin) and has made it a matter of pride to have attained "topless villainy" against such precedents. His supreme consciousness of existing within a theatrical tradition transforms him, in less than 100 lines, into a comic figure.

The problem that such dramaturgy creates is clear. How do we respond to a character who expresses himself in reference to an artificial role, becomes funny in doing so, yet remains a serious threat within the world of the play? Some years ago, R. A. Foakes argued that *Antonio's Revenge* must be regarded as literary parody if we are to make sense of its stylistic excesses and the frequent undercutting of conventional attitudes that mark its dialogue.[55] Though persuasive, his argument tends to negate the undeniable seriousness of much of the work and assumes that literary parody must be directed *outside* the play, mocking a moribund tradition, while at the same time deflating the work in which it appears. Ignored is the possibility that Marston's literary parody may have functioned not just as externally directed satire but as a way of casting light upon certain aspects of human behavior. There is considerable evidence in the text to suggest that he was very much interested in how men tend to assume imaginative postures as a way of dealing with the evil in which they find themselves, and that "parody" may be a character's most appropriate

55. The parody was intensified, in his view, by the fact that children were playing parts reserved to adult actors in the public theaters ("John Marston's Fantastical Plays," *PQ* 41 [1962]: 229–239).

mode of expression. This is, in fact, implied by Strotzo, as he finally
wedges his way into Piero's monologue:

> I would have told you, if the incubus
> That rides your bosom would have patience:
> It is reported that in private state
> Maria, Genoa's duchess, makes to court. . . .
>
> (91–94)

His words indicate that Piero is not just a comic grotesque, but an obsessive—as the triple epistrophe of "revenge" in his preceding speech has
already suggested—and that his delight in his achievements is a function of
his determination to play out the role that best befits his situation ("And
therefore, since I cannot prove a lover . . . I am determined to prove a
villain"). Marston is careful to sketch in this situation: Piero has been
brooding for years over the loss of Maria to Andrugio, which he considers his "honour's death" (1.1.20–29). This is not an Iago-like will o'
the wisp, for he repeats his grievance to Maria on the eve of their marriage, ending on a curiously wistful note: "Dost love me, fairest? Say!"
(5.3.8–17). These brief glimpses at an earlier time suggest that he has
become another man—a stage revenger—under the influence of his in-
cubus.[56]

What we are probably seeing, then, is another instance of *ethopoeia* being used to master difficult circumstances. The phenomenon is explicitly
drawn in the characters of Pandulpho and Antonio. When Antonio hears
that his father is dead and his betrothed accused of lust, he simply despairs
and refuses to be comforted. But Pandulpho, seeing his son Feliche hanging in Mellida's window, responds with laughter. His nephew Alberto
is astonished at this reaction, and so Pandulpho invites him to understand
the event with him:

> PANDULPHO: Come sit, kind nephew; come on; thou
> and I
> Will talk as chorus to this tragedy.
> Entreat the music strain their instruments

56. Philip Ayres observes that Piero becomes more sympathetic toward the end
of the play, especially in his grief at his children's deaths ("Marston's *Antonio's
Revenge*: The Morality of the Revenging Hero," *SEL* 12 [1972]: 371).

With a slight touch whilst we—say on, fair coz.
ALBERTO: He was the very hope of Italy,
(*Music sounds softly*)
　The blooming honor of your drooping age.
PANDULPHO: True, coz, true. They say that men of hope
　　are crush'd,
　Good are suppress'd by base desertless clods,
　That stifle gasping virtue. Look, sweet youth,
　How provident our quick Venetians are
　Lest hooves of jades should trample on my boy;
　Look how they lift him up to eminence,
　Heave him 'bove reach of flesh. Ha, ha, ha.
ALBERTO: Uncle, this laughter ill becomes your grief.
PANDULPHO: Would'st have me cry, run raving up and
　　down
　For my son's loss? Would'st have me turn rank mad,
　Or wring my face with mimic action,
　Stamp, curse, weep, rage, and then my bosom strike?
　Away, 'tis apish action, player-like.
                                    (1.2.298–316)

The scene offers a skillful portrait of a human being turning actuality into artifice. Specifically, Pandulpho transforms murder into tragedy by acting the part of the moral chorus, and drawing from Seneca's *De remediis fortuitorum* a reasonable thesis to encompass the present moment. It is only in this way that he can understand the horrid spectacle before him and ease his grief.

　He strains hard to maintain this Stoic projection upon reality. When Piero asks him in the next act to swear he knew Antonio was plotting Andrugio's death, he refuses to perjure himself and disputes manfully the duties of subject and king in the classic stichomythic pattern. But then he delivers so ringing and passionate a speech on the invulnerability of virtue before physical threats that it begins to appear as if his stoicism is not so deeply ingrained as he insists. And this is confirmed in the fourth act when Pandulpho, finding Antonio mourning the death of Mellida and Alberto the death of Feliche, finally collapses and weeps:

　　Man will out, despite philosophy.
　　Why, all this while I ha' but play'd a part,

Like to some boy that acts a tragedy,
Speaks burly words and raves out passion;
But when he thinks upon his infant weakness,
He droops his eye. I spake more than a god,
Yet am less than a man.

(4.2.69–76)

Here the stage metaphor is explicitly used to define the art of accommodation Pandulpho has been practicing—unsuccessfully—through his Stoic *ethopoeia*.[57]

The third major character who must transform himself imaginatively
in order to meet the extraordinary circumstances of his situation is Antonio, the hero of the play. During the first two acts he simply laments
his father's death and Mellida's defamation, helpless before the assaults
of fortune. Then, at his friend's behest, he samples Seneca's *De providen-
tia* to see if this will remedy his anguish, but finds it too drily academic.
When, however, Andrugio's ghost reveals in Act 3 that he has been
murdered, that Mellida was declared unchaste only to prevent her marriage to Antonio, and that his own mother has consented to marry the
villain Piero, he passes beyond mere despair at misfortune to a state of
total anomie. Vowing to think only upon vengeance he, too, becomes an
obsessive, convincing himself when he kills Piero's small son that he is
spilling only the father's blood and releasing the child's soul to heaven.
This act, brought to a pitch of horror by Julio's innocent trustfulness and
Antonio's clearly demoniac rationalization, marks the turning point of
the play. From now until the final atrocity, Antonio will act as if there
is, at the heart of reality, only a moral void.

Characteristically, he assumes a role that will enable him to function
in the new world he perceives. Warned by his father's ghost to flee the
court and return in disguise to "invent some strategem of vengeance,"
Antonio appears in fool's habit, symbolizing his reduction to a purely
subjective standard in a world without standards. His attitude is set forth

57. Marston's interest in exploring the way human beings respond to harsh reality by spinning imaginative cocoons may also be seen in the earlier *Antonio and
Mellida*. For a discussion of philosophical attitude as refuge in the plays, see Allen
Bergson, "Dramatic Style as Parody in Marston's *Antonio and Mellida*," *SEL* 11
(1971): 307–326.

in the moving praise of folly, with which he answers Maria's criticism that he is not behaving seriously enough:

> Even in that note a fool's beatitude:
> He is not capable of passion;
> Wanting the power of distinction,
> He bears an unturn'd sail with every wind;
> Blow east, blow west, he stirs his course alike.
> I never saw a fool lean; the chub-fac'd fop
> Shines sleek with full-cramm'd fat of happiness,
> Whilst studious contemplation sucks the juice
> From wizards' cheeks, who, making curious search
> For nature's secrets, the first innating cause
> Laughs them to scorn as man doth busy apes
> When they will zany men. Had heaven been kind,
> Creating me an honest, senseless dolt,
> A good, poor fool, I should want sense to feel
> The stings of anguish shoot through every vein,
> I should not know what 'twere to lose a father,
> I should be dead of sense to view defame
> Blur my bright love, I could not thus run mad
> As one confounded in a maze of mischief,
> Stagger'd, stark fell'd with bruising stroke of chance,
> I should not shoot mine eyes into the earth,
> Poring for mischief that might counterpoise
> Mischief, murder, and . . . .
>
> (4.1.38–60)

The speech expresses the psychology of a man who has glimpsed unimagined evil and is driven beyond conventional human boundaries to deal with what he has discovered. Although Antonio cannot share the fool's insensibility, like the fool he pretends to be he exists in a moral void to be filled at his own "discretion."[58] The loss is total, and that is why *Antonio's Revenge* seems to be such an unbalanced play, careening wildly

58. The debate marks an interesting moment in the development of dramatic composition. We have met such defenses of folly before—in Heywood's interlude and in Erasmus's encomium. Here it has traveled the whole route from sophistic set piece to a dramatically integrated expression of the hero's moral loss.

between feverish wit and utter bleakness. In Kyd's play, the tragic is essentially ironic: those in power are men of good will who cannot understand. In Marston's play, they are not good, and there is no alternative to the corrupt establishment of the Court other than the anarchic impulses of the despairing revenger. It is a frightening perception that is perhaps the product of Marston's satiric habit of mind, perhaps the expression of an actual fear that human life is, in fact, evil wherever you look. This is the view suggested in the prologue, where Marston warns:

> If any spirit breathes within this round
> Uncapable of weighty passion
> (As from his birth being hugged in the arms
> And nuzzled 'twixt the breasts of happiness)
> Who winks and shuts his apprehension up
> From common sense of what men were, and are,
> Who would not know what men must be—let such
> Hurry amain from our black-visag'd shows;
> We shall affright their eyes.
>
> $(13-21)^{59}$

What men were, are, and must be is self-serving and cruel; even the good ones are goaded by the evil of others to commit horrors. And therefore horror must be metamorphosed into art, which is the *modus vivendi* within this world. Hence the diabolical masque, Ovidian glossotomy, Thyestian banquet, vexation, and triumph.

This last sequence is overseen by Andrugio's spirit, who acts as chorus to the tragedy, in the manner of Kyd:

> Here will I sit, spectator of revenge,
> And glad my ghost in anguish of my foe.
>
> (5.3.53-54)

He watches with profound relish as the masquers bind Piero and pluck out his tongue—

59. G. K. Hunter argues that Marston's realism draws upon the realities of political life as presented in Guicciardini's *Storia d'Italia* ("English Folly and Italian Vice," *Jacobean Theatre*, ed. John Russell Brown and Bernard Harris [London, 1961], pp. 85-111). This theme is further developed by Lever, *Tragedy of State.*

> I have't, Pandulpho; the veins panting bleed,
> Trickling fresh gore about my fist

—and exults in the atrocity:

> Blest be thy hand. I taste the joys of heaven,
> Viewing my son triumph in his black blood.
>
> (65–68)

The juxtaposition of heaven and black blood is so patently perverse that
Marston can only be intensifying the moral crudity of Kyd's underworld
spirits. But the spectacle he watches is equally insane. At first, the conspirators torment Piero by displaying his severed organ before him; then
Antonio uncovers the dish containing Julio's limbs, and as Piero laments
his son, each of the conspirators rehearses his motive for revenge and
heaps abusive epithets upon him. Once they rush at him, only to draw
back, sadistically prolonging his agony. When each has finally driven a
knife into his tortured body, the Ghost declares with a sigh of satisfaction:

> 'Tis done; and now my soul shall sleep in rest.
> Sons that revenge their father's blood are blest.
>
> (114–115)

And he disappears from view.

His ethical complacency in the face of such an orgy is only compounded, however, when the grave Venetian senators arrive a moment
later to demand "whose hand presents this gory spectacle." One now
anticipates the restoration of a normal viewpoint, leading to the punishment of the murderers, but instead the senators congratulate the conspirators and offer them

> What satisfaction outward pomp can yield,
> Or chiefest fortunes of the Venice state. . . .
>
> (140–141)

Indeed, they compare Antonio to Hercules, the great political savior.[60]
Has Marston lapsed into complete moral anarchy? So it would appear,
but for Antonio's own astonishment at the senators' reaction:

60. "Thou art another Hercules to us In ridding huge pollution from our state"
(5.3.129–130).

We are amaz'd at your benignity.

(145)

Strangely enough, it is the revenger who provides the normative view. And this is because Marston's dramaturgy has taken a very strange turn. Like his sophistic forebears he has split the perspectives on the action, but in such a way that unless the play is performed with an eye to his intention its meaning is quite likely to be lost. Both audiences to Antonio's act lack sufficient comprehension of what has transpired. The Ghost is, in effect, part of the deed; it is under his influence that revenging madness takes hold at the beginning of Act 3 and sweeps to execution in Act 5, and it is within this perspective that "sons that revenge their father's blood are blest." The senators, on their part, operate in a world of reason, and they have gathered enough evidence of Piero's tyranny to exonerate Antonio and his accomplices. But Antonio, like the Hercules incited by Juno to slay his wife and children, has experienced the unthinkable. Now he has come out of his frenzy, and though technically he may be exonerated of his crime he has moved too far beyond the conventions by which ordinary men define their actions to accept the proferred reward. Instead, as Hercules withdraws to Athens in repentance ("O faithful friend, Theseus, seek a hiding place for me, remote, obscure"[61]), he and his companions in atrocity retire to an unnamed monastery, there

> to meditate on misery,
> To sad our thought with contemplation
> Of past calamities.

(163–165)

The demoniac invention designed for victory has in fact proved to be an instrument of final defeat.

It becomes evident in this last sequence that a new way of arguing *in utramque partem* has entered English dramaturgy. What shapes our final response to Antonio is not explicit debate or even a literal shifting of perspective—as in *Cleopatra*—but palimpsestic exposition. Marston wishes us to see the atrocity of Guicciardini's Venice in the light of Seneca's *Hercules Furens*—the Ghost shadowing Juno, Antonio the possessed Hercules, and the Senators the rational Amphytrion. The three views of the

---

61. *Herc. Fur.*, 1334–1335.

revenge are *their* views—testimonies of ancient witnesses who have been invoked to make us see the particulars of the present action against an archetypal murder in which the agent, though technically innocent, remained tainted by an evil he could not excuse. We are asked to judge Antonio as we judge Hercules, a rhetorical *imago* adduced in proof to urge an equitable decision from us. Like the image of the undesirable lovers in *The Play of Love*, the palimpsestic image says, "This is the *kind* of case you have before you. Adjudicate appropriately."[62] In Marston's hands, the device is so subtle as to be almost cavalier, since he provides the clues so late in the action. But it is not entirely unexpected in a mimetic drama growing out of sophistic argumentation, and its sudden exfoliation is in keeping with the violence of the composition as a whole. Marston's predilection for shocking his audience led him to exploit with evident gusto the disjunctive manner of the neo-Senecan tradition, but it was his very real ethical sensibility that moved him to reveal just as abruptly the Senecan scenario that underlay his plot. In its light, the moral never-never-land turns out to be a surprisingly thoughtful exercise in *grand guignol*.[63]

IV

George Chapman's *Bussy D'Ambois* (1604) is perhaps the most problematic of these sophistic tragedies, if only because it is so undoubtedly serious—and therefore will serve as a fitting *terminus ad quem* in our survey of their development. Its difficulties revolve primarily around Chapman's treatment of his hero, whose shabby career seems strangely at odds with the noble concepts he is intended to embody. These difficulties have been only partly resolved by recent scholars who argue that Bussy is not meant to represent the "complete" Senecal man of Chapman's later work, but a natural, prelapsarian hero whose "virtue" is closer to the *areté* of Achilles than to Christian virtue. For even so, the play seems to fall into two often contradictory modes of talk and action, the hero's moral status remains exceedingly doubtful, and the nature of his tragedy is unclear. The questions persist: why did Chapman, that skilled comic dramatist, write

62. Cf. Ch. IV, p. 116.

63. Forewarned of this device, an intelligent director could, in fact, exploit the

a play whose moral design and dramatic fable appear to conflict with one another[64]—and how did he expect us to respond to his elusive hero?[65]

In addressing these problems, it should first be noticed that the composition of *Bussy D'Ambois* is governed by a more explicitly speculative intention than we have encountered before. Its action opens in a pastoral setting, with stage directions supplied by Monsieur:

> I follow'd D'Ambois to this green retreat;
> A man of spirit beyond the reach of fear,
> Who (discontent with his neglected worth)
> Neglects the light and loves obscure abodes. . . .
>
> $(1.1.45-48)$[66]

It is here, in the traditionally clarifying milieu of the *selva oscura*, that Bussy asserts the thesis that "Fortune, not Reason, rules the state of things," and pictures the great of the world as hollow men vainly engaged in the pursuit of power.[67] From the relative safety of this retreat he is

---

play's "theatricality" by staging the whole revenge sequence in a way that suggests the reenactment of an earlier ritual under the influence of a demonic psychology. In doing so, he would restore to the work the dimensions that have been lost on the printed page. Marston anticipated just such a loss when he expressed concern to the reader of *The Malcontent* that "scenes, invented merely to be spoken, should be enforcively published to be read."

64. Ornstein's contention (*Moral Vision*, p. 54).

65. The most suggestive studies are Elias Schwartz, "Seneca, Homer, and Chapman's *Bussy D'Ambois*," *JEGP* 56 (1957): 163–176; Peter Ure, "Chapman's Tragedies," *Jacobean Theatre*, pp. 227–236; Irving Ribner, *Jacobean Tragedy* (New York, 1962), pp. 19–35; Eugene Waith, *The Herculean Hero in Marlowe, Shakespeare, Chapman, and Dryden* (New York, 1962), pp. 81–111; Nicholas Brooke's introduction to the Revels Plays edition (London, 1964); and Raymond B. Waddington, "Prometheus and Hercules: The Dialectic of *Bussy D'Ambois*," *ELH* 34 (1967): 21–48. The following discussion is indebted to them all, though the approach via sophistic tragedy will show, I believe, that the play is less idiosyncratic than is generally assumed, and will clarify its dramatic function.

66. All citations are from Brooke's edition of the original 1607 quarto.

67. The antithesis *hollow* and *full* is used repeatedly through the play to differentiate Bussy from the conventionally ambitious politician. Cf. 1.1.5–17; 2.1.165–166; 5.3.21–25, 34, 42–48, 143–145.

tempted forth on an adventure by Monsieur, who plays to his conviction that Fortune must be seized for the accomplishment of any good action, and persuades him to accept promotion at Court. Knowing full well the corrupt society awaiting him there, he determines to make his own way in it:

> I am for honest actions, not for great:
> If I may bring up a new fashion,
> And rise in Court with virtue, speed his plough. . . .
> (125–127)

Then, accepting Monsieur's earnest money from the insolent Maffe, he leaves the contemplative sphere and enters the heroic. The scene states the premises of the play. A man of spirit declares his concern for "virtue," is bribed by a politician to enter his service, but privately denies that he will serve. What then befalls him is matter for the ensuing action. The procedure is familiar to us: it is that of the speculative thesis explored through hypothesis. Chapman is posing a nondidactic, imaginative question—what might happen if a naturally virtuous man came out of the garden and entered contemporary society?—and he is using Bussy D'Ambois as his chief image. It is a question squarely in the tradition of such speculative moralists as More and Castiglione, and consonant with Chapman's interest in the "prelapsarian" heroes Achilles, Prometheus, and Hercules.[68] To entertain this proposal, he takes the way of Sidney in the *Arcadia*, figuring forth the question through mimetic action. He places his hero in two distinct but related situations—a political struggle for power and a love affair with a court lady—which lead to a third: confrontation with divine powers. Within each setting, he explores the impact of such a man upon normal members of the society and the problems his own unique characteristics hold for him, allowing the hero and his interlocutors to interpret—in dialogue fashion—the significance of the encounter. That the exercise emerges as a strangely moving tragedy is due to Chapman's unblinking honesty in contemplating the results of his experiment and his skillful exploitation of sophistic procedures to make us feel the greatness of his hero.[69]

68. See Schwartz, Waith, and especially Waddington, for the mythic resonances within the text.

69. Chapman's intention is suggested by several peculiarities of the work. First, there is no energizing plot: ostensibly Bussy is hired to help Monsieur obtain

Recognition of Chapman's neutral, interrogative stance is necessary if we are to apprehend the kind of judgment we shall ultimately be asked to make. This will be a tragic judgment, not a moralistic one, or—in the terms used earlier in connection with tragedy—one based on equity and not the letter of the law. It is demanded by the original question, which seeks neither praise nor blame—though these are the inevitable concomitants of any human endeavor—but rather, illumination and understanding. In a sense, Bussy is an Homeric Raphael Hythlodaeus, come to pursue reform in the Court of the French king—and we must judge him in the light of his intention as well as his more dubious achievements. How Chapman elicits such judgment is our next concern.[70]

When Bussy enters the Court of Henry III, he appears to be a changed

---

the crown, but Monsieur has no plan to get it. His offer of service is simply a device to bring Bussy into the Court milieu. Second, the play is divided almost schematically among three concerns: in the first episode, Bussy is involved in a dispute of courtiers in order to raise questions of public justice; in the second, the love intrigue poses problems of private morality; in the third, his defeat is the occasion for cosmological speculation. Chapman weaves them together artfully by allowing the enemies Bussy has made in the first sequence to utilize the events of the second to bring on his fall in the third, but they do not feel like parts of the same wave moving toward its crest. Instead, they convey that sense of "going on to the next topic" that we find in the literary dialogue. That the reviser of the 1641 text sensed this awkwardness is indicated by the new passage between 2.1 and 2.2, in which Bussy claims a long-standing love for Tamyra. Yet at 2.2.10–11, Montsurry reveals that Bussy's brief address to her in the Court scene was their only encounter, and the Friar (2.2.184–185) confirms the fact that Bussy does not yet know her familiarly. Finally, the play is filled with active debate about the hero, as though he were a subject "proposed" for examination. Not only is he variously regarded as noble, ambitious, savage, gallant, fearless, and heroic—he also becomes the center of a controversy about the order of the universe: his career will determine whether Nature works blindly or with purpose. In short, he is the theme for moral speculation on all sides, much like the hypothesized figure of the literary dialogue.

70. The comparison with Raphael is apt in several respects. Like his sixteenth-century forbear, Bussy must decide whether to exercise his contemplative virtue in the active world of the forum, though he goes beyond Raphael's speculations and actually ventures the deed. Also like Raphael, he is not only "learned," but skeptical, self-appreciative, and thoroughly impolitic. He pursues to their bitterest consequences More's genteel conjectures about the effect of such radical innocence in the practical world.

man. Wearing finery provided by his benefactor, he flirts at first with Montsurry's Countess, and then turns his attention to the Duchess of Guise, inspiring the jealousy of the Duke and the mockery of Barrisor, L'Anou, and Pyrrhot, seasoned courtiers. Yet he insists that he is still the same man inside. Chapman's problem here is to maintain a double focus on his hero, who has only accepted Monsieur's accoutrements so that he may attract the eye of the King and exercise his "virtue" at the center of power.[71] He achieves this partly by means of Bussy's heated exchange with the Guise, but more significantly through Monsieur's peculiar remark as the two men nearly come to blows:

> His great heart will not down, 'tis like the sea
> That partly by his own internal heat,
> Partly the stars' daily and nightly motion,
> Ardour and light, and partly of the place
> The divers frames, and chiefly by the Moon,
> Bristled with surges, never will be won
> (No, not when th'hearts of all those powers are burst)
> To make retreat into his settled home,
> Till he be crown'd with his own quiet foam.
>
> (1.2.138–146)

In their immediate context, these words seem quite overblown: to speak of uncontrollable elemental energy being loosed in a court squabble is hardly decorous. But the simile of the sea is not meant to characterize the present exchange; rather it is a *complementary* image which, when perceived in relation to the present scene, is intended to point toward a quite different meaning. Although the circumstances appear trivial— "Come Madame, talk; 'sfoot, can you not talk? Talk on I say, more courtship, as you love it"—the underlying issue, we are to understand, is not. It is the provocation of a natural hero by a shallow politician who will be unable to deal with the enmity he has aroused. What has happened in this passage is that the fully hypothesized quarrel has been swiftly reduced *ad thesin* through the imagistic aside of Monsieur so that its generic significance may be glimpsed. The procedure is based upon the rhetorical concept of similitude: a simile is used in argument because it "implies

71. Cf. 1.1.106–112.

some mutual principle in diverse things."[72] Our discovery of generic principle does not obviate the arrogant Bussy of the "surface," but it makes us deal with him on two levels at once—that experienced familiarly by his fellow courtiers and that perceived by the few who share an insight into his nature. Such modulation between thesis and hypothesis— not unlike that seen in *The Courtier*—is Chapman's way of exploring Bussy's full impact upon the Court. And by revealing both the particulars of Bussy's personality and its underlying significance, he enables us to form a more qualified judgment of the action.

This procedure recurs in various forms throughout the play. In the next scene, having effectively shattered the mannered gaiety of the Court, Bussy moves on to confront the braveries of its young bloods, Barrisor, L'Anou, and Pyrrhot. Their arch taunts to one another—"Come sir, we'll lead you a dance"—hardly prepare us for the kind of battle described to the King shortly afterward:

> But D'Ambois' sword (that light'ned as it flew)
> Shot like a pointed Comet at the face
> Of manly Barrisor; and there it stuck:
> Thrice pluck'd he at it, and thrice drew on thrusts,
> From him, that of himself was free as fire;
> Who thrust still as he pluck'd, yet (past belief!)
> He with his subtle eye, hand, body, scap'd;
> At last the deadly bitten point tugg'd off,
> On fell his yet undaunted foe so fiercely,
> That (only made more horrid with his wound)
> Great D'Ambois shrunk, and gave a little ground;
> But soon return'd, redoubled in his danger,
> And at the heart of Barrisor seal'd his anger.
> Then, as in Arden I have seen an Oak

72. Quod in rebus diversis similem aliquam rationem continet (*De inv.* 1.49). Aristotle, too, comments upon this function of simile and metaphor: "When the poet calls old age 'a withered stalk,' he conveys a new idea, a new fact, to us by means of the *general notion* of 'lost bloom,' which is common to both things. The similes of the poets do the same. . . ." (*Rhet.* 1410b13, trans. W. Rhys Roberts, *The Rhetoric and the Poetics of Aristotle* [New York, 1954], my emphasis). In effect, the disparity between the two images compels us to infer their hidden relationship, and thus we discover the general idea underlying both.

Long shook with tempests, and his lofty top
Bent to his root. . . .

$$(2.1.81-96)$$

Past belief indeed. The image of Barrisor fighting on with Bussy's sword embedded in his face, while Bussy valiantly tries to retrieve it, and *does*, and then thrusts home with it, is so horrifying as almost to appear ludicrous. Almost, but not quite, which means that it engages our imaginations and evokes that sense of wonder which characteristically attends the exploits of the epic hero.[73] The difference between this epic *narratio*, however, and its literary forbears, is that it is so patently incongruous in the circumstances. Chapman's setting is not Troy but the court of a complacent French king. The classical nuntius's speech, therefore, is an extended *imago*, aimed—as Cicero, Quintilian, and Erasmus recommended —at influencing the judgment of the audience. The clue to its function is the King's response. "These willful murders Are ever past our pardon," declares Henry, totally untouched by *admiratio*. The abrupt transition from epic wonder to legalistic censure reveals that just as in the preceding scene Monsieur's remark about Bussy's energy was meant to focus *our* attention upon the heroic issue underlying the petty court quarrel, so the messenger's speech, too, is essentially a sophistic persuader intended to inspire *us* with awe at the deeds of an epic hero, and not an internal dramatic device that develops the characters' attitudes toward one another.

In the sequence immediately following, Chapman descends swiftly from imagistic persuasion to dialectical argument, reducing the particulars of the battle to the more abstract level of debate thesis so as to lay bare its ethical and political implications. As might be expected, the singular heroism so persuasive in the sublimity of epic presentation seems decidedly less so in the medium of disputation. Henry pragmatically designates the action "willful murder." Monsieur, adapting the *status definitivus*, argues that it is but "manly slaughter," and justifies it by claiming that positive law does not provide satisfaction for all wrongs. In this case, the wrong is "murdered fame," and a "true man" must supply its defi-

---

73. Aristotle, it may be recalled, allows more of the marvelous in epic than in tragedy specifically because one does not have to *show* the improbable—which would appear ridiculous in dramatic action (*Poet.* 1460a13).

ciency by his valor. To Henry's objection that all men may therefore murder and claim to be law-menders, Monsieur replies that only "full" men should have such power. The difficulty in applying such a code is obvious, and Henry is unconvinced. Nevertheless he pardons Bussy, warning him not to presume upon his escape in the future.

Bussy, however, is not satisfied with a pardon. Persuaded of an important destiny, he pleads for the right to use the gifts which God and Nature have bestowed upon him:

> since I am free
> (Offending no just law), let no law make
> By any wrong it does, my life her slave:
> When I am wrong'd and that law fails to right me,
> Let me be King myself (as man was made)
> And do a justice that exceeds the law:
> If my wrong pass the power of single valour
> To right and expiate; then be you my King,
> And do a Right, exceeding Law and Nature:
> Who to himself is law, no law doth need,
> Offends no King, and is a King indeed.
>
> (194–204)

His eloquence—and his deference to the King—wins Henry over. But the argument has revealed, as the epic battle could not, the fundamental problem that arises when a man of "virtue" is introduced into a fallen society. Bussy assumes that his inner law—"nature"—will conflict with no just positive law. If, however, he is indeed "man in his native noblesse," then he is walking across a transformed landscape marked by laws that must inevitably appear repressive to him. In which case, he will demand the right to follow inner conviction—as he has just done—and violate social convention. It is this prospect that so alarms the Guise, who hurries to consult with Montsurry on the implications of the King's decision:

> D'Ambois is pardon'd: where's a King? Where law?
> See how it runs, much like a turbulent sea,
> Here high, and glorious, as it did contend

> To wash the heavens, and make the stars more pure:
> And here so low, it leaves the mud of hell
> To every common view.
>
> (2.2.24–29)

Such is the "justice" licensed by the King's new dispensation. In Guise's cry of outrage, we hear not the voice of Huguenot persecutor, but that of postlapsarian man for good and ill. It is the response of *nomos* to the view of *physis* laid open by the debate; Chapman is now arguing the other side of the question, and we must give his words due weight.

Modulation between thesis and hypothesis, then, becomes in Chapman a way of arguing *in utramque partem* within the play proper. More consistently than in Marston's work, extended similes and allusions remind us of the heroic nature, even as we are made aware of the difficulties such a nature presents to its contemporaries. This is achieved by juxtaposing the particulars of the Court scene with particulars of a mythic or natural scene, which together suggest the generic meaning. But the adduced particulars also *attract* us to the hero, and this response is carefully qualified by examining the principle he represents in the more abstract passages of debate.

Similar methods of exposition govern the section dealing with the love affair, where Chapman explores the personal implications of the conflict between *physis* and *nomos*. Tamyra is shown to be a person of conventional moral convictions who has countenanced the vanities of the Court (she has been wooed by both Monsieur and Barrisor), but has retained a deep sense of personal honor. Monsieur attempts to persuade her that honor is only a word (2.2.60–69), but is unsuccessful. The reason for this becomes clear only when Tamyra, awaiting her assignation with Bussy, steps back from the action and reveals in an analytic *pathopoeia* that her honor is an instrument of self-definition. When she loses it, she loses herself:

> I love what most I loathe, and cannot live
> Unless I compass that that holds my death:
> For love is hateful without love again,
> And he I love, will loathe me, when he sees
> I fly my sex, my virtue, my renown,
> To run so madly on a man unknown.

> See, see the gulf is opening, that will swallow
> Me and my fame forever. I will in,
> And cast myself off, as I ne'er had been.
>
> (170–178)

What she loves is the elemental nature which, if embraced, will destroy the conventional notion of virtue by which she has identified herself. Ironically, it is Tamyra who undergoes the metamorphosis that Bussy has been able to withstand, and must contrive various subterfuges to maintain the illusion that she has not abandoned her nature. For all these, she emerges from their lovemaking terrified of her sin. Bussy attempts to reassure her by denying its reality:

> Sin is a coward Madam, and insults
> But on our weakness, in his truest valour,
> And so our ignorance tames us, that we let
> His shadows fright us.
>
> (3.1.18–21)

His insistence that sin is simply an establishment chimera is a striking expression of that innocent point of view which Monsieur calls soul-less in their later flyting:

> in thy valour th'art like other naturals,
> That have strange gifts in nature, but no soul
> Diffus'd quite through, to make them of a piece. . . .
>
> (3.2.348–350)

Indeed, Bussy *is* soul-less, insofar as his soul is not that battleground of moral forces which constitutes the soul of fallen creatures like Tamyra. And his argument reveals an unsuspected irony: *in effect*, the amoral innocent is not very different from the immoral machiavel. Bussy's words against sin echo those Monsieur expressed to Tamyra earlier, although the latter were not offered in so worthy a cause as native noblesse. *Physis* is *physis*, it would seem, whatever justification may be laid upon it.

On the grounds of Bussy's thesis, one might be tempted to collapse any distinction between the romantic rivals, and regard his love affair with Tamyra as an exercise in cynicism. But Chapman casts an aura of nobility upon it which prevents our doing so. Although Tamyra clearly

reveals the depth of her passion, Bussy's involvement is not presented as a
fall into sensuality. Rather, it is a gallant service, quite in keeping with
the heroic nature. The Friar, leading Bussy from the vault, expresses
joy that Tamyra's affections have settled upon him, whose

> wit and spirit can adapt
> Their full force to supply her utmost weakness:
> . . . .
> Though then she seek their [her affections'] satisfac-
> tion
> (Which she must needs, or rest unsatisfied),
> Your judgment will esteem her peace thus wrought,
> Nothing less dear, than if you yourself had sought.
> (2.2.182–183, 188–191)

His words suggest that Bussy is not seducing Tamyra but relieving her,
and it is in this light that Bussy sees their relationship. He is Tamyra's
"servant" in more than just the courtly sense: he is her benefactor—a
role reflected in his veiled allusion to service during the second Court
scene (4.1.34–41), in his response to her deadly summons (5.1.70–72), and
in his strange attempt to prove her blameless against slanderous tongues
(5.8.105–107). This rhetorical *color* has the effect of qualifying their adultery, as does the powerful image of night with which it is associated. It
is another example of Chapman's two-pronged dramaturgy, and reflects
the principle of equitable argument. While Bussy's act is a crime against
the social order, the perspective from which it is presented removes it
from the sordid and compels us to suspend legalistic judgment.[74]

In the last two acts of the play, as Bussy's enemies are closing in on

---

74. This process of qualification is implied in Chapman's theory of poetry.
In the preface to *Ovid's Banquet of Sense*, he compares poetry to painting in this
way: "it serves not a skilfull Painters turne, to draw the figure of a face onely to
make knowne who it represents; but hee must lymn, give luster, shaddow, and
heightening; which though ignorants will esteeme spic'd, and too curious, yet
such as have the judiciall perspective, will see it hath motion, spirit and life" (*The
Poems of George Chapman*, ed. Phyllis Bartlett [New York, 1941], p. 49). The
painting analogy reveals that his poetic method follows the "judiciall" procedure
of adducing qualifying circumstances in order to perceive the total meaning of
the act portrayed. On the symbolism of night, see the following note.

him, a new question comes to the foreground: what is the cosmic significance of Bussy D'Ambois? It is introduced obliquely by Monsieur, after he and Bussy have exchanged veiled threats in the King's presence:

> O my Love's glory: heir to all I have—
> That's all I can say, and that all I swear—
> If thou outlive me, as I know thou must,
> Or else hath Nature no proportion'd end
> To her great labours: she hath breath'd a spirit
> Into thy entrails, of effect to swell
> Into another great Augustus Caesar:
> Organs, and other faculties fitted to her greatness:
> And should that perish like a common spirit,
> Nature's a Courtier and regards no merit.
>
> (4.1.93–102)

Monsieur, of course, is enjoying his own private joke. Having discovered
the love affair and taken steps to entrap his man, he is convinced that
Bussy will die before he can begin his threatened program of reform.
His defeat, therefore, becomes a matter for serious philosophical speculation, and—as in the first act—the play now tends to become polarized
into hypothetical action and argument *a thesi*.

On the level of action, Bussy's "fate" is presented as a complex inter-
weaving of subjective and objective forces. Chapman plots his decline and
fall with great care. Instead of involving him in the mean machinery of
household spies, he allows Bussy to play out his destiny in the heroic
arena of human and divine interaction. This is accomplished when Friar
Comolet invokes occult spiritual powers to come to the lovers' assistance.
Again the act is suspect: we see the friar-pandar abetting adultery with
the aid of demons. But again, Chapman's language suggests that this is
not the significance of the scenario at all. Behemoth reveals that he is no
devil, but a more powerful and neutral agent:

> I am Emperor
> Of that inscrutable Darkness, where are hid
> All deepest truths, and secrets never seen,
> All which I know. . . .
>
> (4.2.48–51)

Behemoth is thus the spirit of divine knowledge, denizen of that realm which Chapman had celebrated in *The Shadow of Night* as the repository of the most profound truths.[75] In so neutralizing the demonic, he established a context for tragedy that is quite new to the English stage. Until now, tragic falls had usually been ascribed—if they were ascribed at all—either to fortune or to sinful denial of Christian morality. By deliberately making it impossible for his audience to identify Bussy's deity with the Christian god, Chapman invites us to see his troubled relationship with the supernatural not as an instance of sin, but rather as a conflict between the cosmic order and heroic virtue.[76]

Bussy is given three warnings. Behemoth, the great spirit summoned by Friar Comolet, predicts that

> If D'Ambois' mistress stain not her white hand
> With his forc'd blood, he shall remain untouch'd.
>
> (4.2.131–132)

It is against this cryptic admonition (whose blood is "his"?) that the action in the following scene is played. Tamyra steadfastly refuses Montsurry's demand that she invite Bussy to her chamber, offering one excuse after another to avoid the trap, but her very loyalty brings about the fulfillment of the first fatal condition. For as she offers Montsurry her outstretched arms, pleading with him not to force her to betray Bussy, he stabs her in fury. Even then she tries to warn her lover that fate is closing in, writing in blood,

75. See Roy W. Battenhouse, "Chapman's *The Shadow of Night*: An Interpretation," *SP* 38 (1941): 584–608, for the general background; also Waith's excellent discussion of the episode, pp. 96–104. A dissenting view is offered by Peter Bement, "The Imagery of Darkness and of Light in Chapman's *Bussy D'Ambois*," *SP* 64 (1967): 187–198, who argues that it is a "stepdame Night of minde" to which Chapman refers in the latter part of the play and not essential night. While the scene does contain certain ambiguities, their force is not sufficient to cast serious doubt upon Behemoth's identity.

76. Daniel had hinted at this in the final chorus of *Cleopatra*, and Shakespeare, perhaps, envisioned Hamlet's fall in such a context. I am thinking of the divine warning Hamlet describes to Horatio, which saved his life on shipboard. Only moments later he feels similar misgivings about his heart, yet finally wearied of a life of circumspection he ignores them, and heroically goes to meet his fate (cf. 5.2.5–11 and 210–222).

that he may see
These lines come from my wounds and not from me.

(5.1.169–170)

Before Bussy receives the message, however, he is given another warning. He is visited by the ghost of the Friar, who has died mysteriously at
the spectacle of Tamyra's torture. "Note what I want, my son," he tells
him, "and be forewarn'd" (5.2.11). But Bussy cannot make out his
meaning:

Note what he wants? He wants his utmost weed,
He wants his life, and body: which of these
Should be the want he means, and may supply me
With fit forewarning?

(15–18)

For clarification, he summons Behemoth again, who informs him,

if thou obey
The summons that thy mistress next will send thee,
Her hand shall be thy death.

(54–56)

It is yet another veiled message, echoing ironically the oracle given to
Hercules,[77] and Bussy interprets it literally:

shall the hand
Of my kind mistress kill me?
(65–66)

On this assumption, he first rationalizes the sweetness of such a death,
whose summons he could not refuse. But then he considers how un-
likely it is that Tamyra should be the agent of his death, unless her hand
were forced. And *if* such danger were present, she would hardly lead
him into it. Yet *granted* that she might send for him, whom would she
send, seeing that her go-between, the Friar, is dead? The transition is
clumsy, but Chapman's intention is surely transparent: Bussy is asserting,
through the exercise of rhetorical proof, his independence of divine warning.

77. "By the hand of one whom, conquering, thou hast slain, Alcides, one day
shalt thou lie low" (*Herc. Oet.*, 1476–1477).

By the time that Montsurry, disguised in the "utmost weed" of the dead Friar, arrives with Tamyra's letter, he is quite ready to believe that Behemoth lied and that blood is indeed the ink of lovers. He has dismissed all three admonitions.[78]

Bussy's "fate" is now essentially determined. As he moves toward his doom guided by Montsurry, Monsieur and the Guise appear above to serve as Chorus to the tragedy, and once again the exposition withdraws behind the particulars of the action to debate the underlying principles at issue. Monsieur, the nominalist, is confident that Nature shapes men with no end in mind—and frequently "that which we call merit in a man" is an accidental quality that effects his ruin. The rationalistic Guise, however, argues that Nature would no more fashion an heroic being without a noble destiny than create a headless man. Then Monsieur points to Bussy as an instance of his thesis:

> as the winds sing through a hollow tree,
> And (since it lets them pass through) let it stand;
> But a tree solid, since it gives no way
> To their wild rages, they rend up by the root:
> So this full creature now shall reel and fall,
> Before the frantic puffs of purblind Chance,
> That pipes through empty men, and makes them
> dance.   (5.3.42–48)

Their colloquy offers an illuminating glimpse of the common need to discover some understandable—and therefore usable—principle behind the perplexing events of human life. But Chapman's action has already pointed elsewhere—not toward a lesson, but a fact: there is something in

---

78. Why Chapman opposed rhetorical to "poetical" utterance in this way is an interesting question. In the preface to *Ovid's Banquet*, he does contrast "perviall" (perspicuous) oratory to "significant" poetry, which can be understood only by "searching spirits" (*Poems*, p. 49). Bussy's literal-minded response would indicate that he is not one—but then, neither was Hercules. The cryptic nature of Behemoth's pronouncements and his association with darkness suggest that Chapman is employing the "significant" mode of poetry to represent divine truth. In this light, his obviously crude mimesis of the traditional technique of argument by varying propositions is probably intended to reveal the impotence of the earthly *logos* before ultimate reality.

the nature of heroic man that clashes with the Other of divinity and brings about his fall. All Guise and Monsieur can do is attempt to moralize that fact, and the significance each finds in it is a function of his own needs and perceptions.

Their choral debate does not end the inquiry, for it is resumed in the ensuing action as Bussy comes to meet Tamyra, still confident of his personal destiny. Here, two kinds of argument *in utramque partem* inform the text. In one—the mimetic—Bussy and the Friar explicitly pose theses in an attempt to understand the terrible turn events have taken. In the other, argument is woven into the texture of the verse itself, as in earlier parts of the play. Both shape our final response to the hero.

At first, Bussy is successful against his enemies. He kills a hired murderer, then pins down Montsurry himself, granting his life only at Tamyra's request. But in the very act of magnanimity he is shot in the back by one of the Duke's henchmen. The Friar's ghost reviles Montsurry for his impious treachery, but Bussy recognizes in the act the work of Fate's ministers:

> Forbear them, Father; 'tis enough for me
> That Guise and Monsieur, Death and Destiny
> Come behind D'Ambois.
>
> (123–125)

Believing the fates have conspired against him, he declares that the soul is simply instrumental to the body and not made for "good actions" after all—echoing Monsieur's very words:

> let my death
> Define life nothing but a Courtier's breath.
> (131–132)

But this is simply the *positio* of a man engaged—another attempt to assess the meaning of his defeat. We have seen that his "fate" is woven of a far more intricate fabric than he assumes.

Bitterly, he then attempts to escape "meaning" by reasserting his heroism, and determines that he shall at least meet death standing upright. Like the Chorus in *Hercules Oetaeus*, he commends his fame to the distant quarters of the world, that all may thunder a sigh to requite his "worthless fall." It is at this point that Chapman reveals most explicitly the

Herculean palimpsest—inviting us to see in this brash courtier shot in the back by a jealous husband the splendid figure of a universal savior. The disparity between action and rhetoric is at its most disturbing here, for Bussy has simply not accomplished anything worthy the fame of Hercules. But characteristically, Chapman has substituted allusion for deeds to keep the generic nature of his hero before the audience, as the particulars of his career recede from consciousness. Though lacking the logic of Aristotelian mimesis, the tactic is rhetorically persuasive.

This Herculean focus is maintained until Tamyra asks Bussy's forgiveness for leading him to so unworthy an end, and displays her bleeding hands. Then something strange happens. That Tamyra's hand would kill him if he heeded its summons was part of Behemoth's prophecy. But Bussy does not appear to connect the prophecy with his *voluntary* act. He responds not as a tragic hero who has been granted an insight into his fate, but as a lover horrified at the torture he has caused his mistress:

> O, my heart is broken.
> Fate, nor these murtherers, Monsieur, nor the Guise,
> Have any glory in my death, but this,
> This killing spectacle, this prodigy.
>
> (178–181)

Though simply another thesis, it is his most moving gesture in the play, for he now explicates his plight not as a mythic figure but as a human being—the "surface" hero of the love affair—denying that any cosmic force could have power to hurt equal to the sight of Tamyra's suffering. Chapman has shifted focus so that we may respond with deeper sympathy to his hero—which we will do if exposed to the human particulars of his situation, not to his universal significance.[79] By modulating thesis and hypothesis in this way, Chapman secures both our intellectual and emotional assent. The hero is seen to be one who transcends conventional human morality and yet affects us by his very human devotion.[80]

And still the debate goes on. It is in his "nominalist" frame of mind that Bussy—yet unable to comprehend his fate—decries the "frail con-

---

79. We may recall that the same principle was at work in our response to Hieronimo.

80. Even here, we do not lose the second viewpoint entirely, for Tamyra's blood—palimpsestically that of Nessus—is also a reminder of Bussy's archetype.

dition of strength, valour, virtue," echoing Monsieur's conviction that the heroic man is an accidental phenomenon without an end commensurate to this worth. But the last word is reserved to the Friar, that curiously sainted bawd, who shifts the perspective a final time:

> Farewell brave relics of a complete man:
> Look up and see thy spirit made a star,
> Join flames with Hercules: and when thou set'st
> Thy radiant forehead in the firmament,
> Make the vast continent, crack'd with thy receipt,
> Spread to a world of fire: and th'aged sky,
> Cheer with new sparks of old humanity.
>
> (268–274)

From the viewpoint of one who was literally transfigured by the advent of the hero from the garden, Bussy's destiny quite fulfills his great spirit, in accordance with Guise's theory.

Obviously, no amount of rationalization can reduce *Bussy D'Ambois* to a well-made play. Its logic becomes apparent only when it is seen at the end of a long line of developing Elizabethan tragedies. For Chapman is using the drama in time-honored fashion to conduct a liberal inquiry. He places before us (and himself) a model of ancient heroic virtue, introduces him into the familiar world we know, and supposes what is likely to befall him and the host society in the encounter. The state of mind is that of the *quaestio*; the manner, that of sophistic tragedy. The play opens in thesis and develops in hypothesis, but now within the action proper we find a more fluid shifting between the two modes of inquiry. Gone are the neat five-part separations of thesis-seeking choruses and hypothesized episodes. Instead, the argument *in utramque partem* is conducted in a variety of ways: in the traditional manner of explicit mimetic debate; by introducing contrastive rhetorical *imagines* to suggest other levels of meaning; through palimpsestic exposition.

The final judgment we make upon Bussy is based upon all of this. We consider not only his bluster and infuriating moral certitude, but also his underlying nature; his Herculean prowess and the very human tenderness that surfaces in the last scene; the evils of the French Court and the unquestionable pain his "virtue" brings to its most well-meaning inhabitants. This is why Chapman, for all his clumsiness and obscurity, performs a worthy service in *Bussy D'Ambois*. Free of tendentious motive, he sets loose a dangerous ideal and countenances the worst it can do without losing admiration for it—in either the modern or the ancient sense. In making us do so, too, he fulfills the function of humanist *psychogogue*.

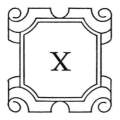

"If Words Might Serve":
Marlowe's Supposes

It is appropriate to conclude this study of explorative drama with Christopher Marlowe. Certainly no Elizabethan playwright exploited his medium more freely to speculate upon human possibility. Yet built into this endeavor is a curious paradox. Although Marlowe uses all the devices of sophistic dramaturgy to enrich *our* emotional response and enlarge *our* understanding of the problems he poses, it is evident that for *him* the chief of these problems is precisely the value of such an exercise. The play of mind had begun with the assumption that inventing alternate views could lead to a fuller apprehension of reality. But tragedy after tragedy—and many comedies in the period—reveal the inadequacy of invention before the "facts" of life. Marlowe was peculiarly concerned with this matter from his earliest collaboration with Nashe; indeed, we can mark its first troubling appearance. Aeneas is preparing at last to depart for Italy. Dido pleads passionately with him to remain true to their love as he had promised, and bitterly recalls all she has done for him: "O speak like my Aeneas, like my love." But Aeneas cannot speak like himself, or rather the self that Dido has known—for he now recognizes that he is the agent of destiny and not his own master. He expresses this fact in a distinctly Marlovian way. "If words might move me," he tells Dido, "I were overcome." Against the absolute, he suggests, arguments of even the most pathetical nature, if they serve a merely human desire, can avail nothing.[1]

1. *Dido Queen of Carthage*, ed. H. J. Oliver (London, 1968), 5.1.112, 154.

This moment—and the emphasis is Marlowe's, not Virgil's[2]—adumbrates a theme that haunts virtually all the succeeding plays. Invention is variously characterized as persuasive power, poetic conceit, witty doubletalk, imaginative capability, incantatory rite—reflecting the late sixteenth-century conflation of the term; but regardless of its local coloration, one can trace through the canon a growing anxiety about the capacity of wit, in its fullest sense, to master ultimate reality. In this respect, Marlowe's plays are literally dramatized *suppositions*, each examining in its own way the ability of the human wit to "grow a second nature," as Sidney puts it—to discover and sustain a true universe. Beginning in great excitement at the possibility of such transcendence, Marlowe comes to express in his last play a deep sense of futility about the project, for he seems to have discovered the humbling truth which has been lurking beneath the surface all along—that all invention is essentially self-referential.

In the present chapter, I shall attempt to sketch this ironic development, focusing primarily upon the terminal plays *Tamburlaine the Great* and *Doctor Faustus*. At the same time, I shall also suggest how Marlowe exercises *our* wit, so that we may form a wide and understanding judgment of his hero's endeavor.[3]

I

The first question confronting a student of *Tamburlaine* marks it unmistakably as a specimen of explorative drama. It is posed in the prologue, where Marlowe invites his hero's auditors to

> View but his picture in this tragic glass
> And then applaud his fortunes as you please.
> $(7-8)$[4]

2. In the epic, Aeneas simply says, "Cease to fire thyself and me with thy complaints. Not of free will do I follow Italy" (4.360–361). *Virgil I*, trans. H. R. Fairclough, L.C.L. (London, 1934).

3. The order of discussion follows Greg's late dating of *Doctor Faustus* in his parallel-text edition of 1950, a position that is supported, it seems to me, by the pattern that will be examined here. My argument does not depend, however, upon the veracity of his hypothesis; it will only be less neat. J. B. Steane, *Marlowe: A Critical Study* (Cambridge, 1964), offers reasonable arguments to refute Greg, though so far as I know the critical consensus has not been overturned.

4. All citations refer to John D. Jump's edition (Lincoln, Neb., 1967).

The suggestion to pass whatever judgment one likes upon the hero is novel enough, considering the moral directives of the prologues extant up to this time,[5] but it masks an even greater puzzle that is not fully evident until the action draws to a conclusion: in what sense is the play a tragedy at all? For the prologue introduces Part 1, which conforms to no notion of tragedy the Elizabethan stage had yet entertained, ending as it does not in the hero's disease or death but in his triumph. Even supposing that Marlowe had already envisioned the second part when he wrote the first,[6] his audience could not share this vision, and was therefore presented with a tragedy that ostensibly ends happily.[7] Thus a fundamental problem exists at the outset. Either *Tamburlaine*'s generic credentials are to be sought simply in the conventional trappings of battles, deaths, and exiles —of which there are plenty—or we are to take Marlowe's tragic intention more seriously and try to find dramatic and psychological meaning in the paradox that the play represents not the tragic fall but the tragic *rise* of a great man. Ultimately, that is, we must locate the tragic in the hero's success.

The latter path is potentially the more rewarding, and is the one I propose we explore. What constitutes a "tragic rise," and how does Marlowe shape our apprehension of such an action? First he creates, from the historical Timur Khan, a protagonist who possesses not only extraordinary physical power and a commanding presence, but above all a mind of "heroic conceit." It is this singular conceit that seems to make possible all Tamburlaine's accomplishments; for while everyone in the play is capable of imagining himself a creature of power, all others subordinate themselves to some ethical norm (cynically or otherwise), and their imaginings bear no fruit. Tamburlaine alone does not measure his behavior by normative standards; on the contrary, he adduces whatever *irregulari-*

5. Cf. the prologues to *Jocasta*, *Gismond of Salerne*, *The Misfortunes of Arthur*, and such "tragedies" as *Cambises* (1561), *All for Money* (1577), and *The Conflict of Conscience* (1581).

6. Despite evidence that he consumed most of his relevant source material in this play and the testimony of the second prologue that the success of Part 1 had inspired a sequel.

7. And in no way resembling the Italian experiments with *tragedia di lieto fin*. See Marvin T. Herrick, *Tragicomedy: Its Origin and Development in Italy, France, and England* (Urbana, Ill., 1962), pp. 63–114. For a detailed account of Marlowe's sources, see Una Ellis-Fermor's edition of the play (London, 1930), pp. 17–41.

ties exist in nature or the supernatural as precedents for his actions, which means, in effect, that he is his own agent. His is the thoroughly liberated imagination—pointing at one moment to Jupiter's deposition of Saturn, at another to Heraclitean strife, at another to reckless Phaeton, as evidence that he simply reflects the way things are—and as we watch him succeed, Marlowe allows us gradually to become convinced that perhaps thinking does make it so.[8]

From his first entrance, Tamburlaine engages in a continuous act of self-creation. In response to Zenocrate's arch reference to his "lordship" ("for so you do import"), he visibly becomes a lord, laying aside his shepherd's weeds for the complete armor and curtle-axe which "are adjuncts more beseeming Tamburlaine" (1.2.43). The logical-rhetorical term is especially fitting, for Tamburlaine seems intent upon fashioning a personage for himself by literally annexing the "accidents" appropriate to his inward vision. Armor is one such adjunct; rich treasures are another; Zenocrate herself is at first simply an addition to the hero's equipage—

> But, lady, this fair face and heavenly hue
> Must grace his bed that conquers Asia
> And means to be a terror to the world
>
> (36–38)

—and she is followed by the annexation of Theridamas and his thousand horsemen, for the conqueror must have the physical strength to accomplish his dreams. But he must possess a manner as well. Tamburlaine's recognition of this political fact is represented by the white, red, and black regalia which signify to the world that his

> customs are as peremptory
> As wrathful planets, death or destiny.
>
> (5.1.127–128)

Together, armor, gold, mistress, warriors, and charismatic ritual compose the full panoply the Scythian shepherd gathers about him to prove

8. In this respect, he bears a remarkable resemblance to the sophist Eteocles in Gascoigne's *Jocasta*. Eteocles' major speech in that play (2.1.359–368) may well have influenced Tamburlaine's "earthly crown" speech (2.7.12–29), since Gascoigne's king-drawn chariot in the third dumb show found its way into Marlowe's play.

that he is indeed a lord, and Marlowe is clearly fascinated by the possibility of such self-creation. In a sense, the whole play is designed as an extended "confirmation" of Tamburlaine's vision.

But counterproof also lurks within this design. To what extent is such ethopoetic realization possible, Marlowe asks, and at what price? He directs our attention to these concerns by focusing upon the chief weapon in Tamburlaine's enterprise—his way with words. It is through language that Tamburlaine most characteristically masters his environment— commanding, persuading, asserting. How absolute is this power? With what kinds of situations can it deal? What imaginative processes lie behind its capacity to effect transformation? These issues, hidden beneath the astonishing succession of Tamburlaine's victories, finally surface in the fifth act when Marlowe pauses for the first time to give us a glimpse of his hero's psychology—and discloses that within his rhetorical strength lies tragic potentiality.

In order that we may appreciate this discovery when it is made, Marlowe lavishes much care upon cultivating our sense of Tamburlaine's rhetorical power. While he does not explicitly establish an ascending scale of personal rhetorics, he does provide certain touchstones of style by which we may measure the hero. Mycetes, for example, produces only the most ludicrous kind of speech when he expresses his "conceiv'd grief":

> Then hear thy charge, valiant Theridamas,
> The chiefest captain of Mycetes' host,
> The hope of Persia, and the very legs
> Whereon our state doth lean as on a staff
> That holds us up and foils our neighbor foes.
>
> (1.1.57–61)

Such a tripedalian vision is bound to foil itself, as Mycetes does quite early in the play. Bajazeth, on the other hand, is nothing if not grandiloquent:

> You know our army is invincible;
> As many circumcised Turks we have
> And warlike bands of Christians renied
> As hath the Ocean or the Terrene sea

> Small drops of water when the moon begins
> To join in one her semicircled horns.
>
> (3.1.7–12)

Yet this claim seems to require extensive shoring-up:

> Tell him thy lord, the Turkish emperor,
> Dread lord of Afric, Europe, and Asia,
> Great king and conqueror of Graecia,
> The Ocean, Terrene, and the coal-black sea,
> The high and highest monarch of the world,
> Wills and commands (for say not I entreat)
> Not once to set his foot in Africa. . . .
>
> (22–28)

The parenthesis reveals that Bajazeth's titles are just so much bombast between the hostile world and his uncertain soul (there is a touch of Lyly's Sir Tophas here), and he repeats it—"(say I bid thee so)"—just a few lines later, to reassure himself once again of his power to command. Although Tamburlaine is equally given to hyperbole, there is never any suggestion that it is protective padding. His characteristic locution, as he himself points out, is "will and shall," for his is a rhetoric of confident expectation:

> Forsake thy king and do but join with me,
> And we will triumph over all the world.
> I hold the Fates bound fast in iron chains,
> And with my hands turn Fortune's wheel about,
> And sooner shall the sun fall from his sphere
> Than Tamburlaine be slain or overcome.
>
> (1.2.72–77)

No other speaker in the play lives so familiarly in the distant regions of the natural and imagined universe, and it is quite true, as Lodge's Sulla later boasts, that

> men of baser metal and conceit
> Cannot conceive the beauty of [his] thought.[9]

9. True even of the Soldan, a man who is neither ridiculous nor wicked, but who, upon hearing of the white, red, and black ritual, can only exclaim, "The slave usurps the glorious art of war" (4.1.67).

If Tamburlaine's rhetoric were only the rhetoric of self-assertion, however, he would not be the master orator that he is. His speech seems capable of seducing chastity itself, as the wooing of Zenocrate indicates:

> With milk-white harts upon an ivory sled
> Thou shalt be drawn amid the frozen pools
> And scale the icy mountains' lofty tops
> Which with thy beauty will be soon resolved.
> (1.2.98–101)

Upon his lips, rape is so purified that even Techelles is convinced:

> What now? In love?

But Tamburlaine reassures him that it is only a matter of art—

> Techelles, women must be flattered

—and pats his trusty sword familiarly:

> *But this* is she with whom I am in love.
> (106–108, emphasis mine)[10]

Marlowe begins to shape a "tragic rise," then, by presenting an heroic figure who visibly "invents" himself before our eyes and is able to do so because his intense conviction of innate nobility expresses itself in "astounding terms" that compel others to obey his will. The dimensions of this figure, though, are also limned, in sophistic fashion, by the views others hold of him. Each of these views works in a different way upon our sensibilities to qualify our judgment of his actions. The most memorable is probably Menaphon's description to Cosroe early in Act 2:

> Of stature tall, and straightly fashioned,
> Like his desire, lift upwards and divine;
> So large of limbs, his joints so strongly knit,
> Such breadth of shoulders as might mainly bear

---

10. Tamburlaine's attitude toward Zenocrate changes, of course, as his great fifth act soliloquy reveals. Nor is the icy grandeur of this speech pure calculation; it is Tamburlaine's version of a wooing speech and therefore reflective of his own essential chastity—a quality suggested more fully at the end of Part 2. But the speech is intended to persuade, and does.

Old Atlas' burden. 'Twixt his manly pitch,
A pearl more worth than all the world is plac'd,
Wherein by curious sovereignty of art
Are fix'd his piercing instruments of sight,
Whose fiery circles bear encompassed
A heaven of heavenly bodies in their spheres,
That guides his steps and actions to the throne
Where honor sits invested royally.
Pale of complexion, wrought in him with passion,
Thirsting with sovereignty, with love of arms,
His lofty brows in folds do figure death,
And in their smoothness amity and life.
About them hangs a knot of amber hair,
Wrapped in curls, as fierce Achilles' was,
On which the breath of heaven delights to play,
Making it dance with wanton majesty.

(2.1.7–26)

Our experience with Chapman will alert us to the function of this set piece. It is another rhetorical *imago*, this time an extended hyperbole, through which Tamburlaine rises in relief from the field of desert warriors to become a creature apart. For Menaphon's words describe not a man but a colossal work of art: its limbs are fashioned in human form, but are huge as Atlas's; where its head should be there is instead a pearl; and in place of eyes, astrological instruments which the idol employs to guide its movements toward a high destiny. Once enthroned, constriction of brows signifies death, dilation life—the responses of some strange, living machine. Notice the verbs of art: "fashioned," "knit," "plac'd," "fix'd," "wrought." Even its hair is framed by "curious sovereignty of art," for it is a knot of amber, which miraculously blows in the wind like real hair. The effect of the speech is not merely to elevate Tamburlaine but to locate him in an *aesthetic* realm beyond the reach of moral judgment. This is the genus to which he seems to belong, having become something quite other than human—a rare artifice operating through its own inexorable law.

In contrast, Zenocrate's description of him in the third act reveals human qualities hitherto unsuspected:

> As looks the sun through Nilus' flowing stream,
> Or when the morning holds him in her arms,
> So looks my lordly love fair Tamburlaine;
> His talk much sweeter than the Muses' song
> They sung for honor 'gainst Pierides,
> Or where Minerva did with Neptune strive. . . .
>
> (3.2.47–52)

Here the image of Tamburlaine becomes soft and diffuse—warm sunlight seen through a rippling curtain of water—and fresh and young—radiant sunrise still cradled on the horizon. His thundering speech is not rhetorical bombast, but poetic striving after Apollonian honors. Zenocrate's similitudes are crucial to our perception of Tamburlaine's character, for they suggest a tenderness in him that is never publicly revealed, and which has evidently touched springs of love in the very conventional princess he has captured. It is largely through her sense of him that we can respond to him as to a human being.

The third major perspective upon Tamburlaine—important because it comes from an untainted foe—is one that characterizes him as a beast:

> Methinks we march as Meleager did,
> Environed with brave Argolian knights,
> To chase the savage Calydonian boar;
> Or Cephalus with lusty Theban youths
> Against the wolf that angry Themis sent
> To waste and spoil the sweet Aonian fields.
>
> (4.3.1–6)

The words are those of Zenocrate's father, addressed to her betrothed as they set out to rescue her. Both are injured parties surveying from the viewpoint of common humanity the depredations wrought by the inspired marauder in their collective orchards. The speech is especially telling because it comes at a time when Tamburlaine's quest for glory is beginning to exhibit increasing signs of cruelty, and the softness which we have been assured underlies his ferocity appears to have been only a lover's illusion. But in fact it is not; the greatness of Tamburlaine lies in his being all these things—a law unto himself, a tender suitor to Zeno-

crate, a pillager of kingdoms.[11] It is only when he feels compelled to reduce his own complexity in pursuit of *ethopoeia* that he begins to approxi-
mate the judgment of his enemies.

This moment comes at the siege of Damascus. Having waited too long
for aid from his allies, the Governor sends forth four young virgins to
beg pity of Tamburlaine, despite the black streamers that signify the
city's imminent destruction. The warrior responds to their plea by ordering the virgins killed, and does so in a particularly nasty way:

> TAMBURLAINE: Behold my sword, what see you at its
>   point?
> 1 VIRGIN: Nothing but fear and fatal steel, my lord.
> TAMBURLAINE: Your fearful minds are thick and misty
>   then,
> For there sits Death, there sits imperious Death,
> Keeping his circuit by the slicing edge.
>   [*He pauses.*]
> But I am pleas'd you shall not see him there.
> He is now seated on my horsemen's spears,
> And on their points his fleshless body feeds.
> Techelles, straight go charge a few of them
> To charge these dames and show my servant, Death,
> Sitting in scarlet on their armed spears.
>   (5.1.108–118, S.D. supplied)

In making of murder a kind of puppet show of the mind—in which the
magistrate-executioner bestrides first his sword, then his horsemen's
spears—Tamburlaine introduces the aesthetic note that has come to be
characteristic of his actions. But in the soliloquy that follows, he reveals
that the substitution of the aesthetic for the moral is not native to his
soul, nor is it achieved without a terrible struggle. The speech is worth
our study, for it is the only intimate glimpse of Tamburlaine's psychology
that Marlowe provides, and is crucial to our understanding of the nature
of his tragedy.

He begins by contemplating the *human* meaning of the destruction of
Damascus, as it is reflected in Zenocrate's tears. And immediately his
desire is to turn this image, too, into artifice:

11. Cf. Eugene M. Waith's remarks on Hercules, *The Herculean Hero in Marlowe,
Shakespeare, Chapman, and Dryden* (New York, 1962), quoted in Ch. 8, n. 15.

Ah, fair Zenocrate, divine Zenocrate!
Fair is too foul an epithet for thee,
That in thy passion for thy country's love
And fear to see thy kingly father's harm
With hair dishevell'd wip'st thy watery cheeks;
And like to Flora in her morning's pride,
Shaking silver tresses in the air,
Rain'st on the earth resolved pearl in showers
And sprinklest sapphires on thy shining face. . . .
(5.1.135–143)

As he traces in his imagination the influence of this beauty upon the surrounding heavens, he is inevitably reminded of its disturbing effect upon his own "tempted thoughts," and realizes he must come to terms with it. So he attempts to define it, for verbal articulation has always been for him a means of mastery. He begins by posing a venerable *quaestio*:

What is beauty, saith my sufferings, then?

There is a pause, and perhaps a sigh of perplexity:

If all the pens that ever poets held,
Had fed the feelings of their masters' thoughts,
And every sweetness that inspired their hearts,
Their minds, and muses on admired themes;

—suddenly he is a man at a standish, searching for the right word—

If all the heavenly quintessence they still
From their immortal flowers of poesy,
Wherein as in a mirror we perceive
The highest reaches of a human wit;

—he glances at the *flores poetarum* here—

If these had made one poem's period,
And all combin'd in beauty's worthiness,
Yet should there hover in their restless heads
One thought, one grace, one wonder at the least,
Which into words no virtue can digest.
(160–173)

—though he speaks of *their* restless heads, his imaginative posture suggests that he has momentarily merged with "them." It is *his* restless head to which he immediately refers, *his* incapacity to render beauty into words.

It is a stunning admission. What had begun as an exercise in definition ends in bathetic acknowledgement that he simply lacks the power to "digest" beauty, which must remain forever elusive. It is especially poignant—though appropriate—that Tamburlaine should suffer his first defeat in what can only be termed his rhetorical invention, for this is where Marlowe has located his peculiar strength. And he fails, it would seem, because beauty is the first absolute he has encountered. King, sultan, emperor—all these can be conquered by the superior human being. The power of beauty upon the human soul is essentially uncontrollable.

The exercise having revealed the limits of his power, he quickly turns away from such humiliating speculation:

> But how unseemly is it for my sex,
> My discipline of arms and chivalry,
> My nature and the terror of my name,
> To harbour thoughts effeminate and faint!

But irresistibly he is drawn back:

> Save only that in beauty's just applause
> With whose instinct the soul of man is touched. . . .

There is reluctant hesitation, and then the mind turns once again, hitting upon the happy thought that sets the problem at rest:

> And every warrior that is rapt with love
> Of fame, of valor, and of victory
> Must needs have beauty beat on his conceits.
>
> (174–182)

The very line structure of this final period reveals the difficult rationalization that is taking place. The first line, a completed dependent clause ending on *love*, suggests that the speaker is still lingering imaginatively on the amorous temptations of beauty; the second line abruptly qualifies the thought with three prepositional phrases offering appropriate objects of love; and by the third, beauty has been transformed into an urgent weapon of warfare. It is with obvious relief that Tamburlaine then can say:

> I thus conceiving and subduing both
> That which hath stopp'd the tempest of the gods,
> Even from the fiery-spangled veil of heaven
> To feel the lovely warmth of shepherds' flames
> And march in cottages of strowed weeds

—a last look back, for the shepherd determined to be a hero—

> Shall give the world to note, for all my birth,
> That virtue solely is the sum of glory
> And fashions men with true nobility.
>
> (183–190)

Overcoming one's background takes its toll. The speech finally converts defeat into victory, but one achieved only at great cost. For in translating the moral message of Zenocrate's tears as symbols of heroic encouragement, Tamburlaine is attempting to withdraw into a private aesthetic world. Hermaphroditically, he will both "conceive"—literally, "generate" and "entertain"—beauty, and then use it to further his own ethopoetic quest. In doing so, he must inevitably reduce his own nature, and lose touch with the wider concerns of the world outside.[12]

Tamburlaine's "tragic rise," then, is compounded of *two* major movements—the hero's spectacular external progress toward power and his concomitant need to narrow his sensibility in order to consolidate that power. Marlowe shapes our awareness of the process by building up the strength of Tamburlaine's rhetoric and the complexity of his nature, and allowing us to see the delimitations of both. He directs our response in other ways as well. His need as the play proceeds is to make us feel the evil that has resulted from Tamburlaine's increasing *libido dominandi*,[13] and also to secure our acquiescence in his triumph. He achieves these ap-

12. Notice how the transition from "conceit" to "conceive" in lines 182–183 implies a kind of infanticide. Beauty "beats" on the "conceit" as on a womb; Tamburlaine then "conceives" and conquers ("subdues") his own progeny. Though unintentional, the image foreshadows his reaction to Calyphas in Part 2.

13. Harry Levin's term, *The Overreacher* (Cambridge, Mass., 1952), p. 36 and *passim*.

parently incompatible ends by means of two devices already familiar to us—the sophistic vignette and the palimpsest. Through the first of these, Tamburlaine's actions are placed in a recognizably "tragical" context. This begins to emerge late in the third act when Theridamas takes Zabina's crown and presents it to Zenocrate. Zabina, he says, is no longer empress, and Tamburlaine concurs, in a tone that he has not used before in addressing the Turks:

> Not now, Theridamas, her time is past.
> The pillars that have bolstered up those terms
> Are fall'n in clusters at my conquering feet.
> (3.3.228–230)

For the first time his words suggest the destruction not merely of the boasting *miles* Bajazeth has appeared to be, but of a dynastic edifice. Clearly, Marlowe is imposing a "tragic glass" upon the action. As a result, the Turkish rulers are transformed in the relatively short space of three scenes from comic objects of mockery to pitiable wretches whose torment at Tamburlaine's hands demands serious attention.

Marlowe's changing attitude toward the Turks can be observed in their language. Bajazeth begins as the unregenerate infidel:

> Ye holy priests of heavenly Mahomet,
> That sacrificing, slice and cut your flesh,
> Staining his altars with your purple blood,
> Make heaven to frown and every fixed star
> To suck up poison from the moorish fens
> And pour it in this glorious tyrant's throat!
> (4.2.2–7)

This follower of the priests of Baal cannot possibly win our sympathy, but after he is stepped upon, taunted, and starved by Tamburlaine, his utter desperation is something we can comprehend feelingly. When Zabina asks

> Then is there left no Mahomet, no god,
> No fiend, no fortune, nor no hope of end
> To our infamous, monstrous slaveries?
> (5.1.238–240)

her repeated *no, no, no* drums hopelessly in our ears; and as Bajazeth reviews the lamentable change that has overtaken them—his speech breaking down as he thinks to comfort his queen with words of love—we are unexpectedly touched by his pathos. What has happened is that Marlowe has literally *magnified* the two victims before our eyes (he leaves them onstage alone for 105 lines), and thus has altered their function in the play. For the first time, we are permitted to observe closely the physical pain and mental deterioration which is the product of Tamburlaine's lust for power. And we are able to do so because the "rules" of sophistic dramaturgy allow the playwright to shift focus upon his characters without actually changing their "character"—if he wishes to point up new considerations for his audience's edification.

Zenocrate supplies the chorus for this changed focus. Her speech upon discovering the dead bodies of Bajazeth and Zabina contains no hint of the pompous Saracen and his "boss," only woe at the sight of fallen majesty:

> Earth, cast up fountains from thy entrails,
> And wet thy cheeks for their untimely deaths;
> Shake with their weight in sign of fear and grief.
> Blush heaven, that gave them honor at their birth
> And let them die a death so barbarous.
>
> (347–351)

She makes no attempt to smooth over Tamburlaine's cruelty, nor is she slow to educe the thesis underlying the spectacle:

> Oh, mighty Jove and holy Mahomet,
> Pardon my love! O, pardon his contempt
> Of earthly fortune and respect of pity,
> And let not conquest, ruthlessly pursu'd,
> Be equally against his life incens'd
> In this great Turk and hapless emperess!
>
> (363–368)

Her words mark an important moment in the course of events. For whatever her position in the eyes of the world, Zenocrate is the moral touchstone in this play. Her concern serves to articulate our own growing malaise about Tamburlaine's status in the cosmic scheme. Though he still commands our awe, he has so transgressed human decency that in strict justice, we feel, he must be punished.

It is on this deeply troubled note that the play enters its final episode. The tension is extraordinary—too great, in fact, to lead to a satisfactory conclusion unless it is eased. And so Marlowe does ease it, by introducing an idea that allows us to judge Tamburlaine in a somewhat different light. He accomplishes this through Zenocrate's psychomachia. Immediately following her lament for the Turkish monarchs, Philemus announces that the Soldan and Arabia have arrived to challenge Tamburlaine:

> th'Arabian king,
> The first affecter of your excellence,
> Comes now, as Turnus 'gainst Aeneas did,
> Armed with lance into the Egyptian fields,
> Ready for battle 'gainst my lord the king.
> (5.1.378–382)

The news brings Zenocrate face to face with her own moral predicament, as "shame and duty, love and fear" flood her consciousness. For whom should she pray in the coming conflict, she asks—her father and betrothed, or her paramour? But then she recalls the messenger's simile. Perhaps all will turn out well; for just

> as the gods, to end the Trojans' toil,
> Prevented Turnus of Lavinia
> And fatally enrich'd Aeneas' love,
> So, for a final issue to my griefs,
> To pacify my country and my love,
> Must Tamburlaine by their resistless powers
> With virtue of a gentle victory
> Conclude a league of honor to my hope;
> Then, as the powers divine have preordain'd,
> With happy safety of my father's life
> Send like defense of fair Arabia.
> (392–402)

The speech is very carefully formulated to reveal a mind earnestly attempting to reassure itself. In effect, Zenocrate solves her problem by casting herself in the role of Lavinia, and Tamburlaine in that of Aeneas.

Then, having convinced herself of the *truth* of this analogy ("as the powers divine have preordain'd"), she ignores its further implication and prays for the safety of Turnus-Arabia. It is charming intrusion of compassion upon logic. Naive as it may be, however, the speech serves as more than a simple expression of wish fulfillment. In a play in which there is no authorial point of view, Zenocrate's epic perspective lends a certain purposiveness to Tamburlaine's embattled career, which begins to take on the shadowy form of Aeneas's establishment of peace in Italy. This impression is reinforced by Tamburlaine's actual magnanimity toward the Soldan and by the emotional colloquy between Zenocrate and the dying Arabia that immediately follows her speech. It is virtually a dramatized *Heroides*—"Turnus to Lavinia," "Lavinia to Turnus"—in which the former lovers exchange affectionate farewells.

It is significant, however, that even within this new generic context, Marlowe does not let us forget the particular, problematic history he is recounting. In victory, Tamburlaine reasserts himself all the more forcefully—as if his magnanimity must not be mistaken for anything but a temporary acquiescence:

> The god of war resigns his room to me,
> Meaning to make me general of the world;
> Jove, viewing me in arms, looks pale and wan,
> Fearing my power should pull him from his throne;
> Where'er I come the Fatal Sisters sweat,
> And grisly Death, by running to and fro
> To do their ceaseless homage to my sword. . . .
>
> (450–456)

To support his claim he points to the visible evidence—the deluge of blood, the millions of bodies, and the new display of the Turk, his great empress, and the dead Arabia—now "sights of power to grace my victory." Though the spectacle seems to prove his success complete, his triumph is qualified and finally "placed" for us as he crowns Zenocrate with these brave words:

> As Juno, when the giants were suppress'd
> That darted mountains at her brother Jove,
> So looks my love, shadowing in her brows

337

Triumphs and trophies for my victories;
Or as Latona's daughter bent to arms,
Adding more courage to my conquering mind.

(510-515)

In this final elevation of the gentle and passionate Zenocrate to the woman behind the throne—or more outlandish yet, a warrior Artemis—Tamburlaine reminds us sharply of the one defeat he has suffered in his heroic progress. Unable to master beauty, he has imaginatively domesticated it to the needs of heroism. The full effects are yet to be seen. Although he has spared the Soldan for Zenocrate's sake, Tamburlaine's pursuit of *ethopoeia* poses a serious danger to his humanity. And this quality is as important to our admiring eyes as his heroism. Being a hero may mean being more than a man, but it must never offer less than men value. This is the tragic implication seen at the end of *Tamburlaine I.*

II

In Part 2, the matter of invention and reality is explored more fully, and in a necessarily altered context. Tamburlaine is still the wondrous, restless figure fashioned by his own words and the admiration of others. In Theridamas's plea to Olympia, Marlowe employs once again the hyperbolic image to enhance the hero,

On whom Death and the Fatal Sisters wait
With naked swords and scarlet liveries;
Before whom, mounted on a lion's back,
Rhamnusia bears a helmet full of blood
And strews the way with brains of slaughtered men;
By whose proud side the ugly Furies run,
Hearkening when he shall bid them plague the
    world;
Over whose zenith, cloth'd with windy air,
And eagle's wings join'd to her feathered breast,
Fame hovereth, sounding of her golden trump,
That to the adverse poles of that straight line
Which measureth the glorious frame of heaven
The name of mighty Tamburlaine is spread. . . .

(3.4.54-66)

While in Part I, this device brought to mind an intricate bejeweled machine, here Tamburlaine is represented as an emblem. The description is pictorial—"on whom," "before whom," "by whose proud side," "over whose zenith"—and the elaborate figures of emblematic heraldry are used to further abstract the hero from the world of contingency and and make us regard him as an absolute force.

But along with this continuing insistence upon the uniqueness of Tamburlaine, Marlowe now introduces issues that cast doubt upon his self-sufficiency, and thus he begins to supply appropriate contexts for a "tragic fall." The first to become apparent is the problem with his sons—two parts warrior, one part amorous malingerer. It is just the proportion we might have predicted from our experience of Part I, but the embodiment in Calyphas of the repressed element in his own nature so alarms Tamburlaine that from the very outset he threatens violence to restore his homogeneity:

> TAMBURLAINE: And, sirrah, if you mean to wear a
>   crown,
> When we shall meet the Turkish deputy
> And all his viceroys, snatch it from his head,
> And cleave his pericranion with thy sword.
> CALYPHAS: If any man will hold him, I will strike
> And cleave him to the channel with my sword.
> TAMBURLAINE: Hold him, and cleave him too, or I'll
>   cleave thee. . . .
>
>   (1.3.99–104)

This is no idle threat, as the events of the fourth act prove. Marlowe defers development of the issue until then, introducing it only as a disturbing prologue to the welcome given Tamburlaine's returning companions and their preparations for a new campaign. As the quest for mastery is resumed, we are to understand, dissolution proceeds within.

It is Zenocrate, however, who once again provides Tamburlaine with his first resounding defeat. As she lies dying, the world darkens in his imagination, and he supposes all the lights of heaven drawn upward to grace the reception at which Zenocrate shall be divinely entertained. It is the old aestheticizing impulse reasserting itself, but Zenocrate pulls him violently down to earth:

> I fare, my lord, as other empresses,
> That, when this frail and transitory flesh
> Hath suck'd the measure of that vital air
> That feeds the body with his dated health,
> Wane with enforc'd and necessary change.
>
> (2.4.42–46)

Such words as "transitory," "measure," "dated," and "wanes" are not beseeming Tamburlaine, and he revolts against her application:

> May never such a change transform my love,
> In whose sweet being I repose my life. . . .
>
> (47–48)

But change does inevitably impinge upon him, and as with all previous foes, he responds to death with persuasions truly pathetical:

> Behold me here, divine Zenocrate,
> Raving, impatient, desperate, and mad,
> Breaking my steeled lance with which I burst
> The rusty beams of Janus' temple doors,
> Letting out death and tyrannizing war,
> To march with me under this bloody flag.
> And if thou pitiest Tamburlaine the Great,
> Come down from heaven and live with me again!
>
> (111–118)

It is an extraordinary speech. For the first time in his life, Tamburlaine the Great is begging for *pity*. The extended biography of his broken lance serves only to point up the anomaly and to reveal the true depth of his feeling for Zenocrate, so carefully sublimated in heroic valor. But his eloquence has no effect. As Theridamas tells him,

> If words might serve, our voice hath rent the air;
> . . . .
> Nothing prevails, for she is dead, my lord.
>
> (121, 124)

Words, grief, tears—all the components of the successful pleader can achieve nothing against the absolute of death. The thought is intolerable:

"For she is dead!" Thy words do pierce my soul!
Ah, sweet Theridamas, say so no more,
Though she be dead, yet let me think she lives
And feed my mind that dies for want of her.

(125–128)

And this is precisely what he does. Conceiving and subduing both, he immortalizes Zenocrate in a casket lapped with gold and carries her picture with him, that as "Bellona, goddess of the wars," she may beat on his conceits. It is a major victory of the imagination, but cut off so desperately from reality that it can only appear artificial and insubstantial.

In Tamburlaine's salvation of Zenocrate, the process adumbrated in Part I—the domestication of the absolute—becomes fully articulated. His difficulty with Calyphas, however, cannot be resolved simply by an act of imagination, for Tamburlaine's integrity is touched more nearly by his son's insufficiency than by the loss of Zenocrate. Having turned again to the wars, he is teaching his boys the arts of assault and fortification when Calyphas shrinks in dismay from even the prospect of basic training: "We may be slain or wounded ere we learn" (3.2.94). Tamburlaine is so enraged by this cowardice that he is moved to do what no enemy has yet been able to achieve: he wounds himself, to demonstrate the paltriness of such affliction, and sees in his flowing blood "the god of war's rich livery" (116). Despite his eulogy, the significance of the wound is evident: he will have to cut away a part of himself in order to maintain the illusion of unalloyed *virtù*.

And this he does when he confronts Calyphas following his defeat of Callapine and the four contributory kings. Marlowe has difficulty with his presentation of Calyphas. On the one hand, he embodies the amiable qualities of life, an extension of Zenocrate and whatever in Tamburlaine had responded to her beauty. So he sometimes utters strangely touching remarks. At the spectacle of Tamburlaine's flowing wound:

I know not what I should think of it.
Methinks 'tis a pitiful sight.

(3.2.130–131)

To Amyras's urging that he enter the field against the Turk:

> I know, sir, what it is to kill a man.
> It works remorse of conscience in me.
>
> (4.1.27–28)

Yet the context in which these remarks are made causes us to question their sincerity. Calyphas *is* a seeker of ease, a card player who would kiss the concubines others have won. The amorous man, insofar as Marlowe is able to conceive him in this play, is a miscegenated thing, indecorous to his soul. And so Tamburlaine's slaying of his son is an act that we attend with mixed feelings. He is clearly unworthy, an

> Image of sloth and picture of a slave,
> The obloquy and scorn of my renown!
>
> (4.1.90–91)

But, at the same time, Tamburlaine's very words tell us that he is committing a kind of suicide in killing Calyphas:

> Here, Jove, receive his fainting soul again,
> A form not meet to give that subject essence
> Whose matter is the flesh of Tamburlaine. . . .
>
> (110–112)

Not only is Tamburlaine rejecting a soul more akin to his own than he wants to admit; he is also finishing the job begun earlier in the tactics scene—butchering his own flesh in a violent act of *ethopoeia* which reduces yet further the dimensions of his nature. The assertive, expansive mode that dominated Part 1 is gradually turning into a dominant mode of denial.

The pattern of "tragic fall," then, places Tamburlaine much more fully upon the mercies of his imagination—an imagination no less liberated than it was in Part 1, but narrower, and all too frequently a means of escaping unpleasant reality rather than a vehicle for creating new possibilities. This does not mean, however, that such a life, forged in the imagination, is not a viable mode of existence if one can carry it off. Marlowe spends much of the remainder of the play making us wonder if Tamburlaine can.

The medium through which he poses this question is the moral subplot. The maneuvers of Orcanes of Natolia and Sigismund of Hungary in the first two acts function as rhetorical exempla against which Tamburlaine's later actions are designed to be viewed.[14] As the play opens, the two monarchs meet on the banks of the Danube to conclude the truce they both desire, and Orcanes requests that Sigismund confirm it with an oath. He complies:

> By Him that made the world and sav'd my soul,
> The son of God and issue of a maid,
> Sweet Jesus Christ, I solemnly protest
> And vow to keep this peace inviolable.
>
> (1.1.133–136)

Orcanes swears a similar oath, "By sacred Mahomet, the friend of God," and the two armies retire to their tents to banquet. At the beginning of the second act, Sigismund is urged by Frederick and Baldwin to attack the unsuspecting Orcanes, who has dismissed the bulk of his troops, so that they may be revenged for a recent massacre of Christians. Sigismund's first response is to ask if they have forgotten the treaty just concluded,

> Confirm'd by oath and articles of peace,
> And calling Christ for record of our truths?
> This should be treachery and violence
> Against the grace of our profession.
>
> (2.1.29–32)

Baldwin argues that Christians are not bound to keep faith with infidels, and that a pagan oath is not to be regarded as an assurance of safety anyway. Again Sigismund protests:

> Yet those infirmities that thus defame
> Their faiths, their honors, and their religion
> Should not give us presumption to the like.
>
> (44–46)

14. "An example supports or weakens a case by appeal to precedent or experience, citing some person or historical event" (*De inv.* 1.49, trans. H. M. Hubbell [London, 1949]).

But Frederick, citing dubious Scriptural evidence that Saul and Baalam were punished for refusing to kill the enemies of God,[15] persuades the pious Sigismund to press the advantage he has been given. This is not simply malicious sniping at Christianity by the atheistical Marlowe, but a serious presentation of the ethical issue involved in such perjury. That Marlowe takes the issue seriously is indicated by the quality of Orcanes's speech when he discovers the treachery:

> Can there be such deceit in Christians
> Or treason in the fleshly heart of man,
> Whose shape is figure of the highest god?
> Then if there be a Christ, as Christians say
> But in their deeds deny him for their Christ,
> If he be son to everliving Jove
> And hath the power of his outstretched arm,
> If he be jealous of his name and honor,
> As is our holy prophet, Mahomet,
> Take here these papers as our sacrifice
> And witness of Thy servant's perjury.
> Open, thou shining veil of Cynthia,
> And make a passage from the empyreal heaven
> That he that sits on high and never sleeps,
> Nor in one place is circumscriptible,
> But everywhere fills every continent
> With strange infusion of his sacred vigor,
> May in his endless power and purity,
> Behold and venge this traitor's perjury!
>
> (2.2.36–54)

Sigismund's Christian piety appears prosaic beside this. Here is no Bajazeth rant, but a passionate hymn to divinity that distinguishes bad Christians from worthy Christianity, and links Christ, Jove, and Mahomet in an essentially monotheistic vision. Calling upon Christ for victory, Orcanes leads his men to confront the perfidious Hungarian.

The next image we see is the dying Sigismund, acknowledging that he has been punished for his perjury and attempting to repent before he

15. See Roy Battenhouse, "Protestant Apologetics and the Subplot of 2 *Tamburlaine*," *ELR* 3 (1971): 40.

dies. Orcanes, too, sees in his victory the justice of Christ, and the whole three-scene sequence draws toward its close as a vignette of divine retribution for violence against the godhead. It is not to Marlowe's purpose, however, to present a *didactic* exemplum—he is offering a context for thought rather than an instance in proof—and so he carefully qualifies its effect. When Orcanes asks Gazellus what *he* thinks of their victory, his companion replies:

> 'Tis but fortune of the wars, my lord,
> Whose power is often prov'd a miracle.
>
> (2.3.31-32)

Orcanes, on his side, remains humbly grateful, and vows to continue honoring Christ in his thoughts, "not doing Mahomet an injury."

The episode indicates a major change of concern from Part 1 to Part 2. In Part 1, the "gods" functioned mainly as just so much decorative rhetoric—names to toss about in defiance or indignation. Cosroe, Bajazeth, and Tamburlaine himself swore by the gods and vowed to vindicate them, but there was never any serious interest in probing the implied relationships. Even the rival prayers of Zenocrate and Zabina (3.3.189-200) could not be taken seriously because Bajazeth and his wife presented such ridiculous figures. The first sign that the gods might be taken seriously appeared in Zenocrate's fervent prayer "to mighty Jove and holy Mahomet" (5.1.363) to pardon Tamburlaine, and as we have seen, the tone of her address had changed drastically because Marlowe was deliberately darkening the tragic context of the play.

This change in tone is apparent at the opening of Part 2 and in the subsequent scenes we have examined.[16] Significantly, the earlier linking of Jove and Mahomet by Zenocrate and the Soldan now also becomes common. The epithet "Mahomet, friend of God" is used by Orcanes in vowing fidelity to his truce (1.1.137) and in crowning Callapine

---

16. Douglas Cole characterizes it well: "By opening with this episode [of Orcanes and Sigismund], Marlowe establishes at the very start a broad vision of the universe which looks beyond mere human agency for the source of suffering" (*Suffering and Evil in the Plays of Christopher Marlowe* [Princeton, 1962], p. 115). Although he tends to dismiss the skepticism of Gazelles regarding the outcome of the battle, his treatment of the relationship between this event and Tamburlaine's final malady (p. 116) is tactful.

(3.1.3); Callapine twice refers to the joint revenge of Jove and Mahomet (3.5.55–57, 5.2.11); and even Tamburlaine swears to Jove "By Mahomet, thy mighty friend" (4.1.120). This suggests that Marlowe is attempting to unify the concept of godhead that informs the play, and that the distinction between Christian, Turk, and pagan, which was gleefully exploited in Part 1, is no longer meaningful. The impression is reinforced by the dignified character of the four Turkish kings, who bear no resemblance to Mycetes, Cosroe, and Bajazeth, functioning instead to point up Tamburlaine's increasingly violent behavior.

Their criticism is borne out by Tamburlaine's changed view of himself as the play progresses. Gone is the exhilarating self-creation we admired, even amid its cruelty, in Part 1. In its place is the pursuit of a distinctly punitive role:

> Nor am I made arch-monarch of the world,
> Crown'd and invested by the hand of Jove,
> For deeds of bounty or nobility.
> But, since I exercise a greater name,
> The scourge of God and terror of the world,
> I must apply myself to fit those terms,
> In war, in blood, in death, in cruelty,
> And plague such peasants as resist in me
> The power of heaven's eternal majesty.
>
> (4.1.149–157)

At this point, there is little left of the attractive Tamburlaine. It is not so much that his actions have changed, but rather the spirit in which he carries them out. To be ruthless in the pursuit of nobility is one thing; to be so in the self-assumed role of cosmic executioner is another. The curses of Natolia, Soria, Trebizon, and Jerusalem are not those of the mean-minded Persians and the irascible Turk. They are cries of outrage from the civilized community.

Because of this, the death of Tamburlaine becomes a matter of deep interest. After besieging Babylon, shooting its foolish governor, and drowning every inhabitant in town, he orders a monumental book-burning:

346

> Now, Casane, where's the Turkish Alcoran
> And all the heaps of superstitious books
> Found in the temples of that Mahomet
> Whom I have thought a god? They shall be burnt.
>
> (5.1.171–174)

The speech is deliberately cast to make it sound like an act of apostasy. Tamburlaine, of course, did not believe in Mahomet in Part 1; in Part 2, however, he treated him as one of his household gods, swearing by him and threatening him, as he did Jove. The denial and derision of the present scene, therefore, is new—a direct challenge to one of the prevailing deities of the play to assert his power. And Marlowe links this apparent act of apostasy to Sigismund's by recapitulating verbally and visually Orcanes's supplication of Christ in Act 2:

> Thou, Christ, that art esteem'd omnipotent,
> If thou will prove thy self a perfect God,
> Worthy the worship of all faithful hearts,
> Be now reveng'd upon this traitor's soul. . . .
>
> (2.2.55–58)

Tamburlaine uses much the same language, but on his tongue it echoes the taunts of the Jews to the crucified Christ:

> Now, Mahomet, if thou have any power,
> Come down thyself and work a miracle.
>
> . . . .
>
> Why send'st thou not a furious whirlwind down
> To blow thy Alcoran up to thy throne,
> Where men report thou sitt'st by God himself?
> Or vengeance on the head of Tamburlaine
> That shakes his sword against thy majesty
> And spurns the abstract of thy foolish laws?
>
> (5.1.185–186, 190–195)

The last remark recalls directly Sigismund's spurning of the sanctified treaty, and it becomes apparent that in burning the Koran, Tamburlaine is visibly reenacting Orcanes's presentation to Christ of the violated protocols—"take here these papers as our sacrifice"—which were probably also burned to propitiate divine wrath. In effect, this is an ironic travesty of the scene in Act 2: there, a pious man offered evidence of apostasy and solicited revenge; here, a contemner of the gods blasphemes and dares revenge.[17]

At first, nothing seems to happen, and Tamburlaine, satisfied that his personal god, the god "full of revenging wrath," is the only godhead, prepares to depart for Persia. But then, only fifteen lines after delivering his challenge, he feels himself "distempered suddenly." Whether he is stricken by an avenging deity or simply by natural disease remains unclear;[18] the Sigismund analogy itself, we must recall, was problematic. Marlowe created it to compel consideration of Tamburlaine's ultimate autonomy, which involves not only his ties to mortality but, more importantly, to larger moral concerns. And in prosecuting this final question he seems to have remembered the celebrated Mitys of Aristotle's *Poetics*. This figure appears in that discussion of plot where Aristotle remarks that a tragedy is not simply an imitation of a complete action,

> but also of incidents arousing pity and fear. Such incidents have the very greatest effect on the mind when they occur unexpectedly and at the same time in consequence of one another; there is more of the marvelous in them than if they happened of themselves or by mere chance. Even matters of chance seem most marvelous if there is an appearance of design as it were in them; as for instance the statue of Mitys at Argos killed the author of Mitys' death by falling down on him when a looker-on at a public spectacle; for incidents like that we think not to be without a meaning.[19]

17. Battenhouse has shown that perjury and blasphemy were treated as related sins in Protestant tracts ("Protestant Apologetics," pp. 37–38).

18. Though it has become the subject of unending critical debate. See, for example, Battenhouse, *Marlowe's "Tamburlaine"* (Nashville, 1941), who offers the fullest argument for the case of divine retribution; he is rebutted by Paul Kocher, *Christopher Marlowe* (Chapel Hill, 1946), who considers the Koran episode "one final burst of religious pyrotechnics" in Marlowe's war against religion (p. 87). Irving Ribner, "The Idea of History in Marlowe's *Tamburlaine*, *ELH* 20 (1953): 251–266, maintains that Tamburlaine is overcome simply by his mortality, a view shared by Helen Gardner, "The Second Part of *Tamburlaine the Great*," *MLR* 37 (1942): 18–24, and by Madeline Doran, *Endeavours of Art* (Madison, 1954). Steane more subtly states the case for retribution (pp. 114–115), while Levin remains equivocal (pp. 51–52).

19. *Poet.* 1452a1–11, trans. Ingram Bywater, *The Basic Works of Aristotle*, ed. Richard McKeon (New York, 1941).

Aristotle is suggesting how the playwright may best induce tragic pleasure in the spectator. The emotions constituting this pleasure are described
as pity and fear, which are most strongly aroused by an unexpected, apparently irrational turn of events. But the primary response to this surprising turn of events is wonder—τὸ θαυμαστὸν—which Bywater translates as "the marvelous." The degree of wonder that is felt is measured
not simply by the shock of the unexpected, but precisely by our sense
that the accidental may in fact be purposeful. We are stimulated to make
inferences. A modern Aristotelian scholar provides us with the most useful gloss:

> The marvelous is to be attained *through* rationality, not in defiance
> of it. The events are to be surprising at first glance, or in themselves,
> but the surprise is to come from, and be heightened by, the reflection
> that they are perfectly natural and logical in the light of what went
> before.[20]

The similarity between this concept and Tamburlaine's blasphemy,
apparent reprieve, and sudden distemperature need not be belabored.
We are moved to infer the causality of the event because it follows Tamburlaine's challenge and because we would have it conform to Sigismund's earlier punishment under similar circumstances. We may even
remember the King of Soria's sinister curse—

> May never spirit, vein, or artier feed
> The cursed substance of that cruel heart;
> But, wanting moisture and remorseful blood,
> Dry up with anger and consume with heat
> (4.1.176–179)

—which seems to be realized in the physician's diagnosis of Tamburlaine's illness:

> Your artiers, which alongst the veins convey
> The lively spirits which the heart engenders,
> Are parch'd and void of spirit, that the soul,
> Wanting those organons by which it moves,
> Cannot endure by argument of art.
> (5.3.93–97)

20. G. F. Else, *Aristotle's Poetics: The Argument* (Cambridge, Mass., 1962), p. 332.

The entire episode, with its visual and aural links to the Orcanes-Sigismund sequence, reveals Marlowe's great care to shape our response to the central question of the play, and finally challenges us to act upon the invitation extended in the prologue to Part I. But we do so at our own risk, remembering the equivocal nature of the paradigm.[21]

Whatever *our* speculation, Tamburlaine himself never repents or even acknowledges that he has met an insuperable foe in death. Instead, he triumphs one more time through his own personal mode of accommodation:

> In vain I strive and rail against those powers
> That mean t'invest me in a higher throne,
> As much too high for this disdainful earth.
>
> (120–122)

Visible failure again breeds imagined success, and Tamburlaine's inventive pride overcomes even the limitations of mortality. But the final note is not ironic. Although we may have doubts about the viability of Tamburlaine's imagination, Marlowe prevents any diminution of his hero by recapitulating his entire career, as it were, on the face of Ortelius's map. As Tamburlaine retraces his progress, the old excitement begins to shine through again and he becomes once more the ardent seeker, pushing back the boundaries of possibility:

> Lo, here, my sons, are all the golden mines,
> Inestimable drugs and precious stones,
> More worth than Asia and the world beside;
> And from th'Antarctic Pole eastward behold
> As much more land, which never was descried
> Wherein are rocks of pearl that shine as bright

21. Whether or not Marlowe knew the *Poetics* is, of course, a matter for speculation. By the 1580s it was available both in Latin and in Italian, and the passage in question was also cited in other critical contexts. In any event, he stimulates the act of inference in much the way the author of the *Poetics* suggests, encouraging us to formulate a thesis by which we can understand the events of the play. He differs from Aristotle, however, in the uncertain basis he provides for inference, and this must not be glossed over. It suggests that he was more concerned to elicit wonder than to lead his audience to a conclusion. This is just what we should expect of Marlowe.

> As all the lamps that beautify the sky,
> And shall I die, and this unconquered?
>
> (5.3.151–158)

There is, finally, poignancy in the death of such a hero.

There is also nobility. For in passing the command to Amyras, Tamburlaine now makes manifest that purity of spirit which was only hinted at in his earlier relationship with Zenocrate. Without warning, he is suddenly the chaste sun king, and the dignified Orcanes and Jerusalem are reduced to Phaeton's unruly beasts:

> Scourge and control these slaves,
> Guiding thy chariot with thy father's hand.
> As precious is the charge thou undertak'st
> As that which Clymene's brainsick son did guide,
> When wand'ring Phoebe's ivory cheeks were
> scorch'd,
> And all the earth, like Aetna, breathing fire.
> Be warn'd by him, then; learn with awful eye
> To sway a throne as dangerous as his;
> For if thy body thrive not full of thoughts
> As pure and fiery as Phyteus' beams,
> The nature of these proud rebelling jades
> Will take occasion by the slenderest hair
> And draw thee piecemeal like Hippolytus
> Through rocks more steep and sharp than Caspian
> clifts.
>
> (228–241)

His words suggest that he is handing over to Amyras not merely the reins of state but the care and guidance of the heroic soul itself. Although Phaeton's disastrous ride was frequently allegorized in the Renaissance as a cautionary exemplum for ambitious princes,[22] Tamburlaine is certainly not dissuading his son from ambition here. Rather he is exhorting him to purify his being lest the unruly "nature" of his steeds destroy him. If anything, his language recalls Plato's figure of the soul in the *Phaedrus*. There, a parade of gods and their followers ascends the vault of heaven,

22. Cf. Conti, *Mythologiae*; Alciati, *Emblemata*; Sandys, *Ovid Englished*.

each one in a chariot drawn by two horses. The gods attain the top and behold truth, but many of their followers, because of their recalcitrant charges, do not:

> another now rises, and now sinks, and by reason of her unruly steeds sees in part, but in part sees not. As for the rest, though all are eager to reach the heights and seek to follow, they are not able; sucked down as they travel they trample and tread upon one another, this one striving to outstrip that. . . . Whereupon, with their charioteers powerless, many are lamed, and many have their wings broken, and for all their toiling they are balked, every one, of the full vision of being, and departing therefrom, they feed upon the food of semblance.[23]

It is the lesson that may be drawn from this myth that Tamburlaine wishes to impart to Amyras in his valedictory. For he begins his speech confronting not his son, but the hearse of Zenocrate:

> Now, eyes, enjoy your latest benefit,
> And when my soul hath virtue of your sight,
> Pierce through the coffin and the sheet of gold
> And glut your longings with a heaven of joy.
>
> (224–227)

He is saying that the material vision of which his mortal eyes are now capable will soon be transcended by a spiritual vision that shall penetrate to the real beauty of Zenocrate. And his next words, directed to Amyras, continue the thought: "So reign, my son." Reign, that is, with a transcendent vision, the vision vouchsafed only to the heroic aspirant. Tamburlaine speaks out of experience; he has conducted his own struggle with passion. And while we may have felt *at that time* that his triumph was in some sense a defeat, *now* Marlowe makes us feel no such thing. At this moment, whatever may lie outside the periphery of the heroic vision is unimportant, for the playwright has adduced his final sophistic proof to "place" Tamburlaine in our minds.[24]

23. *Phaedr.* 248b, trans. R. Hackforth, *The Collected Dialogues*, ed. Edith Hamilton and Huntington Cairns (New York, 1961), p. 495.

24. The analogy with Hippolytus in ll. 240–241 reinforces this reading. It does not appear in Ovid, but it does in Seneca's *Phaedra*, where Hippolytus's helpless race along the seashore is compared to Phaeton's ride (1091–1092). His

III

Marlowe's concerns and methods in the intermediate plays bear a strong family resemblance to those in *Tamburlaine*, although the territory he explores is less grand and he exploits more obviously certain recognizable dramatic conventions for his own highly individual ends.[25] In *The Jew of Malta*, he conflates, with bizarre results, the mode of late vice comedy and that of *The Spanish Tragedy*. It is an exercise in wit run wild, first figured forth in the prolocutor Machiavel and afterward in Barabas and his adversaries. Indeed, in this play "there *is* no sin but ignorance"—the ignorance signified by Barabas's failure of wit in the fifth act. Machiavel had warned what happens to people who cast him off when they attain to Peter's chair—when, that is, they begin to trust others and thereby place themselves at their mercy. This is precisely what Barabas does when he realizes that he cannot safely enjoy the political power he has achieved, and decides to ease himself out:

> Barabas, this must be looked into;
> And since by wrong thou gott'st authority,
> Maintain it bravely by firm policy;
> At least, unprofitably lose it not. . . .
>
> (5.2.34–37)[26]

In choosing the second option, he follows his besetting vice, and as a result he ends up in his own boiling kettle. But his is not a case of *moccum moccabitur*, as Heywood would say; the moral of the story is not that vice will be punished but that knavery which looks only to its present good is folly—and that is something quite different.

Marlowe's characterization of Barabas has always been something of a puzzle. In recent years, the Jew has come to be looked upon as a "hybrid vice," a term coined by Spivack and enlarged upon by Bevington.[27] It

---

extraordinary wound—a sharp stake driven through the groin (1098–1100)—symbolizes his destruction by passion.

25. *The Massacre at Paris* has been omitted from this discussion because it survives in too mutilated a state for meaningful analysis.

26. Citations refer to *The Complete Plays*, ed. Irving Ribner (New York, 1963).

27. Bernard Spivack, *Shakespeare and the Allegory of Evil* (New York, 1958), pp. 346–353; David Bevington, *From Mankind to Marlowe* (Cambridge, Mass., 1962), pp. 218–233.

is a useful way to account for the strangely contradictory aspects of his behavior. The only problem with this concept is that while it acknowledges that a layering of greater psychological complexity has been imposed upon Barabas, and thus *seems* to free itself from a strictly homiletic interpretation of his actions, it still insists upon the presence of an *unchanging* alter ego beneath or beside the secular layer. Therefore it does not really allow a flexible view of his function in the play. Inevitably his un-Vice-like behavior ends up being characterized as deception.[28] Without questioning the obvious Vice-like qualities that *are* his, I think that we can refine this view of him—and consequently liberate ourselves from the restrictions that the designation suggests—if we approach the play in the light of Marlowe's sophistic habits of composition.

The first image we have of Barabas is that of the usurious Jew diligently counting his treasure. But as the initial monologue proceeds, an unexpected tone enters. Barabas scorns the "paltry silverings" of the traders with whom he has just dealt:

> Give me the merchants of the Indian mines
> That trade in metal of the purest mold,
> The wealthy Moor that in the eastern rocks
> Without control can pick his riches up
> And in his house heap pearl like pebble-stones,
> Receive them free, and sell them by the weight.
> Bags of fiery opals, sapphires, amethysts,
> Jacinths, hard topaz, grass-green emeralds,
> Beauteous rubies, sparkling diamonds. . . .
> (1.1.19–27)

This is the old Tamburlaine vein, in which glittering images lift the speaker out of the moralistic emblem in which he has been placed, and deposit him, somewhat disconcertingly, upon "the sweet felicity of an

28. See Bevington's discussion of the taxation scene and its aftermath (pp. 224–225). Although he concedes that Barabas reveals "something far more subtle and lifelike than the type of unrepentant Worldly Man," he goes on to say, "Nevertheless the need for providing motivation should not obscure the purely Vice-like conception of Barabas' original character" (p. 225). He is not speaking here of Barabas's dramatic origins, but of his underlying *nature*, which is, by virtue of his designation, evil.

earthly crown." In this case, the hero's aspiration is ultimately to enclose "infinite riches in a little room"—the same parody of Christ *in utero* that we encountered in the sales pitch of *The Four PP*.[29] There, however, it was an inside joke which could be enjoyed from the vantage point of a moral norm. In this play, where no moral norm is ever firmly established (although there is one good person in it), the point of the joke is not clear. The phrase may not even be a joke at all, but may have acquired a validity all its own, for Barabas's obsession is as great as Tamburlaine's was. Thus we must suspend moral judgment until we can better perceive the concomitants of such an obsession, as we did in the case of Tamburlaine.

These begin to be apparent in Barabas's speech following his interview with the two merchants. Here he reveals that he is hated for his wealth, but that it is the only source of dignity available in the world he inhabits:

> Rather had I, a Jew, be hated thus
> Than pitied in a Christian poverty;
> For I can see no fruits in all their faith,
> But malice, falsehood, and excessive pride,
> Which methinks fits not their profession.
>
> (1.1.112–116)

It is, he claims, an amoral world anyway, and material comforts are the only security. Although his words reveal his own characteristic concern for tangible profit, what he says of Christian behavior is borne out by the action of virtually every Christian in the play. To squeeze money from the Jewish inhabitants of Malta, the Governor employs the casuistry that Malta has been afflicted for its tolerance of Hebrews, "who stand accursed in the sight of heaven" (1.2.64). Mathias's mother, who should profess charity, refuses even to speak with Barabas because "he is cast off from heaven" (2.3.156). Friar Barnardine violates the sacrament of confession (4.1.48) and Friar Jacomo promises Barabas an easy life in his strict religious order if only the Jew wills it his money. Even Lodowick and Mathias are quite unconcerned with the impropriety of courting Abigail when she is a novice in the nunnery (2.1.387)—a venial sin, but typical of the disparity between profession and action in the Christian community. That the Turks are not really any better is indicated by the

29. See Ch. IV, p. 120.

foreclosure tactics with which they initiate the action of the play.[30] The fact is that Barabas is quite right about the moral atmosphere in Malta, as Abigail observes unequivocally:

> But I perceive there is no love on earth,
> Pity in Jews, nor piety in Turks.
>
> (3.3.47–48)

In this light, the dramatic cue provided by Barabas's religious allusion becomes quite clear: it tells us that Marlowe is examining the condition of people who have forgotten the moral referents of their language.[31] As a result, the rhetoric of imagination and the rhetoric of reason are used without check to pursue the desire of the moment, for right and wrong have become purely subjective concepts. Thus at one moment Barabas can comfort his fellow Jews at the news of the Turkish embassy—

> Why let 'em come, so they come not to war,
> Or let 'em come, so we be conquerors,

and then add in an aside:

> Nay, let 'em combat, conquer, and kill all,
> So they spare me, my daughter, and my wealth.
>
> (1.1.148–151)

Or, more interestingly, he can defend his cause before Ferneze with the most apparent sincerity—

> What, bring you Scripture to confirm your wrongs?
> Preach me not out of my possessions.

30. This impression of their character is reinforced by the First Knight's remark in 2.2: "This truce we have is but in hope of gold" (26), and confirmed in the Bashaw's greeting to Ferneze in 3.5:

> FERNEZE: What wind drives you thus into Malta road?
> BASHAW: The wind that bloweth all the world besides,
>   Desire of gold.   (2–4)

31. The phenomenon recurs repeatedly. See, for example, the allusion to "Iphigen," 1.1.134–135; to the shepherd watching over his flocks, 2.1.39–42; to "the first beginner of my bliss," 2.1.50. For more examples, see Wilbur Sanders, *The Dramatist and The Received Idea* (Cambridge, 1968), pp. 38–60. His chapter on *The Jew* is detailed and sensitive to the issues raised in the play.

> Some Jews are wicked, as all Christians are;
> But say the tribe that I descended of
> Were all in general cast away for sin,
> Shall I be tried by their transgression?
> The man that dealeth righteously shall live.
> And which of you can charge me otherwise?

—only to be soundly refuted by Ferneze, who recognizes a pleader of his own stamp and can offer him a counter-argument in kind:

> Out, wretched Barabas!
> Sham'st thou not thus to justify thyself,
> As if we knew not thy profession?
> If thou rely upon thy righteousness,
> Be patient, and thy riches will increase.
> Excess of wealth is cause of covetousness,
> And covetousness, O, 'tis a monstrous sin.

Significantly, Barabas does not deny the charge implied: usurious extortion. Instead, he answers Ferneze's sanctimonious rebuke with a serious counter-claim:

> Ay, but theft is worse. Tush, take not from me then,
> For that is theft. And if you rob me thus,
> I must be forced to steal and compass more.
>
> $(1.2.111-128)$

This is a *disputatio* of thieves, and each knows it. To defend his cause, Barabas first demands, as the Plowman did in *Gentleness and Nobility*, that Ferneze keep holy writ out of the debate. He then offers a proposition in which he attempts to differentiate himself from "bad" Jews. Next, granting for the moment that all Jews were historically damned, he questions whether he must be judged by their legacy, and confirms the question with a pious *sententia*. The technique is familiar to us, but the fact is, as Ferneze shows, that while his argument is good it is not founded on reality. This does not mean that the Jew is without a real grievance; he *is* being victimized, but his Jewishness is simply the medium of his victimization, as it is of his defense: at base, he is not the man he pretends to be.[32]

32. This distinction between argument and reality is explored more subtly in

The foregoing suggests that Marlowe is not so much concerned to expose the sham grievances of a "universalized genius of evil"[33] as to explore the ramifications of an invention thoroughly liberated from conventional morality. At present, the product is pure sophistry, in which differences are finally resolved not by reason but by brute force.

The progressive pattern of the debate between Barabas and the Governor reflects verbally the pattern of action in the play: one moral outrage committed in self-interest is countered by another until only Ferneze survives, the surprised beneficiary of Barabas's lapsed policy. In this respect, *The Jew of Malta* resembles *The Spanish Tragedy* with Hieronimo strangely metamorphosed. The Governor's action against Barabas incites the Jew to revenge by murdering his son; when Abigail discovers the murder, her repentant departure to the nunnery persuades Barabas that she will reveal his crime to the Christians, and he attempts to circumvent this by poisoning her; she confesses, however, before she dies, thus leaving Barabas prey to the avaricious friars whom he attempts to control, first through bribery and then through murder. Ithamore, Barabas's accomplice in these crimes, then turns on him, and his efforts to dispose of *him* bring Barabas into Ferneze's power.

It is at this juncture that Marlowe symbolizes the vapidity of all this witplay by rescuing Barabas through the agency of a sleeping potion. His astonishing recovery after being thrown from the walls of the palace of Malta instantly reduces the action to farce, and the intricate double plot which he engineers first with Calymath the Turk and then with the Governor himself, is simply an extension of the new mode. Although this last episode has been seen as the final stage in degeneration of the morality play's Worldly Man, the degree of the change—not only from the seriousness of the first three scenes, but also from the witty melodrama of the central section of the play—suggests rather one of those sophistic shifts that we have observed in *Tamburlaine* and other tragedies of the nineties. It is made so that we can clearly perceive the radical folly of Barabas's activity.

The technique is not new to this play. It first appeared in Barabas's opening soliloquy, as he apotheosized worldly gain. Then, at the be-

the court scene of *The Merchant of Venice*, where the satirical tone has disappeared but the perception, I believe, remains much the same.

33. Bevington, p. 226.

ginning of Act 2, having cunningly plotted the theft of his hidden treasure from the newly founded nunnery, he suddenly enters, speaking the language of the restless malcontent:

> Thus, like the sad presaging raven that tolls
> The sick man's passport in her hollow beak,
> And in the shadow of the silent night
> Doth shake contagion from her sable wings,
> Vexed and tormented runs poor Barabas
> With fatal curses toward these Christians.
> The uncertain pleasures of swift-footed time
> Have ta'en their flight and left me in despair,
> And of my former riches rests no more
> But bare remembrance, like a soldier's scar
> That has no further comfort for his maim.
>
> (2.1.1–11)

The speech is about the loss of mere money, but the rhetoric creates a moving impression of a man profoundly suffering the effects of fortune's mutability. The homely simile of the scar adds a deft touch of pathos, and the prayer to the God of Israel that follows removes the speech from the realm of parody. We are meant *in this instance* to feel the sorrows of a Barabas who is no longer fortune's favorite. The technique is familiar to us from Lodge's treatment of Marius in *The Wounds of Civil War*, but here the vignette is thematically related to Marlowe's larger inquiry: profound suffering at the loss of mere money *is* the concomitant of living as Barabas says he does: *Ego mihimet sum semper proximus* (1.1.187).

When Barabas next appears at the beginning of 2.3, he is yet a different figure. Now, having regained his wealth and come to an apparent understanding with Ferneze, he confides in the audience that he is secretly plotting revenge against the governor and his son, and reveals a hitherto unsuspected biography:

> I learned in Florence how to kiss my hand,
> Heave up my shoulders when they call me dog,
> And duck as low as any barefoot friar. . . .
>
> (2.3.23–25)

He expands upon this only a few moments later in his interview with Ithamore:

> As for myself, I walk abroad 'a nights
> And kill sick people groaning under walls.
>
> . . . .
>
> Being young, I studied physic and began
> To practice first upon the Italian.
>
> . . . .
>
> And after that I was an engineer,
>
> . . . .
>
> Then after that I was an usurer. . . .
>
> (171ff.)

Bevington points out quite rightly that Barabas could not possibly have enjoyed so diversified a career, and that Marlowe is drawing here upon the generalized history of the Vice-cum-machiavel. But it is necessary to distinguish this local characterization and its function from the total character of Barabas if we are to follow Marlowe's looser speculation. Here he is clearly an evil Vice. But through most of the play it is not his evil character Marlowe is interested in; it is his *lack* of character, because —like Diccon before him—he exists in an essentially amoral universe. In such a situation he is whatever he chooses to be, and his comic degeneration exhibits the final emptiness of a wit uninformed by broad ethical concerns. It is the tragic counterpart of the phenomenon with which Chapman amused us in *All Fools*, and in many respects prefigures Jonson's preoccupation in *Volpone*, whose wily protagonist also reveals a profound moral void. Both Marlowe and Jonson's characters may be Vice-like, but they have outgrown the general designation and reflect the larger worries of a critically sophisticated generation of poets.

If *The Jew of Malta* offers an amusing yet serious glimpse of the grayer aspects of Tamburlainian *ethopoeia*, *Edward II* is a drama very much *engagé*. One senses immediately that the critical detachment of *The Jew*, and even the admiring but generally circumspect attitude in *Tamburlaine*, is gone. Marlowe is very deeply involved with Edward—cognizant of his failures, yet far more sympathetic toward him than his actions warrant—and in the last acts of the play he creates for him a first-person voice that explores its condition with an amplitude not granted to any previous character.

The central issue in the play is the consciousness behind the voice. Its characteristic impulse is described by Edward's most implacable enemy, Roger Mortimer, in the fourth scene. Here, after the barons have re-called Gaveston at the Queen's behest, the elder Mortimer counsels his nephew to be more tolerant of the King, and cites a long list of venerable masculine friendships to show that Edward's private peccadillo need not preclude honorable conduct. But Mortimer Junior replies that it is not the King's homosexuality that bothers him:

> But this I scorn, that one so basely born
> Should by his sovereign's favor grow so pert
> And riot it with the treasure of the realm,
> While soldiers mutiny for want of pay;
> He wears a lord's revenue on his back,
> And Midas-like he jets it in the court,
> With base outlandish cullions at his heels,
> Whose proud fantastic liveries make such show,
> As if that Proteus, god of shapes, appeared;
> I have not seen a dapper jack so brisk.
> He wears a short Italian hooded cloak
> Larded with pearl, and in his Tuscan cap
> A jewel of more value than the crown;
> While others walk below, the king and he
> From out a window laugh at such as we
> And flout our train and jest at our attire.
>
> (1.4.402–417)[34]

The speech starts out as the conventional complaint of the proud noble against the commoner exalted by the king, but quickly Mortimer betrays his real discontent. It is not just that the royal treasury is being drained: public monies are being spent on *clothes*—actually *costumes*—employed in a theatrical display that permits the wearer to disguise his real-life identity and recreate himself in whatever shape he pleases. Even more infuriating, these fantastical players reverse the usual relationship of actor and audi-

34. Citations refer to the New Mermaid edition of W. Moelwyn Merchant (London, 1967).

ence and amuse themselves by making fun of their earth-bound spectators. The final image of the high window from which Edward and Gaveston overpeer Mortimer and his followers fuses the theme of social rise
with which the speech began and the vision of purely imaginative self-
liberation toward which it soon moved, reinforcing the impression that
it is the King's scornful retreat into his friend's private scenarios that really disturbs Mortimer.

In one sense, this is the familiar hostility of the practical man of affairs
toward the inveterate dreamer. But Mortimer's unwavering hatred of
Edward suggests something deeper—the resistance of the moral world
to any departure from "the way things are": a man has his place, and
only in his imagination—and at his own risk—does he rise above it.
Mortimer himself is a good citizen of this world until he, too, begins to
have exalted notions of his capacities. The moment can be designated
quite clearly:

> What Mortimer! can ragged stony walls
> Immure thy virtue that aspires to heaven?
> No, Edward, England's scourge, it may not be;
> Mortimer's hope surmounts his fortune far.
>
> (3.3.70–74)

This is the opening declaration in an ascent that sees gentle Mortimer
transformed into an evil genius, and that ultimately ends in a high fall.[35]
What Marlowe seems to be suggesting here is that imaginative roman-
ticism and "inventive pride" are two faces of the same tragic activity,
and that different men will take the paths their natures dictate but the
quotidian world will reassert itself in either case.

In this play, his interest clearly lies in Edward's activity, for he goes to
a great deal of trouble to shape our attitude toward him, and expends no
imaginative power upon Mortimer's *virtù*. Edward is a curious mixture
of Mycetes, Tamburlaine, and Calyphas. Like the ineffectual Persian king,
he is a poor public speaker. When he commands, one of his favorite

---

35. Though the change in Mortimer's character has been much debated, its
reality may be seen by comparing Edward's reluctant admission in the second act
that "the people love him [Mortimer] well" (2.2.234) and Mortimer's gloating
remark at the height of his power, "Feared am I more than loved, let me be
feared" (5.4.51).

locutions is a combined optative-conditional phrase—"I would wish you grant," "I would wish thee reconcile" (1.1.119, 1.5.156)—which double-distances him from the imperative mood one expects of a king and reveals his inclination to retire from the field of conflict. Like Tamburlaine, he is continually expressing his will—"I will have Gaveston" (1.1.95)—but lacking force, it has the ring of petulance rather than assertion. Like Calyphas, his tastes betray a languid cosmic indecorum:

> Music and poetry is his delight,
>
> . . . .
>
> And in the day when he shall walk abroad,
> Like sylvan nymphs my pages shall be clad,
> My men like satyrs grazing on the lawns
> Shall with their goat feet dance an antic hay;
> Sometime a lovely boy in Dian's shape,
> With hair that gilds the water as it glides,
> Crownets of pearl about his naked arms,
> And in his sportful hands an olive-tree
> To hide those parts which men delight to see,
> Shall bathe him in a spring. . . .
>
> (1.1.53, 56–65)

Unlike Calyphas's hermaphrodism, however, the objects of Edward's delight are presented as attractive and piquant; in the penultimate line quoted above, one has even lost track of whether it is male or female genitalia which men delight to see, for the emphasis is on change and fluidity rather than perversion, in an imaginative universe that escapes the insistent demands of the ordinary world for clarity, definition, and hierarchy.

The central contention between Edward and his nobles, then, is envisioned by Marlowe not as a political or even a strictly moral issue; for all the rancor between them there is remarkably little discussion concerning the duties of kings and their subjects.[36] Essentially, the conflict remains one between willful, mean-minded peers determined to preserve

---

36. This anomaly is remarked by most commentators. See, for example, Clifford Leech, "Marlowe's 'Edward II': Power and Suffering," *CritQ* 1 (1959): 181–196; Sanders, *Dramatist*; E. M. Waith, "Edward II: The Shadow of Action," *TDR* 8 (1964): 59–76.

their ancient prerogatives and a willful king jealous of his right to feed his fantasies, at whatever cost to others.

If this were all there were to it, however, *Edward II* would not be so interesting or troubling a play, for the narrow interests of the barons would tend to justify the King's own self-indulgences which—superficially, at least—are far more attractive. What concerns Marlowe here is not simply Edward's talent for imaginative withdrawal, but the quality of his imagination. It is first indicated in Edward's greeting to Gaveston when he returns from France:

> Now let the treacherous Mortimers conspire,
> And that high-minded Earl of Lancaster;
> I have my wish, in that I joy thy sight,
> And sooner shall the sea o'erwhelm my land
> Than bear the ship that shall transport thee hence.
> I here create thee Lord High Chamberlain,
> Chief Secretary to the State and me,
> Earl of Cornwall, King and Lord of Man.
>
> (1.1.148–155)

Edward's figurative destruction of his kingdom, followed by so frivolous a distribution of titles, sounds more like the dialogue of a child's game than the speech of a reigning monarch, and shocks his brother Kent into protest. That the nature of his activity with Gaveston is perhaps exactly this is again implied a few scenes later in his desperate offer to the barons:

> Make several kingdoms of this monarchy
> And share it equally amongst you all,
> So I may have some nook or corner left
> To frolic with my dearest Gaveston.
>
> (1.4.70–73)

When asked why he loves the universally detested Gaveston, he replies:

> Because he loves me more than all the world.
>
> (77)

With this remark, it becomes apparent that Edward's desire to retreat into the fantasies that Gaveston supplies is actually regression into a child's world of security and narcissistic play. His passion for masquerade, for fluid shapes and shows, represents not so much a transcendent metaphorical sensibility as it does a comfortable relapse into irresponsible prelogical thought.[37]

It is disquieting that in this third, possibly fourth, examination of invention, Marlowe should see it as the instrument of childish wish-fulfillment, but it is symptomatic of the growing skepticism concerning the viability of imagination that we have seen gradually infusing his work. Edward's imaginative activity is not only puerile in motive, but also in scope. Beyond helping him to envision a frolic with Gaveston, it cannot take him anywhere. Instead, it is forever hemming him in. The "nook or corner" image is our first glimpse of this shrunken world. But later, when once again threatened by the barons, Edward declares:

> Do what they can, we'll live in Tynemouth here,
> And so I walk with him about the walls,
> What care I though the earls begirt us round?
>
> (2.2.220–222)

And in a pattern precisely the reverse of that in *Tamburlaine*, Edward's restricted imaginings lead him to actual restriction in Killingworth castle. Here he speaks pathetically of his "dauntless" mind, which

> The ambitious Mortimer would seek to curb
> And that unnatural queen, false Isabel,
> That thus hath pent and mew'd me in a prison.
>
> (5.1.16–18)

But his mind has always been a self-limiting instrument, and now he finds himself exactly where it has been taking him all along.

It is here, in fact, that the final poverty of Edward's imagination is revealed. Leicester suggests a traditional *consolatio*:

> Be patient, good my lord, cease to lament;
> Imagine Killingworth Castle were your court,

---

37. This is not simply a post-Freudian distinction, as may be seen in the folly of young Moros, the hero of W. Wager's *The Longer Thou Livest The More Fool Thou Art*. The nonsense songs and doggerel babble he spouts are creditable imitations of the infantile imagination. The tradition of the unteachable wit that informs this play may well have infiltrated Marlowe's thinking.

> And that you lay for pleasure here a space,
> Not of compulsion or necessity.
>
> (1-4)

But Edward can imagine no such thing, though Kent is quite capable of doing so when he comes to visit him later:

> Where is the court but here, here is the king. . . .
>
> (5.3.59)

Instead, Edward miserably remarks,

> Leicester, if gentle words might comfort me,
> Thy speeches long ago had eased my sorrows. . . .
>
> (5.1.5-6)

And he explains that a wounded lion does not heal itself but vexes further its own flesh, leaping into the air to complain to the gods. It is a serviceable enough image to maintain one's self-esteem, but even as he uses it he admits that the simile is not working for him, because he always remembers that as a king he should take revenge, not simply plead for help:

> But what are kings when regiment is gone
> But perfect shadows in a sunshine day?
>
> (26-27)

The awful disparity between words and reality lies dismally before him. As he contemplates this emptiness, he retreats once again into himself, and the very sequence of his thoughts reveals a collapse toward the only reality he knows:

> My nobles rule, I bear the name of king;
> I wear the crown but am controlled by them,
> By Mortimer and my unconstant queen,
> Who spots my nuptial bed with infamy,
> Whilst I am lodged within this cave of care,
> Where sorrow at my elbow still attends
> To company my heart with sad laments,
> That bleeds within me for this strange exchange.
>
> (28-35)

Deep, deeper, deepest. It is the imagination of the Chinese box.

As we might expect, it is not only spatially limited, but ethically undeveloped as well. Although his heart may be an anvil unto sorrow, at no time does Edward hammer out an insight into his problem, as Shakespeare's Richard does. And this is because his sin is ultimately not a moral or political matter, but one of consciousness. The limited imagination cannot discover its own insufficiencies. All it can do is attempt to preserve its illusions. This is why Edward's mind keeps circling unsuccessfully around the image of the crown. He first conjures the sun to halt the coming of night that he may keep the diadem eternally, but then notices that "day's bright beams doth vanish fast away" (69). He attempts to regain his old sense of mastery by placing the crown on his head once more, but perceives that no one cringes. His only comfort is the familiar feeling of the crown as it rests there—a purely sensible consolation which reveals better than anything else that his ultimate failure as a king was that he had no *idea* of kingship. This characterization is deliberate on Marlowe's part. He had a fine example in Holinshed of an Edward who admitted that "he was fallen into this miserie through his owne offences, and therefore he was contented paciently to suffer it. . . ."[38] But he did not use it. His Edward, the major representative of imagination in the play, cannot win through to such self-awareness; he reaches only a dull blank, asking pitifully,

> how have I transgressed
> Unless it be with too much clemency?
> (122–123)

Paradoxically, the more he exhibits his blindness the more sympathetic this child king appears, which suggests that Marlowe understood his problem and forgave him it. That he could make us sympathize as well —if not, perhaps, to the same degree—is the achievement of a most intricate dramaturgy. Marlowe's chief avenue to this goal is his conception of Edward as victim. In the first part of the play, when Edward is acting so irrationally toward the peers and so heartlessly to Isabella, Marlowe depends primarily upon the figure of Gaveston to maintain in us a modicum of sympathy for his protagonist. It is clear that Gaveston exploits

38. *The Chronicles of England, Scotlande, and Irelande* (London, 1577), p. 882, quoted by Cole, *Suffering and Evil.*

Edward's desperate need for love. His opening speech reveals a strange mingling of devotion and cupidity, but significantly the latter comes first:

> What greater bliss can hap to Gaveston
> Than live and be the favourite of a king?
> Sweet prince I come; these, thy amorous lines
> Might have enforced me to have swum from France.
> And like Leander gasped upon the sand,
> So thou wouldst smile and take me in thy arms.
>
> (1.1.4–9)

So, too, his proposed entertainments, fitted to Edward's delight, are designed to "draw the pliant king which way I please" (52). If Gaveston appears sinister to the barons, he is calculated by Marlowe to appear so to us as well. Playing upon Edward's instinctive jealousy of the aggressive Mortimer, he feeds his fears of Isabella's infidelity until Edward's distrust literally "suggests" her into the arms of her importunate suitor.

Edward's love for Gaveston, though perverse, is real, and commands compassion. So does his loyalty to the Spencers in the second part of the play. Their relationship, which is not marked by the sexual overtones of the first, broadens our view of this man who feels so keenly the value of friends. When he is captured at Neath Abbey, he offers his own life if only his companions may go free:

> Here man, rip up this panting breast of mine
> And take my heart in rescue of my friends.
>
> (4.6.66–67)

And when he is being degraded in puddle water he consoles himself by considering it just requital for the deaths of friends who lost their lives for his sake.

Marlowe's development of these relationships constitutes what we might call a mimetic approach to persuasion, since he guides our attitude toward the protagonist by revealing the psychological agencies that inform his actions. But there are other, obviously "artificial" elements that affect us also. One of these is Edward's sudden conflict with the Holy See. His attack upon the Bishop of Coventry is ruthless and somewhat absurd, since he makes Gaveston Lord Bishop in his place. The nobles, who up to this point have appeared to be right-minded men, are aghast at the action, and join with the Bishop of Canterbury to banish Gaveston. When Edward refuses to heed their request, the Bishop demands that he subscribe to the decree "on your allegiance to the see of Rome." Mortimer inelegantly translates the religious and moral issue involved here into the harshest political terms—

> Curse him if he refuses, and then may we
> Depose him and elect another king.
>
> (1.4.54–55)

—and Edward is forced to capitulate, lest the Bishop discharge the nobles of their duty to him. As a result, we discover that the wrong-headed, despotic king has suddenly become a Protestant martyr:

> Why should a king be subject to a priest?
> Proud Rome, that hatchest such imperial grooms,
> For these thy superstitious taperlights,
> Wherewith thy antichristian churches blaze,
> I'll fire thy crazed buildings and enforce
> The papal towers to kiss the lowly ground. . . .
>
> (96–101)

It is the traditional sophistic vignette. The speech clearly caters to the most vulgar Elizabethan prejudices, and is calculated to make Edward appear victimized from yet another quarter at a time when the audience is hardly likely to feel kindness toward him. Exploited by his friend, opposed without understanding by his nobles, he is now the prey of the hated Roman Church. The opposition is deliberately painted in the most glaring colors so that the really serious issue involved will not be looked into. What is important at this juncture is to restore a degree of sympathy for the King.

A similar function is served by the short scene between Spencer and Baldock, who are being groomed by the playwright as Gaveston's replacements. Marlowe lets us know what kind of men they are beforehand so that we have no doubt that they, too, will be cankers upon the royal oak. Thus Spencer catechizes Baldock:

you must cast the scholar off
And learn to court it like a gentleman;
'Tis not a black coat and a little band, [but]
A velvet-caped cloak, faced before with serge,
And smelling to a nosegay all the day,
Or holding of a napkin in your hand,

. . . .

Can get you any favour with great men.
You must be proud, bold, pleasant, resolute,
And now stab as occasion serves.

(2.1.31–36, 41–43)

Yet in the scene at Neath Abbey, there is no trace of this cynicism:

Oh is he gone? is noble Edward gone,
Parted from hence, never to see us more?
Rent, sphere of heaven, and fire, forsake thy orb,
Earth melt to air, gone is my sovereign,
Gone, gone alas, never to make return.

(4.6.99–103)

Spoken out of Edward's presence, these overwrought words are meant not to flatter him, but to persuade us of the immensity of the speaker's loss. That Spencer's "character" can change so drastically reveals that his relationship to Edward is literally a rhetorical construction designed to affect *our* response.

The same method is applied to the characterization of Mortimer, rising to power in the political vacuum left by Edward. Rather than show, as Shakespeare does in Bolingbroke, a man gradually succumbing to the pressures of political existence and committing a crime he had probably not dreamt of earlier, Marlowe produces an instant machiavel. Harry Levin, examining this phenomenon, remarks that "Somewhere, conceivably during his short imprisonment in the Tower, Mortimer has picked up his sudden flair for disguises, equivocating letters, and other ruses of Machiavellianism."[39] But we need not attempt to locate exactly where or when Mortimer acquired the tools of his new trade. It suited Marlowe's purposes to use the shorthand of machiavel both to inform the audience

39. *The Overreacher*, p. 100.

of Mortimer's emergence as a ruthless political realist and to exploit the
evil associations of the image to increase our sympathy for Edward. Edward, as we have seen, changes not a whit, but only reveals more fully
the dead end of his understanding. It is the world around him that changes,
and while this change comes about for valid psychological and political
reasons, the felt need to maintain a tragic focus upon the King leads
Marlowe to employ rhetorical devices which may be counted upon to
produce reliable results in his behalf.

As a consequence, the figure of Mortimer, a would-be Tamburlaine,
is considerably reduced. But his "inventive pride"—manifested in such
simple-minded devices as the unpointed letter and in his mechanical
rant—

> The prince I rule, the queen I do command,
> And with a lowly congé to the ground
> The proudest lords salute me as I pass
>
> (5.4.47–49)

—is simply the more obviously rhetorical counterpart of the King's own
diminished consciousness. He is, in his own way, quite the appropriate
foil. As Edward before him, he frames his fall in a conventional tragic
attitude that requires no self-examination. Edward had sought comfort
in a *de casibus* vision; Mortimer finds it in Machiavellian fatalism. Like
Edward, he goes to his death without any insight into his own condition:

> Base fortune, now I see, that in thy wheel
> There is a point to which when men aspire
> They tumble headlong down; that point I touched
> And seeing there was no place to mount up higher
> Why should I grieve at my declining fall?
>
> (5.6.59–63)

If the world of *Edward II* does not seem to have room for very high
flights of the imagination, neither does it admit any inner discovery space.
Its atmosphere is distinctly claustrophobic.

IV

With *Edward*, Marlowe has arrived at the threshold of *Doctor Faustus*,
a drama whose universe is both congruent with and contiguous to the

individual imagination. This means, in effect, that it has become para-doxically *reduced* to the limits of human invention. Ultimately, Faustus's exhilarating assertion that the dominion of the magician "stretcheth as far as doth the mind of man" becomes a profoundly ironic epigraph, for the reaches of human wit prove to be astonishingly short. This is not only revealed in the protagonist's speech and actions, but it is also re-flected in the structure itself, where for the first time Marlowe reverts to the moral frame technique of the older drama, so that his action proper is "contained" in a way that it has never been before.

Although this frame appears un-Marlovian in sentiment—conservative, even harsh[40]—it would perhaps be more accurate to describe it as the thesis-seeking element in the play. For the Chorus appeals to our "pa-tient judgments" while it performs "the form of Faustus' fortunes, good or bad"—indicating that judgment *will* be sought, though only when the full story is known. Then, in the manner of an advocate delivering his *narratio*, it proceeds to outline Faustus's case. The narration is qualified by *colores*: the defendant is "swollen with cunning of a self-conceit," "glutted" with learning's gifts, surfeited upon "cursed necromancy." The description sounds highly prejudicial, but when we encounter Faus-tus in his study a few moments later, we find it not entirely unjustified, for Faustus himself uses much the same language. What is missing in his speech is the ethical interpretation, for that is not *his* concern. The per-spective of the Chorus, therefore, is not nearly so myopic as it is in *The Spanish Tragedy*. This is because Marlowe has created a more conven-tional legal structure, in which thesis and hypothesis serve different func-tions, but do not reflect ironically upon one another. While in the action proper, Marlowe provides evidence of character, motivation, and ex-tenuating circumstances—indulging in the detailed and sensitive exami-nation that hypotheses allow—through the Chorus he submits this in-formation to "patient judgments" so that an appropriate thesis may be drawn. The two procedures are different in aim, tone, and emphasis, as they must be. But they are not—as we shall see—necessarily incompati-ble, given Marlowe's view of Faustus's problem.

As Faustus reviews the four major fields of scholarship that have con-

40. A recent editor, Roma Gill, remarks that "the Epilogue, with its cosy smug-ness, is bitterly inadequate" (The New Mermaid edition [New York, 1965], p. xxvii).

stituted his academic endeavors, what disturbs him most is their contingency:

> Is to dispute well logic's chiefest end?
> Affords this art no greater miracle?

A deeper subject fitteth Faustus's wit, and so he turns to physic. But medicine aims only at preserving the body's health:

> Couldst thou make men to live eternally,
> Or being dead raise them to life again,
> Then this profession were to be esteem'd.

He has already, he claims, eased a thousand desperate maladies,[41] and impatiently goes on to Justinian. But law, too, is a contingent science:

> *Exhereditare filium non potest pater, nisi—*
>
> . . . .
> Too servile and illiberal for me.
>
> (1.8–9, 24–26, 31, 36)[42]

Each discipline represents a category of knowledge that can help man to manage his present condition, but not to make any essential change in it. A useful gloss upon Faustus's response to these arts is provided by Sidney's discussion of what he calls "serving sciences" in the *Apology for Poetry*. Each of these has "the works of Nature for his principall object, without which they could not consist, and on which they so depend, as they become Actors and Players, as it were of what Nature will have set forth." Thus, "The Lawyer saith what men have determined . . . the Rhethorician and Logitian, considering what in Nature will soonest prove and persuade, thereon give artificiall rules, which still are compassed within the circle of a question, according to the proposed matter. The phisitian waigheth the nature of a mans bodie, and the nature of things helpful or hurtefull unto it."[43] What all these sciences have in common is their dependence upon man's experience of the phenomenal world. Their sys-

---

41. The verb is the A-text's, which expresses more fitly than the B-text's "cur'd" the frustratingly palliative nature of his achievement.

42. Citations refer to scene and line numbers in John D. Jump's edition (London, 1962).

43. *Elizabethan Critical Essays*, ed. G. Gregory Smith (Oxford, 1904), 1. 155, 156.

tems of knowledge are built upon the epistemological capacity of fallen humanity, and this hampers them from fulfilling the end of every art: "to lead and draw us to as high a perfection as our degenerate soules, made worse by theyre clayey lodgings, can be capable of."[44] For the arts, as Christian commentators from Augustine to Milton repeatedly assert, were given to man to help restore him to his prelapsarian state. According to Sidney, the art that can best achieve this goal is poetry, because the poet is not dependent upon nature; indeed, "he goeth hand in hand with Nature, not inclosed within the narrow warrant of her guifts, but freely ranging onely within the Zodiack of his owne wit." Through the power of his poetical invention, he is freed from the obscuring force of natural phenomena and can perceive an ideal world, in the fullness of truth.[45]

Now Faustus has opened with a similar interest in liberation. Finding each of the traditional academic disciplines subject to fallen nature—divinity especially, which promises not restoration, but death—he turns to magic. What is particularly interesting here is that the clarifying power attributed to the poet by Sidney is the exact analogue of the power of the magician, who "brings forth into the open the miracles concealed in the recesses of the world, in the depths of nature, and in the storehouse and mysteries of God," just as if he himself were their maker.[46] And curiously, Faustus uses the Horatian formula always associated with poetry—"O what a world of profit and delight"—to describe the rewards of magic. This suggests a certain conflation in Marlowe's mind of the arts of poetry and magic—a development not surprising, given his concern with the capacity of the imagination to "invent" reality.[47]

44. *Ibid.*, p. 160.

45. *Ibid.*, p. 156. Invention is specifically the faculty that conceives the poetic image, as in Heliodorus' "Sugr'd invention of that picture of love in *Theagines and Cariclea*" (p. 160)—a point to remember when considering Faustus's activities.

46. Pico della Mirandola, "Oration on the Dignity of Man," in *The Renaissance Philosophy of Man*, ed. Ernst Cassirer, Paul Oskar Kristeller, John Herman Randall, Jr. (Chicago, 1948), p. 249. Henry Reynolds makes the analogy explicit in *Mythomystes* (1632), drawing from Pico his argument that poetry reveals "the generation of the Elements, with their Vertues and Changes, the Course of the Starres, with their Powers and Influences, and all the most important Secrets of Nature" (*Critical Essays of the Seventeenth Century*, ed. J. E. Spingarn [Bloomington, Ind., 1957], 1. 167).

47. I am not suggesting that magic literally depended upon imagination, or

If the conflation proposed here seems a reasonable assumption, then it becomes apparent that far more is involved in *Doctor Faustus* than a condemnation of Renaissance aspirations to learning, wealth, and power. Essentially, Marlowe is testing the viability of an imagination that seeks to liberate itself from the trap of a fallen history and reassert its dominion over nature. This is why Faustus abjures the divine and liberal arts and essays magic. The nobleness of this endeavor is shadowed, however, in several ways. It is apparent from the first that Faustus himself is a piece of fallen nature; though a part of him wishes spirits to "resolve me of all ambiguities," another part wishes them to

> Ransack the ocean for orient pearl,
> And search all corners of the new-found world
> For pleasant fruits and princely delicates.
>
> (1.82–84)

Thus the very terms in which he envisions transcendence cast doubt upon the possibility of its realization. Even sentiments that express intellectual frustration—

> Philosophy is odious, and obscure,
> Both law and physic are for petty wits,

---

upon human wit. Historically, the practice drew upon a traditional body of knowledge transmitted to the initiated. (On this matter see Hiram Hayden, *The Counter-Renaissance* [New York, 1950], pp. 176–190; D. P. Walker, *Spiritual and Demonic Magic from Ficino to Campanella* [London, 1958]; Frances Yates, *Giordano Bruno and The Hermetic Tradition* [Chicago, 1964].) I am suggesting, however, that Marlowe did make such a connection. There is further internal evidence to support this view. Faustus's world of profit and delight is one that awaits "the studious artisan." When Valdes promises him that "these books, thy wit, and our experience Shall make all nations to canonize us" (1.18–19), he is invoking the *trivium* of *ars, ingenium,* and *imitatio* that was the tradit ional basis of rhetorical education. Just afterward, Cornelius suggests that they first teach Faustus "the words of art" which are the keys to necromancy, and as we shall see, words are of far greater importance than books in the action that follows. Perhaps most significant, Faustus's whole endeavor is a pursuit of the image. Grounded in theoretical sciences, he wishes to see for himself—to take in the concrete image of truth. But this is simply another way of saying that he is dissatisfied with the "wordish description" of philosophy and desires the "perfect picture" of a clarified fiction—which is the basis of Sidney's argument for the didactic and persuasive power of poetry.

> Divinity is basest of the three,
> Unpleasant, harsh, contemptible, and vile
> (105–108)

—also reveal a preoccupation with the self that renders the gesture of renunciation extremely ambiguous, and darkens the character of the venture Faustus is about to undertake.

So, too, do his scholarly habits. His examination of Mephostophilis, for example, more closely resembles a catechism than the ardent pursuit of new knowledge:

> Speak, are there many spheres above the moon?
> Are all celestial bodies but one globe? . . .
>
> . . . .
>
> But have they all
> One motion, both *situ et tempore*?
> (6.35–36, 44–45)

The very structure of the questions implies the correct answers, and though Faustus appears disappointed when he receives them, he is unable to resist parading his own expertise before Mephostophilis in an intellectual riposte, before falling back on a new series of tendentious questions. Not unexpectedly, his astrological "investigations" end on a note at once bathetic and properly professorial:

> Well, I am answered.
> (69)

The quality of mind suggested here has led one recent critic to argue that Faustus does not really want to learn—"the tragedy of Faustus is that he hates 'learning' though he loves 'knowing.'"[48] But Faustus's "academic imagination" is not simply the obnoxious occupational disease of a second-rate scholar; it is, more profoundly, the decorous manifestation of a psyche which, like its Marlovian ancestors, is bound by its own egoism. It is, literally, the academic counterpart of Barabas's cupidity

---

48. H. W. Matalene, III, "Marlowe's *Faustus* and the Comforts of Academicism," *ELH* 39 (1972): 504. For evidence that Faustus's Ramist definition of logic was meant to strengthen the impression of scholarly sloth, see Michael Hattaway, "The Theology of Marlowe's *Doctor Faustus*," *RenD* n.s. 3 (1970): 55–56.

and Edward's narcissism, all the more appalling because Faustus is Marlowe's great representative of intellectual achievement, of imaginative yearning, of "experiential" science. What means his show? It can only indicate Marlowe's ultimate pessimism concerning the possibilities of true invention. For while Faustus's spiritual forbears had lived their mental lives in *counterfactual* worlds and thus enjoyed, in varying degrees, the illusion of autonomy, he is denied even this dubious pleasure: his imagination is thoroughly informed by the quotidian world. This is why he cannot discover a fulcrum outside his mind to lift him beyond the contexts of familiar thought and why he is finally unable to invent a viable heterocosm. It is the most frightening discovery of the play.

The congruence of Faustus's imagination and the external world is revealed not only in the questions he asks Mephostophilis,[49] but in the rhetoric of his common discourse. Faustus's venture is premised on his ability to redefine the things of historical experience. Thus he abjures divinity, and declares that "necromantic books are heavenly" (1.49); he expects Cornelius and Valdes to make him "blest" with their sage conference (1.98), and anxiously awaits "glad tidings" from Lucifer in response to his proposed hell compact (5.28); most daringly, he declares "Consummatum est" when he actually signs the deed of gift (5.74). We have encountered such semantic manipulation before, in the speech of Tamburlaine and Barabas. In the first case, we were led to feel that the inversions were perhaps viable after all, for Tamburlaine is, on the whole, successful in inventing an alternate reality for himself. In the case of Barabas, we found the inversions symptomatic of the moral limbo that characterized a mean-minded society; nonetheless there was no evidence they were *perversions* of a norm rather than simply random memory traces in a world cut loose from its ethical moorings. In *Doctor Faustus*, they clearly are perversions, for they are set against a context in which they retain their original meaning. Since this context not only surrounds Faustus, but constitutes the warp (if not the woof) of his own mind, only by a supreme act of will can he ignore the logical absurdity of what he is doing. In his first conversation with Mephostophilis, for example, it rapidly becomes evident that he seeks to transcend the contingencies of

49. *And* in his scientific experiments: surely coasting the *primum mobile*, as invigorating as that activity may be, is the perfect realization of his sense of cloture, for he whirls around *inside* the final sphere of the known universe.

fallen nature by enlisting the aid of those whose power is even more fallen and confined than his own:

> FAUSTUS: Tell me, what is that Lucifer thy lord?
> MEPHOSTOPHILIS: Arch-regent and commander of all spirits.
> FAUSTUS: Was not that Lucifer an angel once?
> MEPHOSTOPHILIS: Yes, Faustus, and most dearly lov'd of God.
> FAUSTUS: How comes it then that he is prince of devils?
> MEPHOSTOPHILIS: O, by aspiring pride and insolence,
> For which God threw him from the face of heaven.
>
> (3.65-71)

The referents of this conversation reveal the impossibility of Faustus's revolt, yet he will not acknowledge it. Despite the fact that he is conversing with a fallen angel, he attempts to restrict the significance of Mephostophilis (and Lucifer) to that of an instrumentality without a theological history. But the past is always slipping out. The first piece of information he desires after the pact is sealed is the location of hell. When he is answered, he attempts to assert his own will over the truth that Mephostophilis is enjoined to give him: "I think hell's a fable." It is a cruelly comic moment, telling the suffering devil that damnation and hell torment are old wives' tales—a measure both of Faustus's need to deny history and the futility of the attempt. Faustus is, in fact, so much a creature of that history that when he seeks relief from Mephostophilis's morbidity in sexual pleasure, he asks, of all things, not for a concubine, nor for a courtesan, but for a wife. He is incorrigibly conditioned to think in sacramental terms. Similarly, when promised the spectacle of the Seven Deadly Sins, he exclaims, "That sight will be as pleasant to me as Paradise was to Adam the first day of his creation" (6.108). Blasphemy indeed. But more importantly, evidence of the historical imprisonment of an imagination seeking new experience in a world that can only rehearse the old. Mephostophilis's moving account of damnation describes Faustus's condition exactly:

Hell hath no limits, nor is circumscrib'd
In one self place, but where we are is hell.
And where hell is, there must we ever be. . . .

$$(5.122-124)$$

This is the cardinal truth of which Marlowe's audience slowly becomes aware, but Faustus never recognizes it.

The revelation of the enclosed self takes other forms as well. Perhaps the most bathetic is the satisfaction Faustus experiences in the conjuror's tricks he performs. Some of these, it is true, are substantial (ontologically, if not axiologically): Bruno's escape from the Roman Pope, the Duchess of Vanholt's delicious grapes, Benvolio's horns. But the tricks that arouse most wonder are illusions: the shadows of Alexander and his paramour, the Duchess's castle in the air, and above all, the appearance of Helen. It is the image he himself has created that Faustus rhapsodizes in the play's most famous lines, and then—in the consummate autoerotic act—embraces, moaning: "Her lips suck forth my soul" (18.102). If this be the sin of demoniality,[50] it is also an explicit image of ultimate sterility, for the neoplatonic commonplace Faustus invokes usually implies an exchange of souls, not the exhaustion of *anima*. Again, Sidney provides an illuminating gloss. Speaking of the poet's ability to manifest an image of his fore-conceit, he remarks:

> Which delivering forth is not wholly imaginative as we are wont to say by them that build Castles in the ayre: but so far substantially it worketh, not onely to make a *Cyrus*, which had been but a particular excellence, as Nature might have done, but to bestow a *Cyrus* upon the worlde, to make many *Cyrus's*, if they wil learn aright why and how that Maker made him.[51]

There could be no better contrast between an imagination that ends in itself and one that succeeds in inventing a world. But Marlowe's poet— the black magician who serves not a wonder-working nature, but his

50. See W. W. Greg, "The Damnation of Faustus," *MLR* 41 (1946), rpt. *Marlowe: A Collection of Critical Essays*, ed. Clifford Leech (Englewood Cliffs, N. J., 1964), p. 106. His argument is rebutted by T. W. Craik, "Faustus' Damnation Reconsidered," *RenD* n.s. 2 (1969): 189-196.
51. *Elizabethan Critical Essays*, I. 157.

own appetite—cannot create "substantially." He must remain literally a "divine in show."

Even Faustus's appetite for beauty has a shrunken quality. Compare these lines of praise—

> O, thou art fairer than the evening's air
> Clad in the beauty of a thousand stars,
> Brighter art thou than flaming Jupiter
> When he appear'd to hapless Semele,
> More lovely than the monarch of the sky
> In wanton Arethusa's azur'd arms,
> And none but thou shalt be my paramour
> (18.112–118)

—with Tamburlaine's hymn to Zenocrate's face,

> Where Beauty, mother to the Muses sits
> And comments volumes with her ivory pen,
> Taking instructions from thy flowing eyes,
> Eyes, when that Ebena steps to heaven,
> In silence of thy solemn evening's walk,
> Making the mantle of the richest night,
> The moon, the planets, and the meteors, light.
> There angels in their crystal armors fight
> A doubtful battle with my tempted thoughts. . . .
> (Part I. 5.1.144–152)

The expanding hyperbole, spilling into many lines in the earlier passage, has given way to a much more conventional *copia*—"fairer than," "brighter than," "more lovely than"—contained within neat two-line periods, and as attractive as the images are, they neither convey movement nor open new vistas as do Tamburlaine's lines. The relentless, almost heedless pursuit of the image upward has been replaced by a carefully controlled, basically static description. More importantly, while Faustus clearly exhibits awe before the shadow of Helen, there is no indication that he is morally touched by beauty, as Tamburlaine is. This would be the moment to reveal the real purchase of his sensibility, yet all that is suggested in his last, abrupt line is a literal desire for appropriation —further evidence of his reduced capacity for experience.[52]

One aspect of Faustus's enclosure, then, is revealed in the self-defined limits of his scientific questions, his rhetoric, his vapid magic tricks, and the quality of his amorous verse. These exemplify the congruence of his imagination with the real world: he can invent nothing that is substantially new. The degree to which his imagination is *contiguous* to the world —reality flowing outward from his psyche and back from the world into him—is revealed by a dramaturgy that effectively combines old morality play techniques with the conventions of Kydian frame drama. In the early moralities, spiritual beings such as angels and devils had an objective reality quite external to the psyche of the protagonist, just as the personified vices and virtues were understood to exist within him. There was no tension between a personal, subjective consciousness and these forces because it was explicitly acknowledged that Everyman's psyche was neutral territory for which the agents of good and evil contended.[53] Representation of these forces in the traditional way becomes decidedly ironic, however, when the protagonist is attempting to assert his psychic autonomy, as Faustus does. Five times in the play a Good and Bad Angel appear onstage beside him. On each occasion Faustus remains unaware of their presence, although it is obvious that they are influencing his thought. On the first occasion, the Good Angel warns him not to "heap God's heavy

52. Observes Steane: "The glamour of earth and sky links with the glamour of the proper names, but it is all to make essentially (though not in Donne's sense) 'some lovely glorious nothing'" (p. 150).

53. Cf. Mankind's exposition in *The Castle of Perseverance*:

> Two angels been assigned to me.
> The one teacheth me to good;
> On my right side ye may him see;
> He came from Christ that died on rood.
> Another is ordained here to be
> That is my foe, by fen and flood;
> He is about in every degree
> To draw me to those devils wood,
> That in hell been thick.

(*English Morality Plays and Moral Interludes*, ed. Edgar T. Schell and J. D. Schuchter [New York, 1969], ll. 301–309).

wrath upon thy head" (1.71), a monition he clearly recalls in the final scene when he begs for mountains and hills to hide him "from the heavy wrath of God" (19.53). But even more obviously, he responds immediately to the Bad Angel's exhortation to be "on earth as Jove is in the sky" with the reflection:

> How am I glutted with conceit of this!
> Shall I make spirits fetch me what I please,
> Resolve me of all ambiguities,
> Perform what desperate enterprise I will?
>
> (1.77–80)

In each subsequent appearance, Marlowe juxtaposes angelic comment and Faustian echo, and in each instance it is apparent that Faustus does not know that his integrity is being violated. Only in their last exchange, when psychic distance is rapidly collapsing, does a dazed Faustus actually seem to converse with the Bad Angel, but even then he does not recognize that he is communing with an external voice.[54]

Faustus's psychic relationship with the devils is represented even more effectively. Having prepared with care the ceremonial elements requisite to conjuring, he enters to test the power of magic words:

> Faustus, begin thine incantations,
> And try if devils will obey thy hest. . . .
>
> (3.5–6)

But unknown to him, as the B-text reveals, Lucifer and four devils are already present. They are not creatures who must be commanded to appear from hell, but a willing audience to the show he provides—a psychological as well as a physical presence, as Mephostophilis reveals when he admits to Faustus in the death scene that he had originally turned the pages of Jerome's Bible to cause the hero's desperate syllogism. This is not a contradictory explanation of that fatal event. It is a haunting reminder that no autonomous act can take place in the world of this play.[55]

54. Cf. 5.4 and 5.19–20; 5.22–23; 6.13–14; 6.17–18; 6.80–81; and 19.125–129.

55. Technically, this intrusion, too, was only *per accidens*—for Faustus's weakness of faith was what attracted the devil in the first place:

As the goodly consideration of Predestination, and our election in Christ, is full of sweet, pleasant, and unspeakable comfort to godly persons. . . . So, for

But Faustus's mind is not disposed to acknowledge this. His willful ignorance is represented almost comically following his first Latin invocation, when a dragon appears in the air, unnoticed by him, and he cries out impatiently, "Quid tu moraris?" This initiates another round of rather simple-minded Latin *while the infernal powers look on*—and when at last a devil does appear to him, departing to return in a more pleasing shape, he is satisfied that "there's virtue in my heavenly words" (3.29).

The disparity between words and reality, however, is borne in upon him with increasing urgency in the course of the play. The first disillusionment occurs when Mephostophilis informs him that it was not his conjuring speech that forced the devil to appear, but his moral dereliction:

> the shortest cut for conjuring
> Is stoutly to abjure the Trinity
> And pray devoutly to the prince of hell.
>
> (3.54–56)

Similarly, in a moment of apparent repentance, he prays to Christ for help only to discover Lucifer, Beelzebub, and Mephostophilis at his elbow—visible testimony the devil has been in his heart even while he prayed.[56] This contrast between psychological-ontological truth and the insubstantiality of willful words is also reflected in the pact Faustus signs with his blood. Lucifer craves the security of a deed of gift (5.37) not because the written word is really binding, but because Faustus believes it is.[57] This is made abundantly clear in the Good Angel's persistent re-

---

curious and carnal persons, lacking the spirit of Christ, to have continually before their eyes the sentences of God's Predestination is a most dangerous downfall, whereby the devil doth thrust them into desperation, or unto a wretchlessness of most unclean living, no less perilous than desperation (*Article Seventeen of the Thirty-Nine Articles*, quoted by C. L. Barber, "The Form of Faustus' Fortunes, Good or Bad," *TDR* 8 [1964]: 105).

56. For other views of this incident, however, see Max Bluestone, "Libido Speculandi: Doctrine and Dramaturgy in Contemporary Interpretations of Marlowe's *Doctor Faustus*," *Reinterpretations of Elizabethan Drama*, ed. Norman Rabkin (New York, 1969), pp. 65–69.

57. In *The Discoverie of Witchcraft* (1584), Reginald Scot writes that agreements between conjurors (witches) and devils are not binding. Evidently this was commonplace doctrine (see Hattaway, p. 76).

minder that Faustus need not surrender his soul to the devil, deed notwithstanding, if he repents. But Faustus, persuaded otherwise by the Bad
Angel, will not believe this. His pathetic offer to renew the oath in blood,
following his eleventh-hour colloquy with the Old Man, only confirms
his blind faith in the reality of "working words."

The greatest test comes in the last scene. As it opens, the devils enter
Faustus's chamber to claim their victim according to the terms of their
agreement:

> LUCIFER: Thus from infernal Dis do we ascend
> To view the subjects of our monarchy,
> Those souls which sin seals the black sons of hell,
> 'Mong which as chief, Faustus, we come to thee,
> Bringing with us lasting damnation
> To wait upon thy soul; the time is come
> Which makes it forfeit.
> MEPHOSTOPHILIS: And this gloomy night
> Here in this room will wretched Faustus be.
>
> (19.1–8)

As Bluestone has pointed out, hell has now physically encroached upon
earth.[58] Earlier the devils were intruders in Faustus's room, visible reminders of the psychological influence they were exerting upon him.
Now they declare it their rightful territory, making manifest the gradual
expansion which that influence has undergone. What Marlowe seems to
have done here is to have adapted the mechanism of the neo-Senecan
choral frame as realized by Kyd, but in a way diametrically opposed to
Kyd's witty use of the device. For in this case, the presence of the three
devils as chorus to Faustus's tragedy is meant to visibly represent the
world of his imagination—which, by fatal coincidence, is also the real
world—pressing in on him. Like Andrea and Revenge, Lucifer and his
associates will be audience to this tragedy—

> And here we'll stay
> To mark him how he doth demean himself
>
> (9–10)

58. "Libido Speculandi," pp. 72–74.

—but unlike their predecessors, they do not exist on a separate psychological plane. They are the determining components of Faustus's psyche, shaping his reponse to the possibility of salvation in his last hour.[59]

After the scholars have taken their leave, Mephostophilis tells Faustus directly that he no longer has any hope of heaven, and exits, presumably from "above." So, apparently, do Lucifer and Beelzebub.[60] Upon the departure of the devils, Marlowe rapidly closes down the world upon Faustus until he literally gasps to death in a kind of cosmic suffocation. Although he feels himself alone on the stage, his reflections upon Mephostophilis's words are represented by the Good and Bad Angels who now enter at different doors. The Good Angel's voice is no longer hopeful but elegaic, reminding Faustus of the heavenly promise he has lost, as a glorious throne descends from the heavens to the sound of music. But this vision is quickly closed over as hell is discovered and the Bad Angel invites Faustus to look into "that vast perpetual torture-house" (117). Most subtly, in the course of this speech, the heavenly throne is transformed into an "ever-burning chair . . . for o'er-tortur'd souls to rest them in" (121–122),[61] and the Bad Angel departs.

Faustus is now indeed physically alone. The hell mouth yawns before him. Before this vision of the future he attempts, as Edward had done earlier, to conjure time to stop:

> *O lente lente currite noctis equi!*
> (142)

59. Notice how, in the above quotation, Lucifer addresses Faustus, but Mephostophilis speaks simply as a detached Chorus, referring to Faustus in the third person. This seems to be Marlowe's cue that the devils have both psychological and ontological reality.

60. The stage direction at l. 98 is in the singular, but at the very end of the scene there is another S.D. "Enter Devils," and these are identified by Faustus as Lucifer and Mephostophilis (19.189–190). In the A-text, evidently simplified for performance on a provincial stage, the earlier sequence of the devils "above" is omitted, but essentially the same lines of dialogue are present at the end, indicating that it is Lucifer and Mephostophilis who have come to drag Faustus off to hell.

61. There is no stage direction indicating its removal, although most editors supply one; the dialogue suggests that it remains onstage, as the objective correlative of Faustus's changing vision.

Why Ovid? More pedantry? Perhaps. But to a mind fired by the melodious lays of Homer and Amphion (a natural magician, according to Agrippa[62]), what more natural than to enlist the mantic cry of the amorous poet? Yet even these words avail nothing:

> The stars move still, time runs, the clock will strike,
> The devil will come, and Faustus must be damned.
>
> (143–144)

He tries physically to escape:

> O, I'll leap up to my God. Who pulls me down?

He fancies he sees Christ's blood streaming in the firmament and cries out to him, "Ah my Christ!"—but then feels himself attacked by the adversary:

> Rend not my heart for naming of my Christ,

There is momentary relief:

> Yet will I call on him . . .

and attack again:

> O spare me, Lucifer!

Then, having prayed to the devil for mercy, he turns back to the symbol of Christ's mercy and finds that it has vanished. In its place he sees only

> where God
> Stretcheth out his arm and bends his ireful brows

and runs frantically about to find some refuge.

All this upon a bare stage. There is no visible threat, but Faustus is clearly enclosed in the hell of his own mind, attempting now to escape the punishment of God, now to overreach the devil.[63] His final words suggest the grim paradox behind this whole venture:

> My God, my God! Look not so fierce on me!
> Adders and serpents, let me breathe awhile!

62. Hattaway, p. 61.

63. Mephostophilis provides the choral commentary on this last desperate exercise in inventing escape clauses (19.13–14).

Ugly hell, gape not! Come now, Lucifer;
I'll burn my books!—Ah, Mephostophilis!

(187–190)

The angry face of God instantly gives way to the vision of suffocating hell serpents. The attempt to run headlong into the earth to escape God's punishment is realized in the reluctant entry into hell mouth. In this sudden contraction of the forces of deity, Mephostophilis is revealed for what he always was—not an alternative to the eternal death Faustus once brooded over, but the instrument of eternal death. Thus the initial flight from God's restricted universe into forbidden delights has turned out to be the most direct path into God's angry arms. Faustus's intimations of entrapment were right.

The Chorus that enters after the scholars have tenderly gathered their colleague's earthly remains (reminding us that he was not really a bad man) offers us some food for thought:

> Cut is the branch that might have grown full straight,
> And burned is Apollo's laurel bough
> That sometime grew within this learned man.
> Faustus is gone; regard his hellish fall,
> Whose fiendful fortune may exhort the wise
> Only to wonder at unlawful things,
> Whose deepness doth entice such forward wits
> To practice more than heavenly power permits.

What are we to make of these words? The first thing to notice is that they are not unsympathetic to the hero. Gone are the slightly sneering epithets of the prologue, and in their place is a new soberness. The opening lines are elegiac, regretting the loss of what might have been. And the verbs used place the responsibility upon external forces; Faustus is passive. *He* is the branch that has been cut, *his* the laurel that is burned. The Chorus, therefore, is not placing blame on Faustus. Rather, it is coming to a prudential conclusion. Having fully shaped (*performo*) the form of Faustus's fortunes, it now abstracts an appropriate thesis from the experience and offers it for our consideration. We are urged to wonder, not to do. To play with the possibility of transcendence may be well and good, but to take our forward wits seriously enough to believe that

387

we can actually invent reality is a usurpation upon deity that will surely provoke cosmic reaction. It is a reasonable enough response, considering what we have seen.

But is it the meaning of the play? The answer to that must be equivocal. It is *one* meaning if, like the Elizabethans, we wish to draw a useful guide for living from our experience of the drama—and may even represent Marlowe's chastened view. But if—also like the Elizabethans—we wish to participate imaginatively in the lives of other human beings so that we may more fully appreciate the complexity of our own, then the play offers another meaning. It lies in the contrast between the hero's humanistic attempt to restore his freedom and his sadly diminished capacity for true freedom; in his ignorance of his own inadequacy; and, above all, in the discovery that hell is really the circumscribed consciousness. This is tragic knowledge, the knowledge that evokes pity and fear. This knowledge, these emotions, Marlowe clearly wished us to share with him, and they are the play's other meaning.

Conclusion

In the preceding pages, I have attempted to draw together a number of themes that can help us to assess more judiciously the nature and function of a large body of Tudor drama. Since we have ranged over a period of some one hundred years and nearly half as many literary works, it might be helpful if I now stated the main ideas briefly—cognizant, as I hope the reader will be, of the necessarily reductive character of theses.

Central to my argument is the notion of drama as a medium of liberal inquiry, in both the sociological and the cognitive sense. The freedom to pursue ethical and scientific questions, released from the practical considerations of daily life, comes to the stage from several related traditions —scientific, political, legal. At their source lies the Aristotelian distinction between theoretical and productive (poetic) wisdom, on the one hand, and prudential wisdom on the other. The former kinds, which govern the arts of logic, rhetoric, and poetry, are in themselves morally neutral powers—the one concerned with scientific investigation, the other with discovering and arranging arguments or with securing the pleasure proper to a certain type of poem. Prudential wisdom, however— which informs the arts of ethics and politics—acts "with regard to the things that are good and bad for man."[1] That is, it specifically concerns moral action. While it is true that logic, rhetoric, and poetry may be applied to both good and evil ends, nonetheless *as arts* they may be cultivated without immediate and obvious reference to external cultural values. This distinction is inherent in Aristotle's definition of a tricky speaker: "What makes a man a 'sophist' is not his faculty, but his moral purpose."[2] It is a crucial point, and lies behind all subsequent defenses of rhetoric and poetry.[3]

1. *Nich. Eth.* 1140b5, trans. W. D. Ross, *The Basic Works of Aristotle*, ed. Richard McKeon (New York, 1941).
2. *Rhet.* 1355b17, trans. W. Rhys Roberts, *ibid.*
3. For discussion of the *duplex peccatum poesis*, by which a man may exercise the autonomy of an artist in reference to his art, but is responsible to the com-

The freedom allowed the speculative and productive arts was always the indispensable precondition for fulfilling their cognitive function. Philosophers argued their speculative *quaestiones* and rhetoricians their *theses* and *hypotheses* on both sides of the question "in order that we may see clearly what the facts are."[4] Cicero, in particular, emphasized the "shaping power" of such a procedure, which in weighing various opinions against one another might arrive at a probable truth—the desired end when dealing with subjects of only "calculable" knowledge.[5] He urged further that it was not enough to examine the particular question in any case—whether so-and-so did such-and-such, or should do such-and-such—but that it was necessary to seek the universal consideration behind the particular instance in order to understand its significance. Correlatively, by considering *all* the particulars of an act—the full set of circumstances—one could discover a new way of seeing the case which might drastically alter one's judgment of its nature, and result in the establishment of virtually a "new kind of Law."[6] Such was judgment in equity. These doctrines, constituting the more philosophic tradition in the transmission of rhetoric, informed the practice of judicial and deliberative oratory in the succeeding centuries. They even permeated the practice of declamation, whose speakers, pursuing their unreal, fictional questions, tirelessly adduced sonorous *loci communes* and *sententiae* to support their particular arguments, and infused their facts with persuasive *colores* which gave them new ethical significance. Thus, inquiry was "liberal" also in its capacity for exhaustive examination.

Not unexpectedly, among the plays that emerged from this rhetorical culture, many were literally constructed as *questions*—which is my second theme. The early humanist dramatists revealed their spiritual affinities in

---

munity in reference to its use, see Wesley Trimpi, "The Quality of Fiction," *Traditio* (1974): 113–118. This Aristotelian tradition, descending in its most specific form from *Poet.* 1460b13–22, had a profound influence upon medieval as well as Renaissance fiction.

4. *Rhet.* 1355a32.

5. *Acad.* 2.7. The distinction between fixed and variable objects of knowing is made by Aristotle in *Nich. Eth.* 1139b14–1140a23; it is reflected in the remark of Sidney's Philanax that the affairs of men "receyve not Geometricall certentyes" (*The Complete Works of Sir Philip Sidney*, ed. Albert Feuillerat [Cambridge, 1912–1926], 4. 337).

6. *Ad. Her.* 2.20, trans. Harry Caplan (London, 1954).

no more direct way than by turning *quaestiones infinitae* into *finitae*, and playing them before audiences. In doing so, they can hardly be said to have realized the potential for complex understanding that is inherent in mimesis, but the structure of their plays often reveals more clearly than those of their successors the main outlines of this process. For they all follow the *via inventionis* of Aristotelian-Ciceronian-Agricolan logic. In invention, it will be recalled, one begins with a particular proposition and seeks to discover why a certain thing is predicated of its subject. This is accomplished by inferring the relationship between them with the aid of the topics, and establishing a more comprehensive proposition that will articulate the nature of the relationship. The process continues until the most comprehensive proposition is reached, and then one sees in succession the "reasons" hidden in the original statement.[7] Thus, the particular question "Who is gentler—this Merchant or this Plowman?" leads the inventor to ask in what way merchants and plowmen may be considered gentle, and when this is established, whether men engaged in commerce or in manual labor may be styled gentle, then whether commoners as a class may be gentle, which finally leads to a definition of *gentillesse*. In this way, the content implied in the original question is laid bare. Were one to move down from the most comprehensive proposition to render a decision about the original question, one would be following the *via judicii* or the process of syllogistic proof, which is the second part of logic, and is reflected in the structure of the morality play. But this is never done in these debate plays—although the characters in them may argue syllogistically—for the questions are merely starting-points for the activity of invention itself. The aim of the play is discovering the most comprehensive truth, not proving the validity of one side or the other. This is why the "answer" usually embraces both.[8]

In the comedy and tragedy that stems from this tradition, the explorative process is similar, but it is manifested in different ways. Comedy, as we have seen, was described by the humanist critics as the imitation of efforts to resolve a *status*—a question in controversy. Should, for example, Pamphilus wed Glycerium, having promised to obey his father's wishes in the matter of marriage? Here, an important change in the manner of

7. See Ch. II, pp. 51–52.
8. Even in *Fulgens and Lucres*, where a clear-cut decision is required, it is not made without a qualification that includes the other side.

arguing *in utramque partem* has taken place—and this is my third theme. Thesis (the abstract question) has been "actualized" in hypothesis (the particular question) through mimesis. We do not ask whether a young man should follow his heart or heed filial duty, nor even whether Pamphilus should; rather, we observe him acting out the question. This has important effects upon our sense of the problem. We see the kind of young man Pamphilus is through his concern for his mistress, his feeling of guilt in deceiving his father, his loyalty to his friend Charinus. We see the kind of man his father is in his dealings with his son, his slave, and his friend Chremes. Mimesis itself, then, has the effect of qualifying our response to the question—and thus complicating it—by revealing the "qualities" of the people involved. This process, as we have seen, is directly related to the rhetorical principle of invoking the *status qualitatis* in order to discriminate more finely the actual rights and wrongs in a given case.[9]

But the plot of the play is also a medium of discovery. Resolving the *status* involves acting out "arguments" *pro et contra*, as each side attempts to reason its way to victory. Some of these are ethical (Glycerium is pregnant, Pamphilus has given his word); some legal (Glycerium is an Athenian citizen, the son is *in potestate patris*); some merely expedient (Chremes will not want his daughter to marry a frequenter of courtesans). Each of these inventions is a more comprehensive proposition that seeks to confirm one side or the other of a particular *status*. As in the debate play, however, the *status* is answered by none of them—but only by the most general proposition of all, unknown to the partisan advocates of either side: Glycerium *is* Chremes' daughter, and therefore Pamphilus may marry her with his father's blessing. The discovery of this truth clearly reveals the cognitive striving underlying the plot. For in learning the single fact that de-knots the issue, the participants attain to a new vantage point—a *status divinitatis*, so to speak—in which all the partial views entertained by human beings and the conflicts these generate dissolve to form one harmonious vision. The most general proposition is God's, or Destiny's. This is the lesson of Shakespeare's *Comedy of Errors*.[10]

9. See Ch. III, pp. 66–67 and n. 7.

10. Given the plots of these plays—involving the search for lost parents and children, the identity of husbands and wives—the cognitive process might be described even more appropriately as a movement toward *anagnorisis*—re-cogni-

Latinate comedy may differ, then, from the debate play not in its cognitive structure, but in the provenance of its first premise. Which brings us to the fourth theme with which this book has been concerned. It is the recognition that the *via inventionis* may be insufficient to master the *status* life frequently imposes upon us. Though a play like *Every Man in His Humour* celebrates the procedure, many other comedies, and all tragedies, acknowledge its inadequacy. In comedy, the solution to impasse is the revelation of a transcendent truth which dissolves the conflict. In tragedy, no such truth is obtainable, and the conflict can only be ended in some painful way, through death or separation from the human community. This is the deeper resonance of Donatus's remark that "comedy teaches us to embrace life, tragedy that life must be shunned."[11] For tragedy seems to be composed from a distinctly human perspective from which it never fully escapes. Cognition, if it comes at all, comes after the fact. Even then, a Richard II may gain a momentary insight into the character "flaw" that caused his fall, but find no way of synchronizing his time with Time itself. Nor can Othello, though he learns *how* Iago tricked him into murdering Desdemona, discover *why* he did so—"what you know, you know"—nor what there is in him that enabled Iago to prevail. First causes remain hidden.

The epistemological assumptions underlying comedy and tragedy have a profound effect upon our role as audience to these plays— which is my fifth theme. In comedy, the conflict ideally arrives at a judgment that is enacted *for us*, within the play. We may assess the rights and wrongs of the case as it unfolds, and may even be troubled by our divided loyalties as our perceptions of the characters and the issues involved become more refined through the qualities of language, circumstance, and motivation; nonetheless comedy will take care of these difficulties for us by offering a solution that allows us to acknowledge all our concerns. When it fails to

---

tion. It is the *rediscovery* of relationship that they solemnize. It would be interesting to study further the connections between this dramatic concern and the logician's assumption that "reasons" may be found if only one searches the hiding places diligently enough. Both the comic and speculative traditions express a faith that there lies within man's reach an embracing truth that will resolve his perplexity as he stands before the opaque particulars of this world.

11. In tragoedia fugienda vita, in comoedia capessenda exprimitur (ed. Paul Wessner, [Leipzig, 1902], p. 21). The phrase is quoted in virtually all Renaissance comparisons of tragedy and comedy.

do so, something is wrong, and we call that result "dark" comedy. In such a play, the basic *status* is answered, but the solution does not take into account the ethical considerations that have been evoked through the mimetic exposition of the issue. In this sense, both *All Fools* and *The Merchant of Venice* are dark comedies, for we are not satisfied that the plays' resolutions are adequate to the human problems that have been revealed. Our critical recourse in such cases is to pose our judgment against the one made in the play and infer ironic intention, if the author seems in other respects to know what he is doing.[12]

Dark comedy points directly to tragedy, for here judgment is thrust almost wholly upon the audience. Theses are educed within the work, to be sure, but they are only partial propositions in the ongoing inquiry, not the most general premise. This can be invented only by the audience, responding to the play in its entirety. It is a humanizing, and therefore sobering experience. Deprived of the key proposition that might resolve the conflict, and confronting only the evil it has generated, we become painfully aware of the necessity to "make a profitable event" of our limitation, as Musidorus tells Euarchus. The events we have witnessed reveal that a "correct" course of action cannot be secured through the discovery of a proposition that will satisfy both sides. If the hero is to realize his subjective "right," some other "right" must be violated, and this violation is acknowledged in the death penalty or exile imposed by the playwright. But the fact of punishment does not end the matter. We must generate a proposition through which, if we cannot save the hero, we may at least "understand" him—stand, that is, beneath or behind his act and perceive its underlying nature. In doing so we do not attain the *status divinitatis*, since we have not discovered a way to prevent the conflict that has been enacted. But we do the next best thing; we reach an equitable judgment that acknowledges his guilt and sympathizes with his existential predicament. And in the process, we find that the hero is indeed "a man like ourselves"—or, more precisely, that we are like him. For though we

12. The *Arcadia* explicitly invites us to do so, since Sidney's narrator reminds us that "justice" has been achieved largely in ignorance of the circumstances and has left many false impressions. But less obviously, many of Shakespeare's comedies, and some of Jonson's, operate in the same way. The likelihood is that the more complex the play—in terms of fullness of characterization and the thoroughness with which its issues are expounded—the "darker" it will be, since our wide variety of responses can never be fully accounted for.

are vouchsafed a wider view than ever he is granted, we, too, can never rise above a merely human perspective. That is the limitation, and perhaps the peculiar strength of tragedy.

These, then, are the major themes I have tried to bring to the reader's attention in this book. It should be remarked in conclusion that the play of mind was, of course, not exclusively a Tudor phenomenon. Its roots lay deep in the past, and some of its features may even be seen in the purposefully dislocating drama of our own time. But in its most distinctive qualities, it was the special child of a rhetorical culture which flourished in England in the sixteenth century, and slowly disappeared in the seventeenth. The faith of this culture in the power of discursive reasoning, its confidence in the capacity of an amoral art to confer long-term moral benefits upon society, and its sheer joy in language, produced an exuberant, frequently uncontrolled drama. This drama led the mind to wider apprehensions through a bewildering variety of rhetorical devices—inductive argument, allegorical witplay, sudden shifts of tone and attitude, improbable but persuasive juxtapositions of images from the past and the present. At its worst it includes some frankly bad plays, but its best work is humanistic in the fullest sense: it is responsible, conducive to learning, and attains an equilibrium between the emotions and the reason to which any culture might aspire. And it produced our best playwright, whose work we have only been able to glimpse briefly in this book. One only has to think of what seems distinctly Shakespearean in *Richard II*, the *Henry IV* plays, *Hamlet*, *Measure for Measure*, *King Lear*, *Antony and Cleopatra*, or *The Winter's Tale* to perceive the affinity between the outstanding dramatist of our period and his worthier predecessors. Ironically, his moment—in which the full potential of the explorative drama is realized by a mind at once wide-ranging and yet strongly centered—also ushers in its decay. As Hamlet tries so desperately to understand man's relationship to evil, Marston's Malevole refuses to look steadily upon it, and turns away; Beaumont and Fletcher's heroes avoid the issue, and Webster's Flamineo tells why: "There's nothing of so infinite vexation As man's own thoughts."[13] The faith in finding out was dying, and this is reflected in the hollowness of so many otherwise exciting Jacobean and Caroline plays. Why this was so, and its specific manifestations in the drama, are important matters that demand further study.

13. *The White Devil*, ed. John Russell Brown (London, 1965), 5.6.205–206.

Index

Academy, Later: relation to Ciceronian rhetoric, 32n; epistemology of, 69; suspension of judgment in, 122; criticized by Seneca, 242

Achilles Tatius, 99n

Acolastus, 148

Adams, Barry B., 270n

Aeneas, 321, 322n, 336–337

Agricola, Rudolph, 45n, 50, 51n

Albertus Magnus, St., 2

Alciati, Andrea, 191n, 351n

All Fools, 174–179; consilium, 175–176; *status*, 175, 177–179; trial scene, 177; as dark comedy, 394

Allegory: educative function of, 9, 201, 203, 206; and *copia* in Lyly, 201–206; of Galatea and Hesione, 210–211, 210n; as wit in *Endimion*, 216–217; physical, in *Endimion*, 218, 221n; 222n; moral, in *Endimion*, 219, 223–224, 224n; religious and political, in *Endimion*, 225; of Hercules, 191n; of the soul, 351–352

Andreas Capellanus, 67n

Antonio's Revenge, 292–302; moral problem of, 292n, 302; theatricalism of, 293–297; parody as *ethopoeia* in, 294–295; tragic chorus in, 295–296; invention in, 297, 301; praise of folly in, 298; Kydian frame, 299; sophistic perspectives in, 301; palimpsest in, 301–302

Aphorisms (style), 43

Aphthonius: writing exercises in *Progymnasmata*, 45–50, 64; distinguishes thesis and hypothesis, 65; and debate play, 108–109; and Terence's *Andria*, 138

Appian of Alexandria, 283

Applicita, 52–53

Aquinas, Thomas, St., 36n, 82n

Arcadia, The Countess of Pembroke's, 8,

67, 87–106, 144, 304, 304n; versions compared, 88; dialogic structure of, 88–90; heuristic exempla in, 90–93; broken disputations in, 93–94; skeptical narrator in, 96; ironic qualification in, 97; trial scene in, 98–104; legislator and law compared, 99–100; equity in, 100, 104; probable judgment in, 100, 370n; status in, 101–103; legal and philosophic judgment compared, 102–103; and use of fiction, 104–106

Aristotle: on wonder in philosophy and tragedy, 1; defense of rhetoric, 31; defines rhetoric, 31; discusses equity, 67n; on artificial and inartificial proof, 146n; on *sententiae*, 243–244; on simile and metaphor, 307n; on marvelous in epic, 308n; *Poetics* and *Tamburlaine*, 348–349, 350n; on theoretical, productive, and prudential wisdom, 389; on *duplex peccatum poesis*, 389n; mentioned, 2, 13, 26n, 68n, 82n, 130, 139n, 196

Arthur, The Misfortunes of, 263–267; debate creates character in, 264, 266; recourse to thesis, 264; sententious argument in, 265; and *Gorboduc*, 266; failure of rhetoric in, 266–67

Augustine, St., of Hippo, 35, 242n, 374

Ayres, Philip, 295n

Bacon, Francis: *Of the Dignity and Advancement of Learning*, 40–41; on rhetorical *loci communes*, 41n, 47n; on hypotheses, 41n; "Of Marriage and the Single Life," 41–42; on "Aphorisms" and "Methods," 43; and Castiglione's dialogue, 76n

Baker, Howard, 230n, 249n, 250n

Baldwin, Thomas W., 3n, 43n, 47n, 131n, 135n, 138n, 148n, 166n

Barber, C. L., 383n